T0305167

The Unfinished Business of Governance

NEW PERSPECTIVES ON THE MODERN CORPORATION

Series Editor: Jonathan Michie, *Director, Department for Continuing Education and President, Kellogg College, University of Oxford, UK*

The modern corporation has far reaching influence on our lives in an increasingly globalised economy. This series will provide an invaluable forum for the publication of high quality works of scholarship covering the areas of:

- corporate governance and corporate responsibility, including environmental sustainability;
- human resource management and other management practices, and the relationship of these to organisational outcomes and corporate performance;
- industrial economics, organisational behaviour, innovation and competitiveness;
- outsourcing, offshoring, joint ventures and strategic alliances;
- different ownership forms, including social enterprise and employee ownership;
- intellectual property and the learning economy, including knowledge; and
- transfer and information exchange.

Titles in the series include:

The Growth of Firms
A Survey of Theories and Empirical Evidence
Alex Coad

Knowledge in the Development of Economies
Institutional Choices Under Globalisation
Edited by Silvia Sacchetti and Roger Sugden

Corporate Strategy and Firm Growth
Creating Value for Shareholders
Angelo Dringoli

The Internationalisation of Business R&D
Edited by Bernhard Dachs, Robert Stehrer and Georg Zahradnik

Corporate Governance, The Firm and Investor Capitalism
Legal-Political and Economic Views
Alexander Styhre

Merger and Acquisition Strategies
How to Create Value
Angelo Dringoli

The Unfinished Business of Governance
Monitoring and Regulating Industries and Organizations
Alexander Styhre

The Unfinished Business of Governance

Monitoring and Regulating Industries and Organizations

Alexander Styhre

School of Business, Economics and Law, University of Gothenburg, Sweden

NEW PERSPECTIVES ON THE MODERN CORPORATION

 Edward Elgar
PUBLISHING

Cheltenham, UK • Northampton, MA, USA

Published by
Edward Elgar Publishing Limited
The Lypiatts
15 Lansdown Road
Cheltenham
Glos GL50 2JA
UK

Edward Elgar Publishing, Inc.
William Pratt House
9 Dewey Court
Northampton
Massachusetts 01060
USA

A catalogue record for this book
is available from the British Library

Library of Congress Control Number: 2018944746

This book is available electronically in the Elgaronline
Business subject collection
DOI 10.4337/9781788113144

ISBN 978 1 78811 313 7 (cased)
ISBN 978 1 78811 314 4 (eBook)

Typeset by Columns Design XML Ltd, Reading
Printed and bound in Great Britain by TJ International Ltd, Padstow

Contents

Preface

The recent political turmoil (when writing in January 2018), including the British referendum in favour of the U.K. leaving the European Union (the so-called "Brexit" ticket), the election of Donald Trump as president in the U.S., and the rise of illiberalism and authoritarian politics in, e.g., Russia and Turkey (whereof the latter experienced a military coup in July 2016) has arguably put an end once and for all to the narrative of "the end of history," entertained by certain liberals since the decline of the communist politico-economic system. The political scientist Francis Fukuyama is arguably the household name *par excellence* associated with this finalist proposition, but there were many others that foresaw no changes whatsoever after say 1990. The Clinton administration's Economic Council even proposed the term "The New Economy," being highly fashionable for a short period around the turn of the millennium until the dot.com bubble burst put an end to the enthusiasm over this term, denoting a liberal, deregulated economy capable of both demonstrating economic growth *and* the ability to regulate itself to minimize the magnitude of the ups and downs over the economic cycle, thus promising "the end of all recessions." Fortunately, most qualified and credible commentators would argue that, today, there is never any "end of anything," and certainly not history per se. Instead, old issues and controversies, not unlike diseases that authorities have claimed have been defeated, such as tuberculosis, are making a return in political and economic debates and discourses. That is, the perhaps last remaining and most persistent *grands récits* of modernity (with Jean-François Lyotard's term), the grand narrative declaring "the end of history" is no longer bankable and should be retired.

This burying of the end of history narrative is still connected to the rhetorical figure of the "unfinished business" of governance. Arguably, the "unfinished business of governance" is an oxymoron, as governance denotes a social practice, rooted in and derived from legislation and regulatory control, and the accompanying development of an institutional framework. Yet, this rhetorical figure emphasizes that governance is, after all, a matter of "business," i.e., rent-seeking, venturing, opportunity-recognition, etc., and, in some cases and less flattering, opportunistic or illicit behaviour (which are what justified the governance in the first place—in a perfectly rational world, governance would become obsolete). To govern a corporation, industry, or a society is thus to admit that there are always of necessity resourceful and strategic actors who initiate action and mobilize resources to shape the governance regime so that it suits the interests and objectives of these actors. The "unfinished business of governance" is thus a ceaseless and ongoing process to balance a variety of interests represented by various stakeholders and their defined agents, and to do so within a shared horizon of temporality. This makes governance a politically charged domain wherein stakeholders actively intervene, either themselves or through their agents, to maximize their own "utility." This, in turn, makes governance as an unfinished business an eminent field of scholarly inquiry.

The last four decades of shareholder activism and the unprecedented growth of the finance industry has led to governance now shifting to being more based on external measures and indices, i.e., data collected by external agencies assigned with the role to monitor industries and corporations, and less based on politically accountable elites (elites here used in a non-pejorative term, which is important to remark in this period of illiberal political campaigns). In the corporate system, the board of directors are today less accountable vis-à-vis the stakeholders, as four decades of shareholder activism has potentially undermined the role and legitimacy of the board; the university system, being affected by changes in industry on the basis of normative and mimetic isomorphism, increasingly relies on "list-and-algorithm governance" wherein allegedly "neutral" and "de-politicized" performance measures are substituting professional self-regulation; on an industry level, say, in the finance industry, a one-sided focus on "efficiency" at the expense of other governance concerns has led to substantial externalities that are probably undesirable for the median voter or tax-payer. In the end, the new governance regime's capacity to generate net economic welfare should be subject to scholarly inquiry.

All these cases indicate that governance is today a field wherein major transformations are taking place, where certain stakeholders' gains are other stakeholders' losses, i.e., in an economy of stagnating economic growth, and governance should therefore be examined as a zero-sum game. This volume therefore explores the recent literature on governance that explores both the corporation, the university (as being a "public sector" or quasi-public sector institution of great importance for economic growth and venturing), and the industry level (most notably finance industry governance, as the finance industry is today dictating the conditions under which nonfinancial firms acquire, raise, and distribute finance capital). In the end, this volume seeks to continue to uphold the role Michel Foucault assigned to Friedrich Nietzsche, "to be bad for stupidity" (cited in Deleuze, 1995: 150).

PART I

On the theory and practice of governance

Introduction: governance regimes and their political, legal, and economic foundations

INTRODUCTION: GOVERNANCE, A MATTER OF JOINT CONCERN

Coffee and Palia (2016) examine how hedge fund managers, holding larger stakes and focused holdings, have an incentive to actively discipline managers and directors in corporations to take a short-term view of their operations and to maximize their return. Economic short-termism here denotes "decisions and outcomes that pursue a course of action that is best for the short term but suboptimal over the long run" (Laverty, 1996: 826. Original emphasis omitted). While hedge fund managers are economically compensated and rewarded on the basis of their ability to maximize short-term rents, what is good for themselves in the short-term perspective may not of necessity be good for the corporate system and the stakeholders dependent on carefully and responsibly managed corporations for their economic welfare, Coffee and Palia (2016) claim. "[W]e are concerned that hedge fund activism is associated with a pattern involving three key changes at the target firm: (1) increased leverage, (2) increased shareholder payout (through either dividends or stock buybacks), and (3) reduced long-term investment in research and development (R&D)," Coffee and Palia (2016: 550) argue. Dallas (2011), in turn, is concerned with how short-termism has become widely endorsed within corporate governance:

> A 2005 survey of 401 financial executives demonstrates the pervasiveness of shorttermism. Financial executives confirmed that they would take an action that is value decreasing for their firms to meet earnings expectations. Over 80% of financial executives said they would decrease discretionary spending, such as advertising expenses, maintenance expenses, and research and development expenses, to meet earnings targets. Over 50% of financial executives said that they would delay starting a new project even if this entailed a small sacrifice in value to meet earnings expectations or to smooth earnings. (Dallas, 2011: 280)

According to Dallas (2011), there are many weaknesses with the short-term governance model, but it is not accurately priced by unregulated markets as short-termism is overpriced, i.e., the efficient market hypothesis does not stand up well against empirical evidence:

> Contrary to the efficient market hypothesis, the study found that markets do not accurately value firms at the time they engage in myopic behavior; the stock market did not value myopic firms less, that is, stock prices did not penalize firms for myopic behavior at the time of their myopic behavior. (Dallas, 2011: 280)

The role played by hedge fund managers in Coffee and Palia's (2016) case, to put pressure on managers and directors to "divest and return" firm-specific resources to shareholders, is based on a long-standing free-market theory model that renders managers as self-serving actors prone to opportunistic behaviour. However, as Coffee and Palia (2016: 550) repeat, "[the] assumption that managements typically engage in inefficient empire building is out of date today and ignores the impact of major changes in executive compensation." However, changes in governance regimes since the 1970s have served to alter the corporate system in fundamental ways, and in ways that are conducive to economic inequality as certain stakeholders (e.g., shareholders, i.e., finance capital owners) have advanced their positions vis-à-vis other stakeholders.

First, Coffee and Palia (2016: 603) argue, corporate governance is "moving from a 'board-centric' system towards a 'shareholder-centric' system"; second, public corporations are increasingly under pressure to "incur debt and apply earnings to fund payouts to shareholders, rather than to make long-term investments" (Coffee and Palia, 2016: 603). This means that shareholder activists such as hedge fund managers are incentivized to discipline managers, endowed with so-called "real" power in corporate legislation, and directors, granted "formal" power, to shift their focus from strategies that balanced short-term gains and performance with long-term goals and investments, ultimately securing the stipulated goal equally for managers and directors, to make the firm survive over time and over economic cycles. The implications from this new regime, rooted in legislation, regulatory control, law enforcement, and day-to-day management and not the least in accounting practices, are considerable: it means that the firm is no longer instituted, as corporate law prescribes, as a team production venture, protected from both outside and inside stakeholders who have an incentive to dissolve and liquidify the firm as soon as they foresee other investment opportunities. Instead, the firm is treated as a bundle of financial assets, formally a set of contracts, whose principal function is to generate a return being paid out to the firm's investors, i.e., the shareholders. This represents an entirely new finance industry-sponsored corporate system that arguably has contributed in substantial ways to raise the well-documented economic inequality in the contemporary competitive capitalism.

As corporate governance practices have shifted gears and deviated from corporate legislation as it is written and intended by the legislators, it is also important to survey the wider field of governance wherein the corporate system is embedded. In the scenario sketched above, the finance industry today executes a considerable real power in determining how corporations invest their so-called residual cash flow and how they manage their assets. Governance as a scholarly and political term, subject to legislation, implementation, and law enforcement, influences and shapes a series of industries and social institutions and should also be examined on the industry level. In addition, trends and tendencies in, e.g., corporate governance carry the seed of coercive, mimetic, and normative isomorphism (DiMaggio and Powell, 1983: 150), i.e., governance practices and devices developed and applied in the corporate system are likely to be imitated and implemented in, e.g., the university system. Kleinman and Vallas (2001) point at such processes:

> Much of the commercialization of the academy is due not to direct corporate investment, but to an array of indirect factors, including the growing and ongoing interaction between the two institutional domains (e.g., the exchange of personnel and pressures from university overseers to model organizational rules and practices along private sector lines), *inducing the university to become isomorphic with its corporate environment.* (Kleinman and Vallas, 2001: 465–466, emphasis added)

This means that studies of corporate governance need to be complemented by a wider understanding of governance as a social and political tool in the hands of policy makers and finance capital investors. More specifically, today, by the end of the second decade of the first millennium, when the economy is increasingly globalized, and where advancement in digital media and the development of transnational governance regimes influence how political accountability can be ensured and inform the polity, governance is becoming a key analytical term for the study of economic activities on the micro, meso, and macro scale. Says Omarova (2011):

> The concept of governance in our polycentric world embodies a collaborative, cooperative enterprise of shaping social outcomes through negotiation among numerous public and private actors with stakes in those outcomes: non-governmental organizations, business and trade associations, labor unions,

technical standard-setting bodies, professional groups, and so on. (Omarova, 2011: 427–428)

In this view, a limited focus on corporate governance per se, a most complex field of scholarly inquiry comprising legal theory, economic theory, management studies, political science, and economic sociology, is insufficient if the objective is to explain how the micro, meso, and macro levels of governance practice are co-produced and entangled, and, not the least, how these entanglements are dependent on the imbrication of theory, practices, and politics, making their constitutive elements most difficult to separate from one another. Thus an analysis of changes in corporate governance theory and practice remains an unfinished business unless embedded in a wider view of governance as an economic–political tool determining standards for political accountability, performance, and resource allocation.

More specifically, the soaring levels of economic inequality,[1] a puzzling phenomenon in the midst of a bountiful economy, spitting out products and innovations (while at the same time being at risk to deplete natural resources, sustainability researchers and activists rightly point out) and raising the standard of living for billions of people, needs to be connected to changes in governance and the mechanisms of governance regimes now put to work in the contemporary economy. This volume therefore examines how governance has been modified over the last four to five decades, beginning in the 1970s and the decline of the managerialist corporate model and the shift to the finance industry-based corporate model and governance regime, and how new ideas regarding governance developing over time has been conducive to increased efficiency in the economy, but also, as an unintended consequence or as a politically designed programme—two complementary views propose—significant growth in economic inequality.

Orthodox economists have claimed over the period that the question of distribution is irrelevant in economic theory and therefore, by implication, also irrelevant for political entities—what matters is exclusively the capacity to generate the largest possible output given the input resources and thus to maximize the efficiency of the transformation of input material into output products. Such economic doctrines may prove their value in analytical models devoid of human beings that respond to, e.g., perceived unfair dealings, but in a real-world economy the question of economic inequality is indeed of great political and economic relevance. For instance, entrepreneurship researchers have shown that entrepreneurs—widely treated as the primus motor of competitive capitalism, following Joseph Schumpeter's intellectual lead—are primarily recruited from a middle to "lower upper class" background where reasonable economic stability and security was assumed, leading to a more pronounced risk-appetite than presumptive entrepreneurs from a less economically privileged class (Valdez, 2015). As a consequence, an economy that is guided by a political system that demonstrates a commitment to promote economic equality (as in, e.g., the Scandinavian welfare state economies) is likely to generate more entrepreneurs and thus become more dynamic. In other words, economic inequality is a key economic and political issue, and it is related to governance regimes in ways that should be examined on the basis of scholarly inquiry (Tsui, Enderle, and Jiang, 2018).

This volume thus makes the assumption that governance regimes are relatively "impure" frameworks that balance practical interest and theoretical input under the influence of policy making processes, including all its imperfections derived from bounded rationality, akrasia (weakness of will) and similar behavioural conditions pertaining to "human nature," and the political waging orchestrated by participants to benefit their own singular interests. In addition, governance is by definition based on a blend of legal theory and practice, economic theory, management studies literature, and economic sociology frameworks, all adding to the practical legislative and everyday work to make governance what it is. This latter view implies that a "mono-disciplinary view" of governance (e.g., to only reference neoclassical economic theory) is insufficient in explaining how governance is structured and implemented, and how its outcomes are to be determined. Therefore, if Omarova's (2011) claim of a "polycentric world" of governance is accepted as a working hypothesis, a pluralistic and heteroglot (in the literature theorists' phrasing) theoretical framework is advisable. If successfully embarking on such an analytical pursuit, it is possible to demonstrate that governance is an analytical term and a domain of practical work that in fact does have strong implications for economic performance along a variety of measures and parameters. For instance, economic stability, economic efficiency, and economic equality are three such parameters that policy makers and their defined regulators, responsive to what is called "median voter preferences" in a politically resilient system, would be interested in to monitor and to balance in ways that are legitimate in the eyes of the largest possible amounts of stakeholders. This casts governance as a legal–political and economic tool and practice, which in turn justifies the characterization of governance as being "impure." That is, the objective of competent governance is to balance a series of objectives and stakeholder interests within a reasonable horizon of temporality. The objective of this volume, in turn, is to demonstrate how governance is today reduced to its economic theory elements and its implied efficiency maximization preference, which tend to underrate the externalities generated by such a one-sided view of governance, burying, e.g., the question of economic inequality, which leads to considerable social and economic costs in the long run.

ECONOMIC INEQUALITY AS A GOVERNANCE PROBLEM

The global economy has been characterized by a sharp growth in economic inequality over the last four decades, by now being back at the level before the Great Depression in the 1930s (Duménil and Lévy, 2004). Despite reforms in the democratic political system to counteract such tendencies, the economic system of competitive capitalism has continued to generate economic wealth that tends to aggregate at the top of the income pyramid (Piketty, 2014). Books such as Saskia Sassen's *Expulsions* (2014), Immanuel Wallerstein et al.'s edited volume *Does capitalism have a future?* (2013), Martin Gilens' *Affluence and influence* (2012), Monica Prasad's *The land of too much* (2012), and Robert H. Frank's *Falling behind* (2007) testify to these changes in competitive capitalism. There is a variety of studies indicating the root causes of this failure to counteract tendencies to amplify economic inequality in the economic system of competitive capitalism. Some studies indicate that the political system, especially in the U.S., has been overtly influenced by campaign donations, lobbyism, and think tank activism, leading to the creation of what Hacker and Pierson (2010) refer to as "winner-take-all politics." Gilens (2012) points at some facts regarding the representation in democratically elected bodies:

> By one recent calculation 44 percent of the members of the U.S. Congress are millionaires. More prosaically, all members of Congress, by dint of their congressional salaries alone, are solidly in the top decile of the American income distribution. Perhaps one reason public policy tends to reflect the preferences of the affluent, then, is simply that policy makers who are themselves affluent pursue policies that reflect their personal values and interests. (Gilen, 2012: 255; see also Carnes, 2013)

Other studies indicate that the institutional restructuring of competitive capitalism (Tabb, 2012) and the increased influence and sheer size of the finance industry has contributed to the present situation (Tomaskovic-Devey, Lin, and Meyers, 2015; Davis and Kim, 2015; Kalleberg, 2015; Lin and Tomaskovic-Devey, 2013; Palley, 2013; Zalewski and

Whalen, 2010). What economic sociologists and others refer to as "the financialization of the economy" is one of the principal drivers of economic inequality, Kus (2012) demonstrates:

> All four indicators of financialisation that we included in our analysis— namely, total value of stock traded on the stock market exchange as a percentage of GDP, bank profitability measured in terms of bank income before tax as a percentage of GDP, securities under bank assets, as well as the aggregate financialisation index that we used—have displayed a significant positive association with income inequality net of conventional explanations under various model specifications we employed. (Kus, 2012: 492)

When the finance industry grows, other industries are disadvantaged and this translates into lower investment in R&D and other development work and fixed (but unfortunately illiquid) production capital (Van Arnum and Naples, 2013). The medium- to long-term consequence is slower job growth and increased economic inequality (Wodtke, 2016; Weeden and Grusky, 2014). Furthermore, policies and campaigns, orchestrated by free-market protagonists as an attempt to weed out so-called rent-seeking agents to "maximize" market efficiency, have served to impair and mute organized labour (Jacobs and Myers, 2014; Rueda and Pontusson, 2000). Such activism has contributed to a tipping of the balance "toward rentiers and away from workers" (Van Arnum and Naples, 2013: 1177). While the blue-collar worker community took the first hit when the American economy was de-industrialized in the 1980s (Bluestone and Harrison, 1982), today, it is increasingly the middle class that suffers the consequences of institutional changes and corporate restructuring (Davidson, 2014).

A third line of studies indicates that it is the restructuring of the corporate system, justified by the maximization of profit (rather than attending to a more diverse set of corporate objectives) and the return of the so-called residual cash flow to shareholders, that explains a substantial share of growing economic inequality (Lin, 2016; Jung, 2016; Bidwell et al., 2013; Bidwell, 2013; Lazonick, 2010; Useem, 1990). Such changes have benefitted managers at the expense of the wider community of salaried workers:

> [R]estructuring influenced production workers' and managers' wage distributions in different ways—production workers as a group experienced a polarization in which the middle part of the distribution shrunk significantly, whereas managers' wage distribution shifted and spread out at the upper tail after the onset of restructuring. (Dencker and Fang, 2016: 482)

Apparently, the corporation as a vehicle for enterprising and economic growth as stipulated by corporate law, and carefully balancing various interests while blocking opportunistic behaviour inside as well as outside the corporation, has lost some of its institutional traction. The corporation is no longer, Morgan (2016: 211) argues, an institution that creates "a shared community of fate" (Omarova, 2011) among its participants and stakeholders; today, Morgan (2016: 211) suggests, "actors have become more diverse and their interest in supporting these old institutions has consequently declined." Ivanova (2017: 1) argues that the 2008–2009 recession (in many publications addressed as "The Great Recession" with capital letters) was not followed by "a typical postwar recovery": "While corporate profits quickly returned to, and surpassed, prerecession levels, investment and employment have been unusually slow to recover" (Ivanova, 2017: 1). Ivanova (2017: 9) explains this phenomenon on the basis of the growth of "total saving originating from the corporate sector" in combination with "the decline in the labor share of national income." The "sluggish wage growth" and falling share of labour national income translates into a higher level of indebtedness among lower- and middle-income households,[2] a credit expansion or "debt-fare" that served to maintain private consumption when real wages stagnated or fell: between 1995 and 2013, "average household consumption in the OECD [Organisation for Economic Co-operation and Development] rose by 7.3 percent each year," while wages rose by only an average of 5.7 per annum (Fuller, 2016: 31), representing on average a 1.6 percent of annual growth in debt-based consumption over the 18 years period. The effect is growing economic inequality in the American economy: "Income inequality has been continuously on the rise since the mid-1970s" (Ivanova, 2017: 12); the Gini index for families reached 0.445 in 2013–2014 versus the post-war low of 0.348 in 1968. At the same time, indebtedness and economic inequality do not themselves explain the staggering economic recovery after 2009. Ivanova (2017) argues that growing corporate profits, an immediate effect of lower compensation for labour, "created an overhang of idle money, eager to lend itself to speculative ventures." When this surplus capital was re-invested in the finance industry, the sub-prime housing market bubble and its secondary derivative market was inflated to unsustainable levels (Lysandrou, 2011), and paved the way for the 2008 finance market collapse. In the end, when the bubble burst and the entire economy suffered the consequences of the leveraged systemic risks in the finance industry, there was no willingness to invest in production capital or in job-generating activities, making the Great Recession a new economic phenomenon in the post-war economy, in many ways different from, e.g., the 2001 dot.com bubble burst. Studies show that the job creation during and after the recession has primarily been in the low-wage services sector, wherein the real wages of the average worker have declined (Bernhardt, 2012: 355); an estimate from the U.S. Bureau of Labor Statistics predicts that 7 out of 10 new jobs will be created in this sector (Bernhardt, 2012: 355). According to Bernhardt's (2012) account, the staggering or declining real wage concern is unlikely to disappear as American employers are now following new "legal and normative standards":

> [T]he main source of America's low-wage problem lies in domestic service industries not impacted by globalization, where the key driver of precariousness is the growing evasion and violation of employers of both legal and normative standards, facilitated by the withdrawal of government's hand in the labor market. (Bernhardt, 2012: 355)

Economic inequality therefore caused by two interrelated corporate decisions, (1) to compensate labour below productivity growth, and (2) to prioritize shareholder value creation and favourable stock market evaluation over long-term investment opportunities. The former tendency in the economy is substantiated by data that reveals that American families are poor not because they fail to find employment, but because they are undercompensated for their work: "61 percent of the officially poor families in the United States contain a worker," Brady, Baker, and Finnigan (2013: 873) report. In fact, Brady, Baker, and Finnigan (2013: 873) continue, "There are more than four times more people in working-poor than unemployed poor households"; between 1974 and 2004, the unemployed poor "averaged only 3.4 percent of the U.S. population," whereas the working poor "averaged 10.4 percent." The second tendency is substantiated by empirical research indicating reduced investment in production capital and in human resources in the corporate system (Gordon, 2015; Stockhammer, 2004). Neither of these two tendencies indicate a very bright future for salaried workers—blue-collar, white-collar, or no-collar.

Regardless of the causes of these changing economic, financial, and institutional conditions, it is questionable whether the present situation with soaring economic inequality is desirable for either stakeholder. Studying the growth of economic inequality in 18 OECD countries over the 1970–2007 period, Perugini, Hölscher and Collie (2016: 251) found "[a] direct causal relationship link between income inequality and debt and thus systemic financial risk." Furthermore, studies indicate that social actors make a distinction between "fair" and "unfair" economic inequality (Osberg and Smeeding, 2006), and that certain degrees of inequality can be tolerated, even encouraged, as a legitimate motivation factor and a mechanism for rewarding efforts and investment in human resources (Bonica et al., 2013: 109), but when economic inequality reaches a critical point, it easily leads to grievances and, in the long run, forms of social unrest or a radicalization of certain disfavoured groups (Jung, 2016; Lin, 2016). The problem is that ideological beliefs affect how policy alternatives are assessed, and the outcome from policies are complicated to predict as there is a lack of empirical evidence to support either strategy, Jencks (2002) argues. Concerning ideology, liberals tend to believe that economic inequality is "unjust or socially destructive," and that policy making and reform is justified on such grounds, while conservatives may believe economic inequality is indicative of a functional performance–reward system that benefits those who contribute the most to prosperity, also benefitting those at the bottom of the income hierarchy. In this conservative view, "Inequality may well rise, but the success of a growth strategy makes the sacrifice worthwhile," Galbraith (2002: 14) says. Concerning the most effective policies to be implemented as soon as the ideological disputes have been settled, this is no easy matter either: most thoughtful liberals do recognize that "rewarding people for producing more goods and services will often improve the absolute well-being of the least advantaged," but to identify the best strategy for "improving the position of the least advantaged" requires complex empirical calculations (Jencks, 2002: 51). For instance, rich democracies such as Western democratic states tend to have lower degrees of economic inequality in comparison to, e.g., Mexico or Russia, but whether this bundling of affluence and democracy always leads countries to adopt somewhat egalitarian economic policies, or if the causality runs in the other direction, suggesting that "extreme inequality retards economic growth,"[3] is yet to be determined (Jencks, 2002: 53).

Taken together, all these changes in competitive capitalism and the political system that regulates and monitors economic affairs indicate that economic inequality and other pressing economic concerns (e.g., lower investment in production capital and R&D, slower job growth, instabilities and imbalances in the finance industry, fewer IPOs (initial public offerings) renewing the stock of public corporations) is a matter of governance. For instance, Perugini Hölscher and Collie (2016: 251) suggest that policy makers who wish to make the financial system (and, by implication, the economic system at large) "more robust" need to "cast the net wider than regulatory reforms and monetary policy," and also consider a wider set of policies including reforms that affect "the distribution of income" and "household indebtedness." Needless to say, such policy reforms demand foresight, integrity, expertise, detailed know-how, and courage. In addition, as Kennedy (2016) remarks, the present situation and its malaises, which need to be understood within the horizon of the remarkable growth of economic welfare over the last four decades for a majority of median voters in advanced, democratic countries, were not always anticipated at the time when the policies were enacted (see, e.g., Krippner, 2011). As a consequence, what in hindsight and with the grace of historical records now at hand appear as unjust or unqualified policies, leading to undesirable conditions, were in many cases unintended consequences of what seemed a reasonable decision at the time: "The world is uncertain and open to elite management. It is also unjust, and … injustice is a byproduct of technocratic—and often enlightened and humanitarian—management" (Kennedy, 2016: 14).

At the same time as unfortunate policy decisions can be forgiven despite their negative yet unintended consequences, policy makers and scholars need to be aware that policy making is in fact a domain of rent-seeking, with certain actors actively promoting solutions to various political problems that benefit their own interests and competencies (see, e.g., Cooper, Graham, and Himick, 2016; Warner, 2013)—otherwise the quickly expanding lobbying industry would not be as lucrative as it is (Drutman, 2015). This makes policy making and governance more widely key mechanisms in contemporary society, occurring and operating at the intersection between stated and implied interests, perceived possibilities, existing know-how and theoretical frameworks, and ideology. At the end of the day, governance is an analytical term and social practice that is sufficiently abstract and malleable, yet distinct and sufficiently operable to bridge and bond such diverse resources and capacities. Therefore, pressing socio-economic concerns such as soaring economic inequality, the destruction of the biosphere, and the depletion of resources are issues that need to be addressed as matters of governance. Such issues can only be handled through governance and the resource that governance as an operative term assumes and deploys; governance is of the essence of the regulating of socio-economic affairs.

THE RISE AND DECLINE OF DE-POLITICIZED GOVERNANCE: THE INDEPENDENT CENTRAL BANKS AND THE QUESTION OF POLITICAL ACCOUNTABILITY

Governance is ultimately a matter of establishing systems that balance agency and decision making discretion and regulatory control that enables the political accountability that makes a governance regime legitimate in the eyes of the median voter. In the case of corporate governance and corporate law, the business charters issued by the state are based on a series of mandatory rules and privileges that taken together protect the business venture from both internal and external opportunism, and that grant the board of directors decision making authority. That is, as the firm is an entity *sui juris*, the board of directors is granted certain constitutional rights to execute formal power within the corporate system, including hiring managers. Governance regimes are therefore based on the legal and regulatory distribution of *formal* and *real* power in, e.g., corporate governance. This view of governance assumes that political power and political concerns are always of necessity irreducible elements in any governance regime. This view has been disputed by free-market protagonists who tend to dismiss the concept of "politics" as being a non-economic concept that creates unnecessary but avoidable complications in governance. In this view, market pricing already does the job for political bodies (i.e., to allocate resources optimally) and therefore politics has no legitimate place in economic policy unless—which sounds like a self-contradictory or paradoxical statement—it serves to insulate economic affairs from political influences. In other words, in the free-market model, politics should be kept at an absolute minimum.

One such domain where the rejection of political influences from economic affairs has become the dominant idea is in monetary policy wherein central bank independence has been ensured. Central banks are widely regarded as one of the key regulatory mechanisms in a national economy, and to protect the decision making authority from being shaped by interest in the political system, central banks have been granted the status of a sovereign economic actor with significant degrees of formal and real power. The idea of an independent central bank is still itself a political or ideological idea associated with the monetarist doctrine that inflation, a particularly troubling economic phenomenon in the 1970s and 1980s, is exclusively a matter of monetary supply (and not premised on any macroeconomic policies and conditions) and that inflation is to be defeated on the basis of the central bank's control of the monetary supply. This idea of inflation being a primary target in economic policy was also largely beneficial for the finance industry as price stability served its interests:

> Since the 1980s, reducing inflationary pressures on the economy has remained a key concern for monetarist economists running the central banks of advanced nations. Since inflation undermined banks' ability for borrowing money from customers and lending it to investors, and ultimately decreased bank profitability, these inflation targeting policies proved favourable to banks and were welcomed by the larger finance community. (Kus, 2012: 485–486)

Polillo and Guillén (2005) claim that the "war on inflation" in the mid-1970s was in fact part of a wider neoliberal doctrine and political programme being rolled out by free-market intellectuals and pro-business activists in the period, i.e., the doctrine of central bank independence was justified by its technocratic ethos and "its purportedly objective, non-partisan, disinterested and depoliticized approach to policy making" (Polillo and Guillén, 2005: 1768). In fact, the new policy was a centerpiece of a new economic regime.

More specifically, the dominant doctrine in the 1970s in leading economic agencies such as OECD, International Monetary Fund (IMF), and the World Bank was that inflation was propelled by excessive demands made by organized labour. To fight inflation was, therefore, indirectly, and concealed under its veil of technocratic disinterestedness, to undermine organized labour and trade unions. To many heterodox economists, Hung and Thompson (2016: 461) remark, "the great monetary tightening in the early 1980s was nothing but part of a war against workers waged by financial capital, which exercised covert power over apparently independent central banks." Central bank independence provided many benefits and managed, in the end, to push down inflation. Still, critics of the long-term war on inflation have pointed at the wider socio-economic consequences of making inflation control the only legitimate economic policy and how this allegedly technocratic policy has benefitted, e.g., the finance industry at the expense of, e.g., organized labour. Regardless of this critique, articulated already in the 1970s, the so-called Washington Consensus, a set of predefined doctrines and policies conducive to greater "economic freedom"—the *cri de guerre* of free-market theorists—including central bank independence, was part of the "terms and conditions" that the World Bank and IMF included in their standard agreements to provide credit to countries in a state of economic distress in, e.g., Latin and South America (Polillo and Guillén, 2005: 1774). What was first advocated as a technocratic policy was suddenly part of a broader political project, thinly justified on the basis of economic doctrines and deeply entrenched ideologies.

In the 1990s, when inflation was no longer a major economic policy concern, central banks "changed tactics," Major (2014: 127) argues, and "began to set explicit targets for the rate of inflation as a guide for monetary policy." Now *some* inflation was good for the economy as a "natural" growth of prices, say in the range of 2 to 3 percent, supposedly created a good balance between price stability and economic growth. Under all conditions, the doctrine that central banks should be independent and that price stability is one of the primary goals has been a policy that has been adopted and enforced across the world of developed economies. Still the central question regarding the role of politics in economic policy, partisan or technocratic in orientation, remains unsolved; should key economic issues be handled by agencies that are insulated from political accountability, or is such a policy to overstate the virtues of the technocratic regulation of the economy? "Moving regulatory and monetary policy-making authority to central banks and financial ministries insulates monetary policy making from mass political pressure," Major (2014: 207) claims. The idea of the prudential and self-disciplined technocratic agency being at the helm during travels in stormy seas as well as in calm waters is per se a politicized view of governance and regulatory control, not least the implicit assumption that technocrats bestowed with great decision making authority are themselves capable of separating polity and wider social beliefs and trends. Zelner, Henisz, and Holburn's study (2009: 405) of economic policy reform in the global electric power industry in the 1989–2001 period indicates that there is no such "political economy policy" devoid of politics, but, in fact, institutions and their political entanglements do matter in decisive and profound ways when new economic policies are implemented:

> Though these agencies [reforming the energy industry] may have as their ultimate goal the implementation of 'pure' neoliberal reforms rooted in neoclassical efficiency criteria, our findings suggest that the long-term success of such reforms requires careful attention not only to economic influences but also to the domestic and global institutional context in which policymaking occurs. (Zelner, Henisz, and Holburn, 2009: 405)

In addition to factual evidence of how politics matter in all domains of economic policy and their positive or negative consequences for economic growth and performance, the normative question whether politics *should* be able to influence economic policies, affecting millions or even

billions of citizens and voters, remains unsolved. For some commentators, such as Major (2014), examining the austerity policy being the
foremost consequence of the Great Recession, it is clearly beneficial if,
e.g., the finance industry was given less authority to regulate itself as
suits their interests and instead re-connects economic policy and political
accountability: "Finance needs to follow, not write, the economic policy
script" (Major, 2014: 208).

After the great financial crisis of 2008, many commentators, pundits,
and laymen would agree with such statements, but as a legal and
economic matter, governance is not easily determined given the heterogeneity of stakeholders and the various time horizons that need to be
balanced in prescribing legal and regulatory frameworks. Nevertheless,
there seems to be an emerging consensus or a new conventional wisdom
that governance needs to be accompanied by political accountability to a
higher extent; the allegedly "blind" but ultimately "fair" mechanism of
market pricing did not provide the self-regulatory and self-correcting
benefits its proponents claimed it would, and the great debacle of 2008 is
indicative of the decline of an economic doctrine wherein market pricing
was the indisputably principal regulatory mechanism. What should come
in its place remains far from clear, but political accountability is back on
the policy agenda anew, as is always the case when governance regimes
fail in spectacular ways (Gerding, 2005).

Corporate Governance as Regulatory Licence

Pargendler (2016: 361) argues that corporate governance is now
advanced as the solution to "a vast array of economic and social
problems," spanning from "economic development," "systemic risk," to
"rising inequality." At the same time, the bulk of corporate governance
scholarship focuses primarily on "internal governance," which relates to
"the balance of power among shareholders, boards of directors, and
managers" (Pargendler, 2016: 362). In Pargendler's (2016: 364) account,
sketching an intellectual and politico-economic history of the awakened
interest in corporate governance since the 1970s, the upsurge in corporate
governance advocacy "did not result from the invisible hand of the
market." Instead, this shift towards corporate governance "resulted from
the visible hand and voice of policy entrepreneurs," constituting an
emerging "corporate governance industry" that promoted corporate governance reform (Pargendler, 2016: 364). The neoconservative and pro-
business political and economic mobilization of the 1970s, crowned by
Ronald Reagan's presidency beginning in January 1981, was unified in
its disregard of government, and instead declared that "the cure for

economic woes had to lie in the private sector" (Pargendler, 2016: 365). However, as Pargendler (2016: 365) notices, in the case where markets fail and governments offer no better alternative, corporate governance may appear as an attractive alternative for a heterogeneous group of social actors, but in this "hydraulic system," governance may "partly substitute for government, at least in the level of discourse." That is, seemingly paradoxical and in conflict with the free-market credo of many of the neoconservative and libertarian economic advisors and functionaries, the corporation was now expected to act like a government but on the corporate scale. Pargendler (2016) can be cited at length here:

> [T]he growing concern with corporate governance partly compensates for the misgivings about government intervention in the policy arena. Ironically, it does so by treating the corporation as a metaphor for government in two ways. First, it transposes to the corporate form the same traditional formulas for controlling and legitimizing power in the political sphere—"checks-and-balances" through strong independent boards and (shareholder) democracy—in the hope of tackling numerous economic and social problems. Second, the internal workings of the corporation become the focal point of public debate, as well as the presumptive remedy. Indeed, a key promise of the corporate governance movement is that, once the proper decision-making processes internal to the corporation are in place, external substantive regulation of corporate action will become increasingly superfluous, as corporations will be in the position to govern themselves. (Pargendler, 2016: 365–366)

This corporate governance agenda is palatable to political entities, as it combines a private sector focus with "a reformist overtone" (Pargendler, 2016: 366); as such, Pargendler (2016: 366) continues, "corporate governance change appeals to progressives as a path for social and economic change in the face of political resistance to greater state intervention, while pleasing conservative forces as an acceptable concession to deflect growing governmental intrusion in private affairs."

As a practical matter, corporate governance issues are as old as the corporation itself, and probably much older than that if the idea of "agency costs" (an abstract and hard-to-measure construct, yet guiding much of the orthodox corporate governance scholarship grounded in neoclassical economic theory), is understood as a generic administrative concern. The corporate governance is based on the tripartite separation between shareholders, boards of directors, and managers, whereof the last category, the orthodox model suggests, has "gone unchecked" (Pargendler, 2016: 375). To amend this situation, primarily for the benefit of the shareholders who are claimed to suffer the largest losses from undisciplined managers, the directors are to be empowered. The outcome

is a corporate governance model based on checks and balances to
strengthen the role of the board of directors, but also, to afford "a
meaningful role to shareholders" (Pargendler, 2016: 375). This generic
model proved to be a remarkably resilient recipe put forth during the
decades after the 1970s as a candidate for the solution of various
economic problems at hand. Proponents of the orthodox corporate
governance model claimed that extant corporate legislation and court
rulings were inefficient in making real-world directors monitor their
managers (a claim rejected out of hand by legal scholars at every single
point of inquiry) and, therefore, they argued, directors should not merely
serve as "the pawn in the managers' game," but should be more tightly
connected to the shareholders to better monitor managerial decision
making.

The virulent anti-statism of the 1970s in the U.S., fuelled by economic
downturn caused by the oil crises, the political turmoil of the Watergate
scandal, the City of New York being on the brink of bankruptcy, and the
embarrassing end of the Vietnam War (to list a handful of events), was a
seedbed for new corporate experiments deviating from the path laid out
by New Deal policies. The wave of hostile takeovers in the 1980s, caused
by a high-interest rate policy and great overseas savings flooding into the
U.S. economy (Stearns and Allan, 1996) and a de-regulation of the
finance industry, enabling the junk-bond financing of takeover and
corporate restructuring activities, indicated that shareholder-led governance was not of necessity more efficient than, e.g., governmental
regulation—the new model merely distributed economic wealth to the
benefit of a few stakeholders at the expense of the many stakeholders—
but the 1980s' free-market euphoria failed to contain any self-reflexive
thinking in policy making quarters regarding the long-term effects of the
new economic and monetary policies. Instead, the wave of hostile
takeovers in the mid-1980s was understood by this new conventional
wisdom to be the new order of things.

In the 1990s, the "decade of corporate governance" (in Pargendler's,
2016: 379, account), the widespread belief in the free-market based
governance model continued uninterruptedly, now further fuelled by the
take-off effects from previous investment in computer science technology, digital media, and the introduction of Internet on a broad scale.
By the mid-1990s, American scholars and policy makers were convinced
that the U.S. could take pride in having the best possible governance
model known to mankind, possibly only challenged by the German
model (as the Japanese economy, a previous contestant, stagnated in the
1990s and displayed structural problems). The triumphalist American
1990s of the Clinton presidency, marking an end to the Republican 12

years' reign but certainly not the end to free-market ideology, further cemented the idea of the superiority of the U.S. model. "In the 1990s, as the U.S. economy recovered, the Anglo-Saxon model of corporate governance turned into a blueprint for financial and economic development around the world, particularly in emerging markets and transition economies," Pargendler (2016: 367) writes. The sordid bankruptcies of Enron, WorldCom, and a handful of other companies during the first years in the new millennium thus sent shock-waves across the American policy making and legal communities, as the U.S. was widely understood, not the least in the U.S., as the "international paragon of good corporate governance" (Pargendler, 2016: 383). The greed and corruption of the Enron scandal was particularly daunting, as Enron did everything by the orthodox corporate governance theory book, was the rising star of the new de-regulated finance market, and had ample connections in Washington and other branches of the U.S. political system (Aven, 2015; Dembinski et al., 2006; Watkins, 2003; Gordon, 2003; Coffee, 2003). Only a few years after Enron had wiped out $60 billion in market capitalization and "$2 billion in pension plans" (Pargendler, 2016: 383), the crisis struck anew during the fall of 2008, marking the end of the faith in free-market ideology, but not, as Pargendler (2016) emphasizes, in corporate governance as economic remedy and political tool. Corporate governance was a unifying theme for the full political spectrum, serving as both "the identified culprit for the crisis" and as "a recipe for reform" (Pargendler, 2016: 386). Corporate governance thus rather reinforced its role as a universal remedy after the fall of 2008, serving as a balancing point between increased governmental regulation (with a politically unattractive centralization of the economy) and an increased free-market dependency (on an empirical basis most likely to generate its own intolerable political consequences, in the end being passed on to the tax-payers as indicated by a robust financial crisis track record; Calomiris and Haber, 2014; Pontusson and Raess, 2012; Gerding, 2005):

> [I]t was the financial crisis of 2008—and its immense costs to taxpayers and deleterious implications for macroeconomic performance—that has disseminated growing skepticism of the shareholder primacy norm. At least with respect to financial institutions, the pursuit of shareholder value maximization no longer appears conducive to the promotion of social welfare even to advocates of shareholder primacy. (Pargendler, 2016: 397–398)

Pargendler (2016) here echoes the concern of Berle and Means (1934/ 1991), being sceptical regarding salaried managers' ability to monitor social welfare, a concern that applies also to directors being recruited by and large from the same pool of professionals deemed qualified for corporate governance responsibilities. Therefore, rather than blindly trusting that firms and their boards of directors, especially when joining hands with shareholders, are in the best position to act like governments on the smaller scale, Pargendler (2016: 400) calls for an analysis of how corporate governance fares "compared to alternative mechanisms to further the same objectives," including strengthening government regulation or market forces. "[T]he obsession with corporate governance may still be harmful to the extent that it crowds out more meaningful modes of reform," Pargendler (2016: 400) alerts us.

Pargendler (2016) thus calls for a scholarly programme that at least examines the root causes of this widespread enthusiasm over corporate governance as the assigned and favoured model within a series of domains. Pargendler (2016) also reviews to what extent *the claim* that corporate governance (and, by implication, governance more widely) is in fact capable of solving economic problems where government or markets run short can be substantiated. This volume is located within such a programme, targeting governance as a historically and culturally contingent solution to perceived problems and, therefore, also including the exclusion of equally important problems, not comfortably sitting within the proposed governance model.

DEFINING KEY TERMS

The Concept of Governance

Bevir (2009: 3) defines governance quite generally as "the construction of social orders, social coordination, or social practices." In addition, governance refers to "all patterns of rule," including the "kind of hierarchical state that is often thought to have existed prior to the public sector reforms of the 1980s and 1990s" (Bevir, 2009: 3). Benton (2016: 661–662), in turn, uses a definition of governance that emphasizes the role of the public corporation (i.e., the corporation with dispersed ownership): "Corporate governance refers to the practices and structures within and around public corporations that allocate power among organizational participants, particularly shareholders, directors, and managers." In a more recent publication, Bevir (2012) makes a distinction between *government* and *governance*: the former term is used in the situation wherein "people believe in a unified sovereign state" and in its ability to monitor all economic and political affairs; the latter term is used when analysts "do not believe in the state," and therefore choose to "concentrate more on the complex and messy processes of governance" (Bevir,

2012: 12): "Governance here differs from government because social organization need not involve oversight and control, let alone the state. Markets and networks might provide governance in the absence of any significant government," Bevir (2012: 3) argues. More specifically, Bevir (2012: 78) actively discredits and undermines the idea that the sovereign state is capable of being in control of the wide diversity of issues and affairs that fall under its authority:

> The notion of the central state being in control of itself and civil society is a myth. The myth obscures the reality of diverse states practices that escape the control of the centre because they arise from the contingent actions of diverse actors at the boundary of state and civil society. (Bevir, 2012: 78)

This re-locates the state—no longer being "monolithic"—as one actor that negotiates with "networks of organizations" (albeit still an influential and centrally located actor), including actors from the public, private, and voluntary sectors in policy making processes; "the boundaries between state and civil society are blurred," Bevir (2012: 79) contends. As a consequence, Bevir (2009: 29) is sceptical regarding the ability to define governance in lexical terms that fit any domain of practice: "[T]he term governance can be used at various levels of generality and within various theoretical contexts. The diversity of uses exceeds any attempt to offer a comprehensive account of governance by reference to its properties." Governance is thus a fluid and malleable concept, by and large contingent on the context wherein the practices are situated.

In a review of the literature on governance, Fukuyama (2016: 90) follows Bevir's (2009) claim that it is complicated to define governance once and for all, and argues that there is "no consistent understanding of the meaning of the word governance today, which indicates a degree of disarray in the field that purports to study it." The term is "applied promiscuously," Fukuyama (2016: 90) says, to a whole range of activities that have in common "the act of steering or regulating social behavior." Yet, Fukuyama (2016) identifies three basic meanings of the term, including (1) "international cooperation through nonsovereign bodies outside the state system (international governance)"; (2) "governance as public administration"; and (3) "governance as the regulation of social behavior through networks and other nonhierarchical mechanisms," i.e., what Fukuyama (2016: 90) calls "governing without government."

Lobel (2004: 344) defines governance as a term that "[s]ignifies the range of activities, functions, and exercise of control by both public and private actors in the promotion of social, political, and economic ends." Lobel (2004: 343) also introduces the term "the Renew Deal" (to paraphrase Franklin D. Roosevelt's New Deal programme) to denote a series of changes in governance in U.S. administrative agencies at federal and state levels, prompted by changing market conditions. These initiatives share the quality of being "outreach programs and issuing nonbinding guidelines," not substituting traditional "top-down rule promulgation, implementation, and enforcement activities" (Lobel, 2004: 343). Lobel continues:

> At the beginning of the twenty-first century, against the backdrop of global competition, changing patterns in market organization, and a declining commitment to direct government intervention, contemporary legal thought and practice are pointing to the emergence of a new paradigm—governance— that ties together recent developments in the political economy with advances in legal and democratic theory. (Lobel, 2004: 344)

In this scenario, governance becomes distributed inasmuch as "multiple stakeholders" (including not least what Lobel refers to as "norm-generating nongovernmental actors") are encouraged to participate in governance activities, serving to transfer responsibilities to the private sector, including private businesses and nonprofit organizations (Lobel, 2004: 344–345). In Lobel's (2004: 345) optimistic view, lawmaking therefore "shifts from a top-down, command-and-control framework to a reflexive approach, which is process oriented and tailored to local circumstances."

Lobel's (2004) vision of a "Renew Deal" governance regime is rooted in free-market ideology and the firm belief in the market as the most efficient arbiter in any economic system. The Renew Deal programme is therefore *reactive*, i.e. is based on the premise that "as the world changes, patterns of law and governance must change with it." Governance is therefore not a matter of being part of a political agenda wherein political entities are granted the authority to influence market behaviour on basis of democratic interests. Lobel (2004: 361) is sceptical towards such an active polity and judiciary system, not the least on the ground of alleged inabilities of such entities to handle practical concerns: "Under the traditional regulatory model, law itself has become so complex and dense that it is inevitably self-defying." In contrast, the Renew Deal is grounded in legal thought that is "adopting a practice patterned after and correlated with the changing American market as an analogous sphere of good practices to be replicated in other spheres of life" (Lobel, 2004: 366). Lobel continues:

> [a]s scholars and reformers increasingly observe private-sector developments, regulatory agencies and public officials are facing heightened pressures to

imitate the efficiencies of the private sector. For example, government is urged to become lean and flexible through the reduction of size and costs. One central way to reduce the size of the public sector is through accelerated privatization projects, reducing the size of bureaucracy primarily by contracting out public functions to private parties. (Lobel, 2004: 366)

What Lobel (2004: 361) refers to as the "the thick regulatory state" is thus under pressure to adapt to various market-based conditions, and "the political economy" accompanied by social and legal theory have "motivated these changes in policy aspirations and the techniques for their realization" (Lobel, 2004: 365). In Lobel's view, the new governance model is no longer exclusively bound up with political entities and state-controlled agencies, but governance becomes a form of distributed systems of interrelated activities. Yet, the state is expected to continue to play an active role as a centrally located actor, held responsible for an operable and efficient judiciary system. Furthermore, this Renew Deal agency model undermines governance as a political tool, controlled by democratically elected political entities, as the nature of this governance regime is essentially determined by market conditions: "The model enables practices that dislocate traditional state-produced regulation from its privileged place" (Lobel, 2004: 344). In Lobel's view, governance is an activity or a practice wherein principally all market-based actors can participate; it is a form of libertarian image of governance that challenges many assumptions of traditional governance regimes. The Renew Deal governance regime represents a decisive step towards the vision of "governing without government."

Corporate Governance

The literature on corporate governance offers a variety of concepts and terms that are applicable when examining also governance. Campbell and Lindberg (1990: 636) define governance quite broadly as "[t]he institutionalized economic processes that organize and coordinate activity among a wide variety of economic actors." Campbell and Lindberg (1990: 636) also introduce the term *governance regimes* to denote "combinations of specific organizational forms, including markets, corporate hierarchies, associations, and networks," and that consequently "coordinate economic activity among organizations in an industry or economic sector." To better flesh out the term governance, Kogut (2012: 8), separates "two related but distinct sets": one *set of practices*, including the board of directors and the various governance decision practices such directors make use of, and one *set of institutions*, constituting the supportive social and political system, "such as the rule of law or politics." While the legal system (i.e., the second set) dictates and enforces governance rules, the first set (e.g., boards of directors) translates such rules into governance practices and renders abstract law meaningful within an organization's activities (Edelman, Fuller, and Mara-Drita, 2001; Dobbin and Sutton, 1998).

Examining an even more detailed level of analysis, Du Gay, Millo and Tuck (2012: 1085) propose the term *governance devices* to denote a variety of tools and heuristics, including decision protocols, accounting standards, legal strictures translated into an operative and managerial vocabulary, being used in governance work.[4] In Du Gay, Millo and Tuck's (2012) use of the term, such *governance devices* are not passive resources in the hands of governing bodies or individuals, but such tools assume distinct agencies that make corporate governance a matter of blending humans and non-humans (in an actor–network vocabulary; Latour, 2005) into productive *governance assemblages*. These governance assemblages are thus "[c]lusters of people, machines, and institutionalized processes that operate interactively towards an organizationally defined goal," Du Gay, Millo and Tuck (2012: 1085) suggest.

Transnational Governance

A growing body of literature examines how governance is increasingly becoming a transnational activity, with the institutions anchored in the sovereign national state and ultimately granted authority by democratically elected decision making bodies now in some cases only playing a secondary, advisory role (Slaughter, 2004; Büthe and Mattli, 2011). In areas such as environmental regulation (e.g., Bartley, 2007) and finance market monitoring (e.g., Singer, 2007; Abdelal, 2007), much regulatory licence is granted to networks of transnational regulators, sharing information, and establishing international standards and assisting one another in enforcing standards (Bignami, 2005: 809–810). "The state is not disappearing, but it is disaggregating into its components' institutions, which are increasingly interacting principally with their foreign counterparts across borders," Slaughter (2004: 18) writes, pointing at the new governance practices. One primary concern regarding the growth of transnational governance is that the modern understanding and acceptance of legitimate public administration is tied to national democratic institutions, with the persistent critique of "democratic deficit" haunting transnational regulators: "The sharing of powers among national and supranational regulators in networks makes it difficult for national publics and parliaments to hold such regulators accountable," Bignami

(2005: 811) argues. As also national governments and other local governmental agencies have a hard time keeping track of the advancement of transnational governance activities, it is even more complicated for the general public to monitor and overview these changes. In the end, what is arguably the only meaningful approach to the regulation of transactional markets, that of transnational governance, easily becomes discredited or rendered suspicious as the traditional ties between democratic institutions and their regulating agencies become loosely coupled and tenuous.

Another concern is that, e.g., global financial governance (see e.g., Abdelal, 2007) is highly technical–legal in character, making it almost impenetrable for laypeople but also to some extent for policy makers and journalists (Riles, 2011: 10), lacking the expertise needed to understand, e.g., highly technical and legally complex domains such as securities market regulation (Keys et al., 2009; McCoy, Pavlov, and Wachter, 2009; Paredes, 2003; Rock, 2001). In such cases, Riles (2011: 232) argues, regulatory policy is enacted as something that is "stipulated in principle," while de facto being "something to be left to lower-tier implementers or even to market participants themselves." In the case of finance market regulation, a long tradition of market actors regulating themselves on the basis of, e.g., credit rating (Naciri, 2015; White, 2013; Bolton, Freixas, and Shapiro, 2012) or reputation-impairing mechanisms ("shaming") (Hunt, 2009; Paredes, 2003; Sikka, 2009), has accomplished little to stabilize global finance markets or to discipline speculative behaviour (Fligstein and Roehrkasse, 2016; Gerding, 2005), making finance market regulation a precarious activity, subject to much criticism from scholars and commentators (Alp, 2013; Crotty, 2009). As consequence, Riles (2011: 246) summarizes, "[l]egal governance is ultimately not so much a matter of grand design as it is a set of lived practices and techniques— techniques that are often disparaged or ignored but in fact are far more interesting, subtle, and full of transformative potential than we habitually recognize."

Yet another concern regarding governance, both on the transnational level and in the corporate setting, is that the governance practices commonly seek the full commitment of the actor subject to governance activities, and such an acceptance of various forms of detailed control demands a tolerance for paternalist governance, i.e., a belief in the efficacy of, e.g., organizational goals and objectives and the means provided by the employer, the sponsor, or the sovereign state (see e.g., Karlsen and Villadsen, 2016). As such paternalism runs counter to, e.g., professional and academic liberties and jurisdictional discretion, the new regime of governance needs to "sell itself" on the basis of both personal

and societal interests and benefits, a bundling of interests that is beset by
tensions and contradictions.

Governance and the Spectre of Paternalism

"Paternalistic policy aims to affect choice either by changing the set of
available alternatives among which an agent can choose or by employing
non-rational means to influence how the agent chooses among an
unchanged set of alternatives," Hausman and Welch (2010: 129) write.
Therefore, "paternalistic actions" either "coerce people" or use "imperfections in their deliberative abilities to shape their choices" (Hausman
and Welch, 2010: 129). In either case, paternalism is based on the
principle that some regulating body or agency is endowed with the
legitimate right and intellectual capacity to determine choice alternatives
that are favourable for *all* participants. Rizzo and Whitman (2009a: 907)
use the term "new paternalism" to examine how academic work in the
field of behavioural economics has served to define new governance
practices, based on the predefined and theoretical "rational behavior"
model dominating economic theory. In behavioural economics, human
actors are enacted as autonomous decision making agents, yet suffering
from "various cognitive biases, insufficient willpower, and difficulties of
information processing" (Rizzo and Whitman, 2009a: 907). To overcome
or neutralize such deficiencies of "human nature," behavioural economics
seeks to provide standards for paternalist government policies that do not
impose choice alternatives "from above," formulated by some external
agency, but instead actively identify and formalize the agent's own
preferences. In Rizzo and Whitman's (2009a) sceptical view, such a
behavioural–economic model of governance is encountering formidable
challenges, and many of the elementary research methodologies being
used, including the ordinal ordering of stated preferences and slippery
slope problems in setting standards, are yet to be handled.

Despite a variety of theoretical and methodological shortcomings and
failures, the idea of a new paternalist governance has struck a chord in
policy making quarters, and its principal elementary idea, that governance works best when the subject of governance shares objectives,
norms, and ideologies with the governing agency, is today conventional
wisdom in the governance literature. As will be discussed in the
following section, paternalism is today paired with calculative practices
and the construction of "lists and algorithms," a set of practices that
fashion a halo of scientific respectability around what are in fact
governance practices and objectives riddled by controversy. In other
words, in order to bury controversies and to mute opposing views,

governance practices are based on the enactment of supposedly "object-ive" performance measures that are widely taken for granted and that institute goal congruence among heterogeneous actors and communities, in many cases articulating opposing interests or otherwise sharing few concerns. The use of numerical governance devices such as ranking lists and track record calculations are thus part of what Merry (2016, 2011) refers to as the "politics of measurement" that is supposed to work as an infrastructural system, i.e., it should be peripheral in public debates and be recognized as a natural order of things within the realm of the regulator's jurisdiction.

OUTLINE OF THE VOLUME

This book is structured into three parts and five chapters in addition to this introduction. The first part of the book, "On the theory and practice of governance" consists of the Introduction and Chapter 1, wherein the philosophical and legal roots of governance, and more specifically corporate governance are discussed. Chapter 1 discusses the two legal traditions derived from the writings of the English philosopher John Locke and the German philosopher George Wilhelm Friedrich Hegel as the starting point for the two dominant pathways for governance theory and practice, the free-market based governance model dominating the Anglo-American world of liberal market economies, and the more statist governance model rooted in the continental tradition of coordinated market economies. The first chapter thus emphasizes that the deviations between liberal market economies and embedded market economies need to be traced back to its intellectual roots and the wider institutional structure wherein such governance traditions are anchored.

The second part of the book, "Governing the economy" includes Chapters 2 through 4 and examines governance doctrines and reforms in three separate, yet intertwined practical domains, including corporate governance (Chapter 2), university governance (Chapter 3), and the governance of industry, and more specifically the finance industry (Chapter 4). The three chapters demonstrate that new governance regimes are by no means implemented without unanticipated consequences, externalities, and social and economic costs imposed on various actors. By the end of the day, governance reform and changes in governance practices, intended to accomplish certain economic objectives, are often-times accompanied by consequences that were not fully anticipated by the reformers and policy makers. Alternatively, governance reformers who campaign to establish new governance practices and doctrines may on purpose understate certain consequences, including the tilting of the balance of power between various stakeholders. The second part of the volume contains the principal empirical cases serving to substantiate the claim that governance remains an unfinished business.

The third part of the volume, "Theoretical and practical implications," includes only one final summary chapter wherein some of the shortcomings of the extant governance regime, operating on the micro (firm or production unit), meso (industry), and macro (transnational) levels of the global economy are examined. The chapter reviews some of the literature that discusses the theoretical doctrines and underlying ideologies that guide governance reform and new legislation in the contemporary period, but also points at some hands-on, practical reforms being advocated by, e.g., legal scholars. In the end, the volume advocates and calls for more scholarly research that examines practical shortcomings and theoretical doctrines that sub-optimize and/or serve to imbalance the delicate distribution of formal and real power between constituencies, accomplished on the basis of legislation, regulatory control, and governance. As governance is politics pursued by other means, governance is, to paraphrase the former French Prime Minister Georges Benjamin Clemenceau, a matter far too important to be left to a small group of insiders, especially when, e.g., changes in corporate governance practices instituted over the last four decades have proved to generate considerable externalities that befall others than the primary benefactors of such reforms. Seen in this view, governance scholarship needs to survey the full consequences of governance reform and not only myopically emphasizes singular measures such as efficiency.

SUMMARY AND CONCLUSION

The last four decades of governance reforms are entangled with two primary socio-economic changes: the unprecedented growth of the global finance industry and the shift in institutional logic towards finance industry interests, and the ideological discrediting of the sovereign state as a market maker and market regulator, enticing legal reforms and new governance practices increasingly relying on market-based self-regulation. The long-term consequences of these changes in the conventional wisdom and doctrines and ideologies remain disputed, but robust factual evidence indicates growing economic inequality and levels of debt now being at unprecedented levels. Instead of explaining the growth of systemic risk on the basis of microeconomic models, rendering, e.g., soaring household debt a consequence of inadequate decision making, or on the basis of "over-regulation" and similar state-led excesses (two favoured explanatory models in the moderate right to libertarian quarters), systemic risks are arguably created on the basis of systemic reforms and changes. Although governance, here defined as a term indicative of a polity substantially reducing the legitimacy of the sovereign state, is a composite term, including a variety of heterogeneous elements and operating within a temporal horizon wherein short- to long-term objectives are not easily reconciled, it is still argued that changes in governance on the micro, meso, and macro scales do deserve a closer scholarly analysis. While governance is, *ex hypothesi*, what is of necessity "unfinished," i.e., it is creaseless and ongoing, never fully stabilized but always "in the making," governance traditions and practices can still be examined in terms of their ability to generate economic and social welfare. Expressed differently, governance is neither the remedy nor a poison, but is a potion that can do good or do harm dependent on under what conditions it is applied. Making governance an issue beyond human influence is a form of defeatist fatalism, but to believe that governance is a universal solution to all kinds of social and economic malaises (see e.g., Pargendler, 2016) is not a viable way forward either; only acting with moderation ensures sustainable outcomes.

NOTES

1. The concept of inequality and its implied normative associations, i.e., that inequality is either inducing economic inefficiencies or morally questionable (or both), need to be explained and justified. Frankfurt (1987), a philosopher, is critical of the idea that "economic equality has considerable moral value in itself," and treats economic inequality not so much as a factual condition (and therefore a policy making matter), as it is a "moral idea" that needs to be examined on such grounds. In contrast to this inherited liberal view, Frankfurt (1987: 21) argues that "economic equality is not, as such, of particular moral importance." This view is consistent with Jencks' (2002: 50) claim that "[t]reating inequality as a moral issue does not make the empirical questions go away, because the most common moral arguments for and against inequality rest on claims about its consequences." In the next stage, if these claims regarding the consequences cannot be supported by evidence, Jencks (2002: 50) continues, "skeptics will find the moral arguments unconvincing," regarding moralist claims being factually unsubstantiated. What matters is, Frankfurt continues, is that all individuals "have *enough*," not that all individuals should "have *the same*," a position that Frankfurt (1987: 22) refers to as "the doctrine of sufficiency." To assume that all individuals deserve the same is not only an error, but is also a belief that "tends to do significant harm," Frankfurt (1987: 22) claims. For instance, Frankfurt (1987: 22) argues, "egalitarianism distracts people from measuring the requirements to which their individual natures and their personal circumstances give rise." Instead, egalitarianism as a "moral idea" encourages people "to insist upon a level of economic support that is determined by a calculation in which the particular features of their own lives are irrelevant" (Frankfurt, 1987: 22). This means that egalitarianism undermines a broader recognition of the various conditions under which a certain level of wealth is generated, but also that the

question of how to supply sufficient resources to individuals who need them are less prioritized.

While Frankfurt makes a valid point in emphasizing the slippery slope of the egalitarian argument (e.g., how much economic equality is enough, and at what point are enterprising incentives generating the economic resources at hand undermined by egalitarian policies and legislation?) and the is–ought fallacy (Volokh, 2003) inherent to the moral idea of economic equality as a desirable state, Frankfurt's argument is assuming that a call for some economic equality implies that all should "have the same." That is not the case, as most proponents of economic equality recognize the need to discriminate differences in income and entitlements, while the span for such differences of necessity is a political issue; some tolerate and justify larger economic inequality, while others may be more concerned about the consequences. Regardless of Frankfurt's (1987) critique, egalitarianism comes in many versions.

Therefore, when economic inequality is invoked to justify a scholarly analysis of governance regimes in this volume, it is based on the economic idea that excessive economic inequality (i.e., at the point where considerable proportions of accumulated finance capital is excluded from productive circulation, e.g., it is not used for consumption or invested in production capital and human resources, but is saved or re-invested in the finance industry) is harmful for a dynamic economy inasmuch as it undermines the long-term capacity of generating economic welfare for a majority of the stakeholders or citizens. That is, this proposition is consistent with Jencks' (2002: 53) liberal critique of economic inequality that predicts that inequality, above a certain, yet hard-to-define level, "retards" economic growth. In addition, as no economy can be examined in a social, cultural, or historical vacuum, social norms regarding tolerable degrees of economic inequality (see, e.g., Bonica et al., 2013)—very few individuals actually do believe that all should have "the same"—cannot be conspicuously violated without considerable social costs that in turn translate into economic costs. That is, regardless of the idea of economic equality being an economic theory proposition, a "moral idea," or something else, humans tend to construct norms regarding what Frankfurt (1987) calls "enough" economic resources, and as they live according to such norms, violations of the norms may have unanticipated consequences. Economic equality is therefore an actual and legitimate concern pertaining to scholarly inquiry and, more specifically, the question of governance addressed in this volume, despite its inability to provide a waterproof case when being subject to a stern analytical procedure.

2. Karabarbounis and Neiman (2014) report that between 1975 and 2012, in the 59 countries included in the sample, 42 "exhibited downward trends in their labor shares." Brennan (2014) observes a similar tendency in his sample, and points at a divergence between productivity growth and real-wage growth. In the U.S., Haskel et al. (2012: 120) show, there has been "a dramatic acceleration in aggregate labor productivity growth since the mid-1990s," with nonfarm business sector output per hour growth being at 1.4 percent per year over the 1973–1995 period, but thereafter taking a leap to 2.5 percent per year over the 1996–2009 period. Despite this productivity growth, Haskel et al. (2012: 120) speak of "[p]ervasive real-income declines for the large majority of Americans in the past decade." Furthermore, Kristal (2013: 383) reports that U.S. productivity grew 80.4 percent between 1972 and 2011, while the median worker's hourly compensation "grew just by 10,7 percent." Weil (2014: 16) writes that productivity rose by 23 percent between 2000 and 2012, but only 0.5 percent real-wage growth could be secured for the median worker.

Karabarbounis and Neiman (2014: 62) claim that the decline in labour share cannot be explained on the basis of exogenous factors (e.g., technological shifts or the globalization of the economy), but are instead for most parts "attributable to within-industry changes rather than to changes in industrial composition." Brennan (2014: 249) suggests that "[t]here is a shift in power in the economy away from traditional wage-earning workers and towards those who make money from non-work activities": "[F]rom 1966 to 2001 ... the top 10% of wage and salary earners were gaining at the expense of everyone else, including the median workers" (Brennan, 2014: 249–250). Kristal (2013) and Wolff (2003) argue that waning unionization has been the main force behind the decline in labour's share: "[A] reasonable presumption might be that an equal division of power between capital and labour should lead to real wages increasing at about the same rate as overall labour productivity. If wages increase more slowly, we might suspect that the balance in power has shifted towards capital," Wolff (2003: 497) argues. Also Karabarbounis and Neiman (2014: 102) stress the trade-off between labour shares of income and business earnings and corporate saving, and suggest that "[t]his large change in the flow of funds between households and firms may have important macroeconomic repercussions."

3. Scheidel's (2017) magisterial overview of economic inequality in historical societies provides a rich number of examples of how excessive economic inequality is caused either by overbearing political crises or natural disasters (such as the plague in the fourteenth century in Europe), or correlates with various sorts of political conflicts or economic crises. In this overview, spanning from the Neolithic age over antiquity and into late-modern competitive capitalism, economic inequality is not a signature of a vital economic and social system. On basis of such historical records, economic inequality should be taken seriously. On the other hand, economic inequality is widely taken as an indicator of a dynamic economy, providing life chances and opportunities for the venturesome or clever, whose acumen and enterprising capacities benefit also, in the end, the poorer income strata. Furthermore, the level of economic inequality (measured in terms of the Gini index) is substantially lower in most democratic, industrialized states than in the historical societies that Scheidel (2017) examines.

4. The literature provides a number of examples of "governance devices" including "managerial ownership" (Bhagat, Bolton, and Romano, 2008: 1838), "the market for corporate control" (Fisch, 2010: 942), and "fiduciary duties" (Macey, 1991: 41).

1. Governance varieties: Locke and Hegel's philosophy of right and the roots of governance traditions

INTRODUCTION

The so-called Great Recession (Redbird and Grusky, 2016; Suárez, 2014; Biven and Shierholz, 2013; Mian and Sufi, 2010), now looming for close to a decade, especially in parts of Europe, and materializing into political consequences (the "Brexit" referendum in the U.K., and the anti-free trader Donald Trump surprising the "political establishment" in Washington by defeating Hilary Clinton) has also generated a renewed scholarly interest for the elementary governance mechanisms underlying the economic stagnation and soaring economic inequality now being widely recognized as undisputed conditions of the contemporary period (Jacobs and Dirlam, 2016; Wodtke, 2016; Stockhammer, 2015; Bartolini, Bonatti, and Sarracino, 2014; Gilens, 2012; Alderson and Nielsen, 2002). Among many things, the enforcement, not so much *de jure* as de facto, of a shareholder primacy model (court rulings in, e.g., Delaware, the state of choice for incorporation for the majority of Fortune 1000 companies, still provide strong support for the "board-centric corporate system"; Levitin, 2014: 2059), stipulating that governance enriching shareholders, the firm's investors, not only minimize the risks of management opportunism but also benefit *all* stakeholders, has been fortified as the dominant corporate governance doctrine. While the popularity of the shareholder primacy model coincides with (some would say *precedes*; see, e.g., Tomaskovic-Devey, Lin, and Meyers, 2015; Dobbin and Jung, 2010) a series of worrying tendencies in advanced capitalist economies, including declining economic growth, soaring economic inequality, the loss of blue-collar and white-collar jobs, and declining investment in long-term ventures including R&D and human capital, the advocacy of the shareholder primacy model seems unrelenting; shareholder primacy advocates do still, notwithstanding the remarkable success they have had in advancing their reform agenda, Cremers and Sepe (2016: 135) say, "see shareholder empowerment as not yet accomplished." Against this wider institutional and socio-economic foregrounding, there are reasons to examine the intellectual and doctrinaire roots of the shareholder primacy model. The history of the shareholder advocacy from the mid-1970s and the publication of the seminal paper of Jensen and Meckling in 1976, is well covered in the corporate governance literature, but this more "recent history" needs to be complemented by the analysis of what the renowned Annales-school historian Fernand Braudel (1980) refers to as *la longue durée*, the long duration wherein intellectual ideas gain a foothold in historical processes only over time but may suddenly spring forward, at times seemingly from nowhere (as in the case of the recurrent waves of American conservatism in the eyes of liberal commentators; see Philips-Fein, 2009: 725) when "their time has come," as the saying goes.

The purpose of this chapter is therefore to discuss how the so-called "Berle–Means firm" was established in the New Deal framework (Hawley, 1966), wherein the legal scholar Adolf Berle served as an advisor in the Roosevelt administration. Prior to the Wall Street crash of 1929, and the depression that lasted well until the Second World War served to blow life into the American economy, there was a debate initiated by the leading American economist Thorstein Veblen and liberals such as the lawyer Louis D. Brandeis regarding the relationship between finance capital investors and "real economy actors," voicing worries that in an economy dominated by "passive shareholders," enterprising and entrepreneurial impetus would be undermined or compromised in undesirable ways. This debate was in turn animated by inherited intellectual traditions in the U.K. (and dominated by the philosophy of right of John Locke, the great British empiricist and proponent of liberalism) and in continental Europe (primarily Germany, and with George Wilhelm Friedrich Hegel's *Philosophie des Rechts* as its intellectual foundation), both being important influences for the New Dealers. Only by examining how the concerns addressed by Veblen and Brandeis in the 1910s, and how their critique of "the Money Trust" was muted in the depression era and post-Second World War period can the present day concerns regarding the long-term consequences of the shareholder primacy model be fully understood. In essence, economists expressing a firm belief in the efficacy of market-pricing, i.e., an economic model by-passing or ignoring the role of the sovereign state, were more attracted by John Locke's "minimal theory of rights" in comparison to Hegel's "extended theory of rights," which granted the sovereign state a more active and affirmative role. While Roosevelt advisors by and large were sympathetic towards continental European doctrines of statism (Adelstein, 1991: 165), the intellectual and cultural climate in the U.S. undermined a meaningful application of, e.g., governance doctrines rooted in, e.g., Hegel's thinking. In the end, the received American model was constructed and operated on the basis of a minimal state doctrine. The consequences for corporate governance practice and theory are considerable, for instance, rendering legislative practices and regulatory control orchestrated by the state suspect in the eyes of, e.g., free-market protagonists.

THE PHILOSOPHY OF RIGHT: THE LIBERAL/BRITISH AND THE STATIST/CONTINENTAL TRADITIONS

While paying attention to philosophical doctrines may appear a concern for a handful of academic specialists or seminarists in defined disciplines, the connection between philosophical doctrines and latter day governance practices is not a moot question. In fact, like in the case of biological systems, also human cultures and social institutions are "built from the bottom up," originating with elementary mechanisms and differentiating over time. Therefore, the economic system of competitive capitalism, intimately bound up with modern democracy and the emergence of a scientific worldview, in brief, *modernity*, needs to be traced to its roots to explain contemporary conditions and practices.

As Duggan (2003: 4) explains, "liberal theorists, such as John Locke and Adam Smith, provided a set of metaphors, an organizing narrative, and a moral apologia for capitalism." The British liberalism tradition, leveraged by the dominance of the Britons in international trade from the early eighteenth century, has many thinkers on its pantheon, including not least John Locke, formulating the foundational liberal principle that any man has the right to the fruits of the work he has invested in or laid down in, say, ploughing and sowing a field, building a clock, or baking a batch of loaves. The concept of property rights in the modern sense of the term, central to Locke's work, was first developed by the Dutch scholar Hugo Grotius (1583–1645). Grotius developed his concept of property rights from natural law. In this view, humans had the "natural right" to use communal resources, say, "apples, land, cloths, chattels, etc." not yet claimed by anyone (De Araujo, 2009: 356). However, this right to use such resources does not per se justify property rights in the modern sense of the term: "In the state of nature, to say that an object is 'common' does not mean to say that everyone possesses it but, rather, that it does not belong to anyone. If an object belongs to everyone, then it is called 'public,'" De Araujo (2009: 356) writes. To overcome the limitations of natural law, Grotius regarded property right a human institution, derived from humans' interactions with one another (De Araujo, 2009: 356). In other words, property rights is not "a natural state of affairs" but is constituted on the basis of human reason; private property, Grotius argued, "arises out of collective recognition that a person is entitled to retain or keep for oneself an object he or she has occupied in the first instance" (De Araujo, 2009: 358). Human interactions, which gradually become more intense as society "thickens," generate the need for property rights, Grotius argues, and consequently a variety of social institutions such as laws, commerce, and the state are created "for the protection of the institution of private property" (De Araujo, 2009: 364). The epistemic leap in Grotius' legal theory of property rights is thus from the foundational idea of "natural law" to the institutional view of legislation, a bond between theology-inspired legal theory and a modern institutional legal theory that Grotius, despite his brilliance, could not dissolve. Jeremy Bentham (1748–1832), for instance, writing two centuries later, rejected all propositions regarding natural law, stating that "Rights are ... the fruits of law, and of the law alone. There are no rights without law—no rights contrary to the law—no rights anterior to the law" (Jeremy Bentham, cited in De Araujo, 2009: 366). Despite having one foot left in scholastic legal theory and Aristotelianism, Grotius' legal theory of property rights still paved the way for later generations of legal scholars—the Scottish Enlightenment scholars including e.g., David Hume and Adam Smith recognized Grotius' work (Haakonssen, 1996, 1985)—and the philosophy of right presented by Locke and Hegel.

In the Anglo-American liberal tradition, Locke is a saintly figure that justifies human integrity and elementary rights vis-à-vis authorities and elites such as the aristocracy. Locke is also explicitly enacting political power, materialized into "a right of making laws with penalties of death, and consequently all less penalties," as a privilege and prerogative granted only for the benefit of "the public good" (Locke, 1690/2003: 101, Book II, §3). That is, the legislator, first the sovereign and thereafter democratically elected parliaments, must not use legislation to benefit their own interest. In contrast, Hegel's philosophy of right, formulated 13 decades after Locke's *Two Treatises on Government* appeared, recognizes private property as a basic legal right, but unlike Locke who stipulates ownership rights as an end in itself, and being of limited interest or concern for the sovereign state once such rights have been enacted by law, Hegel presents a considerably more complex theory of property and property rights. Hegel starts with a fictive individual in a pre-social condition, and asserts that this individual has the right to property; indeed, the right to property is "the origin" of the person's "right to life and liberty" (Stillman, 1988: 1032)—for Hegel, property is "essential for an individual's freedom" (Stillman, 1988: 1032). This is essentially where Locke's philosophy of right ends, being a "minimal theory" of rights based on the proposition that "[E]very man has a *property* in his *own person* ... The *labour* of his body, and the *work* of his hands, we may say, are properly his" (John Locke, *Two Treatises on Government*, Book II, Ch. 5, cited in Stillman, 1988: 1040). In Hegel's thought, this pro-social recognition of the property right is merely the starting point, an axiomatic first principle in his elaborate philosophy of right. Through his property, Hegel argues, "the person goes forth from himself to relate to other men and to build social institutions" (Stillman, 1988: 1036), i.e., property is the *vehicle* for the construction of an autonomous self and the individual liberties are the basis for the free individual. At the same time, which is a key complexity of Hegel's dense writing, property must, to serve its political, social, and economic purposes, be *aufgehoben* (derived from Hegel's central philosophical term *Aufheben*, meaning "to sublate," to preserve by transcending or to preserve by "destruction" or "cancellation")—it must be both preserved and transcended, become part of the life of the individual and an element within "the structure of society" (Stillman, 1988: 1037). This is a most complex point made by Hegel:

> Hegel's political philosophy is founded on property; but it is founded on property only so that it can transcend property. The fully developed individual—active outside the sphere of abstract rights, the system of needs, and the administration of justice—has moral and ethical ideals and human interactions (for example, family and state) that are not based on private property. But property nonetheless remains a permanent apparatus for carrying out a life plan, for giving reality to a conception of his own good, for his further development, and for his self-satisfaction. (Stillman, 1988: 1037)

The decisive point is that Locke and Hegel represent the two freedoms identified by Isiah Berlin (1958), with Locke speaking of property in terms of *negative freedom*—freedom from oppression and the governance of the sovereign or the government—and Hegel emphasizing how property rights enable and justify participation in civil society. As Stillman (1988: 1040) remarks, "Locke's person is socially and psychologically somewhat static and protective because he already has everything that he needs," while Hegel's person, in contrast, is "dynamic and developmental"; Hegel's person must work to "appropriate and apprehend himself," tasks which, to be fully accomplished, "require not only the content of the prepolitical condition but also, and necessarily, moral attitudes and practical experience in a range of rational social institutions" (Stillman, 1988: 1040). In this latter enactment of the private and public self, society and by implication the state has a much more significant role to play. Locke postulates that the right to property is original and an end in itself, and the individual is thus independent or separated from the individual's social relations "in the state of nature and in civil or political society." In brief, neither individuality, nor property rights are constituted within the realm of social relations. In the Lockean universe, "the preservation of the person's property is a constant and unchanging goal for citizens and for political society," Stillman (1988: 1041) summarizes. This position is central to the Anglo-American tradition of liberalism and its scepticism towards statism in any form, especially in American conservativism and libertarian intellectual traditions.

In Hegel's thinking, social relations, society, and the state are granted a more central and a more positive role. Hegel does not, however, reduce or equate the constitution of fully developed individuals and individual freedom with the functioning of the surrounding society and the state. Just like with the fully developed individual, realizing his or her potentiality, Hegel envisions a social and political world that must grow progressively richer, more complex, and more various in order to "generate the values and relations that can enrich the developing individuality that citizens pursue and that politics encourages" (Stillman, 1988: 1041). For a hard-core latter day libertarian, this vision may sound either naïve or as a *carte blanche* for the development of an authoritarian state, but what Hegel arguably advocated was possibly something more like the liberal welfare state, wherein all the individuals are given certain liberties and possibilities (i.e., through the education system) to become the fully developed person they have the capacity to become. In Locke's view, property right is the basis for a liberal society, but for Hegel, the same property rights are merely the stepping stone for an ongoing project to constitute individuality and a functional society supportive of the development of an autonomous and fully capable person.

The Image of the Market and the Legal Device of the Contract

The deviations that Locke and Hegel's philosophies demonstrate beyond the shared recognition of property right as a constitutive right have considerable economic and policy making implications. While Locke is relatively silent regarding the relationship between the individual and the wider economic system (while being commonly understood as taking an affirmative view of, e.g., commerce, a proposition induced from Locke's statement regarding the rights to property as derived from an investment in labour), Hegel is more explicitly separating the economy from civil society, Stillman (1988) argues:

Hegel does not wish to impose images, metaphors, or models of private property and free contract throughout all social life. Nor does he wish to follow economistic theorists in asserting, without much argument or context, that free alienating and contracting are always desirable. (Stillman, 1988: 1054)

Again, Hegel's thinking is sophisticated and demands careful examination, and while he is sceptical of reducing property right to economic conditions and mechanisms (e.g., contracting), he still regards "the corporation" as being one of the key institutions of the civil society: "The *family* is the first ethical root of the state; the *corporation* is the second, and it is based in civil society," Hegel (1999: 379) declares. In this context, it is important to keep in mind that "corporation" does not primarily denote the modern firm with defined features such as limited liability, distributed ownership, and salaried managers overseeing operations, but the corporation denotes a wider set of organized activities such as churches, townships, schools, and voluntary organizations. For instance, the development of corporate law, the legal protection of incorporated business ventures against various external and internal opportunistic behaviour and providing additional legal rights and privileges, originally enacted in the late eighteenth century and, being widely established by the mid-nineteenth century in the U.S. (Blair, 2003: 425–426), did not originally incorporate business ventures at all (Kaufman, 2008: 404). Instead, all kinds of civil organizations including churches and townships were granted such business charters. Still, Hegel (1820/1981: 189) emphasizes "the corporation," defined as commercial and professional as well as municipal organizations employing "officials, directors, managers, and the like," as playing a key role in civil society. More specifically, in the corporation, defined as "voluntarily organized groups" including "business corporations, churches, interest groups, charitable societies, etc.," the corporation member finds scope for "liberality and rectitude," Hegel claims (Stillman, 1988: 1048). Within this context of the corporation, private property is *aufgehoben*; it is simultaneously put to use and affected by the norms and goals of the corporation, and the individual must actively contribute to receive *recognition*, and not only maximize personal profit.

Despite this affirmative view of the corporation in Hegel's philosophy of right, Hegel is, unlike social contract theorists in the British tradition (Hobbes, Locke, Adam Smith, etc,) not willing to use the legal device or, alternatively, metaphor of the contract as a meaningful mechanism in his analytical model. This in turn is rooted in Hegel's scepticism towards the idea of the market, widely recognized as an ethically neutral arbiter and efficient resource allocation mechanism in the British liberalism tradition (most notably captured by Adam Smith's metaphor of the "invisible" but ultimately benevolent and fair "hand," directing resources to their best use and thus transcending and neutralizing instrumental self-interest). In contrast to this liberal view, Hegel does not see how the market can provide sufficient agency for the free individual. This is in turn because market transactions, enabled by the use of the legal device of the contract, are based on inequality of power and do not demonstrate what Hegel calls the requirement of "double competition"—competition among "both buyers and sellers." As markets are tilting to benefit either buyers or sellers (as conveyed by the expression, "It's a buyer's/seller's market today"), Hegel anticipates governmental intervention to make markets operable and efficient (Stillman, 1988: 1056). Furthermore, even if markets hypothetically *would* demonstrate fair competition and an absence of power imbalances, Hegel does not believe the legal device of the contract can serve as a metaphor for the state and civil society, simply because the contract is too narrow and too focused on defining mutual rights and obligations (not least because this functional simplicity enables legal enforcement) to fully apprehend how the individual develops socially, intellectually, and emotionally within the realm of the state. Therefore, for Hegel, the market and its contract device/metaphor does not provide adequate possibilities for individuals choosing, which is a *sine qua non* for individual independence and self-determination (Stillman, 1988: 1053). By and large, Hegel is also sceptical towards the idea that freedom of choice would be a legitimate or qualified candidate for the constitution of the free and autonomous individual, on the one hand because the market does not provide possibilities for authentic choices, and on the other hand because the idea of "freedom of choice" is beside the point within Hegel's philosophy of right: "Membership in civil society is not a matter of choice" (Stillman, 1988: 1054).

In summary, Locke provides a minimal liberal theory of negative freedom ("freedom from"), wherein the right to the fruits of one's own labour is a constitutive right in civil society. Hegel, in contrast, offers an extended liberal theory of positive freedom ("freedom to"), wherein property right is stipulated as the basis for civil society, but wherein social organizations such as the corporation and the state play a more central role in materializing individual liberties. Many things do separate Locke and Hegel, but they are unified in their firm stance on property rights, being at the core of the philosophy of rights. While the minimal theory of Locke has been the beacon for generations of Anglo-American liberals, conservatives, and libertarians, Hegel's scepticism about the market and the alleged virtues of freedom of choice (not least being some kind of slogan for the Chicago school of economics tradition, following Milton Friedman's charismatic lead; see, e.g., Friedman and Friedman, 1979) has been less recognized. Yet, Hegel's argument about property rights as being a *constitutional right*, still being only the starting point for the participation in and continuous development of civil society and, *ipso facto*, the individual, is haunting policy makers and theorists, perhaps because it indicates that private property without a surrounding society and functional state would be an oxymoron, as the very term "private" is introduced as a contrast to "public," and "property" is per se a legal term that presupposes at least a minimal state supplying jurisprudence, or at least the presence of collective norms. As will be discussed below, the Hegelian scepticism towards the market and the concern for the corporation as a vehicle for the fulfilment of collective pursuits has been a perennial issue in the corporate governance literature. That is, Hegel's thinking may receive limited recognition in comparison to Locke's, but the issues Hegel addresses within his philosophy of right remain of relevance for corporate governance practice, policy, and scholarship.

THE PRE-DEPRESSION CORPORATE GOVERNANCE DEBATE

The modern concept of the firm including all its defined features was enshrined by corporate law that was developed during the nineteenth century. In addition to corporate law, developed to promote business venturing and enterprising in societies quickly being transformed by the industrial revolution, corporate governance denotes a set of practices, standards, legislation, and regulatory activities that serve to monitor the business venture—the corporation. While corporate law is relatively stable over time to enable a transparent corporate system and law enforcement, yet accompanied in the Anglo-American common law tradition by court ruling cases that further substantiate and clarify the legislation, corporate governance is subject to continuous modifications and ongoing discussions and scholarly analyses. Much of the modern corporate governance practices were developed in the depression era and in the post-Second World War period, characterized by what has been called "managerialism" (Marris, 1964) and the development of the "Berle–Means firm," characterized by the separation of ownership and control. Also in the period preceding the Wall Street crash and the reforms that followed to restore competitive capitalism, there were concerns regarding the governance of industry and the corporate system.

Thorstein Veblen, for instance—"quite probably the most famous American economist in the first quarter of the twentieth century," in Ebenstein's (2015: 28) account—expressed his concern regarding what he referred to as "absentee ownership," i.e., finance capital owners' investment in companies to reap the benefits without being actively involved in the day-to-day management. In Veblen's view (1919/1964: 44), in this regime, ownership has become "denatured" and "no longer carries its earlier duties and responsibilities." The dominance of "absentee ownership of anonymous corporate capital" means that the corporate system loses some of its legitimacy, as wealthy investors can now "control the conditions of life" of the majority of the population, but without taking any responsibility. In another publication, Veblen (1916: 16) criticized the new "financial captains of industry," who demonstrate that an "[a]ddiction to abstract and unremitting valuation of all things in terms of price and profit leaves them, by settled habit, unfit to appreciate those technological facts and values that can be formulated only in terms of tangible mechanical performance." In Veblen's (1916: 16) scathing critique of these finance capital investors, "they are experts in process and profits and financial manoeuvers; and yet the final discretion in all questions of industrial policy continues to rest in their hands." There are thus two major concerns that Veblen addresses: first, that finance capital investors are granted significant power and authority in the economic system of competitive capitalism, now being able to serve, Veblen (1919/1964: 45) says, as "an anonymous pensioner on the enterprise." Second, Veblen (1916: 16) is worried that this singlehanded emphasis on "profits and financial manoeuvers" leads to "the financial captains of industry ... losing touch with the management of industrial processes, at the same time that the management of corporate business has, in effect, been shifting into the hands of a bureaucratic clerical staff." In the end, Veblen believes the corporate system is now being hi-jacked and taken over by investors exclusively concerned with generating finance capital rents, but otherwise having little expertise in how liquidity is generated on the basis of highly illiquid capital such as machinery, input materials, and human resources.

Veblen was not the only liberal in the period who worried about the dominance of the finance industry and the hegemony of finance capital investors. The liberal lawyer Louis D. Brandeis (1914/1967: 43), an outspoken critic of what he referred to as the "money trust"[1] claimed that "industrial and political liberty" was "imperiled" by the money trust. Like Veblen, Brandeis was critical of the finance industry's claim that they supplied the finance capital needed to fuel the capitalist economy, while, in fact, Brandeis claimed, "the great banking houses" only "come into relation" with enterprises, "either after the success had been attained, or upon 'reorganization' after the possibility of success had been demonstrated," or when the funds of "the hardy pioneers, who had risked their all, were exhausted" (Brandeis, 1914/1967: 91–92). Such claims are consistent with and substantiated by more recent scholarly works demonstrating that finance capital enters industries only *after* most of the risks have been discounted by the state, or where the state serves to socialize losses (Roy, 1997; Evans, 1995; Dobbin, 1994; Levitin, 2014). In other words, liberals such as Veblen and Brandeis were concerned already during the first decades of the twentieth century that finance capital investors were granted liberties that were possibly not optimal for overall economic efficiency, as they undermined the incentives of business entrepreneurs. In the 1920s, and especially after the Wall Street crash of 1929, this discussion about the relationship between passive capital owners and active entrepreneurs, business promoters, and their assigned executives would be even more animated, not the least on the basis of the works published by the legal scholar Adolf A. Berle.

THE DEPRESSION-ERA RESOLUTION: THE QUESTIONS OF THE SEPARATION OF OWNERSHIP AND CONTROL, MANAGERIAL ACCOUNTABILITY, AND THE INSTITUTIONALIZATION OF THE "BERLE–MEANS FIRM"

Just like Veblen and Brandeis two decades earlier, depression-era liberal scholars and intellectuals were equally concerned with the governance of industry and the role of capital investors. What has been known as the Dodd–Berle debate between the Harvard Law School Professor E. Merrick Dodd Jr. and President Roosevelt's advisor Adolf A. Berle has been emphasized as a watershed discussion between advocates of state regulation and a market-oriented governance model. Following Veblen and Brandeis' strident advocacy of a more detailed monitoring of the finance industry, Dodd (1932: 1153) argued that shareholders, "who have no contact with business other than to derive dividends from it," were particularly unsuitable for playing a key role in contributing to social and economic welfare. Rather than promoting shareholder-centric or finance industry-based governance in the corporate system, Dodd (1932: 1153), proposed that "incorporated business" could only be "professionalized" (i.e., play a wider role than merely generate rents for its investors) if the managers were involved in such a project. For instance, one such welfare-generating effect, of acute interest during the depression era when unemployment soared to unprecedented levels, was how to make "the economic security of the worker" one of the obligations of the incorporated business, Dodd (1932: 1151–1152) argued. For Dodd (1932), such questions were not simply of academic or theoretical interest but concerned the question of whether "capitalism is worth saving" and can "permanently survive under modern conditions"; for Dodd, writing in 1932, such eschatological themes were by no means far-fetched or beyond the issues at hand.

Berle, a liberal legal scholar, shared many of Dodd's worries and concerns, and yet his response to Dodd has been widely interpreted as a clear defence of a shareholder-based corporate governance model. This interpretation of Berle's work has been disputed in the corporate governance literature, where some scholars emphasize that Berle did in fact not endorse shareholder primacy governance, as advocated by agency theorists and contract theorists from the 1970s. Similar to Dodd (1932), concerned about the efficacy of the governance function of the corporate system, Berle (1932: 1366–1367) speaks of the "great industrial managers, their bankers and still more the men composing their silent 'control'" (i.e., shareholders), and claims that this group today serves "more as princes and ministers than as promoters or merchants." In addition, Berle (1932: 1367) is sceptical towards the recent view, taken by corporate lawyers—"mainly in New York," Berle adds—that managers are "trustees" for "corporate security holders." This can be seen as a critique of early attempts to downplay the role of managers in the corporate system. Yet, Berle (1932) is a staunch defender of the economic system based on individual ownership of property, and he deplores the lack of concern regarding "the subject of private property" in "American enlightened juristic thought." This negligence is a "great misfortune" in Berle's account, because "a society based on the individual" can only be maintained on the basis of a "vigorous protection of the property that he has" (Berle, 1932: 1368). However, consistent with Veblen's previous critique, Berle makes a distinction between "active" and "passive" property, whereof the latter is exemplified by a "stock certificate or a bond," each representing "an infinitesimal claim on massed industrial wealth and funnelled income-stream" (Berle, 1932: 1368). At the same time—and this is probably the reason for his being portrayed as a shareholder primacy governance advocate—Berle says that "the owner of passive property" has limited possibilities for securing the value of such assets, but can only sell off the asset if he is dissatisfied with the performance of the management team of the firm, issuing the stock; furthermore, this predicament "[l]eaves him [the shareholder] entirely in the hands of the factual possessor or administrator of the massed wealth" (Berle, 1932: 1370).

Berle (1932: 1370) then proceeds to claim that the present regime of corporate management has generated a social and professional class that can seize power "without recognition of responsibility." That is, it is reasonable to claim that Berle (1932) is more sceptical towards unchecked managerial authority than he is concerned with shareholders drawing the shortest straw; the subordinate position of the shareholder is merely invoked to indicate the power balance in favour of top management in American corporations. Berle (1932) is thus sceptical towards Dodd's (1932) belief in the managers as social reformers and functionaries within the emerging welfare state:

> Most students of corporation finance dream of a time when corporate administration will be held to a high degree of required responsibility—a responsibility conceived not merely in terms of stockholders' rights, but in terms of economic government satisfying the respective needs of investors, workers, customers, and the aggregated community. (Berle, 1932: 1372)

Furthermore, Berle advocates mechanisms that would impose checks and balances on managers, or else they would be able to claim substantial authority in the corporate system, and, *ipso facto*, wider society, now dependent on the corporate system for its subsistence:

> Unchecked by present legal balances, a social-economic absolutism of corporate administrators, even if benevolent, might be unsafe; and in any case it hardly affords the soundest base on which to construct the economic commonwealth which industrialism seems to require. (Berle, 1932: 1372)

Berle's (1932) staid critique of unregulated managerial authority has been widely interpreted as a favourable attitude towards shareholder primacy governance, especially after the publication of Berle and Means' seminal work *The Modern Corporation & Private Property* in 1932—"[o]ne of the most influential social-scientific works of the twentieth century" (Moore and Rebérioux, 2011: 86)—at the height of depression and within the political project to restore the faith in competitive capitalism. Competitive capitalism was both seriously impaired by the system-wide consequences of the Wall Street crash of 1929, and was now rivalled by both socialist and communist economic models and the corporatist fascist economic model being developed in, e.g., Italy and Germany in the 1930s.

Still, against this background, Berle's concern for shareholders has been overstated, Hill and Painter (2009: 1178) claim:

The emphasis on stock-based compensation reflected that in many influential quarters, shareholder primacy had become the norm. To overstate the case (but not by much), many believed that making managers shareholders would solve everything. Thus, one of the problems that Berle identified—that managers too often do not do what stockholders want them to do—was supposedly solved, with enormous, some would say grotesque, stock compensation plans. The broader problem that Berle, Dodd and Brandeis had discussed—that corporations and particularly banks were sometimes run in a socially irresponsible manner—was largely ignored. (Hill and Painter, 2009: 1178)

When advocating this interpretation of Berle's work and his intentions, Berle's response to a critique of his work published by legal scholar Henry Manne in 1962 is key to Berle's normative view of the balance of power between shareholders and managers (and, thus, the firm *sui juris*). Being a head-on assault on *The Modern Corporation & Private Property*, Manne (1962) claims that a lack of "traditional economic analysis," and an overstating of corporate law issues undermine the practical relevance of the book. By implication, Manne continues, Berle and Means (1934) advocate a corporate governance model that keeps managers "safe from outside interference" (i.e., market evaluations of their performance). This, in turn, Manne (1962: 405) argues, leads to predictable and systematic managerial opportunism: "If this situation exists for all firms in the industry, then … incumbent managers will be able to capture for themselves this greater-than-competitive return for their services." Here, Manne (1962: 404) does not spare the reader numerous examples of how this managerial opportunism may materialize into squandering of resources, including the buying of "[e]xpensive office furnishings, lavish expense accounts, company yachts, time off from day-to-day business concerns, and a variety of other nonpecuniary rewards." In short, Manne (1962) portrays Berle and Means (1934) as being lax on managerial accountability and naïve regarding allegedly escalating opportunist behaviour in executive suites.

Needless to say, Berle (1962) does not let such accusations pass without a proper response, and stepwise disassembles Manne's argumentation. First of all, Berle is critical of Manne's inability to take into account the wider socio-economic and historical conditions that brought forward Berle and Means' (1932) seminal work:

Professor Manne and his contemporaries did not live through World War I and the decade of the twenties, and the crash of 1929, culminating in the breakdown of the American economic system in 1933. They have not experienced a corporate and financial world without the safeguards of the Securities and Exchange Commission, without systemization and enforced

publicity of corporate accounting, without (more or less) consistent application of antitrust laws, without discouragement of financial pyramiding, and
which tolerated conflicts of interest to a degree unthinkable now. (Berle,
1962: 433)

Berle (1962) thus argues that Manne (1962) is guilty of the so-called
"whig history" fallacy, wherein the present situation is understood to be
the outcome of a series of inevitable and historically determined events
unfolding, and where the situation today is accomplished on the basis of
an almost mechanical finalism. As opposed to this view, commonly
treated as an overtly naïve historical view, it could have been possible
that history would have taken a different turn, leading to entirely different
scenarios and outcomes.

Second, Berle (1962) grapples with the implicit objective of Manne's
(1962) critique, to advocate and render legitimate an economic theory of
law that should trump inherited legal traditions and legal theory on the
basis of instrumental rationality and calculations derived from rational
choice theory: "Professor Manne and his academic supporters are, of
course, accepting and crusading for an academic theory of economics,
and are trying to place the modern corporation within it" (Berle, 1962:
435). This attempt to overturn legal theory and to subsume it under some
generic "economic theory of law" (pioneered by the law and economics
tradition initiated at the law school of the University of Chicago by
Aaron Director in the 1950s, originally concentrating on criticizing
anti-trust law; Van Horn and Emmett, 2015) does not impress Berle. In
Berle's view, the critique of what he refers to as "the industrial system"
on the basis of orthodox economic theory overlooks and marginalizes the
role of institutions being developed over time, and ignores the separation
of "ownership from management" as being a legal innovation (Berle,
1962: 436), protected by law in business charters issued by states (in the
U.S.) or the federal state (in, e.g., the U.K.). Rather than being inefficient
and impaired by clumsy and self-sufficient managers, this corporate
system, being under the guidance and control of both finance market
actors and regulatory agencies (whereof many were instituted within
various New Deal initiatives), Berle (1962: 437) says, "has done more for
more people, has made possible a higher standard of living for the vast
majority of a huge population in a huge country, has preserved more
liberty for individual self-development, and now affords more tools
(however unused or badly used) from which a good society can be forged
so far as economics can do so, than any system in recorded history." At
the same time, Berle (1962: 437) admits, despite such accomplishments
and benefits, the industrial system is still "eons from perfection."

In the sections that follow, Berle proceeds to respond to and reject a series of technical issues brought up by Manne (1962) and consistently avert his criticism regarding the protection of managers, and undermines Manne's own theory of the market for management control. In making this argument to support the received corporate system as stipulated by corporate law, Berle (1962) enforces the authority and discretion of managers vis-à-vis shareholders; in Berle's view, Manne (1962) and his collaborators fail to present any credible argument justifying legal reforms. That is, the authority and discretion of managers stand fast and in fact represent a balancing force against "free market pricing":

> In assuming responsibility for certain aspects of community life, in making gifts to charity, in playing any role in economic statesmanship not dictated by market considerations, the corporate management traitorously departs from the discipline of seeking the highest possible profit, regarded by classicists as the motive driving all into the court of the 'free market'—the supreme and beneficent arbitrator. When these recreant managements depart somewhat from their devotion to making the last market-dollar for their stockholders, they denigrate the market mechanism and are thus faithless to their profit-seeking trust. (Berle, 1962: 442)

When revisiting Berle's article (1962), Berle does not emerge as a proponent of shareholder primacy, nor as a sponsor of shareholder activism. On the contrary, Berle's work represents a legal theory view of the corporate system that does not seek to reduce the relationship between the legal device of the business charter, its finance capital supply, and its executive function to a mere price-setting mechanism. In Berle's view, the legal device of the corporation, developed over decades and even centuries, cannot be abandoned simply on the basis of fictive cases of allegedly rampant managerial malfeasance, as the institutional framework of competitive capitalism is a social and legal system that has evolved over time and with the intention of striking a balance between, e.g., stability and economic growth, enterprising and finance industry rent-seeking, individual and collective objectives, etc. While Berle (Berle and Means, 1932/1991) argued that managers—but also their bankers and shareholders—are now "the princes" of the economic system, it does not follow that he is willing to discard the entire legal innovation of the chartered business as soon as some legal scholar inspired by economic theory or an economist airs the idea that legal theory would benefit from economic analyses. On the contrary, Berle (1962) maintains that the industrial system, despite its imperfections, remains a major accomplishment that needs to be recognized in its full complexity, rather than simply being dismissed on the basis of marginal concerns (i.e., the perceived risk of managerial opportunism). Seen in this view, Berle remains a key figure in the corporate governance literature, and a figure whose seminal contributions remain disputed.

BERLE'S LEGACY: THE "BERLE–MEANS FIRM"

Adolf A. Berle's work and the joint work of Berle and Gardiner Means, a skilled statistician, have remained subject to perennial scholarly debate since their publication. While some shareholder primacy advocates regard Berle as a forerunner and proponent of the finance market-based model they champion, others see Berle as a defender of the legal theory view of the firm as prescribed by corporate legislation. As, e.g., Mizruchi (2004: 581) points out, "Berle and Means's concern about the separation of ownership from control was not simply about managers' lack of accountability for investors. It was also a concern about managers' lack of accountability to society in general." Such arguments indicate that Berle has been misinterpreted in ways that have benefited certain political and scholarly programmes, pitting Berle as a white knight of free-market pricing against E. Merrick Dodd's call for increased regulatory control of the corporate system, and an expanded role of the state in corporate matters.

Under all conditions, Berle and Means (1932/1991) have been credited for their work under the label of the "Berle–Means firm" (Roe, 2000: 546), denoting the chartered business with dispersed ownership and with directors and defined executives at the helm, serving as the directors' agents. The Berle–Means firm dominated in the era of managerial capitalism of the post-Second World War period until the mid-1970s' economic depression (Marris, 1964). Romano (1984) outlines the components and mechanisms of what she refers to as *corporatism*, the idea that the firm as a hierarchical structure relying on delegation is conducive to economic welfare. For Romano (1984), "the corporatist political ideal" can be "most lucidly illustrated" by the views of Berle: "The organizing principle of Berle's vision is not a market system but the hierarchical corporation" (Romano, 1984: 936). For Romano (1984: 928), a legal scholar, the "business organizations" have an advantage inasmuch as they "may foster cooperative behavior when the individually dominant strategy of noncooperation produces inefficient outcomes." As the firm conducts repeated transactions over time, the "firm's permanence" has "reputation-building effects," which in turn foster "the emergence of the more efficient cooperative outcome" (Romano, 1984: 928). This is the principal contribution of the legal construct of the corporation: it provides better possibilities than comparable market transactions to organize collaborative efforts, and to receive positive feedback in the form of a favourable reputation. For free-market theorists, the crux is still that the hierarchy is more complex to manage than one-on-one market contract relations, and therefore the hierarchy rests on a "substantial delegation of decisional authority" (Romano, 1984: 929). Romano (1984: 929) argues persuasively that information cost, the actors' costs for acquiring accurate, useful, and trustworthy information, makes decentralized decision mechanisms unworkable (direct democracy being one such case). Instead, hierarchical organizations and decision making delegation (and representative government in the case of the democratic political systems) are more efficient mechanisms for optimizing economic and social wellbeing. The delegation of decisional authority thus creates the "master problem" of the hierarchical organization, an agency or representation problem—the problem of how to ensure that "delegation is effective," and that the agent's incentives are aligned with the principal's desires" (Romano, 1984: 929).

This problem is given different weights in the two models of the firms that Romano presents. In the "contract approach," the corporation is treated as a shell or form created by consenting individuals, interrelated and integrated by the explicit and implicit contracts these individuals have agreed to sign. These contracts should in turn represent the "contracting parties' wishes" (Romano, 1984: 933). If contracts are possible to specify in detail and costless to enforce (which they may be in theory, but not in practice, especially not within the realm of the corporation, attending to a vast number of contingencies), there are no costs generated by the decentralized decision mechanism. Furthermore, in this ideal situation, there is no need for a delegation of decision authority, and consequently no agency costs are generated. In contrast, in the "concession view" of the corporation, the corporation is an entity *sui generis*, "something quite different from its individual parts," and serving as an independent economic, political, and social entity. Furthermore, the concession view, at least in its purest form, assumes that all corporate rights are "privileges granted by the state" (Romano, 1984: 933). The contract view is based on an "individualist ideal," rendering the problem of the delegation of the decision authority a matter of aggregating individual preferences to joint decisions that are tolerable for all participants and at a low cost. In the individualist ideal, there is no assumption made about information costs, but an individual knows, and indeed solely knows, "his best interests" (Romano, 1984: 929). In the concession view, in contrast, delegation is not only tolerable but mandated as a pathway to joint and individual economic welfare.

Romano (1984: 934) here introduces the term *corporatism*, a model that combines the individualist ideal of the contract view under the label of pluralism, and the concession view of the corporation as an autonomous legal entity (carefully separated from its European, fascist version), and as an ideal "that emphasizes hierarchical organization and an organic conception of community." Romano (1984: 934) continues: "The corporatist universe is a vertically segmented system of complementary and interdependent social units in which the hierarchical organizational arrangement of the business corporation is fundamental." In this vision of the corporation, each individual "occupies a niche in a unified social system," namely the corporation, and thereby contributes to the collective production of economic value and welfare. Furthermore, being another deviation from the contract view and its individualist ideal, corporatism accepts that government agencies and industry associations assume the role of market makers and market regulators because such entities have the capacity to collect the information needed to oversee the entire field; the hierarchical model's information processing capacities grant such agencies certain privileges, which translate into net economic welfare when their assigned roles are skilfully executed. A standard critique of such central agencies is that the market, *ex hypothesi*, does this job more effectively, and that the delegation of decision authority of necessity aggregates agency costs that are higher than the benefits, i.e., central agencies do not add to aggregated efficiency as stipulated by corporatists. Romano disagrees that such a critique is substantiated on the basis of empirical data, nor are these propositions theoretically consistent (e.g., all actors may demonstrate opportunistic behaviour, not just actors entrusted with decision making authority at the apex of corporations, nor individuals located in central agencies), but adds that corporatism is based on a pluralist theory of the state wherein central agencies serve a "market-correcting function" that justifies forms of coercion, as such coercion is "necessary to guarantee that individuals attain their optimal consumption bundles" (Romano, 1984: 942). This proposition in turn generates the thorny practical questions regarding (1) justifiable levels of coercion (the risk of "over-regulation" is always a practical concern); and (2) on what grounds market failure can be factually demonstrated, a concept that the corporatist regulatory model depends on. Romano also adds that the corporatist model is bundled with the assumption regarding certain entitlements (associated with welfare state provisions) that the contract view and the individualist ideal oftentimes reject as a mere politicization of the corporation:

State regulation of private activities is justified on grounds of market failure. In addition, in keeping with an individualist perspective, the theory of the welfare state is based on notions of individual entitlements. It emphasizes a political judgment that each member is entitled to a specified minimum bundle of rights or subsistence level, which the operation of markets may not provide. (Romano, 1984: 942)

Despite the critique of proponents of the contract view, accepting neither the ideas about market failure, nor the welfare-generating effects of central agencies, nor the idea about citizenry based on defined entitlements, the corporatist model is relatively freed from additional social or cultural assumptions and ad hoc hypotheses, Romano (1984: 936) argues: the corporation is essentially enacted as a value-neutral vehicle for social betterment, and there are few abstractions being imposed on the model:

> Berle does not draw upon any ethnic or nationalist metaphors, as do other corporatists, to create the spiritual basis that secures the unity of the whole. In his work there is no explicit theory of harmony, no overarching group-legitimating explanation that guarantees the spiritual cohesiveness that is so important to corporatists. The one exception is the abstraction of the corporation itself. (Romano, 1984: 936)

In this corporatist view, advocated by Berle, individualism is, seemingly paradoxically, recognized and enforced on the basis of collective organization, an outcome enabled by the corporation and its intricate governance mechanisms being either mandated by corporate law or established on the basis of market mechanisms: "Legal rules giving power to the board to act in the shareholders' interests to maximize profits ... promote the core elements of a pluralist polity, the realization of individual ends by means of organizations" (Romano, 1984: 953). These legal rules are based on the trust that must always be assumed in what Reynaud (2017: 132) calls a "delegatory relationship." The delegation of decision making authority to directors and managers is still not "committed blindly," as that would be a case of mere "submission" (Reynaud, 2017: 132); instead, the delegation is dependent on the asymmetry and "the reciprocity of commitment" that characterizes all relationships dependent on trust. The corporation is therefore playing a role similar to that of money in Georges Simmel's (1978) seminal account; it is a legal device, sanctioned by the sovereign state, supportive of individualism on the basis of collective agreements. "Money has made it possible for people to join a group without having to give up any personal freedom and reserve," Simmel (1978: 371) argues. In Simmel's case, the trust in the monetary system is the price that needs to be paid to take advantage of its affordances; in the case of the corporatist model, the trust in delegated decision authority and the role of the central agencies enables individualism on the basis of collectivist agreements. As long as such sources of trust can be upheld, all participants benefit.

Concerning the legal entity in question, the corporation granted a business charter, both proponents of the minimal state, mostly adhering to the contract view and the individualist ideal, and welfare state pluralists, endorsing the corporatist model and recognizing the role of the state as a market maker and regulator, value the efficiency gains generated by the corporate organization in the non-public sector and its powerful ability to "augment individual welfare" (Romano, 1984: 944). The efficacy of the corporate system, a major socio-economic and legal innovation constituted by legal, economic, and managerial statutes and practices, is therefore not disputed; the question is instead to what extent such efficiency gains are generated on the basis of, or despite, e.g., the delegation of decision authority and the active central agencies and associations, to what extent market failure can be demonstrated, and what level of coercion such alleged failures may justify. That is already quite a few issues to address.

The Post-Berle–Means Firm

Since the mid-1970s, the corporation has undergone considerable restructuring and reform, and de-regulatory impulses in the finance industry, also globalizing over the last four decades, have altered the governance function of the corporation, now considerably much more responsive to finance market interests. That is, it is today possible to speak about a "post-Berle–Means firm" (Moore and Rebérioux, 2011) wherein the influence and deficiencies of finance market pricing are no longer cushioned by a competent board of directors and their assigned managers, but where the finance market is instead understood and treated as a neutral mechanism for the assessment of managerial decision making quality. This represents a diametrically opposed view of the market to that taken by Veblen, Brandeis, Berle, and the New Deal policy makers, granting the finance market certain capacities and benefits but not being in a position to effectively govern the corporate system:

> [T]he doctrine of shareholder primacy relies for its effective realization upon the functioning of a liquid and efficient stock market: in a sense, while a liquid stock market was perceived as a "problem" in the post-Berle and Means managerialist literature, it is considered by contractarianism as the "solution." (Moore and Rebérioux, 2011: 88)

In the end, Veblen, Brandies, Berle, and the New Dealers advocated a "Hegelian firm," wherein the "corporation" is the favoured and assigned platform for the realization and transcendence of private property; in contrast, shareholder primacy advocates, including a heterogeneous group of agency theorists, contract theorists, and free-market protagonists, all sharing a belief in the analytical benefits of orthodox neoclassical economic theory, have successfully promoted a "Lockean firm," wherein private property is carefully separated from the wider socio-economic, institutional, and cultural conditions that were originally integrated into corporate law.

THE STANDING OF THE BERLE–MEANS FIRMS IN THE NEW MILLENNIUM: HAS MANAGERIAL DISCRETION AND THE BOARD-CENTRIC GOVERNANCE RESISTED SHAREHOLDER ACTIVISM?

A key question in the corporate governance scholarship is to what extent the managerialist and board-centric system that was enacted in corporate law in the nineteenth century and further enforced in the New Deal and post-Second World War era has managed to fend off shareholder activism and its claim to have the right to dictate managerial decision making. One strand of research points at the decline of, e.g., corporate elites, by implication making shareholder activism a successful campaign. In contrast, another body of literature emphasizes that managerial discretion still holds and that the board-centric system is operable despite being under the strain of shareholder activism.

The Decline of Business Elites and the Board-centric Model Argument

Mizruchi (2013) and Mizruchi and Marshall (2016) argue that the traditional "corporate elites" no longer play a central role in governing the corporate system. "Corporate elites" here denotes "a particular subset of presidents, chairmen (and women, where applicable), and what are now called chief executive officers (CEOs) of the largest American corporations" Mizruchi (2013: 12) writes. The post-Second World War period of economic growth, rooted in the New Deal system developed during the Great Depression of the 1930s (Fraser and Gerstle, 1989; Hawley, 1966), generated remarkable economic welfare in the U.S.:

> The average real standard of living of American families was rapidly improving, nearly doubling between 1946 and 1970. Poverty, which afflicted nearly one-quarter of the American population in 1960, was reduced by almost half over the following decade. Millions of Americans became homeowners and began to enjoy a middle-class lifestyle. (Mizruchi, 2017: 105)

When this period of economic stability came to an end in the 1970s, propelled by the politically generated oil-crisis driving up inflation, and accompanied by a political leadership crisis following the Watergate scandal and the failure to bring the Vietnam war to closure, the business elite allied itself for the first time with conservatives and free-market protagonists to develop and advocate a new economic regime. The 1970s campaign to restore the authority of industry was highly successful, and by the time of the election of Ronald Reagan in 1980, "the business community had achieved virtually all of its goals," Mizruchi (2017: 108) writes:

> Organized labor had been significantly weakened. Government intervention in the economy had been delegitimized. Corporate taxes had been sharply reduced. And even with a Democratic president and Democratic control of both houses of Congress, a series of liberal ventures, including the proposed Consumer Protection Agency, had been soundly defeated. (Mizruchi, 2017: 108)

At the same time as "business interests" were carefully attended to in Washington DC during the Reagan presidency, the major American banks started to lose the centrality in the business networks when finance markets were de-regulated as a component of the pro-business policy. Finance industry reforms prompted a process of disintermediation (see e.g., Fang, Ivashina, and Lerner, 2015; Myers and Rajan, 1998), and banks were impaired by their declining importance as a source of capital for industry and had to increasingly turn to fee-for-service activities. In addition, reflecting these changes, banks "reduced their appointments of nonfinancial chief executives to their boards," which ultimately served to marginalize the major banks in the corporate elite network (Mizruchi, 2017: 109). This gradual shift from network-based governance to market transactions undermined the authority and influence of the business elites: "By the early 1990s, the corporate elite was incapable of acting collectively to address the crisis over the cost of health care and this inability to act has persisted into the present" (Mizruchi, 2017: 108).

In Mizruchi's (2013: 8) view, the role of this corporate elite is today substantially reduced: "[T]here [is] no longer a relatively cohesive group of moderate, pragmatic leaders at the top of the American business community." For Mizruchi (2017), the ambition of the *ancien régime* to anchor competitive capitalism within the democratic state apparatus, and to actively endorse and participate in collaborative work between business and government is now discounted, put under erasure by the anti-statist ideology of, e.g., the free-market theorists who had counselled American presidents continuously since the Nixon Administration:

> The corporate leaders of the postwar era believed in a strong cooperative relation between business and government. If critics … saw this alliance as potentially undemocratic, it did have an underlying virtue: it was based on the assumption that any attempt to address seriously the social and economic problems of the society required systematic solutions that were carried out through public policy, that is, through the actions of government. (Mizruchi, 2017: 109)

Patrician and statesmanlike CEOs are no longer actively advocating "collective solutions" for issues of concern to the business community and society as a whole, but instead large corporations address their firm-specific interests through lobbying. Executives are today compensated "at levels far beyond what their predecessors received," Mizruchi and Marshall (2016: 144) argue, and yet, seemingly paradoxical, they experience "less autonomy," i.e., "they face greater scrutiny from their boards of directors and the investment community" than previous generations of executives did:

> During the postwar period and into the early 1980s, the chief executives of the largest American corporations were able to operate with a high level of autonomy. Largely insulated from the pressures of stockholders, these executives were able to consider the long-term implications of their actions for the wellbeing of the larger business community, and even, as I suggested earlier, the society as a whole. (Mizruchi, 2017: 109)

In addition, while becoming CEO used to be the crowning moment of a long and loyal career within a major corporation—the work and career of General Motors' legendary CEO Alfred P. Sloan Jr. being an exemplary case (Sloan, 1964)—the tenure of CEOs has declined substantially. Mizruchi and Marshall (2016: 153) report a decline in mean CEO tenure in the 24–30% range in the 1980–early 2000s period. "[R]egardless of their compensation, today's corporate CEOs face a more volatile and precarious environment than did those of the managerial era," Mizruchi and Marshall (2016: 153) summarize. As detailed by Khurana (2002), the search for new CEOs is today structured around the idea of finding an efficient and preferably charismatic market communicator. Loyalty, industry experience and expertise, and similar "old school" qualifications are rated as being of less importance, despite evidence suggesting otherwise (see e.g., Vuori and Huy, 2016). "The enlightened self-interest advocated by the Committee for Economic Development in 1971 has been replaced by a narrow, short-term self-interest, the consequences of which we are continuing to see," Mizruchi (2017: 114) contends.

The situation for directors demonstrates a similar pattern, Chu and Davis (2016) demonstrate. The "inner circle" of interlocked directors— directors sitting on several boards—has essentially been in decline since the 1990s, indicating a shift in corporate governance activities: "In 1994, at least 75 people held five board seats. By 2012, there was only one director serving on five S&P 500 boards" (Chu and Davis, 2016: 715). Collecting a data sample including 27,000 directors serving on almost 2,500 corporate boards in the United States in the 1997–2010 period, Chu and Davis (2016: 716) find evidence that "the inner circle" of elite directors, being "a durable feature of the U.S. corporate landscape over the 20th century," has now disappeared (Chu and Davis, 2016: 716). This means that "distances between companies on the interlock network" have lengthened to "unprecedented levels" (Chu and Davis, 2016: 716). One of the key implications is that the prospects for "broad-based, moderate political action by corporate elites are lowered," Chu and Davis (2016: 716) argue, a conclusion in line with the work of Mizruchi (2013) and Mizruchi and Marshall (2016). In addition, "multiple interlock ties"— directors sitting on many boards—served to diffuse new corporate practices (say accounting methods or management concepts) between organizations. Today, such mimetic isomorphism is promoted through other channels (e.g., management consultants). Chu and Davis (2016: 726) thus propose that "the disappearance of superconnectors" is indicative of an institutional shift in competitive capitalism: "Much that was true of the interlock network for 100 years became untrue within ten subsequent years. The U.S. corporate interlock network suffered a striking decline in connectedness." The economic and social value of having well-connected directors on the board declined and other mechanisms substituted for the interlock ties. In the end, Chu and Davis (2016: 750) propose, the rapid decline of multiple-board membership prestige is indicative of how "social elite membership" and "corporate power" are separated: the corporate elite is no longer overlapping the social elite. Davis (2015) summarizes the changes in U.S. capitalism as being indicative of the decline of corporate elites, and speaks explicitly about the decline of the Berle and Means corporation:

The "shareholder value" movement of the past generation has succeeded in turning managers into faithful servants of share price maximization, even when it comes at the expense of other considerations. But the shareholder value movement brought with it a series of changes that have undone many core features of the Berle and Means corporation. Corporate ownership is no longer dispersed; concentration of assets and employment has been in decline for three decades; and today's largest corporations bear little semblance to the companies analyzed by Berle and Means. Moreover, there are fewer of them than there used to be: the United States had half as many publicly traded domestic corporations in 2009 as it did in 1997. (Davis, 2015: 155)

Mizruchi (2010: 132) argues that the new corporate elite is today located in the finance community. That community differs substantially from the traditional corporate elites, a "small group of leading, old-line New York commercial banks." Instead, the new corporate elite include "[a] mélange of professional investors, working in the service of institutional stockbrokers, financial analysts, hedge-fund managers, and arbitrageurs" (Mizruchi, 2010: 132). Apparently, this group of finance market actors no longer need interlock ties and "superconnectors" to advance their interests, as they operate through other means and mechanisms to accomplish their goals. In the end, the balance of power in the corporate system is tilted in favour of finance industry actors to marginalize traditional corporate elites. In this analytical framework, the managerialist and board-centric model is in decline, gradually being subsumed under a finance industry interest model that is characteristic of investor capitalism.

Ownership and Governance in Agency Capitalism

Gilson and Gordon (2013) argue that the Berle–Means firm model and the various problems including agency costs is now obsolete in the era of what Gilson and Gordon (2013: 864) refer to as *agency capitalism*, dominated by "[a]n ownership structure in which agents hold shares for beneficial owners." In this new regime, where institutional investors (including pension funds, mutual funds, hedge funds, etc.) hold approximately 73 percent of all stocks in Fortune 1000 companies,[2] "a double set of agency relationships" are established first, between shareholders and managers (the traditional agency theory bilateral relation between defined principals and agents), and, second, between "beneficial owners and record holders" (Gilson and Gordon, 2013: 864). In this new model, the institutional investors act as "governance intermediaries," working to benefit the beneficial owners, but also on the basis of the incentives that the performance–reward system fund managers operate within, which means that fund managers may be more active and may demonstrate a higher degree of risk-appetite than the median beneficial owner in a given fund. This means that institutional investors are not to the same degree "rationally apathetic" as dispersed owners of stock would be on the basis of the information cost associated with shareholder activism. Instead, Gilson and Gordon (2013: 867) argue that institutional investors actively "monitor company performance" and then "present to companies and institutional shareholders concrete proposals for business strategy through mechanisms less drastic than takeovers." At the same time, most institutional investors (e.g., pension funds and mutual funds) are not acting as what Gilson and Gordon (2013: 895) call "governance entrepreneurs," as the "costs, lack of expertise, and incentive conflicts reduce the value of governance rights in the hands of intermediary institutions." Only funds with a high-risk investment strategy, attracting clients that pay a higher fee for a higher return such as hedge funds, may benefit from shareholder activism campaigns and thus participate in such activities:

> Activist shareholders are not control-seekers, in the sense that they are neither motivated by the pursuit of private benefits of control, nor do they anticipate actually managing a portfolio company. Rather they are governance entre-preneurs, arbitraging governance rights that become more valuable through their activity monitoring companies to identify strategic opportunities and then presenting them to institutional investors for their approval. (Gilson and Gordon, 2013: 895)

Only a smaller proportion of the institutional investors are in fact activist shareholders and "governance entrepreneurs," whereas the remainder of the institutional investors can be assumed to be "rationally reticent," Gilson and Gordon (2013: 867) propose; that is, fund managers "will respond to proposals but are unlikely themselves to create them." In practice, this creates a free-rider problem (Olson, 1965) wherein ration-ally reticent institutional investors may benefit from the campaigns orchestrated by, e.g., hedge fund managers operating in concert (see e.g., Coffee and Palia, 2016) but without actively participating in, or carrying the costs of the campaigns.

In this new environment, wherein first the Berle–Means firm model is no longer an accurate depiction of the corporate system, populated by independent but uncoordinated shareholders, the board-centric model is put under pressure by, e.g., highly leveraged hedge fund managers. This in turn implies that managerial decision making discretion can no longer be assumed, as fast-moving finance capital markets undermine the governance structures' ability to adapt to changes; in addition, actors' concern for the protection of inherited privileges and entitlements may play a role, Gilson and Gordon (2013: 873) suggest: "path-dependent institutions move less quickly than markets, in no small part because adaptation negatively affects those favored by existing patterns." The question is still to what extent does the activism of, e.g., hedge funds generate economic stability and welfare in a medium- to long-term perspective,[3] or does the "divest and distribute" policy mandated by shareholder activism lead to a depletion of firm-specific resources and competences (Coffee and Palia, 2016)?

Cheng and Xiong (2014: S185) provide evidence that demonstrates that hedge fund managers, trading commodity futures, a financial derivative instrument used to trade risks in the agriculture industry, make changes in their holdings and in their market positions that are not justified by market price changes: "Our empirical analysis shows that although hedgers' futures positions are much smaller than output, the volatility of their positions is much higher than the output volatility measured by either the year-to-year output fluctuation or month-to-month fluctuation of professional output forecasts." Furthermore, as a factual condition in the agriculture industry, during the harvest season, "output uncertainty" declines, but there is no evidence of hedgers' trading volatility demonstrating an accompanying decline; instead, "trading volatility remains stable throughout the year" (Cheng and Xiong, 2014: S185). In addition, Cheng and Xiong's empirical data (2014: S185) demonstrate that hedge fund managers' trading activities amplify price changes so that they are not in parity with actual supply of commodities, i.e., hedge fund managers tend to "respond strongly to changes in price": hedge fund managers "short more futures contracts when the futures price rises and reduce their short position as the futures price falls." That market behaviour indicates that hedge fund managers participate in speculation: "It is difficult to reconcile such trading behavior as purely that of hedging strategies of risk-averse hedgers seeking to hedge price and output uncertainty," Cheng and Xiong (2014: S185) argue. Based on two sets of empirical evidence, Cheng and Xiong (2014: S185) suggest that commodity futures markets include substantial speculation, as "hedgers frequently change their positions over time for reasons unrelated to output fluctuations." In fact, based on this evidence, Cheng and Xiong (2014: S186) suggest that the theoretical distinction between "hedgers," having "commercial interests" and "speculators," being financial traders, is "less informative than previously thought for benefit–cost analyses of financial regulation." Furthermore, in day-to-day trading, "genuine hedgers" may believe they have "informational advantage" vis-à-vis the "speculators," and this overconfidence may result in excessive trading when hedgers disagree with the speculators regarding future price movements (Cheng and Xiong, 2014: S204–S205). That is, *even if* there are distinctively separated "genuine hedgers" and "speculators" in the market, the hedgers act *as if* they were speculators as they disagree with finance-oriented traders, as the hedgers believe they act under the advantage of superior market information, partially derived from their perceived expertise in the trade vis-à-vis finance traders, partially derived from their actual interest in the underlying commodity. That is, as speculators' behaviour strongly affects the everyday trade of commodities futures, and the distinction between hedgers and speculators demands an understanding of the traders' intentions, or relies on second-guessing the motives and preferences of traders (something commonly excluded from economic theory and frowned upon by economists as a form of psychological or sociological research question, instead assuming endogenous and heterogeneous interests and preferences among actors being separated from market-based pricing and economic incentives), these two categories can be collapsed into one class of commodity futures traders. Expressed in more positive terms, participants in futures markets are not the producers themselves but are "market makers" who trade in futures markets to "hedge forward contracts written with ultimate commodity producers such as farmers" (Cheng and Xiong, 2014: S205). In their role as market makers, serving the interests of third, non-market-based parties, hedgers still engage in "significant non-output-related trading" (Cheng and Xiong, 2014: S204), which generates market price fluctuations beyond what is justified by elementary supply–demand equilibria, theoretically defining the market price. In other words, hedge fund managers and commodity futures traders do add to socio-economic wellbeing but they tend to generate additional informational complexity on the basis of speculation, which imposes costs that befall other actors outside, e.g., the commodity futures trade business.

To summarize the literature, the Berle–Means firm is today a legal entity that is exposed to finance market-based pricing that tends to marginalize the board-centric corporate governance model and downplay the discretion and autonomy of managers. Under all conditions, in the agency capitalism regime, the managerialist model is no longer unrivalled, and the consequences thereof is partially known and partially still in the making.

The Persistency of the Managerialist Model Argument

Another body of literature recognizes the expanding role of shareholder activism but maintains that the managerialist and board-centric model is still operational, and points at empirical data that stress managerial discretion as a factual condition in corporations (Goranova and Ryan, 2014; Shin, 2013; Ertimur, Ferri, and Stubben, 2010). "[a]lthough the shareholder value principle is dominant today, it is far from being hegemonic," Shin (2013: 829) writes. Goldstein (2012: 269) demonstrates that, despite operating under shareholder primacy ideologies, i.e., managers are scrutinized regarding how they allocate financial capital, the proportion of managerial employees in the U.S. private sector "rose steadily from the mid-1980s through the early 2000s by several different metrics." More specifically, the share of total business income "devoted to managerial salaries actually rose from 16 to 23 percent between 1984 and 2001" (Goldstein, 2012: 269). Such data indicates, Goldstein (2012: 269) argues, that executives have been instrumental in re-channelling anti-managerial sentiments within the shareholder primary advocacy into self-enriching outcomes. Gordon (1996) argues that the downsizing activities that were justified and actively promoted by shareholder value programmes, leading to fewer employees yet being subject to more intensive work pressure, demanded *more* rather than *less* supervising managers, leading to corporations increasing their managerial costs. This "more managers chasing fewer employees" scenario leads to inflated professional managerial services cost. Seen in this view, shareholder primacy governance and managerialism are not mutually excluding governance regimes but are instead intimately bound togther.

Benton (2016: 662) portrays corporate governance as the mechanism wherein power is allocated to various participants and stakeholders. Despite being under the pressure to satisfy shareholder interests, "managerialist governance models" remain "surprisingly resilient," Benton (2016: 662) claims. Using a network structure approach that represents the social ties among corporate leaders (and not directors, as in the case of Chu and Davis', 2016, study), Benton (2016: 662) suggests that these social ties are resources that "aid them in maintaining managerialist governance profiles." Benton does recognize the decline in the number of directors holding multiple-board appointments, but there are still norms among directors that enforce managerial discretion and the maintenance of what is called the "business judgment rule" in court ruling, i.e., the managers' ability to make business-related decisions without negotiating with third parties. As a consequence, Benton (2016: 675) continues,

"Directors who have recently participated in implementing shareholder-oriented governance reforms frequently receive social sanctions from other directors." Furthermore, the overall "interlock network" among corporate executives serves the role of upholding management discretion, thus indicating that corporate elites are not totally disarmed in the era of shareholder activism: "Managers hoping to maintain their autonomy may need to rely more on their fellow corporate leaders than ever before, even as those resources fade," Benton (2016: 701) summarizes. The social ties that Benton examines is thus a resource in the hands of corporate directors, supportive of the board-centric governance model, as it reduces shareholder voting rights, installs takeover defences, delays proxy battles, and protects officers (Benton, 2016: 701). More specifically, research conducted by James Westphal and colleagues has demonstrated how corporate executives are able to neutralize or mute the critique of external directors (Westphal and Khanna, 2003), shareholders (Westphal and Zajac, 1998), institutional investors (Westphal and Bednar, 2008), security analysts (Westphal and Graebner, 2013; Westphal and Clement, 2008), and journalists (Westphal et al., 2013). Such managerial skills and competencies arguably contribute in substantial ways to the reinforcement and reproduction of the board-centric governance model. The primary mechanism manipulated by corporate managers is thus to decouple the everyday decision making in the executive suite from finance market evaluation (Westphal and Zajac, 2001).

The work of, e.g., Goldstein (2012) and Benton (2016) indicates that the managerialist governance regime is far from obsolete; while there are new forms of pressure on managers and directors to serve shareholder interest, managerial discretion and the board-centric model are still operable, Goldstein (2012) and Benton (2016) suggest. This leaves the analyst with two alternative models: one wherein corporate elites have lost much of their power and position, now being transferred to the finance industry, and one wherein the core of the managerialist governance regime is maintained, primarily on the basis of corporate executives and directors' ability to co-opt shareholder pressure and turn it in their own favour. Not least the soaring economic compensation of corporate executives is indicative of such political clout on the part of the executives. Still, the question remains to what extent the present corporate governance regime is informed and defined by shareholder interests.

THE CORE QUESTION: DEBATING THE SHAREHOLDER PRIMACY ARGUMENT

The shareholder primacy model, advocated by, e.g., agency theorists and contract theorists, is indebted to Locke's minimal theory of negative freedom, making the question of shareholders' rent the core issue in governance theory and practice. Moreover, in this view, rights are irreducibly individual and can only be secured and preserved on the basis of individual preferences, aspirations, and entitlements. La Porta et al.'s (2000: 4, emphasis added) definition of corporate governance, stated accordingly, "Corporate governance is, to a large extent, a set of mechanisms through which *outside investors* protect themselves against expropriation by the insiders," is by and large consistent with this Lockean view; it is the "outside investors' interest" that is the primary concern, and such interest needs to be "protected." In contrast, theories of corporate governance that emphasize the team production qualities of the chartered and incorporated business are founded on Hegelian ideas wherein foundational rights are fulfilled and rendered meaningful within the domain of the corporation; as such, and through legislation, property rights and other individual rights bestowed upon the individual are only meaningful if they are means to accomplish wider goals—goals that transcend and fulfil the original rights serving as the basis for civil society. In this Hegelian view, represented by Berle himself and a series of legal–managerial scholarships, the corporation is a vehicle for the differentiation of civil society. O'Sullivan's (2000: 1, emphasis in the original) definition of corporate governance is representative of this extended theory of positive freedom, rooted in the corporation: "Corporate governance is concerned with the institutions that influence how business corporations allocate resources and returns. Specifically, *a system of corporate governance shapes and makes investment decisions in corporations, what types of investments they make, and how returns from investments are distributed.*" Rather than simply speaking about the interests of "outside investors," as La Porta et al. (2000) do, O'Sullivan (2000) includes a wider set of "institutions" that all add to the production of economic value. This indicates a Hegelian tradition of thinking, making individual property rights merely the starting point for the corporate system and the wider institutional set-up of the economic system at hand, i.e., in the contemporary period, competitive capitalism.

Based on the distinction between a Lockean and a Hegelian view of corporate governance, a number of objections to the minimal theory of corporate governance can be articulated. First of all, shareholders are neither de jure, nor de facto, the firm's investors (i.e., owners) in the way that the minimal theory suggests: "[F]rom a legal perspective, shareholders do not, and cannot, own corporations. *Corporations are independent legal entities that own themselves*, just as human beings own themselves" (Stout, 2012: 10, emphasis in the original). "By folklore habit we say the buyer of stock of AT&T or General Motors has 'invested in' these companies; but this is pure fiction," Berle (1962: 446) adds. Second, shareholders are not the only residual claimants (as stated by, e.g., Fama and Jensen, 1983) outside the highly specific case of bankruptcy law (Stout, 2013). This is because in a world of incomplete contracts, complicated and costly to write and enforce, not only shareholders are exposed to various market risks: "When contracts are incomplete, residual claimant status is a matter of degree and is not restricted to shareholders" (Garvey and Swan, 1994: 154). Third, by legal statutes, directors are *trustees*, not the shareholders' agents, and managers, whom shareholder primacy advocates want to turn into the shareholders' agents on the basis of the two arguments disqualified above (i.e., that shareholders "own" the firm and that they are the only legitimate residual claimants), are the agents of the directors and no one else: "In the eyes of the law, corporate directors are a unique form of fiduciary who, to the extent they resemble any other form, perhaps most closely resemble trustees," Blair and Stout (1999: 291) say. In addition, in the role of trustees, bestowed with fiduciary duties, the directors are expected to act in ways that contribute to social welfare and not only to enrich certain stakeholders such as shareholders: "[The Board] had an obligation to the community of interests that sustained the corporation, to exercise judgment in an informed, good faith effort to maximize the corporation's long-term wealth creating capacity," a Delaware Chancery Court statement makes clear (cited in Blair and Stout, 1999: 296). As a consequence, shareholders cannot "control" managers, and to build a theory of the corporation on the premise that shareholders have contracted for such rights "grossly mischaracterizes the legal realities of most public corporations" (Blair and Stout, 1999: 260–261). Fourth and finally, as an empirical matter, the assumption that shareholders would be more prudent and demonstrate less proclivity to succumb to opportunistic and illicit behaviour than, e.g., managers—systematically made suspicious of being of such weak moral fibre—is not a tenable proposition. As, e.g., Coffee (1991: 1334) states, "institutional investors should not be mistaken for financial saints"; nor will institutional investors "automatically represent all shareholders," but they are likely to "favor the interests of their employers" in the case of diverging interests (Coffee, 1991: 1334). Therefore, Coffee (1991: 1367) induces, the reduction of agency costs (being the favoured, yet hard-to-measure and thus largely theoretical estimate of the degree of management opportunism in the shareholder primacy literature) "cannot be the sole goal of corporate governance reform," on the grounds that "monitors [e.g., regulators] as well as managers can behave opportunistically" (Coffee, 1991: 1367). In addition, what free-market protagonists at times address as a free-rider problem, and commonly being an argument in favour of de-regulatory reform, is present among the community of shareholders (Coffee, 1984: 1190). Speaking about how a "rational apathy" characterizes the behaviour of shareholders, as no shareholder can, Coffee (1984: 1190) argues, "fully appropriate the gain that his individual efforts might produce," Coffee says that the rational shareholders choose to take no action and thus generate a free-rider problem. In other words, Coffee (1984) argues that opportunistic or self-interested behaviour does not solely exist in the executive suites, but is a human predicament affecting the entire economic system on various levels.

In the end, the question of corporate governance is a matter of how to balance individual interests and rent-seeking, and how to institute and enforce incentives for participating in collective action. Both the minimal Lockean and the extended Hegelian theory provide their own distinct benefits, but the one-sided dominance of the individualistic and reductionist Lockean theory in shareholder primacy advocacy has overstated the benefits of self-interest in this delicate balancing of individual rent-seeking and collective action. On the other hand, a dominance of the extended Hegelian theory in corporate governance theory would easily understate individual interests, with undesirable consequences following. While much agency theory and contract theory literature promoting the shareholder primacy model is unhesitantly Lockean in orientation and in its advocacy, the legal theory and management studies literature arguably does a better job to shed light on the wider field, indeed making corporate governance a matter of the *institutional conditions* constituting and supporting the corporate system and the specific firm in question. That is, a scholarship that contributes to the handling of corporate governance issues must continuously question the very foundation upon which such scholarship rests, and not the least seek the roots of inherited and in many ways taken for granted doctrines and beliefs, or else the balancing of individual rent-seeking and collective action is tilted in either direction.

SUMMARY

The flamboyant and provocative social theorist Slavoj Žižek (2008: 1) advises that theorists should avoid "an arrogant position of ourselves as judges of the past." In the post-Second World War period, Hegelian statism has been widely endorsed within the project to expand and deepen the welfare state and its provisions, and yet has been treated as a thinly veiled argument in favour of a paternalist, even authoritative state by certain commentators, frequently in conservative and libertarian quarters. The recent decline in the faith in the liberal economy and its institutions, indicating that a new conventional wisdom is about to be established, departing from what once was referred to as the "Washington consensus" among political commentators (see, e.g., Babb, 2013; Sheppard and Leitner, 2010), may be equally problematic for the Lockean theory of individual rights. Efficient governance is rooted in both formal legislation and everyday practices (Kogut, 2012), and in each case the balancing of individual benefits and collective accomplishments remains imperative. Therefore, it is important to not abandon the Lockean, liberal inspirations now when the pendulum possibly swings back in this forthcoming period of governance reform. The Lockean and the Hegelian positions are thus complementary rather than mutually excluding frameworks for the establishment of governance legislation, regulation, and practices. However, taking a Braudelian (1980) *longue durée* view of corporate governance breeds an understanding of how perennial issues have been tackled over time and with the ebb and flow of the economic cycles and regulatory reform initiatives. For instance, the role of individual rent-seeking and collective action such as team production efforts, the balancing of the interest of financial and nonfinancial industries, and director and management accountability are a few examples of corporate governance issues that have been debated over time and temporarily handled through specific practices and rules. What worried Thorstein Veblen, Louis D. Brandies, and Adolf A. Berle in the 1910s and the 1930s may essentially be the same thing that worries scholars, policy makers, and commentators at the beginning of the third millennium, despite all the finance industry innovations (e.g., the development of derivative instruments and the expansion of securitization of assets, the implementation of digital media including the recent use of high-frequency trading and "robot trading," and various legal and regulatory reforms; MacKenzie, 2017; Arnoldi, 2016; Lange, Lenglet, and Seyfert, 2016; Lenglet, 2011). This ultimately testifies to the condition that when all things are said and done, human nature and the demand for both recognizing individual self-interest and collaborative action remain stable factors over time. Governance scholarship thus needs to consider this condition and to reconcile various objectives within prescribed policies and practices.

NOTES

1. "Trust" is here a synonym of monopoly and a widely used term following the anti-trust legislation of the Sherman Act of 1890 (see, e.g., Wood and Anderson, 1993; Pitofsky, 1979).
2. In comparison, in 1950, stocks were still held predominately by households, whereas institutional investors, including pension funds, held "only approximately 6.1% of U.S. equities" (Gilson and Gordon, 2013: 874).
3. An empirical literature indicates that hedge fund activism does produce value for shareholders (Brav, Jiang, and Kim, 2015; Klein and Zur, 2009). Klein and Zur (2009: 187) refer to hedge funds as *entrepreneurial activists,* defined as "[a]n investor who buys a large stake in a publicly held corporation with the intention to bring about change and thereby realize a profit on the investment." Hedge funds also target financially healthier firms with higher earnings and with more cash on their balance sheets in comparison to other entrepreneurial activists (including, e.g., asset management groups, private equity funds, and venture capital funds; Klein and Zur, 2009: 190), who tend to target smaller firms in terms of revenues and market capitalization (Klein and Zur, 2009: 205). Pursuing such strategies, Klein and Zur (2009: 209) argue that hedge funds generate "abnormal returns" for their clients in comparison to other entrepreneurial activists. Moreover, Klein and Zur (2009: 211) remark that hedge fund activism is most successful:

   > Hedge fund activists enjoy a 60% success rate. Most strikingly, they gain representation on the target's board 30 out of 41 times, for an achievement rate of 73%. They are 100% successful in getting the firm to buy back its own stock, replace the current CEO, and initiate a cash dividend. Approximately 50% of the time, the target firm changes its operating strategies, drops its merger plans, or agrees to be taken over or merged. (Klein and Zur, 2009: 211)

   Unfortunately, this success does not benefit all constituencies. Brav, Jiang, and Kim (2015) report that labour suffers wage losses after hedge fund campaigns as "improvement in labor productivity" is not translated into real-wage growth. Instead, "workers do not fully capture the value of productivity improvements but instead relinquish most of the surplus to equity investors after hedge fund intervention" (Brav, Jiang, and Kim, 2015: 2726). This loss of return on productivity growth is particularly salient for white-collar workers, whose average wage drops by 5 percent after an activist campaign. In summary, therefore, Brav, Jiang, and Kim (2015: 2753) write, "on average, workers at target firms do not share in the improvements associated with hedge fund activism. They experience stagnation in wages, while their productivity improves significantly." In the end, hedge fund activism and its reduction in productivity-adjusted wages facilitates "[a] transfer of 'labor rents' to shareholders, which may account for a portion of the positive abnormal returns associated with the announcement of hedge fund interventions" (Brav, Jiang, and Kim, 2015: 2753). Such empirical research findings suggests a zero-sum game situation where the shareholders' gain comes at the other constituencies' (white-collar workers in particular) loss. In addition, as healthy and financially sound companies are a primary target (rather than underperforming companies, potentially poorly managed), the hedge funds' aggregated effects on economic welfare should be subject to further scholarly research.

PART II

Governing the economy

2. Governing the corporation: the economic theory roots of the shareholder primacy doctrine

INTRODUCTION

In corporate law, the relationship between the board of directors and the firm's shareholders is based on the mandatory rule of director discretion. In a seminal paper, Eisenberg (1969: 5) states that under the received legal model, "no one acts as agent of the shareholders—that is, of ownership." Managers ("officers" in Eisenberg's terms) are the directors' agents, and the board, in turn, is "conceived to be an independent institution, not directly responsible to shareholders in the manner of an agent" (Eisenberg, 1969: 5). The board of directors oversees an autonomous, discrete legal entity and its managers (including the CEO) are bestowed with so-called *real power*, including the *business judgment rule* enforced in court cases (Stout, 2012: 44; Boatright, 1994: 404; Easterbrook and Fischel, 1981: 1163). Yet, shareholder primacy governance advocates argue that market prices aggregate information effectively, which in turn means that the shareholders' buy or sell decision is a both legitimate and efficient response to managerial decision quality and other firm-specific conditions (Cremers and Sepe, 2016: 72–73). This means that a drop in stock price signals shareholder dissatisfaction, which in turn institutes a disciplinary mechanism in the corporate system (Manne, 1962, 1965). Based on this idea of information-efficient markets and predictably rational investor behaviour (operationalized as a preferences for liquid over illiquid holdings and a short-term perspective), proponents of shareholder primacy governance justify and promote a corporate governance model wherein formal authority is "entrusted to the shareholders" (Cremers and Sepe, 2016: 79-80): "[U]nder the governance model defended by shareholder advocates, shareholders retain the right to subject directors to specific controls on virtually any important aspect of corporate decision making, as well as the right to promptly displace the board," Cremers and Sepe (2016: 82) argue. One of the key concerns with this shareholder primacy model is that the global finance markets are dominated by institutional investors, not individual shareholders holding small proportions of the stock (Davis, 2009), and that institutional investors such as hedge funds tend to be short-term oriented and highly leveraged, as fund managers are incentivized to engage in shareholder activism to maximize the payout to shareholders (Chong and Tuckett, 2015). Such concern regarding short-termism is acknowledged by proponents of shareholder primacy governance, but they maintain that this issue "[s]hould not be placed on equal footing with the much larger problem of managerial moral hazard, which remains a first-order governance problem" (Cremers and Sepe, 2016: 84). As a consequence, shareholder primacy governance advocators claim that the liquidity preference, materializing into short-termism, is a minor problem in the corporate system in comparison to the aggregated costs of managerial opportunism or malfeasance.

The shareholder primacy governance model is disputed on all levels. First of all, information economics scholars such as Stiglitz (1993: 109–110) reject the proposition that financial markets and markets more generally are information efficient; instead, markets are not allocationally efficient (i.e., "Pareto-efficient") as claimed by e.g., Fischel (1978: 1); markets are not always in place, or may be "thin," i.e., include few actors (Stiglitz, 1993: 109); markets are not characterized by efficiency-inducing competition, and rent-seeking plays an active role in market activities. In short, Stiglitz (1993) argues, market prices cannot be assumed to effectively mirror firm-specific managerial decision making quality. Second, even if markets demonstrated such qualities, conducive to information efficiency making stock prices indicators of, e.g., managerial decision making quality, finance markets always attract investors with heterogeneous risk appetite and diverging investment horizons, i.e., shareholders display a great deal of heterogeneity in preferences (Cremers and Sepe, 2016: 110). Third, and perhaps most importantly, when proponents of shareholder primacy governance "essentially assume away the role of the board of directors and cast the interactions among shareholders and managers as a bilateral agency relationship" (Cremers and Sepe, 2016: 82), they render the firm a black-box whose internal processes and specificities are only of anecdotal importance for the pricing process located to the finance market.

This analytical procedure is based on the faulty assumption that a firm is a commodity that can be traded like any security, Biondi (2013: 393) argues. In contrast, the firm is "factually a significant socioeconomic activity" that cannot be reduced to a set of formal contracts (see e.g., Jensen and Meckling, 1976); the firm is a legal vehicle for the amassing of finance capital and other firm-specific resources, mobilized in a team production effort that generates liquid capital *only after* the team production activities have been organized and carried out (Blair and Stout, 1999). In other words, shareholder primacy governance advocators are mistaking the cause and effect of corporate law and the corporate system, assuming that simply because shares and other issuances are traded on the market, the legal vehicle of the incorporated business *per se* is reducible to the contracts and pricing mechanisms that enable such a trade of shares and securities. As opposed to this view, Biondi (2013: 416) advocates an "enterprise entity view," which understands the firm as "a whole" and as "a dynamic system of relationships, not merely comprising contracts or bargaining" (see also Romano, 1984). In contrast, what secures the production of economic value, which in turn is translated into favourable market pricing of the firm's stock, is efficient accounting standards and organizational routines, checking that input resources are effectively transformed into output commodities and services, ultimately generating economic value and thus securing the long-term survival of the firm—the directors' and their managers' foremost objective (Fligstein, 1990: 5).

Unfortunately, the accounting view of the firm is for the most part absent in the shareholder primacy advocacy, emphasizing abstract information efficiency of the finance market as the only legitimate and factual check on mismanagement and so-called agency costs. This inability to recognize firm-specific and managerial practices, including the development, implementation, and everyday use of accounting procedures and organizational routines, undermines effective corporate governance practices. The purpose of this chapter is therefore to critically discuss how shareholder advocacy has systematically overstated the role of markets and relied on the tenuous proposition of market efficiency well beyond the empirical support for the thesis. In making the argument in favour of an "enterprise entity view" of corporate governance, a variety of economic, legal, and management studies literatures are examined, making the point that the shareholder primacy governance model does not stand up well against empirical evidence of various market imperfections as listed by Stiglitz (1993). In the best of possible worlds, the shareholder primacy governance advocate's ideal world, markets may display qualities and self-regulating mechanisms that render the shareholder primacy model an optimal governance mechanism, capable of minimizing managerial opportunism and agency costs, but in real-world economy markets, few of these conditions are fulfilled. This does, in the end, undermine the shareholder primacy model, which therefore fails to optimize the efficiency of the corporate system and to contribute to social wellbeing more widely.

COLD WAR RATIONALITY AND RATIONAL CHOICE THEORY

Erickson et al. (2013) introduce the concept of "cold war rationality" to denote a specific set of propositions, methods, models, and laboratory technologies developed in the post-Second World War decades to explore human behaviour and policy making under determinate conditions. This rationality should be "formal," and therefore "largely independent of personality and context," Erickson et al. (2013: 3) write. Therefore, Erickson et al. (2013: 3) continue, the ideal and purified rationality "frequently took the form of algorithms—rigid rules that determine unique solutions—which were moreover supposed to provide optimal solutions to given problems, or delineate the most efficient means toward certain given goals." A strong tendency in this cold war episteme is thus to examine elementary decisions in order to extract generalized patterns of decision making that arguably also apply to more complex choice situations. That is, the cold war rationality was based on a reductionist epistemology where more complicated decision outcomes can be extrapolated on the basis of empirical data generated in laboratory studies of elementary decision making:

> [c]omplex tasks were analysed into simple, sequential steps; the peculiarities of context, whether historical or cultural, gave way to across-the-board generalizations; analysis took precedent over synthesis. And finally, at least ideally, advocates hoped that the rules could be applied mechanically: computers might reason better than human minds. (Erickson et al., 2013: 3–4)

The "stripped-down formalism" and the "analogical reasoning from experimental microcosms" was thus the principal scientific approach to the understanding of human decision making writ large (Erickson et al., 2013: 5). The military research of the cold war period, in many cases located outside military institutions, had towering ambitions and sought to identify and pin down *real* and *substantive* rationality, the Holy Grail of militarized behavioural research in the era (Erickson et al., 2013: 5). As research programmes and projects, rooted in the cold war rationality, were advanced and penetrated university departments and represented in research fund's board of directors, the reductionist and instrumental rationality rose to dominance, and rendered alternative models being developed in, e.g., sociology and anthropology, emphasizing other features than mere utility maximization in decision making and choice, as merely heterodox accounts of human behaviour. However, by the 1980s and 1990s, the cold war rationality did not really wither away, Erickson et al. (2013: 6–7) argue, but the "forces that had earlier held together the different disciplines, techniques, and policies in the crucible of the Cold War began to slacken." In this new environment of *Glasnost* and evidence of the Soviet communist economic system being on the verge of collapse, "[d]efining rationality was no longer the sacred quest that would unify the human sciences and keep the world safe from nuclear Armageddon" (Erickson et al., 2013: 6–7).

Yet, the long years of a strong sense of urgency among scholars and intellectuals had made their mark on the academy and other research institutions. Reisch (2005) captures the paranoia and unease of the cold war decades, beginning in the 1930s, and how it affected the academy, no longer being a safe haven and a space for intellectual work but being carefully monitored by the authorities to identify individuals deviating from the conventional wisdom and shared beliefs:

> With major campuses conducting formal hearings and FBI agents interviewing faculty and department secretaries about suspicious professors, intellectual life in the 1930s mixed scholarship, fear, peer pressure, ostracism, and sometimes, overt bullying by colleagues. Winners and losers over the long term were not always determined by intellectual talent. (Reisch, 2005: xiii)

In military research institutions such as RAND (an abbreviation for Research and Development), founded in 1948 as an autonomous, military-financed research centre serving to "[i]nsure the continuance of teamwork among the military, other government agencies, industry, and the universities" (Düppe and Weintraub, 2014: 463), but de facto being one of the foremost sites for military research work, a blend of operations research, cybernetics theory, and mathematical modelling was favoured. Among many other contributions, much of economic theory and its rational choice theory model of human decision making was generated and fortified in this milieu of advanced military research, gathering the best minds of a generation (relying primarily on male co-workers, though) in the pursuit to outsmart the communist bloc's scientists and experts. Of all the economic theory contributions from this setting, rational choice theory is arguably the most prestigious and most lasting output. In the eyes of orthodox neoclassical economic theorists, this is the closest the analyst can get to a purified model of *real* rationality, i.e., as rationality *should* be executed in the best of possible worlds. Such a world is in turn characterized by the absence of clumsy governmental interventions within free and self-regulating markets, and devoid of less-than-perfect human cognition and behaviour, being of necessity the rational choice theorist's demon—that is, everyday people's inability to live up to the prescribed standards of rationality, calculated on the basis of logic and cold war rationality reasoning based on examples.

Rational Choice and Neoclassical Economic Theory

Erickson (2010: 386–387) argues that political philosophy and legislative action have historically relied on concepts such as *ethics*, *fairness*, *justice*, and *tradition* to settle disputes and to provide a legal framework making civil society and the economy resilient, yet dynamic and transparent, and to reward enterprising activities and ambition. In the cold war rationality, favouring mathematical formalisms over more convoluted or even murky, narrative forms of historical and contingent knowing, a "thinner" but logically consistent and formalistically elegant model of rationality should preferably displace the older regime of policy making. That is, a set of "axioms of preference ordering" and "utility maximization choices" became principal input variables in the formal definition of instrumental rationality (Erickson, 2010: 386–387). Amadae (2003) argues that rational choice theory (RCT), the common shorthand denominator for such a formalization of instrumental rationality, was generated with geopolitical intentions in mind; for its proponents, RCT was "a philosophy of markets and democracy that was developed in part to anchor the foundations of American society during the Cold War" (Amadae, 2003: 2–3). More specifically, the idea of a "rational choice liberalism" was supposed to play a key role "in the triumphant West's ideological victory over Soviet communism," inasmuch as it postulated "an implicit and inevitable linkage between free-market economics and democratic politics" (Amadae, 2003: 4). RCT was thus originally intended as a liberal and liberating conceptual model that undermined the planned economy idea of a centrally located economic agency, capable of monitoring and regulating industrial production in meaningful ways.

For Amadae (2003: 5), RCT is thus one of the defining marks of the Post-Second World War era: "[T]he degree to which [RCT] has come to pervade the popular discourse by the early years of the twenty-first century cannot be overestimated." For instance, the idea of "rational choices" are not only fortified in the discipline of economics and related "economic sciences" (as the Nobel Prize Committee puts it) and in policy making on various levels, but the idea has also penetrated the everyday lives of billions of humans, even into the most intimate sphere of human lives such as romantic life and dating (see, e.g., Zelizer, 2005), wherein the "choice of partner" is frequently discussed and rendered meaningful in economic terms (i.e., to be "single" is to "be on the market," and browsing dating sites is to "check the supply" of "dateable" men/women, etc.). Under all conditions, the two principal axioms of RCT, that (1) choices are made individually by intellectually and emotionally autonomous and discrete actors, and (2) that such actors use calculative practices to weigh the costs and benefits to determine the overall "utility" of different choice alternatives, are well entrenched in economic theory and policy making. The crux is that such propositions have been notoriously complicated to substantiate by both field data (e.g., available market statistics data) or in laboratory settings. Such "under-substantiation" of the theoretical model indicates that the orthodox RCT model is simplistic and in fact incapable of fully mapping the intricacies of human decision making, partially shrouded in mystery. Alternatively, RCT does prescribe a perfected model of rational choice, but people by and large, having imperfect understandings of statistical induction and cognitive choice processes, act "predictably irrational" (Stiglitz, 2010: 250). But if that would be the case, critics may contend that unrealistic and hyper-specialized, normative decision making models have little analytical and practical value. Instead, they belong to the domain of moralism (bordering on religiosity), wherein human nature is all-too-readily deplored and subject to prolonged lamentation.

Amadae (2003: 5) points at a few shortcomings and analytical challenges with the model:

> Rational choice theory presupposes that rational agents have a consistent set of preferences and act to obtain that which they most prefer. The theory pertains to both parametric environments and strategic environments with other self-interested rational actors, as well as to uncertain and risky circumstances. The term 'self-interest' encompasses both selfish and altruistic preferences, although most often theorists accept that agents are self-interested in a narrowly constructed, self-oriented manner. (Amadae, 2003: 5)

The principal challenge of the RCT model is that it is incapable of explaining a series of well substantiated empirical phenomena regarding non-optimizing utility outcomes (Boudon, 2003: 6), ranging from voting behaviour (in democratic societies, where the democratic principle of *isonomia*—one vote per citizen—precludes the individual's capacity to determine outcomes, voting per se is irrational in this view; Green and Shapiro, 1994) to altruism more generally. Furthermore, RCT normatively prescribes rational egoism and thus cannot accommodate human collaboration, and even in elementary and simplistic scenarios such as the well-known thought experiment of the "prisoners' dilemma," self-interested behaviour is mandated, leading to sub-optimal outcomes. Such evidence casts doubt on the RCT model, and leaves, e.g., policy makers in the dark regarding the efficacy and sustainability of policies based on the assumption of predictable self-interested behaviour.

Under all conditions, RCT is beyond reasonable doubt a military research contribution: "It is no exaggeration to say that all the roads of rational choice theory lead to RAND," Amadae (2003: 11) claims. "[c]learly," Erickson (2010: 387) adds, "military funding and objectives played a role in creating and disseminating theories of rational choice." The concern for commentators is that the very term "rationality" has been appropriated by economic theory, rooted in military research, to the point where "[t]he word 'rationality' has become almost synonymous with 'economic rationality'" (Daston, 2015: 675). Daston uses the example of Ulysses' choice to have himself tied to the mast of his ship while passing the sirens, whereas the rest of the crew of the ship had their ears plugged with beeswax to avoid making them fall prey to the otherworldly beauty of the sirens' song. RCT may recognize the arrangement to have oneself tied to the mast as a "rational choice" (i.e., to resist the lure of the sirens and to evade death is more rational than other choice alternatives), but economic theory and RCT ignore the core question, that is, *why* Ulysses wants to hear the sirens' song in the first place:

> [Ulysses] wants to hear the Sirens, to know their song, though he does not trust himself to resist its lure … It was obviously rational to want to evade the Sirens' deadly trap for seafarers; was it also rational to want to hear their song? Economic rationality is mute on this topic: individual utility functions accommodate all manner of desires, no matter how strange, so long as preferences are consistently ordered. (Daston, 2015: 676)

If humans believe that social resources such as beauty, meaning, aesthetics, friendship, and emotions, i.e., all things that make human lives what they are and that arguably define human nature, then RCT remains limited. "The [rational choice theory] modeling of complex social phenomena often involves simplifying assumptions," Camerer and Fehr, 2006: 47) say: "otherwise, models may quickly become mathematically intractable." There are indisputably situations in military work and in economic activities that are adequately captured by formalist and mathematized models such as RCT (Camerer and Fehr, 2006), but to make the claim that, e.g., RCT provides a universal, standardized, and legitimate image of substantive rationality is quite another matter; what is left outside the model and what is simply dismissed as "irrational behaviour" is simply subjected to a form of paternalism that grants certain elites the authority to make the claim that significant proportions of the population fail to act rationally in predictable ways, i.e., as stipulated by the favoured analytical framework. Such declarations in turn have little to do with the erudition or acumen on the part of the experimenter and theorist, but present a thinly veiled and unflattering return to authoritarian privileges. Such authoritarian privileges are at the same time the anathema of, e.g., neoclassical economists as that is precisely what the cold war science was formed to undermine, the authoritarian socialist or communist regime and the belief in the efficacy of planned economies from the vantage point of the political elites at the apex of the system. This leaves proponents of RCT with the choice to either accept the empirical fact that the proposed model can only explain a subset of economic and other types of choices, and to continue to hope for people to better know their preferences and to e.g., assess short-term and long-term effects of choices, or to enforce their normative model "from above." Neither alternative is attractive, but the solution has oftentimes been to roll out neo-paternalist campaigns (Bergstrand, 2014) to teach citizens how to monitor their health (Monaghan, Hollands, and Pritchard, 2010; Maravelias, 2009; Throsby, 2009), their level of debt (Zinman, 2015), and to cope with other issues in everyday life pertaining to what are operationalized as choice situations.

COLD WAR RATIONALITY REDUX: NEO-PATERNALISM AND BEHAVIOURAL ECONOMICS

Rizzo and Whitman (2009a) address what they refer to as the "new paternalism" in economic theory and in behavioural economics more specifically (see, e.g., Thaler and Sunstein, 2003). As noticed above, RCT was developed and brought into policy making to by-pass historical and contingent knowledge as the primary resource in policy making, regulatory control, and other politico-economic decision making processes. Rather than staying with an elite rule system (see, e.g., Clark, 1989), proponents of RCT made calculative practices capable of revealing real rationalities their major contribution to governance, leaving the *ancien régime* outmoded. Still, Rizzo and Whitman (2009a: 907) say that the increasingly differentiated RCT used in the discipline of behavioural economics (for an overview, see Madrian, 2014; Kamenica, 2012; Wilson, 2011; Jolls, Sunstein, and Thaler, 1998) shares the credo with old-school paternalism that "individuals may not always act in their own best interests," and that they are "not fully 'rational,' as economists understand that term, because their choices are adversely affected by

various cognitive biases, insufficient willpower, and difficulties of information processing." In the regime of traditional paternalism, having its
roots in moral or religious notions of what is good, the preferences—or,
more widely, interests or pleasures—of the actor were simply ignored as
elites claimed the right to know better and to dictate what good,
legitimate preferences were. Even if, say, an individual prefers to drink
alcohol on a daily basis, such a preference needs to be counteracted
because that is simply "a bad preference" in the eyes of elite policy
makers, potentially imposing, e.g., increased taxation on alcoholic bever-
ages to reduce consumption on the basis of such norms. In contrast,
Rizzo and Whitman (2009a: 907–908) say, neo-paternalism overturns this
elite model and "takes the individual's own subjective preferences as the
basis for policy recommendations." The benefits of the neo-paternalist
model are significant, as the individual can now escape heavy-handed
paternalist policies, and policy makers and the law-enforcing agencies
they command no longer need to cope with unruly populations that, say,
smuggle alcohol or grow cannabis in their backyards. At the same time,
the key question remains, does behavioural economics in fact supply the
information needed to amend policy making and legislative reform in
substantial ways? The answer to that question is no, Rizzo and Whitman
(2009a: 909) propose (see also, Mitchell, 2005: 1248, 1254).

The main reason for the dire prospect of a neo-paternalist policy
regime is that it is most complicated to determine what the real or true
preferences of even one single individual are (Hausman and Welch, 2010:
125; Mitchell, 2005: 1251), and when millions of individuals are to be
governed by only a single policy framework, the problems grow logarith-
mically in proportion:

> *If* well-meaning policymakers possess all the relevant information about
> individuals' true preferences, their cognitive biases, and the choice contexts in
> which they manifest themselves, *then* policymakers could potentially imple-
> ment paternalist policies that improve the welfare of individuals by their own
> standards. But lacking such information, we cannot conclude that actual
> paternalism will make their decisions better; under a wide range of circum-
> stances, it will even make them worse. New paternalists have not taken the
> knowledge problems that are evident from the underlying behavioral and
> economic research seriously enough. (Rizzo and Whitman, 2009a: 910,
> emphasis in the original)

For instance, on the elementary level, it is easy to confuse statements
regarding preferences and actual behaviour. For instance, if an individual
says that, "I want to save more, but I am too weak willed," testifying to
the risk of akrasia, then it is unclear whether this is an individual

"expressing a preference or a simple desire" (Rizzo and Whitman, 2009a: 920). While the former statement reflects a willingness to "incur the opportunity cost" (i.e., the individual understands that saving money de facto means that consumption is postponed and re-located in the future), the latter declaration of "a desire to save" is just more generally a "favorable attitude toward something irrespective of opportunity cost" (Rizzo and Whitman, 2009a: 920). That is, to make a statement is not by itself evidence of "true and comprehensive underlying preferences" (Rizzo and Whitman, 2009a: 921). "For the theorist, it is important to distinguish between idle wishes and feasible choices," Riker (1995: 26) argues. These difficulties involved in discriminating between the two meanings of a statement on the elementary level lead to the pressure on the analyst (e.g., the behavioural economists) to be smarter than the subject and to be able to identify the *true* preferences of the subject, something even the subject him- or herself cannot do.

Even if such intellectual superiority would be practically possible to demonstrate, the next problem is that the very notion of preferences as a stable set of dispositions and actualized behaviours may in fact be hard to verify on the basis of empirical data: "Evidence suggests that agents may not have 'true' preferences at all. This, in itself, presents a problem for the new paternalist paradigm; we cannot claim to be making people better according to their preferences if such preferences do not exist" (Rizzo and Whitman, 2009a: 922). If preferences are contingent on historical conditions, local practices, and actual choice situations, the idea of a true preference becomes a moving target, almost impossible to pin down and to translate into meaningful policy making input material, especially if large populations are monitored or empirically tested. This leads to the third problem, that *even if* such contingent and detailed knowledge is possible to obtain, the costs of doing so are significant. Expressed differently, it is costly to measure and evaluate preferences because there is a series of "biases" in preferences (Hausman and Welch, 2010: 125)—which behavioural economists are the first to admit as they commit considerable effort to the identification and description of such biases—but also because it is difficult to determine "a baseline of 'true' preferences" (Rizzo and Whitman, 2009a: 932). To know true preferences, the analyst needs to estimate the magnitude of biases and how they "mislead" the subject from a baseline measure when he or she makes decisions: "The paternalist policymaker also needs to know the *extent* of the bias in order to design the appropriate solution to counteract it" (Rizzo and Whitman, 2009a: 932).

One specific challenge for the behavioural economists is that laboratory studies cannot account for the "debiasing efforts" of the individual

(Mitchell, 2005: 1255), i.e., the work conducted to overcome misconceptions about the role of the information generated and used to make a decision, as such efforts are "context-dependent" (Rizzo and Whitman, 2009a: 932). Mitchell (2005: 1253) speaks about such context as *frames* (see e.g., Tversky and Kahneman, 1981) that strongly influence choices and suggests that what is missing from behavioural economics is "a theory of when choice frames will control choice and when they will not" (Mitchell, 2005: 1253). Such know-how or aggregated theory might educate researchers and policy makers on how to improve decision making quality, which in turn might, as neo-paternalists set as their explicit goal, "foster individual freedom of choice rather than have the central planner make such choices" (Mitchell, 2005: 1254). Unfortunately, laboratory environments are typically devoid of such context to be able to control, with Rheinberger's (1997: 13) apt term, "the experimental situation," but the precision of the data generated does not, Rizzo and Whitman (2009a: 948) argue, outweigh the loss of the external validity of the empirical data. This makes the prospect of laboratory-based studies unpromising: "Even if the experiment designer deliberately structures the experiment to create the illusion of context, this effort cannot capture self-debiasing efforts that seek to achieve *overall* outcomes by differing *across* contexts" (Rizzo and Whitman, 2009a: 948, emphasis in the original).

Finally, even if it would have been possible to provide robust data sets apprehending the situated preferences of a population, the neo-paternalist encounters the problem of how to ensure that the policy makers themselves are not biased in their preferences. Extensive research indicates, for instance, that democratic bodies such as members of parliament do factually not represent the population in terms of, e.g., educational attainment or other credentials (see e.g., Jones, 2011: 77–77; Dacin, Munir, and Tracey, 2010: 1396–1397), and this fact compromises the neo-paternalist argument. That is, behavioural economists make the assumption that "only the choices of the targeted agents are subject to cognitive or behavioral biases" (Rizzo and Whitman, 2009b: 705); policy makers, financiers of research projects, and the behavioural economists themselves, etc., are thus assumed to be capable of escaping the delusion and biases that *all other* citizens are exposed to. For instance, "the theorist may be gullible or cynical or both," Riker (1995: 26) remarks. It is therefore questionable to make the assumption that the "new elites" are somehow immune to "the cognitive and behavioral biases that new paternalists ascribe to most people" (Rizzo and Whitman, 2009b: 705). This assumption reveals one of the great ironies of economics as a scholarly discipline; at the same time as economists render self-interest and self-regarding behaviour prime motivators, the economists' own advice and advocacy are somehow insulated from this otherwise systemic feature (Offer and Söderberg, 2016: 2). In the end, the economist assumes the prerogative to advocate various reforms from some centrally located and neutral vantage point that economists, at least those who pledge allegiance to Friedrich von Hayek's sceptical view of centralized planning, reject as a practically obtainable position in a market-based society:

> Like a socialist planner, an economist ... believes that he can accomplish great feats, because he supposes that he has finally uncovered the fully predetermined mechanisms that drive market outcomes and that his model adequately captures how market participants think about the future. He generally believes that his theory enables him to ascertain whether state intervention is warranted to, say, correct market failures or deal with swings in assets prices. He also uses his theory to prescribe how government should conduct macroeconomic policies on society's welfare. (Frydman and Goldberg, 2011: 67)

This proposition regarding exceptions from otherwise predictable human behaviour is disputable and cannot be accepted out of hand (Hausman and Welch, 2010; Mitchell, 2005).

The work of Rizzo and Whitman (2009a, 2009b) indicates that it is not uncomplicated to escape the difficulties involved in verifying RCT as a universally applicable and accurate model of substantive rationality without returning to a paternalist credo, including assumptions about the analyst's privileges. Green and Shapiro (1994) summarize the lack of empirical substantiation of theoretical propositions and integrated models:

> To date, a large proportion of the theoretical conjectures of rational choice theorists have not been tested empirically. Those tests that have been undertaken have either failed on their own terms or garnered theoretical support for propositions that, on reflection, can only be characterized as banal: they tend to do little more than restate existing knowledge in rational choice terminology. (Green and Shapiro, 1994: 6)

Yet the strategy to shift the burden of proof from the analyst onto the subject remains a viable approach in economic theory, making significant proportions of the population suspicious of, or factually being proved, acting in ways that violate elementary and more sophisticated statistical inductive methods. Such a strategy saves the RCT model but leaves the analyst with an expanding pool of what Thomas S. Kuhn (1962) referred to as *anomalies*, empirical observations that cannot be explained on the basis of the stipulated analytical model. In the following, the work of Daniel Kahneman and colleagues (most notably the late Aron Tversky) will be examined as an example of how the burden of proof is passed on to the experimental subject.

The Experimenter's Fallacy: The Elimination of Contextual Meaning

Buturovic and Tasic (2015) discuss how the concept of rationality in economic approaches easily becomes "a tautological assertion of the existence of subjective preferences," as rationality is simplistically defined as a consistent ordinal ordering of goals (Riker, 1995: 28). Rationality is thus not a term that describes actual real-world economy problems and choice situations, and how individuals cope with such situations under the influence of a variety of contingencies; instead, rationality denotes a *norm* or an *ideal*, and any deviations from such a norm or ideal are by definition treated as evidence of irrationality on the part of the subject. The method used to construct such norms and to test their empirical validity (or, rather, to test to what extent individuals fail to live up to theoretical prescriptions) is based on the assumption that statistical reasoning and an elementary understanding of probability and normal distribution are of necessity more rational than any other comparable good heuristics (Buturovic and Tasic, 2015: 133). When experimental subjects fail to process the information provided in the experimental situation, or prove unqualified to calculate statistically likely outcomes (i.e., to assess the probability of a certain event to occur, say, that flipping a coin would leave the same side of the coin up a certain number of times), such failures to pass the experimenter's "rationality test" are deemed as "cognitive biases," i.e., consistent and predictable misunderstandings of a particular situation or problem. However, Buturovic and Tasic (2015: 134) suggest that rather than being evidence of cognitive bias, "simple ignorance of either quantitative technique or of relevant facts suffices to explain it." For example, what Kahneman (2011) refers to as "a simple puzzle" is exemplary of the experimenter's overinterpretation of the data generated, expressed as follows: "A bat and ball costs $1.10. The bat costs one dollar more than the ball. How much does the ball cost?" According to Kahneman's reasoning, what he calls the "fast mode of thinking" invites humans to say that the bat costs $1 and the ball 10 cents, adding up to total cost $1.10. But the bat costs one dollar *more* than the ball, making the correct arithmetic answer the price of $1.05 for the bat and 5 cents for the ball. For Kahneman, this is an illustrative case how humans tend to rush to conclusions without carefully processing all information provided, even in a simple case. Buturovic and Tasic (2015: 135) object to this conclusion, being made on the premise that this is in fact a "simple" puzzle. Buturovic and Tasic (2015: 135) object that the calculative problem is not as elementary as Kahneman invites his readers to think: "In reality, this is a system of two equations with two unknowns—the type of mathematical problem that, in the United States, is not learned until at least the eighth grade, if ever." By simply rendering mathematical analysis and statistical methods not only as high-status modes of thinking, but also to prescribe them as normatively preferable in comparison to any other heuristic, Kahneman and his collaborators undermine the legitimacy of real-world economy reasoning used by millions of humans on an everyday basis (see e.g., Lave, 1988).

More specifically, much of the so-called cognitive biases that behavioural economists identify, seek to explain, and promote as the root of a series of economic malaises derive from the experimental system per se, fashioned to sort out such "inconsistencies." The lack of contextual information easily invites the experimental subject to "fill in the blanks" in the scenarios and problems described, and these sorts of embellishment of the case situation are interpreted as cognitive biases and analytical failures, i.e., as sources of irrationality. Furthermore, the experimenter needs to account for the possibility that the experimental subject is unaware that he or she is exposed to a series of trick questions that are likely to lead them to the wrong answer; if the experimental subject knew that, it is possible that he or she would have responded in ways that affect the outcome. That is, the subjects of the experiment are assumed to be "naïve" (Riker, 1995: 32), i.e., they do not reflect on the experimental situation as such or the scarcity of information provided to make sense out of the puzzling and unfamiliar event of participating in laboratory experiments. "Designed with only literal interpretation and formal probability theory in mind, such experiments can lead to the interpretation of subjects' rational interpretations of the entire context in which the questions are asked as 'irrational,'" Buturovic and Tasic (2015: 137) suggest. The "entire context" is of great significance, as cognitive studies "in the wild" suggest that human cognition is structured around the human ability to perceive and apprehend an external world in its entirety (Lave, 1988), and that choice situations and decisions are always embedded within such context. To extrapolate how decisions in the wild are made from context-free decisions is a precarious epistemological leap, easily misleading the analyst:

> The prevalence of Kahneman-type phenomena in psychological and decision-making literature does not necessarily reflect their relevance in the actual world. The fragility of the link between the outcomes of laboratory experiments and real-world decision-making has not been a secret, which makes the near-universal acclaim for Kahneman's results and the enthusiastic acceptance of the entire field of behavioral economics all the more puzzling. (Buturovic and Tasic, 2015: 140)

In addition, even if it would be possible to construct meaningful contexts within the experimental system, the experimenter encounters the same demarcation problem between "good" and "not-good" norms as the neo-paternalist policy maker does: it is complicated to establish a "clear norm that would allow a decision to be judged good or bad, let alone rational or irrational" (Buturovic and Tasic, 2015: 140). Therefore, faced with the difficulties in "assessing accuracy of the outcome of social judgments in the real world" (Buturovic and Tasic, 2015: 140), experimenters have generated a variety of norms of judgement against which they assess human decision making performance, but such norms of judgement suffer from a low degree of external validity, as they apply only in "highly artificial settings," i.e., the laboratory setting.

Ultimately, even if it was possible to design more elaborate experimental systems, and if there were jointly agreed standards for hard end-point data and widely recognized norms of judgement to determine human decision making quality, the favouring of mathematical calculation and statistical reason per se, as being superior to any other heuristic and indeed unsurpassable as the basis for human rationality, would still be an idiosyncratic and curious view of human rationality. In fact, an individual who pursues a strictly calculative mode of existence, and who uses statistical methods to calculate the likely outcomes of economic decisions, as well as letting the intimate sphere of human life be organized on such principles would be regarded as odd. Such a machine-like and "super-human" adherence to instrumental rationality would violate widespread ideas of what it means to be human. In addition, most of advanced, higher education is structured around the ability to think freely, in new and creative terms, and to transcend common sense thinking (see e.g., Nussbaum, 2010):

> There is a reason why concern with creative thinking is a staple in business, clinical, and educational contexts, to the point where phrases like 'thinking outside the box' have become clichés. It is in the discovery of options and possibilities where most of the challenge of decision making lies, not in precisely comparing predefined and given options. (Buturovic and Tasic, 2015: 141)

Such objections to the design of the research programme are not trivial but point at fundamental assumptions made in RCT-based scholarship. Behavioural economics does not tackle the more important and sophisticated aspects of human decision making in a real-world economy setting, but merely shows that humans have a problem to effortlessly and with ease use statistical methods and to draw credible conclusions from limited information. That contribution is both interesting and credible, but it does not grant the experimenters the authority to dismiss humans as being predictably irrational *tout court*. Ultimately, Buturovic and Tasic (2015: 141) say, these lines of experimental research "tell us very little about how people think." Instead, behavioural economics experimenters develop what could be referred to as an "epistemology of fault finding," wherein "artificially induced quirks of human cognition are examined in excruciating detail while everyday decision making of great individual and social consequence are ignored" (Buturovic and Tasic, 2015: 141).

Therefore, the primary value of this experimental data lies in the demonstration of how a large proportion of the subjects can be manipulated "with trick questions and clever framing," i.e., the laboratory research provides practical proof of successful and purposeful manipulation (Riker, 1995: 34). Perhaps that insight per se has value for the understanding of human rationality and decision making, but its implications for real-life settings are oblique. Identifying and examining "cognitive blunders" and situations where the capacity to execute instrumental rationality fall short on the part of the experimental subject may live up to scientific standards regarding systematic deviations from rational choice norms, but it says little about real-world decision making quality outside the experimental situation. Therefore, Buturovic and Tasic (2015: 142) argue, behavioural economics experimenters confuse *error* and *mistakes*, which in turn mislead them to dismiss human cognition as being riddled with biases and ultimately irrational. While error is "a deviation from a given standard" (Buturovic and Tasic, 2015: 142), i.e., the rational choice decision making norms and their veneration of statistical induction, mistakes are "incorrect judgements" within a broader and more context-rich horizon of meaning, i.e., in a real-world setting. Therefore, in the end, Daniel Kahneman and behavioural economists have "turned a notion of rationality that started as an absurdly unrealistic assumption in economics into an absurdly unrealistic model of how decisions *should* be made" (Buturovic and Tasic, 2015: 141). This, in turn, is an outcome dependent on the construction of "doable problems" within a confined epistemic community.

THE CONSTRUCTION OF "DOABLE PROBLEM" AND THE ROLE OF EPISTEMIC SCAFFOLDS

The main challenge for behavioural economics is to design experimental situations whose generated data carry *external validity*, i.e., the research output mirrors real-life situations and decisions made in this domain. According to Rizzo and Whitman (2009a, 2009b) and Buturovic and Tasic (2015), the present laboratory-based experimental system used to substantiate RCT fails in predictable ways to provide such data, and therefore, in the end, the know-how regarding real-world economy decision making remains limited and obscure. Nelson (2013) discusses the question of external validity in terms of the construction of an "epistemic scaffold" that serves to uphold the belief that the experimental system does in fact reflect, e.g., actual choice situations:

> Building an epistemic scaffold ... involves a process of building up arguments and evidence to substantiate the use of the model to do knowledge production work. What is stacked in an epistemic scaffold, however, is not a series of increasingly general claims about a particular observation but a series of increasingly risky claims about the relationship of the model and the modeled. To argue for the use of the model as an appropriate tool, researchers select particular facts or observations about both the model organism (the mouse) and the organism being modeled (the human) and attempt to link them together, and these paired pieces of information are stacked to build the epistemic scaffold of greater heights. (Nelson, 2013: 8)

Underlying the concept of the epistemic scaffold is the idea that in order to be able to generate and publish credible research data, the experimenter needs to construct a "doable problem" (Fujimura, 1996) within the stipulated time horizon of the project and on the basis of the resources being committed. Therefore, experimenters make use of pre-defined and standardized "theory-methods packages" including "standard test protocols," "software packages for data analysis," and "existing literature on the test" that taken together reduce the time needed to get started with the experimental, data-generating work (Nelson, 2013: 19). While such standardized theory-methods packages reduce the transaction costs in, e.g., the life sciences and provide the auxiliary benefit of unifying the discipline as a geographically dispersed community of researchers deploying standardized experimental systems or model organisms (see e.g., Rader, 2004; Kohler, 1994), it also leverages the problem regarding *external validity*, the relation between the model at hand and the factual reality that the model purports to represent (Johnson, 2007: 603). For instance, in some scientific disciplines such as astrophysics, oceanography, and meteorology, data generated in simulations of actual processes and events are accepted as input variables in the construction of the theoretical models that are used to explain such phenomena (Sundberg, 2011, 2009), testifying to the difficulty involved in constructing robust experimental systems. In other cases, researchers may encounter what Roth (2009: 315) refers to as "radical uncertainty," wherein there are no external and objective criteria for evaluating the outcome from experimental work independently of the actions of the researcher (see, e.g., Lewis et al., 2013). That is, researchers end up with a "chicken-and-egg" conundrum wherein in order to "evaluate their actions, researchers have to draw on the outcomes of these actions but, for evaluating the outcomes, they have to rely on their actions" (Roth, 2009: 315). The inability to assess whether the model or the experimental system as such can or cannot be trusted until the empirical data is generated and tested *outside* the model leads to a situation wherein it is *assumed* that the model or the experimental system are accurately designed and operated. This assumption enables the experimental work to continue for the time being until the flaws of the model or experimental system are detected, a form of breakdown or failure that Downer (2011: 748) refers to as an *epistemic accident*, the undesirable effect of a fallible design of a technology or experimental system that reveals itself only after the fact, yet is impossible to anticipate from the original vantage point of the researcher or engineer. As a consequence, the actual or reputed relationship between *the model* and *what is modelled* is of key importance for the authority of the scientific community and its long-term ability to raise research funds. Therefore, the epistemic scaffolds, Nelson's (2013) shorthand expression for the advocacy of a tight fit between the model and what is modelled, consequently "often end up becoming permanently provisional structures." That is, such structures are built for "particular pragmatic purposes," but the work that they are needed for often goes on for much longer than expected, turning these temporary structures into "semipermanent features of the scientific landscapes" (Nelson, 2013: 22).

Applying Nelson's analytical model to RCT-based behavioural economics, and using the case of Daniel Kahneman's experimental data one more time, Buturovic and Tasic (2015: 141) make the claim that decision making is always of necessity consequentialist for Kahneman, i.e., any decision always has as its stated and clear goal to maximize the decision maker's "utility function." Using Nelson's (2013) concept of the epistemic scaffold, this consequentialist credo is the foremost "semipermanent feature" of the research model applied. Without the leveraging of the consequentialist norm to be the only legitimate and credible standard for what qualifies as "rational behaviour," and the entire decision making apparatus that comes with it, the access to "all conceivably relevant facts, knowledge of statistical methods, and thinking in an abstract, uncontextual, and overly literal way" (Buturovic and Tasic, 2015: 141), rationality would not reveal itself within the experimental system at hand. Expressed differently, in order to render "human rationality" a "doable problem"—the grandiosity of such a research programme left aside for the time being—rationality had to be defined in instrumental terms and be accompanied by an experimental system.

Unfortunately, the theory that was developed and put to the test of empirical data in many ways defines how the data is to be interpreted in order to save the core theory through the introduction of ad hoc hypotheses. "The vast majority of deviations from results predicated on rational-choice theory fall under … various exceptions. Each allows economists to explain the deviation without abandoning the assumption that decision makers are rational" (Ulen, 1994: 489–490). Murphy (1995) suggests that the attempt to always save the concept of rationality from unfavourable empirical evidence is tangential to the comical, as there is always some handy ad hoc hypothesis emerging in the event of unsupportive evidence surfacing:

> Attempts to modify equilibrium analysis in rational choice theories have been largely comic: if we find that people are ignorant, then ignorance is optimally rational, given the costs of information; if we find that people are impulsive and passionate, then passion and impulse are optimally rational, given the costs of deliberation; if we find that people act out of habit, then habits are optimal decision strategies, given the costs of thought; and so on. These auxiliary theorems modify rational choice theory in the sense that a cat is modified by the mouse it eats. (Murphy, 1995: 172)

In other words, seen in this view, behavioural economists cannot pride themselves with identifying the "really real rationality" on the basis of the consequentialist norm and the RCT methods package they deploy. Indisputably, behavioural economists have called our attention to the concerns regarding the shortcomings of human actors when it comes to inducing statistically relevant information on the basis of available data, but that is also all there is. To make the claim that such predictable failures are indicative of an absence of rationality altogether is quite another matter. Therefore, insights from science and technology studies reveal that behavioural economics is yet to explore the dark continent of human cognition in the wild.

The establishment and enforcement of cold war rationality and the rational choice model is of importance for the analysis of how corporate governance practices were developed in the 1980s and in the coming decades, making finance market monitoring on the basis of the valuation of the corporations' shares the single most important mechanisms for minimizing what is referred to as agency costs. Therefore, the corporate governance literature needs to be examined in some detail to demonstrate that the corporation was a legal invention and a legal device that was never defined in such finance market terms, as finance markets are only secondary to the development of the corporation as a vehicle for enterprising and market making more widely. As a consequence, the "market for managerial control," advocated from the early 1960s in the law and economics literature, is derived from original legal reforms in corporate law, which this literature now criticizes for tolerating "inefficiencies" in the corporate governance and managerial decision making functions. This critique is therefore turning a blind eye to historical conditions and ignores the causality between legal reform and market making, making the faulty assumption that markets in some way pre-exist legislative practices.

CORPORATE GOVERNANCE AS A LEGAL, ECONOMIC, AND MANAGERIAL PRACTICE

The Economic Theory Blind-spot: Recognizing the Work of Managers and Directors

For legal and management studies scholars, the finance theory-based model of corporate governance, based on the proposition that markets are information efficient and that the risks of the moral hazard of managers overshadow and dwarf any other governance concern (e.g., market instabilities, short-termism, evidence of speculation, poor credit rating quality, etc.), is an untenable proposition not justifying legal reform or changes in governance practices. Finance theorists advance the disputed idea of market efficiency as an axiomatic first principle for its normative governance model, and avert criticism regarding strong evidence of less-than-perfect information efficiency in finance markets by claiming that government interventions into supposedly self-regulating and self-correcting markets bias market pricing. In contrast to this view, legal scholars assume that corporate law is "consistently board-centric" (Cremers and Sepe, 2016: 84), i.e., there is no legal support for shareholder primacy governance. In fact, in Delaware, corporate law, the state where the majority of Fortune 500 companies are incorporated,[1] has enshrined the authority and autonomy of the board, with its §141(a) stipulating that "[t]he business and affairs of every corporation ... shall be managed by or under the direction of a board of directors" (cited in Moore and Rebérioux, 2011: 96). In legal theory, shareholder primacy is a venturesome theoretical proposition that in no decisive way has the capacity to by-pass or otherwise compromise the mandatory rules of corporate law.

Management scholars, in turn, and in contrast to finance theorists, have limited incentives or theoretical baggage inviting them to question the conventional wisdom of legal scholars that the mandatory rules of corporate law are and will continue to be enforced in court cases. Instead, management scholars tend to be sceptical of the black-box view of the firm enacted in economic theory, rendering the firm an organization unit "devoid of interesting hierarchical features" (Williamson, 1981: 1539), and thus worthy of little theoretical attention beyond specific engineering concerns. In the end, Daston (2015: 673) argues, "[e]conomists prefer the blind logic (sometimes known as the invisible hand) of the market to the intelligent design of individual actors and governments." Williamson (1981) suggests that the view of the firm as "production function"—and thus being primarily a matter of "engineering interest"—needs to make way for the view of the firm as a "governance structure" that accurately assesses the internal organization and management of the firm (Williamson, 1981: 1539). For instance, Williamson (1981: 1548–1549) argues, "internal organization enjoys advantages over market contracting for transactions that are supported by highly specific assets as both contract-writing and contract-execution stages." As both writing and negotiating contracts are costly and are accompanied by "implementation problems," the firm does have an advantage over comparable market transactions (Williamson, 1981: 1548–1549).

Beyond the more specific practice of negotiating, writing, and monitoring contracts (see e.g., Goldberg, 1976), the firm practically functions as a site where the internal allocation of resources is monitored by the accounting system. In fact, Biondi (2013: 404) says, confusing external market pricing of outstanding stocks and securities and internal accounting practices is a major fallacy in the finance economics governance model,[2] simply "turning the firm inside out," as market prices are treated *as if* they were accurate and legitimate indicators of internal managerial decision quality, as stipulated by the theory of the market for management control (Manne, 1962, 1965). In Biondi's (2013) view, the capacity to generate qualified and reliable accounting information and to use such information is a distinctively managerial competence, conducive to firm efficiency and, by implication, social and economic welfare:

> Representation, organization, and governance of [the] enterprise process require an accounting system, not a price system, because the accounting system defines economic revenues and costs attached to the reference period through "accruals," the determination of the accounting entity perimeter, the retained concept of capital maintenance, and other technicalities that encompass the monetary dimension. Contrary to the black box view, the firm cannot be reduced to a simplistic "nexus of monetary flows (prices)" because the accounting system goes far beyond the cash basis through its definition and application of accruals, consolidation, and other accounting technicalities. (Biondi, 2013: 404)

That is, accounting systems are an integral part of the governance system and serve the key function of making the firm and its management "accountable." Accountability is, as a considerable accounting literature demonstrates (e.g., Miller and O'Leary, 1987), a human and institutional accomplishment that needs to be recognized within the domain of corporate governance practice. In the context of corporate governance theory and practice, "accounting becomes a way to represent, organize, and regulate the dynamic system of the business firm," Biondi (2013: 408) argues. In the "enterprise entity view" that Biondi advocates, the accounting systems assume an active role in "representing, organizing, and governing the ongoing activities of the enterprise entity as a whole"—even in the case of "complete absence of markets and ownership" (and their alleged control over management). In other words, in order to make the team production activities efficient and capable of generating economic value, benefitting all team production participants (whereof the firm's shareholders are the firm's financiers and are thus part of the team), the accounting system is more relevant than the price system, managerial scholars argue.

Furthermore, not only legal and management scholars express their impatience with one-sided and belligerent shareholder primacy advocacy. Also information economics scholars provide evidence that undermines the shareholder primacy as an authoritative governance model. Cremers and Sepe (2016) examine the effect of so-called *staggered boards* and their economic value generating effects, and find that staggered boards, widely criticized by shareholder primacy governance advocates, in fact do generate economic value. First of all, staggered boards are defined as boards where directors are grouped into different classes, "with each class of directors standing for re-election in successive years" (Cremers and Sepe, 2016: 76–77). In contrast, in *unitary boards* all directors stand for re-election at each annual shareholder meeting (Cremers and Sepe, 2016: 76). Shareholder primacy advocates argue that staggered boards de facto serve as a takeover protection clause, leading to an unnecessary obstacle towards an efficient monitoring of managerial opportunism (which is, *ex hypothesi*, the overbearing corporate governance problem at hand): "A staggered board could now function as an antitakeover defense by forcing a prospective acquirer to go through a costly waiting period before being able to appoint a new majority of directors," Cremers and Sepe (2016: 78) explain.

To test whether this shareholder primacy critique of staggered boards is supported by empirical evidence, Cremers and Sepe (2016: 71) collected a U.S. data sample for the 1978–2011 period, and report that "[s]taggered boards are associated with a statistically and economically significant increase in firm value." In order to explain why staggered boards are in fact positively associated with increases in firm value, Cremers and Sepe (2016: 120) propose that finance market short-termism (again, a minor concern vis-à-vis systematic managerial opportunism in the eyes of shareholder primacy advocates), can be mediated by the board of directors. This tendency is particularly pronounced for "corporate-production processes that involve the development of nonstandardized, innovative technology and that rely more on specific human capital contributions," Cremers and Sepe (2016: 120) suggest. Moreover, many firms and industries are today operating on the basis of such nonstand-ardized, innovative technology and specialized human resources—"[h]uman capital is, today, an increasingly specialized resource" (Cremers and Sepe, 2016: 121)—which make staggered boards an efficient mechanism for insulating the corporate system from finance market short-termism. Unfortunately, shareholder activism works to undermine the very same mechanisms (i.e., efficient corporate govern-ance practices) that generate economic value and social and economic welfare: "The recent increase in shareholder empowerment jeopardizes the board-centric model's continuing ability to deliver efficient out-comes" (Cremers and Sepe, 2016: 75). Therefore, drawing on their empirical evidence and theoretical reasoning, Cremers and Sepe (2016: 75) recommend legal reform that would "transform staggered boards into a quasimandatory rule." In order to protect finance market actors, including shareholders, from their own short-term orientation and liquid-ity preference, and also being ignorant of the value that directors and their assigned managers generate within the corporate system, legislative reform is called for. Thus, *less* market pricing, not *more*, is the pathway towards economic efficiency and social and economic welfare, Cremers and Sepe (2016) contend.

Exogenous Market Conditions: Price Volatility as an Impediment to Shareholder Primacy

Fox, Fox, and Gilson (2016) report another empirical study at the intersection of legal scholarship and economics of relevance for corporate governance. As suggested by many information economics and legal scholars, the high-paced, securitized global finance market is prone to derail and demonstrates extraordinary levels of risk during recurrent periods of crisis (King, 2016; Calomiris and Haber, 2014; Friedman, Jeffrey and Kraus, 2012; Gerding, 2005; Shiller, 2003). During periods of crisis, a recurrent phenomenon over the entire 85-year period examined by Fox, Fox, and Gilson (2016), the so-called *idiosyncratic risk* grows in significant proportion. Robust evidence suggests that such growth in idiosyncratic risk is indicative of less-than-perfect market efficiency, i.e., public market information is not assessed in equal terms over the economic cycle, but information tends to be *more highly valued* by market actors and plays a more central role for the price-setting of, e.g., stocks and securities during the "spikes" in idiosyncratic risk. The concern for legal scholars, economists, and policy makers and regulators is that the sharp growth in idiosyncratic risk provides an advantage for insiders, who now have "[s]ubstantially more opportunities to profit from trading on the nonpublic information that they possess and issuers have more opportunities to sell securities at an inflated price" (Fox, Fox, and Gilson, 2016: 332). In short, growth in idiosyncratic risk, a *bone fide* measure of market instability and thus an indicator of market imperfection, benefits insiders, i.e., finance market actors.

While the recurrent spikes in idiosyncratic risk are embarrassing for advocates of information-efficient market theory and undermine the credibility and legitimacy of policies justifying market-based self-regulation, there are more pressing legal concerns of relevance for the corporate system. Finance actors who believe they have suffered losses during periods of soaring idiosyncratic risk need to present solid empirical evidence in court in so-called fraud-on-the-market cases. Unfortunately, Fox, Fox, and Gilson (2016: 346) show that the "event-based method" being advanced as the gold standard to assess such perceived losses emphasizes the factors influencing the price of only the one, single asset in question. In fact, to measure "the price impact of a particular event" requires that the analyst (i.e., the plaintiff or his or her agents) can isolate the effect of "a single item of information—the occurrence of the event under study—from the cacophony of information constantly reaching the capital markets" (Fox, Fox, and Gilson, 2016: 346). In practice, this is a most complicated procedure. Therefore, as a consequence, the reductionist "event-based case" is unlikely to play any actual role in court ruling, Fox, Fox, and Gilson (2016: 362) argue:

> The spike in idiosyncratic risk that occurs during financial crises causes a very substantial decline in the usefulness of fraud-on-the-market class actions in crisis times. These actions allow buyers in secondary securities markets to recover from the issuer losses that they incurred by purchasing at prices inflated by the issuer's misstatements, without individual class members having to prove that they actually relied upon (or even knew about) the misstatement giving rise to their claim. (Fox, Fox, and Gilson, 2016: 362)

In other words, during the period where inside trade is increasingly lucrative, as every single piece of new information is more highly valued, *ceteris paribus*, it is comparatively more complicated to take fraud-on-the-market cases to court, simply because plaintiffs are dependent on the reliability of event studies, whose statistical material includes a considerable proportion of noise during periods of spikes in idiosyncratic risk (Fox, Fox, and Gilson, 2016: 362). The legislation and the court cases thus work less well during the conditions where they are needed the most, that is, when there is a need for restoring the faith in the accuracy and efficiency of finance market pricing. In the end, the study of Fox, Fox, and Gilson (2016) provides a valuable case for how finance markets are volatile over the economic cycle, with periods of stable economic growth and moderate idiosyncratic risks followed by periods of economic crises with spikes in risk measures, a condition that in considerable ways compromises the shareholder primacy governance model. Unfortunately, the legal and regulatory system that provides a final check on inside trade (i.e., the illicit use of non-public information that would harm the interest of third parties) suffers from deficiencies, which leaves the individual suffering losses from, e.g., such trade with a formidable challenge to provide credible, robust evidence in fraud-on-the-market cases.

Governance as a Real-world Economy Problem: Beyond the Efficiency Criteria

One of the standing critiques of the shareholder primacy governance model is that real-world economies do operate differently from the abstract and idealized economic models that dominate textbooks and seminar cases, developed and fine-tuned by card-carrying economists and finance theorists in particular. For instance, even an economist committed to RCT as a meaningful analytical framework such as Riker (1995), argues that, e.g., decisions are not made once and for all and then simply forgotten, as in the laboratory experiment dominating microeconomic theory. In the real world, actors do first of all live with the consequences of their decisions and choices, and, secondly, they do "choose again and again" (Riker, 1995: 35), i.e., there are possibilities for learning how to make sound economic decisions on both individual and collective levels—which in turn justifies the business judgment rule enforced by courts—i.e., insiders such as managers do have the capacity to lower aggregated costs on the basis of their detailed understanding of the idiosyncratic conditions of their industries and businesses.[3]

Based on such theoretical and methodological shortcomings, Hill and Painter (2009: 1186) argue that asking how "hypothetical 'rational' wealth-maximizing bankers" approach the problem of risk is the wrong question; instead, researchers should ask how senior bank managers (and the owners of stock in these banks) are *actually* making decisions that affect the risk exposure of these banks in real-world economy settings. That is, orthodox economic theory is granting too much explanatory value to experimental data, based on fabricated decision making scenarios, at times even using graduate students as a proxy for highly specialized finance professionals, or simply relies on deductive reasoning on the basis of fictive decision making cases. At the bottom line, such preferences and inclinations reveal a preference for a world devoid of impurities and cleansed of human virtue and folly, a fictive world wherein calculative practices and instrumental rationality provide undisputed standard for "rational" and "efficient" decision making, Rowe (1984: 1549) claims in a critique of "equilibrium theory" (see also Kaldor, 1972): "A figment of orthodox equilibrium economics, it posits a timeless universe in balance, with ideal resource use for all. Such harmony, however, can never exist in the real world." Unfortunately, as Herbert Simon (1955: 114) remarks, human beings' ability to cope with an overwhelming complexity in choice situations, amplified by cognitive limitations, introduces a "discrepancy" between the "simplified model and reality." The rational actor is cognizant of this discrepancy and individual cognitive limitations, but, according to Simon, the orthodox neoclassical economist is unwilling to accept the presence of this deviation between the simplified map of the economy and the real-world economy territory. As a consequence, the rational actor falls prey to the fallacy of misplaced concreteness that invites analysts to underrate the fuzziness of underlying conditions.

In the next instance, once the orthodox analyst has assumed that simplified models of, e.g., decision making in, say, corporate governance practices, are valid and legitimate, after the model has been assessed and verified and corroborated by a sufficient number of authoritative actors, there is a determination of which performance parameters the preferred model should optimize. In the case of orthodox neoclassical model of governance, "efficiency" has been the predominant performance benchmark, inherited from the neoclassical doctrine that economic growth is the foremost objective within a governance regime. Unfortunately, measuring social welfare in terms of "efficiency" is a far from trivial challenge, i.e., "efficiency" is not a singular concept, nor an undisputed term. Needless to say, the orthodox economist's claim that "efficiency" is an indubitable performance criterion, legal scholars, management researchers, and economic sociologists are sceptical towards the idea that efficiency is easily measured, as there is significant "noise" in any economic system, or because the term per se is already from the outset defined in politically charged ways that undermine the possibility to generate objective data.

In the field of corporate law, a constitutional law in the U.S. legal system, economic concepts such as "efficiency" poorly sides with legal theory, prominent legal scholars argue: "Understandably, formal legal rules are easier for economists to code, measure, and incorporate into their regression equations, but they may have little to do with the reality of actual practice," Coffee (2007: 244) says. In the same vein, Desan (2005: 23) deplores "[t]he banality employed by economists in describing legal categories." More importantly, such critics argue that that the efficiency criterion was never a legitimate contestant for being the measure *par préférence* in governance practices. That is, governance as a legal term, managerial practice, or agency activity was never enacted and constituted, nor developed, to exclusively satisfy a singular "efficiency criterion."

The birth of the efficiency criterion
In this context, it is important to recognize that the efficiency criterion per se is a disputed and politically loaded term, associated with free market theory and the Chicago school of economics. In Manne's (1962) account, managers are made suspicious of not maximizing the output, as they are assumed to be primarily concerned with their own wellbeing. Alchian (1965: 30) argues that there is "empirical evidence" that indicates that managers and their employees pursue policies directed at "increasing sales, gross assets, employees, expenditures for various equipment and facilities beyond those that yield a profit maximum." For both Manne (1962) and Alchian (1965), such decisions and policies represent deviations from their prescribed, normative free market model and its efficiency criterion, and therefore actors failing to follow these instructions are by definition sub-optimizing the activities. Therefore, by implication, managers are guilty of opportunistic behaviour. But such a

strictness of the assessment criteria has not been assumed across the field of economic theory. In William Baumol's (1959) seminal work, firms do not maximize "efficiency" in the narrow sense prescribed by Manne (1962) and Alchiam (1965), but they are still *effective* inasmuch as they balance the various interests and objectives at hand, and translate such diverse decision making input materials into operative decisions. To accomplish this work, Baumol (1959: 28–29) introduces the concept of "rule of thumb": "Management's difficulty is that it must retain some measure of control over the operations of the firm without, at the same time, tying itself up to operational details. This problem is solved by the frequent use of rules of thumb." As Baumol continues, "these rules of thumb do not work too badly," as they serve to translate "hopelessly involved problems into simple, orderly routines."[4] Moreover, rules of thumb save the executives' time and permit "a degree of centralized control" over the firm's manifold operations, Baumol (1959: 28–29) adds. In this view, managers are far from the self-serving opportunists, creating a situation where they can "enjoy a quiet life" in the executive suites, as they would come to be portrayed in, e.g., the agency theory literature (see, e.g., Bertrand and Mullainathan, 2003). In Baumol's (1959) account, managers are competent professionals with detailed expertise of highly specialized production systems, capable of balancing a variety of interests advocated by a number of stakeholders, at times with opposing objectives (e.g., diversified shareholders who may favour increased risk taking and creditors who can reap no benefits from such a strategy as their contracts are already stipulating their returns).

More importantly, the efficiency criterion as defined by free market theorists is by and large irrelevant in Baumol's (1959: 27) view, as the "competitive situation" is not the primary factor in managerial decision making: "[E]ven in fairly crucial decisions, and almost always in routine policy-making, only the most cursory attention is paid to competitive reactions." For instance, managers, operating under the limitation of bounded rationality and thus using rules of thumb to manage the operations, do not primarily make maximized profit their primary object-ive but seek to expand the firm's sales, growth, market penetration, etc., i.e., they *create possibilities* for higher profits, but such decisions are not primarily guided by a concern for efficiency maximization:

> So long as profits are high enough to keep stakeholders satisfied and contribute adequately to the financing of company growth, management will bend its efforts to the augmentation of sales revenues rather than to further increase its profits. (Baumol, 1959: 50)

In Baumol's (1959) model of the firm, the efficiency criterion is an impractical and thus understated concept within real-world decision making. The tendency to impose an efficiency criterion derived from some abstract theoretical model and to assess the performance on the basis of this model is to ignore the complexities facing managers, and represents a form of hyper-rationalism, a favouring of abstract reasoning over real-world economy conditions.

Leibenstein (1966: 407) lists some of the activities that managers oversee in everyday operations, associated with a series of difficulties from the view of an "efficiency-maximizing" criterion: "(a) contracts for labor are 'incomplete', (b) the production function is not completely specified or known, and (c) not all inputs are marketed or, if marketed, are not available on equal terms to, all buyers" (Leibenstein, 1966: 407). Furthermore, some of the supposedly "inefficient" practices that may be observed derive from information collection costs being higher than the cost to make a decision (see, e.g., Feldman and March, 1981). For instance, when employees negotiate salaries, direct measurement of individual work effort and its efficiency is costly, say, in domains of professional work. In such situations, "managers may pay their workers in excess of what the market demands" (Weeden and Grusky, 2014: 478). This is a form of "overcompensation" of certain individuals,[5] derived from information costs, but such decisions are still rational solutions to practical issues at hand. From a strict and narrower efficiency criterion, though, overcompensation is seen as factual evidence of the squandering of firm-specific resources. But such a statement is firmly rooted in specific economic doctrines and their assumptions regarding the cost to collect relevant information. Operating in such markets and economies, managers cannot translate "efficiency" into practically useful benchmarks guiding their day-to-day work at low cost. In addition, what one school of orthodox neoclassical economists regards as an uncomplicated term and a normatively enforceable benchmark, other groups may treat as a highly disputable proposition that serves no functional role in real-world economies. In the end, governance regimes remain politically informed practices within the horizon of meaning of managers and directors, arguably doing their best to optimize a variety of interests expressed by heterogeneous stakeholders.

Legal scholars' rejection of the efficiency criterion

Budros (1999: 70, original emphasis omitted) says that "efficiency" is a "technico-economic standard of performance" that measures "how well an organization achieves its objectives, given the resources used"; efficiency is thus the ratio between input and output. As such an accounting term already presupposes that the input and output variables can be specified with great precision to make sense, and that such precision is complicated to attain in a real-world economy outside accounting stand-ard procedures, efficiency is a poor candidate for being a benchmark measure within jurisprudence, Rizzo (1980) argues. For instance, in order to enforce legislation being based on an efficiency standard, there is a need for indisputably trustworthy data, i.e., data that can serve a meaningful role within the court system. Unfortunately, as such data is costly and complicated to acquire for all actors, efficiency becomes more of a metaphor than a functional legal term:

> [T]he substantial information requirements that must be satisfied in order to identify efficient legal rules make efficiency impractical as a standard. Unless the efficiency theorists can show how courts can overcome the difficulties outlined here they will continue to argue for a norm that has little operational content. It is all too easy to show that efficiency leads to desirable results within simplified constructs; it is quite another thing to show what this has to do with the world in which we live. (Rizzo, 1980: 658)

Also Elzinga (1977: 1212) is sceptical regarding the use of efficiency as a legal term, and claims that it is, normatively speaking, not a candidate for being the overarching goal of the legal system. Efficiency is "only a means, not an end," Elzinga (1977: 1212) argues. Hovenkamp (1985) argues that the idea that "public policymaking" should be guided exclusively by a notion of efficiency, derived from neoclassical economic theory and its market model, is "naïve." Just like Rizzo (1980) and Elzinga (1977), Hovenkamp (1985: 284) points at both practical and normative limitations with the efficiency model: "That notion both overstates the ability of the policymaker to apply such a model to real-world affairs and understates the complexity of the process by which the policymaker must select among competing policy values." For legal scholars, the economic theory concern regarding the maximization of efficiency is neither practically useful, nor a legitimate candidate for being an operative term in legal practice.

Beyond the specific argument in favour of efficiency as a guiding objective for the legal system and its enforcement, several legal scholars disarm the law and economics scholars' critique that economic models should play a central role in jurisprudence. Aguilera and Cuervo-Cazurra (2004: 434) argue that "codes of good governance" are developed not only because there is pressure from market actors to improve the effectiveness of corporate governance systems, but more importantly because there are "exogenous pressures to legitimate the current system by introducing such practices regardless of their degree of implementation" (Aguilera and Cuervo-Cazurra, 2004: 434). Rock and Wachter (2001: 1622), two legal scholars examining corporate law vis-à-vis economic theory views of the corporation, argue that, as a legal device, the corporation, the business granted a charter from the sovereign state, the raison d'être of firms is "to replace legal governance of relations with nonlegally enforceable governance mechanisms (what are sometimes called 'norms')." This statement runs counter to, e.g., the dominant agency theory view that imposes the efficiency criterion on the corporation, and that operationalizes efficiency as (1) the maximum payout of the residual cash flow to shareholders, and (2) the minimization of agency costs. Rock and Wachter (2001: 1697) argue that the agency theory model is based on the idea of complete contracts, capable of stipulating in detail the rights and obligations of various participants within the business venture, but as the corporation as a legal device rests on *incomplete contracts* (Aghion and Holden, 2011; Hart, 1988), the agency theory model is irrelevant. For instance, the strong emphasis on agency costs as an overbearing and substantial externality in the corporate system in agency theory is rejected both on substantive grounds, as agency costs are in fact complicated to measure, and their magnitude is likely to be considerably lower than agency theorists claim, and on legal theory grounds; "[a]gency costs are not the only thing that matters in corporate law and, standing alone, are either unable to explain major areas of corporate law jurisprudence or are even misleading" (Rock and Wachter, 2001: 1622).

Regarding the claim made by agency theorists that shareholders "own the firm," an argument commonly dismissed by legal scholars as corporations qua legal devices are incorporated *sui juris*, i.e., they "own themselves" and engage directors as their trustees, Rock and Wachter (2001: 1698) argue that in closely held corporations (i.e., corporations with limitedly dispersed ownership, such as in family-owned firms or start-up firms), the shareholders are the "owners" in terms of being granted the right to exercise control over the corporation's assets. In the public corporation, the firm with dispersed ownership and where stockholding is accompanied by voting rights (and being the category of corporations that primarily engages agency theorists), "directors and not dispersed shareholders are the owners in that they exercise control over assets," Rock and Wachter (2001: 1698) state. As a consequence, the agency theory view of the corporation and its emphasis on the shareholders' contractual right to claim the residual cash flow is rejected by Rock and Wachter (2001); the corporation is a legal device based on incomplete contracts, and shareholder interests is merely one concern among many others that directors, endowed with formal power in corporate law, need to consider. In addition, maximized efficiency is merely one objective competing with other stated objectives and the "nonlegally enforceable rules and standards" that the firm relies on in its day-to-day operations (Rock and Wachter, 2001: 1623).

In summary, legislation, regulation, policies, and standards are not only implemented to maximize the efficiency of a specific economic system at any cost and under all conditions, but also serve to signal a commitment to certain norms or beliefs, even goals, internal as well as external to the firm. In the end, legislation serves many ends, whereof efficiency-maximizing outcomes are one objective, siding with many others. Legislation, regulation, policies, and standards are thus human accomplishments developed to serve practical needs and interests, not to conform to some theoretical model preferred by certain scholars and commentators.

The substantive argument: market actors do not emphasize efficiency

In the end, economists fashion a role for themselves as "guardian[s] of rationality" (in Arrow's, 1974: 16, memorable phrase) and easily accept the burden to instruct others how to, e.g., make rational decisions (Offer and Söderberg, 2016: 2). In such situations, the theoretical models enacted and normative statements made need to be carefully aligned with how, e.g., market actors behave under the influence of market competition and with a profit motive justifying certain decisions, or else the legitimacy of their advocacy of specific practices is undermined. If efficiency is the overarching and indubitable criterion for managerial decision making in corporations, then market actors are also targeting efficiency in the same terms—in fact, it is the latter category's preferences that dictate the former category's legitimate behaviour in the free market governance model. Studies of hostile takeovers and tender offers, part of the market for management control (Manne, 1965, 1967), wherein shareholders execute their voting rights and seek to take control over a firm to manage it more efficiently than the incumbent management team, indicate that efficiency is not at all a key parameter when selecting a firm to target. Instead, such data suggests that efficiency is an overstated objective for also shareholders, for whom free market theorists claim to speak when they advocate the efficiency criterion.

Schneper and Guillén (2004: 263) define a hostile takeover as "a corporate acquisition that is actively opposed by the target firm's incumbent management or board of directors." The term tender offer bid, in turn, denotes the attempt to buy large shares of the firm's stock but with the board's approval (Davis and Greve, 1997: 9); when a tender offer bid fails to get approval from the board, it is referred to as a hostile takeover bid. Following pro-business reforms in the 1980s, including more relaxed regulatory control, the inflow of overseas savings in the period, and the finance innovation of the junk bond (made popular by the "junk bond king" Michael Milken), the mid-1980s (*circa* 1983–1988) was the heyday of hostile takeover bids (Zorn et al., 2005: 273, Figure 13.1). However, a nationwide survey presented by Touche Ross & Co. asked corporate directors to rate from a list of specified factors "the characteristics that made a potential target company attractive" (Coffee, 1984: 1212). The result indicated that no less that 98 percent of the informants listed "excellent management" as being either a "major attraction" or a "minor attraction." This empirical evidence indicates that the narrative about managers as self-serving squanderers of the share-holder's residual capital is overstated by, e.g., agency theorists and proponents of the contract theory of the firm, making the propositions regarding managerial malfeasance an integral element of their analytical model and normative prescriptions. More importantly, "the vast majority of responses denied that the perceived inefficiency of the target made it an attractive takeover prospect" (Coffee, 1984: 1212). In short, inefficiency—theoretical, perceived or substantial—is beside the point; rather than acting in accordance with a free market theory model, the corporate directors followed a Baumolian model, and recognized other performance goals than the hard-to-measure efficiency criterion.

Furthermore, empirical studies conducted after the fact, the great upsurge in hostile takeover bids in the mid-1980s, support Coffee's (1984) proposition. Davis and Stout (1992) found that it was not poorly managed, and underperforming firms that were the primary targets of takeover bids as predicted by agency theorists, claiming that under-performing firms have low stock value (a stipulated index of substandard managerial decision quality), which in turn makes them vulnerable to takeover bids. Instead, empirical data indicates that firms with low debt were targeted. This in turn suggests that the takeover bid mechanism does not serve the efficiency-inducing role its proponents claim, i.e., the market for management control does not discipline poorly performing management teams, as such firms were never selected as candidates for takeover bids in the first place (Davis and Stout, 1992: 626). Presenting factual evidence, Davis and Stout's (1992) data undermines the empirical basis of the market for management control argument and its one-dimensional emphasis on efficiency: "There is a great irony in the fact that firms that maintained slack to buffer themselves from environmental uncertainty by taking on little debt were prime candidates for takeover in the 1980s," Davis and Stout (1992: 627) remark. Similarly, Franks and Mayer (1996: 164) conclude from their study of hostile takeover bids, that "[u]sing a number of different benchmarks, we find little evidence that hostile takeovers are motivated by poor performance prior to bids." In summary, hostile takeovers, even at the height of their management fashion cycle in the mid-1980s, never served as a market mechanism disciplining incompetent and opportunistic managers as argued by a variety of free market theory schools (e.g., the market for management control theorists, agency theorists, contract theorists); instead, well-managed firms with low debt that were, by and large, excellent examples of how corporate law has successfully promoted venturing, economic growth, and economic welfare on the basis of the business charter device were targeted.

Implications and moderations
The downplaying of a one-dimensional efficiency criterion in governance theory and in legal scholarship and management studies has several implications. One implication is to once and for all abandon the persistent idea that salaried managers are self-serving beneficiaries of the corporate system. Already at the height of the takeover wave in the mid-1980s, Coffee (1986) argued persuasively that the rejection of the legitimacy of salaried managers is untenable for legal, theoretical, and substantive reasons:

> Implicit in much recent commentary about hostile takeovers has been a view of managers as the villain of the story. Their ability to shirk or consume excessive perquisites or otherwise overreach shareholders is seen as providing the rationale for the hostile takeover. True as it is to say that managers sometimes do all of these things, they also can be presented as the victims of the story. Threatened with loss of job security and expected deferred compensation in a volatile stock market in which few companies are not at some point rumored to be takeover targets, managers have been forced as a takeover defense to leverage up and accept a higher level of risk. (Coffee, 1986: 73)

Coffee does not, on the one hand, say that *all* managers, *all* of the time, of necessity act with prudence, nor make the "correct decisions" (an assessment that can only be made in hindsight), but to assume that they predictably underperform and act opportunistically as a core proposition in a theoretical and normative model is, on the other hand, neither conducive to increased understanding of governance practice, nor consistent with extant legislation, nor empirical evidence. Instead, as the economic growth data over the entire post-Second World War period indicate, the era of "managerial capitalism" (*circa* 1945–1973) is the period with the highest economic growth and the sharpest rise in economic welfare (Gordon, 2015). Such aggregated and widely accepted empirical data indicates that salaried managers are efficient decision makers and that coordination within hierarchical firm structures generate net economic benefits, and that they do contribute to economic welfare. It is also questionable to assume that certain actors (e.g., managers, inside directors, central regulation agency officers) are incompetent and act opportunistically in predictable ways, while others (e.g., outside directors and shareholders), would be more prone, as a systemic feature, to make strictly rational decisions (see, e.g., Rizzo and Whitman, 2009b: 705). First, empirical data and theoretical deductions speak against such claims (Frieden, 2016; Greve, Kim, and Teh, 2016; Rajan, 2006; Klick and Mitchell, 2006; Froot, Scharfstein, and Stein, 1992), and, second, the line of demarcation between these actors is far from clearly drawn; actors do have various roles and positions, and they enter different positions over time during their careers. Thus, the idea that, e.g., managers should be more vulnerable to opportunistic behaviour or akrasia than, e.g., shareholders is a questionable proposition on these grounds.

The Doctrine of Efficiency and the Nirvana fallacy: Implications for Corporate Governance

"Contrary to shareholder value rhetoric, financial crises, scandals, and shortcomings suggest that a market- and ownership-based approach to the firm provides limited understanding," Biondi (2013: 406) argues. This conclusion would be rejected by shareholder primacy governance advocates out of hand, and they in turn would emphasize that shareholders and market pricing serve to minimize agency costs and the risk of managerial opportunism, brought to the forefront of the normative corporate governance model being advocated. Even if such objections, rooted in doctrines and inherited theoretical assumptions regarding, e.g., the benefits of market pricing, are muted, Biondi's (2013) idea of "limited understanding" merits some discussion. "To understand" in both scholarly vocabularies and in everyday language denotes the capacity to apprehend a thing or an event in its full contextualized complexity, and to not reduce it to singular explanations (say, as in the case of a claim, "The Soviet Bloc collapsed because of internal corruption," or similar univocal statements). In Biondi's (2013) enterprise entity view, shareholder advocates confuse (external) market pricing and (internal) accounting practices, which leads to an overstating of the benefits of market pricing as a disciplinary mechanism in corporate governance. This understanding can be complemented by several competing explanations, but Stiglitz (1993) stresses that the economic theory doctrine of what can be called "epistemic self-interest" (see e.g., Daston, 2015)[6] is one strong candidate for explaining why the "hierarchical features" of the firm are ignored and marginalized. In Stiglitz's view (1993: 110–111), "the more ruthlessly individuals pursue their self-interest—the more they behave as we economists teach our students they do behave—the less efficient, in a sense, is the economy." Epistemic self-interest, operationalized as an ordinal ordering of preferences and no inconsistencies in "choice behaviour" (Sen, 1977: 336), is the principal mechanism that explains individual behaviour in neoclassical economic theory, thereby deemed "rational" in the received model. A substantial literature examines the relationship between "the rational man model" and real-world economies, which indicates that the abstract and ideal-type model is incapable of explaining real-world conditions.

Eisenberg (1990: 1324) introduces the term "the Nirvana fallacy" to denote the tendency in economic theory to compare "real rules with ideal markets," i.e., to imbricate reality and fiction in scholarly reasoning. Rizzo (1980) in turn criticizes the use of the economic concept of efficiency, derived from ideal market models, to serve as some kind of absolute fixed Archimedian reference point for jurisprudence: "It is all too easy to show that efficiency leads to desirable results within simplified constructs; it is quite another thing to show what this has to do with the world in which we live" (Rizzo, 1980: 658). In Hovenkamp's (1985: 284) view, discussing the antitrust law re-entrenchment literature (see, e.g., Bork, 1978), the efficiency criterion overstates the policy makers' ability to apply idealized models "to real world affairs," and understates the "complexity of the process by which the policymaker must select among competing policy values." Therefore, Hovenkamp (1985: 284) concludes, "the neoclassical market efficiency model is itself too simple to account for or to predict business firm behavior in the real world." By and large, Rizzo and Whitman (2009a: 909–910) add, overtly simplistic models, derived from deductive reasoning on the basis of thinly theorized human behaviour, lead to economic models that are incapable of apprehending or guiding real-world economic decisions, i.e., economic theories are guilty of the fallacy of misplaced concreteness:

> The most important reason that many economists had failed to appreciate this knowledge problem is that they had been deceived by their own excessively simple models. They had taken models useful in understanding some limited features of the real world, such as the equilibrium reaction of markets to supply or demand shocks, and applied them to the broader problem of

substituting government planning for market processes. They were guilty of
the fallacy of the misplaced concrete: simple models were mistaken for a
simple world. (Rizzo and Whitman, 2009a: 909–910)

Needless to say, also mainstream economists are sceptical about the
Nirvana fallacy in economic theory, and, e.g., Demsetz (1969: 377)
argues that it is a "mistake to confuse the firm of economic theory with
its real-world namesake." In particular, Demsetz (1969: 377) suggests
that neoclassical economic theory may explain how the price system
coordinates the use of resources, but that mechanism fails to explain "the
inner workings of the real firm." The "neoclassical market efficiency
model" has proved to be "particularly inept at identifying many forms of
strategic behavior," Hovenkamp (1985: 284) adds. That is, to treat the
firm as a tradeable security whose market pricing minimizes the costs of
management opportunism is thus not an operative model that of necessity
secures the greatest efficiency in the corporate system, as advocated by
shareholder primacy governance protagonists. One final evidence of the
abstract and inoperable economic models advocated is the sharp growth
of think tank economists and lobbyists, serving as the linchpin between
economic theory and real-world policy making and economic affairs
(Drutman, 2015; Leeson, Ryan, and Williamson, 2012; Vidal, Draca, and
Fons-Rosen, 2010; Smith, 1991). As one think tank policy expert
remarked (cited in Medvetz, 2010: 559), "economists like to build their
models that have nothing to do with the real world and that's one of the
reasons I think the think tanks have risen. [Think tank economists] are
more interested in talking about what the real world is."

At the bottom line, the doctrine of epistemic self-interest, being the
cornerstone and an axiomatic first principle of neoclassical economic
theory, remains a major obstacle for a reconciliation of legal and
management theory and economic theory. Working in the domain of
contract law and contract theory (see, e.g., Brudney, 1997; Easterbrook
and Fischel, 1993; Goldberg, 1976), Kar (2016: 767) makes an important
contribution by making a distinction between the "reasonable" and the
"merely rational" person.[7] Whereas the merely rational person "responds
solely to instrumental reasons," the reasonable person has an additional
motive, Kar (2016: 769–770) argues: "She is inclined to seek out and
abide by a mutually acceptable set of rules for the general regulation of
conduct and treat those rules as generating genuine obligations, given an
appropriate assurance that all others will, too." Expressed in less convoluted terms, the reasonable person is not only "instrumentally motivated," but also has "a sense of justice and interpersonal obligation" (Kar,
2016: 767. See also Macaulay, 1963; Charny, 1990; Bernstein, 1992, for

empirical substantiation). This view of human agency and "rational behaviour" is quite far from *homo oeconomicus* that Sen (1977: 336) refers to as a "rational fool" or "social moron." Instead, in Kar's (2016) so-called "contract as empowerment model," contracting is founded upon an understanding of wider socio-cultural and economic conditions. As many legal scholars, management researchers, and business historians have emphasized time and again, the institutionalization of corporate law was not originally based on the epistemic self-interest that shareholder primacy governance protagonists regard as a warrant for maximized efficiency in the corporate system, but on the principle to commit resources to a joint team production activity for a considerable period of time (Lamoreaux, 1998). That in turn demanded what Kar (2016) refers to as "reasonable persons" and a legal and regulatory system that enforced corporate law, Blair (2003) emphasizes:

> To build sustainable organizations, individuals with sufficient talent and expertise to run a business operation had to be induced to give up their own entrepreneurial aspirations in order to work in a business in which they would not be independent and might now share directly the potential business profits. The corporate form gave stability to the business enterprise, which helped assure those professional managers that their firm-specific investments would be protected, along with the dedicated physical and financial capital, and that they would have substantial input in how the business would be run. (Blair, 2003: 427).

Over time, the shareholder primacy governance model, derived from neoclassical economic theory, has undermined the legislative intent of policy makers. Rather than praising the collaborative and trust-based features of corporate law and the corporate system, shareholder activists advanced a model based on epistemic self-interest as the *only* legitimate basis for the governance of the corporate system, but in the end that model defeated itself when eroding the institutional basis for the corporate system. Only by giving more weight to the scholarship of legal scholars, management researchers, and business historians can the governance of the corporate system be based on reason (in Kar's, 2016, use of the term) instead of epistemic self-interest.

SUMMARY AND CONCLUSION

Despite the remarkable success of the shareholder primacy governance model over the last four decades (Dobbin and Jung, 2010; Daily, Dalton, and Cannella, 2003)—which makes the paper of Jensen and Meckling

(1976) the inaugural point of shareholder activism—advocates of the benefits of the shareholder primacy model, Cremers and Sepe (2016: 135) say, "are not satisfied with the gains they have already made." "Notwithstanding the remarkable success they have had in advancing their reform agenda," Cremers and Sepe (2016: 135) continue, "they see shareholder empowerment as not yet accomplished." As all available public statistics indicate a substantial growth of economic inequality in most advanced economies, and in the U.S. in particular (Perugini, Hölscher, and Collie, 2016; Bonica et al., 2013; Sullivan, Warren, and Westbrook, 2006), one may question what other benefits shareholder primacy governance advocates foresee. From a policy maker's view, the sharp growth in economic inequality and the increasingly unstable economy, whose periods of economic turmoil take longer for non-financial entities (e.g., households) to recover from than for finance market institutions (Peek and Rosengren, 2016; Redbird and Grusky, 2016; Fox, Fox, and Gilson, 2016: 337; Hacker, Rehm, and Schlesinger, 2013; Mehran and Mollineaux, 2012: 219) and that benefit finance industry insiders, need to be examined in terms of their welfare generating effects. Is it the case that an unbridled shareholder primacy governance model has generated socially and economically desirable outcomes, conducive to economic and social wellbeing and stability? Or has the shareholder primacy model been a core component of a deep-seated institutional shift in competitive capitalism (Tabb, 2012), now compensating finance capital investment more generously than any other contributions to firm-specific team production activities? A substantial literature indicates that the shareholders' win corresponds to other stakeholders' loss (Lin, 2016; Jung, 2016; Bertrand and Mullainathan, 2003; Rosett, 1990) as the economic growth has staggered in the period after the mid-1970s (with the notable exception of 1996–2004, caused by previous investment in computer science and technologies; see Gordon, 2015). This data suggests a tilting of the balance of power towards rentiers (i.e., shareholders) and "away from workers" (Van Arnum and Naples, 2013: 1177). While a small group of capital owners may still be dissatisfied with the traction of the shareholder primacy model, more moderate policy makers, scholars, and commentators may follow Cremers and Sepe's (2016: 142) call: "[I]t is time to reverse the *j'accuse* of shareholder advocates." If nothing else, the institutional and cultural changes of competitive capitalism should now, when the Great Recession, following the finance industry collapse of the autumn of 2008, enters its second decade, be subject to detailed scholarly analysis that both covers the minute details and that shine a light over the entire field.

NOTES

1. The dominance of the Delaware corporate law in American industry (Romano, 1985; Cary, 1974) merits some comments. "In a sense," Simmons (2015: 220) writes, "the Delaware brand is to corporate law what the Apple brand is to personal computers." Simmons argues that regulators and courts can be understood in a productionist view as the "producers of law," dependent on the behaviour and reputations of, e.g., courts. Among multinational firms, Delaware is "a global brand of choice for corporate law, dispute resolution, and incorporations," Simmons (2015: 225) says. The state of Delaware also manages to attract the absolute majority of newly incorporated businesses. In 2013, 83 percent of all initial public offerings (IPOs) in the U.S. involved Delaware entities (Simmons, 2015: 221). Delaware corporate law is also a popular source of emulation. Foreign jurisdictions, "seeking to enhance their reputations, elevate their business competencies, and attract foreign direct investment adopt Delaware-style features and precedents," Simmons (2015: 225) writes. Romano (1985) argues that Delaware has been highly successful in maintaining first-mover advantages over more than a century, and that the standardized Delaware model for legal services provides transparency and predictability:

   > Focusing on one jurisdiction allows counsel to specialize and develop expertise, reducing the cost of furnishing advice to clients, particularly where the state's law is as well developed as Delaware's. The stability and predictability of Delaware law that is favorable to managers for planning numerous complicated business transactions therefore also benefits attorneys, and it gives them additional, independent incentives to recommend Delaware if the firm is going to engage in transactions not well defined by a home state. (Romano, 1985: 280–281)

   "The value of Delaware incorporation may come as well from lawyers' familiarity with Delaware law and the ease with which they can provide reliable legal advice," Klausner (2013: 1345) adds.

   Simmons (2015: 225) argues that in today's market environment, trust is a "foundational element," being of foremost importance in market activity, corporate governance, court ruling, and society. Yet, Simmons suggests that the importance of trust remains underestimated. In Delaware, though, where trust is a key resource in the operational legal system, the "implicit understanding" between Delaware, the judiciary, and corporations, referred to as the "credible commitment," holds trust in esteem: "In essence, credible commitment is the belief that Delaware's legal regime and its various actors, including courts, will continue to meet the ever-changing needs of the business community in a non-politicized manner" (Simmons, 2015: 231–232). This mutual agreement translates into high-quality professional services, beneficial for business demands and interests. For instance, in 2012, the average time from submission to a decision by the Delaware Supreme Court was 29.7 days, a comparably short period of time; "other states with intermediate courts have difficulty resolving disputes in an expeditious manner," Simmons (2015: 240) says. In addition, the Delaware Supreme Court for most part adheres to what is called the "unanimity norm," which means that the court "[s]peaks with a single voice and rarely issues separate opinions even concerning controversial issues" (Simmons, 2015: 240).

   The credible commitment rests on the joint agreement that the State of Delaware will continue to invest in legal capital to continue to provide "experienced, skilled judges and lawyers to assist corporations," and that this investment is reciprocated by new business charters and tax revenues financing the mutually beneficial system. The political climate of Delaware, characterized by "a mild conservatism and distrust of large fluctuations" (Simmons, 2015: 232), also serves to buffer uncertainty and volatility. "Corporate law is Delaware's business," Levitin (2014: 2059) summarizes, but adds that the work to uphold the attractiveness of Delaware corporate law jurisdiction in the eyes of both managers and shareholders is ongoing and ceaseless. It should also be noticed that not all commentators are equally pleased with Delaware corporate law. Palan, Murphy, and Chavagneux (2010) refer to Delaware as a "tax haven," comparable to, e.g., Lichtenstein, Jersey, or Cayman Islands, each providing jurisdictions including generous fiscal policies.

2.   One illustrative case of the relationship between finance theory and accounting theory is the discussion regarding the change from historical cost accounting (HCA) to various forms of mark-to-market accounting, and more recently to what is called Fair Value Accounting (FVA) or Fair Value Measurement (FVM) (Bougen and Young, 2012: 392, footnote 4). For accounting researchers such as Michael Power (2010: 197), FVA is more than "just a technical measurement convention," but is rather to be understood as a change process which is "global in aspiration," and that fundamentally changes the nature of accounting (see, e.g., Laux and Leuz, 2009). In traditional accounting methods, the balance sheet represents a form of summary of rights (assets) and obligations (liabilities), and is therefore an attempt to translate an "economic reality" into financial metrics (Barker and Schulte, 2016: 55). With FVA, which represents a shift towards an "accounting as economics" view, not only actual transactions are captured by the accounting information, but also fictive economic assets and liabilities, derived from hypothetical market pricing, should be mirrored in the financial reporting. That is, Barker and Schulte (2016: 56) argue, the logic of financial economics extends its authority to re-define what accounting is by introducing "the market" and "market valuation" as relevant accounting terms. By introducing market-based values into accounting, FVA represents a non-managerial logic wherein the "fair value" is established on the basis of the distance between the entity being measured (e.g., a firm reporting its performance) and the "collective judgment of the market" (Power, 2010: 199–200). This finance market logic is in turn reflecting the underlying liquidity preference of finance theory, making finance markets the ideal-typical market, wherein valuations are made in large measures on an everyday basis. The concern is still that FVA not only includes actual transactions and assets and liabilities but also uses "accepted economic methodologies" to make speculative valuations on the so-called level 2 and level 3 (Power, 2010: 200). The International Accounting Standards Board (IASB) insists that in the case where "data are unobservable," the accountant should prepare a financial statement on the basis of the hypothesis that there exist fictive market actors who would be able to value an asset *as if* such a market existed (Barker and Schulte, 2016: 57). On the level 3, the accounting standard framework IFRS 13 thus mandates what physicists Ernst Mach referred to as a *Gedankenexperiment*, a "thought experiment," but this shift from transaction-based accounting is justified by the sole belief in the accuracy of market pricing *in abstracto*.

In Power's (2010: 201) view, the establishment of FVA as a "new basis for accounting fact production," despite all the articulated resistance, is grounded in "the cultural authority of financial economics." Power continues:

> [S]upporters of fair values managed to occupy a conceptual space which implicitly redefined accounting reliability with the foundational support of financial economics. Fair value at the level of principle is becoming a kind of 'rational myth' in the sense of depending for its efficacy and reality on the fact that it is widely believed ... The many critics of fair values have had no clearly definable alternative abstract rational myth to offer in its place, notwithstanding their appeal to values such as stewardship. (Power, 2010: 205)

One of the foremost consequences of the new market-based accounting framework is that accounting as practice and institutional fact, representing and thus de facto (but no longer *de jure*) being constitutive of "economic reality," is undergoing a process of what Power (2010: 205) refer to as *de-legalization*; in many countries, the balance sheet has been a "juridical" representational device, embedded in corporate legislation, and incomplete or inaccurate accounting practices have consequently justified legal enforcement. In contrast, fair value is not itself a legal concept and it is constructed within broader market-based processes, which invite the sovereign state or supra-state regulators to delegate accounting rule-making authority to agencies that operate outside the national legislation. In this new regime, corporate legislation is no longer the basis for accounting, but regulatory agencies seek "collective recognition" for their standards. In this view, the de-legalized accounting system promotes a form of market-based control that has historically proved to fail to block speculative activities, or to otherwise minimize opportunistic behaviour. "It can be said that the 'shadow of law' is being replaced by 'the shadow of financial economics,'" Power (2010: 205) says: "From this point of view, measurement issues are much more than mere accounting methods but represent an entire basis for re-engineering the intellectual ecology of the balance sheet."

Despite the advocates of FVA being successful in promoting their finance theory-based accounting model, Barker and Schulte (2016) argue that the finance theory-based concept of fair value is unattainable, as there either are or are not markets in place, capable of making market valuations of assets. For markets to exist, there are certain elementary conditions that need to be fulfilled, e.g., an item being traded needs to be supported by property rights and there need to be calculative agents who can assess the economic value of the item vis-à-vis all other available items qua investment objects. In short, a market capable of performing proper market valuations ("pricing") is based on a "complex, subjective social ontology" (Barker and Schulte, 2016: 59). Drawing on the work of philosopher John Searle's institutional theory, a market is constituted on the basis of "the existence of a legal or regulatory framework, standards of conduct and calculation, and some form of physical structure or process that constitutes the marketplace itself" (Barker and Schulte, 2016: 59). When such a "subjective ontology" is in place and in operation, "epistemologically objective" market conditions—"institutional facts"—can be established (e.g., price change observations derived from the ontologically subjective national or regional monetary system, or changes in the stock market index), which enable second-order assessments and a variety of social practices including, e.g., possibilities for arbitrage. However, unless the market based on a subjective ontology (i.e., being established as a collective agreement, or convention palatable to the majority of the actors) is ensured, market assessments cannot be done. This is why the level 3 valuations mandated by IFRS 13 are inconsistent with regular market pricing; there is no market in operation, and consequently the accountant needs to recourse to mere speculation about how fictive market actors would price assets.

What Barker and Schulte (2016: 65) refer to as the "wished-for market ontology" of IFRS 13 cannot functionally substitute the subjective ontology of actual markets; the production of "institutional facts" (e.g., accounting data) presuppose an underlying institutional reality that is not yet established among relevant economic actors. Thus the finance theory model and its acclaim of the efficacy of market actors serve as the only "institutional reality" to support fair value accounting. In Barker and Schulte's (2016) view, a bundle of propositions, theorems, and models, themselves at times highly controversial (e.g., the theorem regarding the informational efficiency of markets) serve as a fragile institutional basis in comparison to the corporate legislation that mandated prudent accounting practices in the regime of historical cost accounting:

> We have here an idea, which is initially born out of economists' theorising about revealed preferences in markets, which is then disembodied from the function of markets in practice and carried into the realm of hypothetical markets, and which is then finally called upon to act performatively in creating accounting representations in its own image. (Barker and Schulte, 2016: 57)

As Power (2010) argues, "being influential" in the policy sphere is not so much about "winning arguments" and demonstrating in broad daylight and beyond reasonable doubt the efficacy of proposed governance models, but rather a matter of selling a "rational myth" that policy makers can believe in and that can guide their decision making in a buzzing and blooming world beset by ambiguities and confusion. In the end, "accounting innovations" such as FVA may be treated as the outcome from the use of persuasive "rhetoric" (Klamer and McCloskey, 1992) or as a mere simulacra (Bougen and Young, 2012), but the tendency to let finance theory dictate market-based solutions to soaring accounting problems (e.g., the massive growth of the derivatives trade) may compromise and bias the construction of economic realities conducive to sustainable economic growth. When accounting becomes a sub-discipline to economics, accounting research is "eating its own tail," (Klamer and McCloskey, 1992: 159) contend.

3. "Even if one believes that management is biased in favor of inefficient growth and expansion, one must still recognize that management has better information than outsiders," Coffee and Palia (2016: 606) argue. They continue; "Asymmetric information is the basic and unavoidable reality of corporate governance: managers know more than shareholders."

4. The organization theory literature on rules (e.g., Martinez-Moyano, McCaffrey, and Oliva, 2014; Mengis and Eppler, 2008) and routines (e.g., Becker, 2004; Feldman, 2000; Pentland and Rueter, 1994) is quite extensive. Reynaud (2006) discusses how rules and routines are complementary mechanisms in organizational practices. First, rules are defined as "explicit and public statements" that trigger an action "with a certain degree of predictability," yet cannot determine the outcome as the agent cannot fully anticipate all contingencies that affect the outcome (Reynaud, 2006: 850). That is, a "rule-following process," Reynaud (2006: 848) argues, is embedded in a "logic of appropriateness" rather than being the agent's "calculation of consequences." Rules are therefore "incomplete" inasmuch as they are to be applied "in the light of knowledge, of information contained in the other rules, as well as custom, and practice and context" (Reynaud, 2006: 850); rules prescribe scripted sequences of practices but do not assume any wider cognitive engagement on the part of the agent. For this reason, Reynaud (2006) argues, rules need to be complemented by *routines*. Reynaud (2006: 857) defines routines as "[t]ransformational devices based on cognitive resources to reach a particular result." While rules prescribe scripted action, the routine re-locates the rule within a wider horizon of meaning and a social context, and therefore fulfils the rule; a rule in itself "neither strictly determines individual choices and behaviours nor guides them," Reynaud (2006: 850) says. Routines, in contrast, are "located devices" embedded in "particular contexts"; routines, complemented by rules, handle problems that are dependent on local and situated knowledge, i.e., a level of practical and technical detail that rules can never reach down to. In Reynaud's (2006) view, rules and routines are complementary mechanisms, to some extent consistent with Feldman's (2000) separation of routines into an ostensive component and a performative component. In Baumol's (1959) model, the rules of thumb guiding everyday managerial work include both the rule and the routine mechanisms and the ostensive and performative component of active decision making.

5. As a matter of fact, some individuals within the same category with a higher degree of competence or work morale may at the same time be undercompensated vis-à-vis less skilled and/or prudent co-workers, thus creating so-called free-rider problems (Olson, 1965).

6. McLevey, 2015, studying think tank economists, proposes the term "utilitarian epistemic cultures" to denote the assumptions made regarding instrumental rationality in this group of professionals, sharing a joint conceptual and methodological framework (see e.g., Hirschman and Berman, 2014; Reay, 2012).

7. The concept of rationality is oftentimes debated in economic theory and in the social sciences. Reason, Philip Selznick (1959: 529) says, "has an old-fashioned ring to it," and it also represents "an authoritative ideal," a form of human thinking and acting that transcends the mere calculability of self-interested outcomes. "Reasonable behavior," Lydenberg (2014: 365), a legal scholar, says, "supposes that one takes into account the effect of one's actions on others." What is reasonable is therefore, by implication, concerned with the protection or enhancement of "the common good." In contrast, Lydenberg (2014: 365) continues, rational behavior, an axiomatic proposition in neoclassical economic theory, is "essentially self-interested and seeks to identify the most efficient means of achieving one's personal ends." Rational behaviour is therefore "primarily concerned with the attainment of private goals" (Lydenberg, 2014: 365). Behavioural economists such as Jolls, Sunstein, and Thaler (1998: 1488) argue that the term "rationality" is "highly ambiguous and can be used to mean many things." For instance, in neoclassical economic theory, an agent is considered rational if he or she "(1) conforms to the axioms of expected utility theory; (2) is responsive to incentives, that is, if the actor changes her behavior when the costs and benefits are altered; (3) is internally consistent; (4) promotes her own welfare; or (5) is effective in achieving her goals, whatever the relationship between those goals and her actual welfare" (Jolls, Sunstein, and Thaler, 1998: 1488). Furthermore, the term rationality can denote both the

choices made by agents and their actual preferences (which may not materialize) "in the light of the prevailing incentives" (Jolls, Sunstein, and Thaler, 1998: 1488). This in turn makes it complicated to separate rationality as a definition of preferences and as a prediction of choice. This epistemological difficulty to discriminate between actual choices on the one hand, and actual preferences or stated preferences and ambitions on the other hand represents a formidable challenge for behavioural economics, its critics claim. Under all conditions, the distinction between reasonable and rational behaviour can be distinguished on the basis of theoretical and legal grounds.

3. Governing the university system: how to blend algorithm governance and social meaning

INTRODUCTION

"If the universe is governed by reason, then there will be no need for coercion; a correctly planned life for all will coincide with full freedom—the freedom of rational self-direction—for all," Isaiah Berlin (1958: 32) said in his famous lecture on "the two liberties," delivered at Oxford University on October 31, 1958. Today, there is little hope for and faith in such a society ever materializing, and instead the social control and regulation of human beings have reached unprecedented heights. This detailed control of social and intellectual life is especially cumbersome in the university setting, wherein scientific investigations are by definition impossible to fully anticipate and predict, making various forms of university governance a blunt tool for securing academic excellence. "A university is a place where scholars seek truth, pursue and transmit knowledge for knowledge's sake irrespective of the consequences, implications and utility of the endeavour," Leys (2012: 398, original italics omitted) states, but such an overtly romantic view of the university system has today little to do with how the university system is actually governed or how academic researchers' activities are monitored.

What is of specific importance in the present governance regime is the concept of *utility*, mentioned in the passing by Leys (2012). Few areas of academic research would today tolerate a disregard or negligence of the utility derived from systematic research. In fact, what Vallas and Kleinman (2008: 284) refer to as the "profit imperative" in the extant university governance model dominates the university governance discourse. In Vallas and Kleinman's (2008: 284) account, the profit imperative "[t]hreatens to erode the freedom and autonomy of scientific inquiry, erect institutional constraints (through patenting and licensing conventions) to the flow of knowledge and information and allow pressures to engage in revenue generation to shape the questions that researchers are likely to pursue." This view of the university deviates in considerable ways from Leys' (2012) ideal model, making the deviation between scholarly ideals and actual governance regimes conspicuous and at times daunting. In Holloway's (2015: 750) account, "commercialization has provided a set of rules and priorities to which researchers must aspire." That is, Holloway (2015: 750) continues, academic researchers are today situated in a broader political structure wherein commercial interests and a "market logic" (Berman, 2012: 291) are the predominant governance principles. While it is not inadequate to assume that academic researchers should be concerned with the practical utility generated on the basis of public and private investment, several scholars and commentators emphasize how the market logic undermines (or, less negatively, complements) traditional professional norms and values in the academy (Mirowski, 2011; Jain, George, and Maltarich, 2009; Owen-Smith, 2006; Smith Hughes, 2001)—norms and values that have historically been remarkably successful in generating scientific research results and in establishing methodologies and routines for scientific verification (e.g., the double blind-review journal system). University governance that rests on a market logic and governance techniques that rely on what Porter (2012) refers to as "thin descriptions" (e.g., forms of calculated quanta, ratios, and induced statistics) is at risk of undermining a most historically successful academic regime of knowledge production and of alienating academic scholars, ultimately leading to a flight from the university as being examined by Vallas and Kleinman (2008) and Fochler (2016a). The new university governance regime thus needs to be examined in greater detail and to be couched in the extant literature on governance, pointing at more deep-seated and wider changes in the governance of the corporate system and public sector organizations, including, e.g., universities.

The purpose of this chapter is thus to examine how recent and profound changes in university governance are today making scholarly inquiry not so much a pursuit based on professional norms and academic standards but rather one organized on the basis of predefined output variables, in turn derived from the assumption that it is practically possible for also sponsors, university management, and functionaries to *ex ante* define meaningful performance measures and targets (Power, 2015). This faith in governance is in turn rooted in the belief in the efficacy and relevance of the "lists and algorithm governance" (Johns, 2016) that are being developed and today serve at the core of university governance regimes. While the "trust in numbers" (Porter, 1995), being at the centre of this governmentality, coincides with the advancement of "numerical literacy" more widely, the unintended consequences of such numerical regimes of control are arguably understated and insufficiently understood. That is, the willingness to govern on the basis of numerical data is suffering from the lack of more detailed understanding of the various consequences derived from such a governance model.

INDICATOR CULTURE AND THE POLITICS OF MEASURING

Fukuyama (2016: 94) argues that New Public Management, one of the key fields of scholarly inquiry in the 1990s (see e.g., Lorenz, 2012; Lane, 2000), is today in decline and now being "[t]aken over by economists or political scientists using econometric techniques or, more recently, randomized experiments to investigate behavior at a micro level." Such new research technologies and frameworks include, e.g., the behavioural economics programme examined by Rizzo and Whitman (2009a, 2009b), which in many ways represents a breach with traditional governance models, granting professional communities a key role. In this new regime, calculative practices are given a significantly more central role, ultimately being a dusting off of the 1960s' concept of "management by objectives" (MBO, see, e.g., Drucker, 1955). However, as Merry (2016: 9) argues, what she refers to as "indicator culture" in transnational governance is a "dimension of what has been labeled audit culture," i.e., the performance measures and accounting standards being enacted within governance regimes are not primarily defined by top management as stipulated by the MBO literature but by *external agencies*, operating from the outside, and that purports to provide an independent check on organizational activities and performance (Power, 1997). While MBO was based on the key idea of joint interests and shared goals enacted *within* the team production activities, auditing as governance technique is based on the mistrust of professional workers and the employees more widely (Kipnis, 2008).

Indicator culture is thus part of an emerging governance regime that renders evidence-based data a core asset and employs calculative practices and numerical *indicators* to govern activities (Merry, 2016: 10). "In contrast to earlier systems, which relied on rules and punishments for violations, this mode of governance works through the collaborative production of standards and the evaluations of outcomes, including the use of self-assessment and ranking techniques," Merry (2016: 11) argues. The indicators, being at the very core of the transnational governance practices that Merry (2016, 2011) studied, are fabricated to provide two benefits from the governing agencies' point of view: (1) to "convey an aura of objective truth," and (2) to facilitate comparisons across samples.

These two objectives also offer the auxiliary benefit to conceal the "political and theoretical origins" of such indictors, a key functional demand that ensures that governance activities run smoothly and evade resistance. Expressed differently, the indicators are founded on "practices of measurement and counting that are themselves opaque" (Merry, 2011: S84), and yet they are put forth as being capable of mirroring supposedly objectively true, underlying conditions.

What Merry (2011: S88) calls *the politics of measuring* is thus based on the capacity of the governing agency to formulate and institute indicators that "submerge local particularities and idiosyncrasies into universal categories," i.e., the capacity to generate standardized indicators that enable commensuration across countries and regions (Merry, 2011: S84). Furthermore, indicators are typically statistical measures that consolidate complex data into a univocal number or rank, being meaningful for policy makers, industry actors, or the public. Standardized measures are thus granted more analytical value and significance than detailed and situated expertise, formulated in narrative terms. In the end, such emphasis on aggregated and processed data further serves to transform a political process of "judging and evaluating" into a technocratic pursuit and a technical issue structured around the "measurement and counting by the diligent work of experts" (Merry, 2011: S88). For Merry (2011), this is precisely the most prominent concern regarding indicator culture: its tendency to substitute political accountability for technocratic governance, based on the faulty assumptions that indicators are conveying "objective information" and that the data "speaks for itself":

> The creation of indicators reveals a slippage between the political and the technical. The slippage occurs in the way issues and problems are defined, in the identity and role of experts, in the relative power of the people engaged in producing and using indicators, and in the power and clout of the sponsoring organization. Through the apparatus of science and measurement, the indicator displaces judgment from governing bodies onto the indicator itself, which establishes standards for judgment. Nevertheless, indicators are inevitably political, rooted in particular conceptions of problems and theories of responsibility. They represent the perspectives and frameworks of those who produce them, as well as their political and financial power. (Merry, 2011: S88)

The concept of politics of measuring indicates that metrics is of necessity a political process that includes values and norms to be substantiated and vindicated through the very practice of measuring. In order to accomplish the social benefits and economic welfare derived from shared standard metrics, and to fully understand its innate mechanisms,

Brighenti (2018: 24) introduces the term *acts of measurement* as being "type of practice that constantly repositions subjects and objects by virtue of its own performance." To unpack this dense passage, Brighenti (2018) suggests that the calculation and creation of metric is in fact a non-linear activity that includes a considerable degree of heterogeneity: "Calculation thus appears as not merely mathematical or metrical in nature, but rather as a composite work made of different stages including objectification, separation, individualization, comparison, association, transformation, disembedding and distribution" (Brighenti, 2018: 24). What Brighenti (2018: 25) refers to as "the measure–value nexus" is thus based on a concept of measurement that is self-referential, that recursively refers back to itself, and is therefore performative inasmuch as a measure shapes the practice it purports to mirror objectively:

> [M]easures are not simply tools in our hands, they are also environments in which we live. While our focal awareness is inevitably attracted towards measures as technical devices and formal procedures, from the moment in which measures become infrastructural they also become an 'air' that we breathe, an atmospheric component of society. (Brighenti, 2018: 25)

In this view, the relation between measure and value is "necessarily circular," or, perhaps better, Brighenti (2018: 25) writes, "entangled": "value exists *before* as well as *after* measure." "Increasingly," Brighenti, 2018: 25) continues, "data loops upon itself, generating a surplus of information that corresponds to novel forms of value creation. But instead of being merely metrical, repertoires or registers of worth are involved in the operation of value creation and value accretion." In addition to the value-based nature of metrics and constitution of "environments," metric is essentially a *ratio*, "a relation" (Brighenti, 2018: 28):

> A measure is an inherently *relational* device, one that defines *relations of value* and assembles disparate beings by bringing them into given *configured relations* within a defined *environment*. Confusion derives from the fact that we end up calling "value" the number produced by an act of measurement, while in fact the number or price is just the way in which the measure we are using helps us in approximating what is reputed to be an invisible real value, something that is of importance to us. Making measures is a way of making *meaning* and, concurrently, of making meaning *visible*. (Brighenti, 2018: 28, emphasis in the original)

When we measure, e.g., the output from two production units, values regarding, e.g., preferences for sustainability or efficiency may be used to determine what production units are better managed, and the use of such values needs to be subject to an ordinal ordering, i.e., either sustainability or efficiency needs to be established as being prioritized over the other (or a combination thereof, still demanding a decision whether sustainability or efficiency is the more trustworthy measure of good management). Brighenti (2018: 29) argues that one of the key concerns regarding measurement is that these values are concealed by the measurement process per se, and credits the French sociologist Gabriel Tarde for making the observation that measures enable the analyst, social reformer, or any end-user to treat in *logical and quantitative* terms things that, in fact, "pertain to the field of aims and ends." That is, measures tend to conceal the confusion of means and ends as *"measures turn what we want into what we believe"* (Brighenti, 2018: 29, emphasis in the original). In this way, in the case above, the independent choice between sustainability or efficiency (or a combination thereof) suddenly appears to be integral to the choice of measure per se, resulting in the choice of measures being insulated from critiques regarding allegedly faulty values or preferences (e.g., sustainability over efficiency for specific reasons) as the measure of choice per se already stipulates a preference for a certain value. Therefore, Brighenti (2018: 29) contends, rather than simply being "epistemic constructs," measures are "a domain of practical action."

In the end, a measure contains three dimensions that are complementary but which tend to be conflated in day-to-day measurement work and activities derived therefrom, such as policy making. First, there is "a *technological–scientific* facet of measure" wherein a measurement unit and a measurement system are enacted as epistemological terms wherein concepts such as truth are invoked in discourse and debates. Second, "the *political–administrative* facet of measure" connects a measure with political decisions or policy making, and stipulates that measures are supportive of certain objectives, or can render such objectives visible. Third and finally, there is a *"moral–judiciary* facet" of measure, wherein virtues and capacities such as "balance, moderation, fairness, and wisdom" are enacted as valuable skills when using measures. In Brighenti's (2018: 29) account, in the pragmatic view of measurement and metrics, these three, mostly overlapping but never fully intersecting, nor conflating facets of measure, are easily confused or mixed up. For instance, a moral–judiciary justification of the preference for sustainability over efficiency may in fact be advocated on technological–scientific grounds, *as if* the preference for sustainability over efficiency is primarily a matter of scientific evidence and not a balanced and moderate moral–judiciary view of the situation at hand. As long as there is a reasonable level of trust in the authorities, agencies, or industry actors making such statements, the practical consequences are minimal, but if third parties question the rationale for making the statement and supplement this critique by an informed analysis of the faulty logic of the statement, mistrust regarding operative practices and ulterior motives may gain a foothold, with social costs ensuing. In the end, therefore, Brighenti (2018) says, the measure–value nexus needs to be handled with moderation to avoid compromising the use of imprecise or inadequate measures to accomplish certain objectives. In this way, the politics of measuring is a domain of disputes and controversies, manifest or latent. In the end, e.g., transnational governance centred on the use of indicators easily becomes a matter of instituting calculative practices that purport to capture factual conditions and qualitative changes, while such indicators may in fact not sufficiently pay attention to what falls outside the indicators, or what assumptions and values the indicators apprehend. This downplays and mutes the suspicion that the indicators per se are politicized accounts of parameters that are in the interest of certain elites to measure and monitor.

ALGORITHM GOVERNANCE

Coombs (2016: 298) uses the term "algorithmic governance" to point at how indicators are increasingly being re-packaged and further processed into more complex and manifold metrics, including the establishment of certain algorithms that stipulate governance objectives (for an overview of the use of "Big Data" and algorithms in governance, see Pasquale, 2015; Steiner, 2012). In many cases, Citron and Pasquale (2014: 4) note, what they refer to as *scoring society* and its "scoring trend" is often touted as "good news." Richards and King (2013: 41) in turn speak about "Big Data evangelists," who use an "overblown" and "utopian rhetoric" to address the possibilities of the emerging algorithm governance (see e.g., Mayer-Schönberger and Cukier, 2013). For instance, scorers often characterize their work as "an oasis of opportunity for the hardworking" (Citron and Pasquale, 2014: 3), and automated systems are claimed to "rate all individuals in the same way," thus overcoming the perennial issue of discrimination. Unfortunately, such accounts are "misleading," Citron and Pasquale (2014: 4) suggest: "Because human beings program predictive algorithms, their biases and values are embedded into the software's instructions, known as the source code and predictive algorithms"; "there is nothing unbiased about scoring systems," Citron and Pasquale (2014: 5) contend.

Johns (2016: 126) examines what she refers to as the *lists-plus-algorithms model* in governance practice, and claims that "[a]lliances of lists and algorithms are, roughly speaking, everywhere" (see also O'Neil, 2016). Johns (2016: 126–127) speaks about *data analytics* as being a "generic descriptor" for governance practices that frequently entail deployment of lists-plus-algorithms, i.e., practices that transform "massive quantities of raw data" into "data about the data" for analytical purposes. Such data analytics serves to generate algorithms on the basis of aggregated collected data, which in turn is used to construct lists employed in governance activities. The "list-plus-algorithm" assemblage is thus "a device of global governance" (Johns, 2016: 130). Zarsky (2016: 121) argues that there is a reasonable critique of algorithms that questions the efficiency-based argument that justifies their use, noting several distinct sets of flaws. First, an "inaccurate set of data" is at risk of biasing the output. Second, the analysis itself "could be mistaken due to errors in predicting individual behavior," since, in specific settings, human conduct may be "unpredictable" (Zarsky, 2016: 121). In this view, Ziewitz (2016: 4) suggests, algorithms cannot be assumed to be either "straightforward tools" to be implemented in governance activities, or a set of "mythologies to be debunked," but are best understood as a concept that "can help us rethink entrenched assumptions about the politics of computation, automation, and control." In particular, Ziewitz (2016) continues, the list-plus-algorithms governance model is embedded in the long-standing Western epistemological tradition, central to, e.g., neo-classical economic theory, concerned with identifying and understanding the "origin of order." For instance, Ziewitz (2016: 6) suggests, Adam Smith's "invisible hand" or Charles Darwin's "natural selection" are two metaphors connected to underlying theories that assume that a defined selection mechanism generates large-scale consequences, being a form of Lucretian clinamen,[1] a small deviation whose consequences are substantial: "Algorithms, it seems, fit in seamlessly with this line of stubbornly seductive stories about the origins of order" (Ziewitz, 2016: 6–7).

Johns (2016) uses the case of airline security governance, being an acute concern following the events of September 11, 2001, wherein all sorts of classified information is used to generate a list of "individuals at risk" and "risk groups" who may encounter interrogations when checking in at airports or entering a country. While evidently not all individuals listed are criminals or at risk of committing criminal acts, they are identified and targeted as "risk subjects," which naturally has implications for personal integrity and other liberal legislative rights. Yet, airline security concerns mostly overrule such issues, leading to millions of individuals facing heavy-handed monitoring and stressful questioning when flying internationally. In Johns' (2016: 135) account, such lists based on algorithms tend to be "[u]nsystematic and unprincipled as knowledge forms, confounding reasoned synthesis or explanation." As emphasized by Merry (2011: S84), the practices of measurement and counting "are themselves opaque,"[2] thus making list-plus-algorithm governance to some extent functionally efficient, and yet incapable of revealing its own underlying logic—its political assumptions and motives. This opacity has two consequences: first, the opacity per se is easily read as a sign of influence and power, Ziewitz (2016: 6) says, leading to the suspicion of understated ulterior motives. Second, the lack of transparency leads persons affected to speculate whether, e.g., algorithmic selection is arbitrary, which in turn undermines the legitimacy of algorithm governance, as the output is questioned and the underlying process is shrouded in secrecy.

Credit Rating Score as Governance

Citron and Pasquale (2014) use the case of credit scoring, commonly based on the generation of so-called FICO scores (Rona-Tas and Hiss, 2010; Keys et al., 2009; Poon, 2007), an algorithm "[u]sed in ninety percent of lending decisions in the United States" (Fourcade and Healy, 2013: 561),[3] to examine how algorithm governance operates in real-world settings. Citron and Pasquale (2014: 5) argue that scoring systems are opaque for the end-users; although some scores are available to the public, "the scorers refuse to reveal the method and logic of their predictive systems" (Citron and Pasquale, 2014: 5).[4] This means that no one can challenge the process of scoring or the output, the FICO score. This is a concern because such scores are of utmost importance for the individual presumptive borrower, as the credit score determines creditworthiness and thus the access to credit, widely understood as a key to full citizenry in American society (Polillo, 2011; Hyman, 2011; Peñaloza and Barnhart, 2011). As Polillo (2011: 438) notes, the concept of creditworthiness is not only a strictly economic or financial term, but is institutionalized "through moral authority." The moral authority that follows from stated creditworthiness implies membership in society and a solidarity between the lender and the borrower and all other participants in the financial system. Expressed differently, the FICO score represents a form of "financial citizenship" rooted in moral categories. As Day (2014: 62) notes, algorithms are both derived from and being the vehicle of certain ideologies (say, the moral claim that "creditworthiness is to be maintained as a form of socio-economic fitness"): "The algorithms do not simply run alongside ideology, but rather, they are designed into ideology, which is to say also, conversely, that ideology is enfolded into the logic of and elements of calculative devices."

As FICO scores can assume such an additional role, as a form of licensing of financial citizenship, it is important that they are used with moderation. Unfortunately, that is not of necessity the case, Rona-Tas (2017: 52) suggests: "Credit ratings recently have found a variety of new uses. Ratings developed in retail lending, called credit scores are now routinely used in fields such as auto insurance assessments, cell phone contracts, residential rentals and even hiring decisions." This use of credit ratings outside the context of credit granting is referred to as *off-label use*, a concept that testifies to how the imbrication of "surveillance and digital self-representation" marks a novel intersection "between the quantified self and financial inclusion" (Kear, 2017: 350). As the financialization of the economy is moving forward, Rona-Tas (2017: 53) says, "many of its instruments, developed in the specific context of a particular financial transaction come to be utilized for novel purposes, outside their original context." For instance, a 2009 study of 433 companies conducted by the Society for Human Resource Management revealed that 60 percent of the companies "conducted credit background checks of job candidates," and that "13 percent did it for all job openings" (Rona-Tas, 2017: 67). In this way, the creditworthiness of the job applicant serves as a proxy for the moral standing of the individual, representing an additional use of the FICO score, arguably never intended by the designers of the original algorithm. In addition to the concerns regarding the drift of creditworthiness ratings, the expanded off-label use of credit ratings first contain measurement biases that in the next instant contaminate new markets when being transferred. To start with the measurement bias, credit rating algorithms emphasize statistical averages at the expense of variance. This results in the amplification of small initial differences, which are tolerable for the user of credit scores on a global scale, including a portfolio of borrowers, whereas *individuals* may be consistently under- or overrated in terms of their creditworthiness:

> Errors may cancel out overall, some actors will be over- others will be underrated, but over time, the same actors will be stuck with the worse-than-deserved ratings, just as the same actors will get to keep their better-than-deserved ratings. The resulting inequalities (variation in economic outcomes) and their ill effects are invisible in models that focus on averages and ignore variances. (Rona-Tas, 2017: 71)

Second, the transfer of credit rating scores to novel markets leads to a situation "wherein externalities spill over to and harm other markets," Rona-Tas (2017: 70–71) says. For a mortgage loan originator or a recruiter, the use of credit rating scores may be a rational response to informational costs in the market, but the linking of credit and the job markets through the use of one joint measure results in certain groups being further disadvantaged, in many cases beyond their actual economic and financial fitness on the basis of the fallacy of overstating statistical significance above and beyond its practical relevance (see e.g., Ziliak and McCloskey, 2008). Based on these mechanisms and the tendency to officially or sub rosa use credit scores in a variety of activities and interrelated markets, it is no wonder that, e.g., Americans are concerned to "work their credit scores," an activity that Kear (2017) accounts for.

Despite this central importance of the credit score in American society, the algorithms that generate the FICO score "are zealously guarded trade secrets" (Citron and Pasquale, 2014: 5): "Credit bureaus routinely deny requests for details on their scoring systems. No one outside the scoring entity can conduct an audit of the underlying predictive algorithms" (Citron and Pasquale, 2014: 10).[5] Consequently, the FICO score cannot be understood, challenged, or audited by the individuals; "working a good credit score" (in Peñaloza and Barnhart's, 2011: 759, phrasing) becomes an impossibility—"consumers cannot determine optimal credit behavior or even what to do to avoid a hit on their scores" (Citron and Pasquale, 2014: 11). In the exceptional cases where finance institutions reveal some parameters in their algorithms, this information is essentially incomplete and cannot be used in any proactive, meaningful way:

> FICO and credit bureaus do, however, announce the relative weight of certain categories in their scoring systems. For example, 'credit utilization' (how much of a borrower's current credit lines are being used) may be used. But the optimal credit utilization strategy is unclear. No one knows whether, for instance, using twenty-five percent of one's credit limit is better or worse than using fifteen percent. (Citron and Pasquale, 2014: 11)

In the end, therefore, credit scoring remains a business based on the regulatory licences granted to a handful of finance institutions, capable of determining the access to household credit in American society. To claim that such privileges and subsidies are beneficial for all American citizens is an overoptimistic account of the efficacy of the present model. Instead, empirical studies indicate arbitrary credit scoring, which casts doubt on the extant model: In a study including 500,000 files, 29 percent of the consumers had credit scores that "differed by at least 50 points between the three credit bureaus" (Citron and Pasquale, 2014: 12). Such variations in credit scoring (taking undisclosed strategies of the three credit bureaus aside) suggest "a substantial proportion of arbitrary assessments" (Citron and Pasquale, 2014: 12). Given the centrality of access to credit in the American market-based society, such arbitrary credit rating is arguably inconsistent with median voter preferences. In addition, it casts doubt over the efficacy of the oligopolistic credit scoring model.

Being based on mathematical-statistical methods, data shortage may be covered by various statistical intra- and extrapolations, and new data emerging, not yet included in the present algorithm, may not be considered. This in turn leads to what Johns (2016: 138) calls "transmissive clunkiness" between, first, the list and the algorithm as such, and, second, between the list-plus-algorithm and other knowledge forms. The "unknowability" and amorphous nature of the object being governed is easily compensated by the capacity to further process and aggregate existing data, whose internal consistency and practical relevance needs to be evaluated outside the list-plus-algorithm assemblage as such. This in turn creates "labyrinthine workings of modern administrative states," which have long been seen as elusive and whose distribution of authority within them is difficult to map (Johns, 2016: 138). That is, the list-plus-algorithm assemblage becomes a machinery preoccupied with its own particular agency, and accompanied by its own sponsors and advocates who still have a hard time proving the efficacy of the governance model. In the end, the technocratic nature of algorithm governance runs counter to stated democratic ideals, as algorithmic decision making raises a set of "fairness-based concerns" (Zarsky, 2016: 129). As algorithms in many cases use personal information without the person's informed consent, the autonomy and dignity of the individual may be harmed. As a consequence, the alleged efficiency gains derived from the use of algorithms needs to be weighed against the privacy and democratic rights of citizens and consumers (Zarsky, 2016: 129). Furthermore, there is a lingering concern that, e.g., credit scoring tends to be arbitrary and to discriminate against women and minorities, systematically underrating the creditworthiness of these groups and therefore excluding them from the credit circuit (Citron and Pasquale, 2014: 8). "We need a healthier balance of power between those who generate the data and those who make inferences and decisions based on it," Richards and King (2013: 45) contend.

One of the foremost virtues of transnational governance, that of *transparency* (Roberts, 2009; Strathern, 2000), widely championed in the literature, is thus one of the first casualties when too much faith is invested in list-plus-algorithm governance, Johns (2016: 140) proposes. Industries, markets, national economies, and populations are thus governed on the basis of data stocks, mechanisms, and tools that are intransparent for all but a small group of technocrats, being granted the regulatory licence to handle such resources. Not only suffering from

democratic deficit, such governance practices more importantly undermine the meaning that well-designed governance practices can convey,
making, e.g., airport security control (an area where individuals are
otherwise likely to tolerate certain integrity violations on rational
grounds) unintelligible, puzzling, or simply acts of integrity violations.
Fourcade and Healy (2017: 23) examine the wider theoretical implications of algorithm governance, and state that "the old classifier was
outside, looking in," whereas "the new classifier is inside, looking
around." In the former model, founded on a paternalist logic, the
traditional governance regime based on surveys and aggregated market
data examined discrete events *ex post facto* and the shortage of information is widely understood to be the overbearing governance problem;
the agent is disfavoured by his or her lack of sufficient and reliable
information and his or her limited information-processing abilities, or
there is noise or poor signalling in the market system that results in
sub-optimal decision making (which in turn leads to political consequences, including, e.g., a considerable stock of home mortgage loans in
an economy). In the new system, in contrast, the access to information is
plentiful, and the sheer mass of market information can be used to
construct behavioural models on both collective and individual levels on
the basis of the concrete and practical action, whose traces digital media
collect, store, and process. In this new model, much of the concerns in
traditional governance regimes are no longer relevant, and Fourcade and
Healy (2017: 24) even go so far as to state that algorithm governance has
generated a "new behaviourism": "Today, a new behaviorism challenges
the assumptions that dominated economics and political science in the
cold war period." In this new behaviourism, Fourcade and Healy (2017:
24) say, "acrimonious debates about the calculative abilities of individuals and the limits of human rationality have given way to an
empirical matter-of-factness about measuring action in real life, and
indeed in real time."

The primary consequence of this shift in perspective, from the *outside
view* from the apex of the governance regime, wherein experts designed
systems supportive of the access to information and information-
processing capacities, to an *inside view* based on the calculability of Big
Data, the "data lakes" that, e.g., corporations collect and access today, is
that there is no longer a demand for, the protagonists of the new model
claim, the expertise located at such centrally located agencies; to some
extent, digital media displace political and technical expertise:

> The computers won, but not because we were able to build abstract models
> and complex simulations of human reasoning. They bypassed the problem of

the agent's inner life altogether. The new machines do not need to be able to think; they just need to be able to learn. (Fourcade and Healy, 2017: 24).

Digital media and the access to "our most intimate and unconscious behaviour" (e.g., shopping records and Internet search activities) enable such pools of data to be explored to construct active metrics rooted in a "new economy of moral judgement." As Kear (2017) remarks, these tendencies are especially pronounced for low-income or otherwise financially vulnerable groups, being provided with goods and services in exchange for "informational transparency," a form of "data voyeurism" that breaches or compromises legally stipulated integrity protection rights:

> Increasingly, those who cannot pay with money pay with privacy and information. Technologies for quantifying the self are paving the way to a convergence of surveillance, finance and distributional politics. A person who wants to buy a car but has bad credit can now get the loan they need by allowing lenders to track and control their movements with so-called starter interrupt devices, which allow lenders to remotely disable a car's ignition. (Kear, 2017: 364)

Algorithm governance thus has implications for social class and the access to various commercial services. In the end, in this new regime of "prosthetic rationality," driven by the advanced calculability of Big Data, "metrics become moral injunctions," Fourcade and Healy (2017: 24) contend. By implication, the behavioural economics conundrum of how to distinguish between choices and preferences becomes obsolete, as choices are all that matters because only choices can be traced by digital media. On the Internet, for instance, you are what you click on, and little else matters in algorithmic governance. Algorithm governance is thus based on a form of interpellation wherein the subject is "coming to understand him- or herself as a subject of reference in response to a particular type of hailing or call" (Day, 2014: 75), namely the hailings and calls of the operational algorithms that increasingly structure and define agency in the era of algorithm governance.

RANKING AS GOVERNANCE DEVICE

In addition to the use of audits in university settings to monitor activities, newspapers and media are fond of using ranking list and league tables as a tool for rendering what is opaque and complicated for the outsider appear transparent and manageable. Rankings are based on what economic sociologists refer to as *commensuration*, the calculative practice of comparing heterogeneous entities with one shared metric to enable a comparison between the entities as if they in fact were more or less homogeneous. For instance, Kornberger and Carter (2010) discuss the use of the rankings of cities and examine the case of the so-called Anholt City Ranking, measuring the quality of life in the different cities of the world. Everybody intuitively understands that individual cities with their own histories, tradition, and geographical locations are unique and idiosyncratic entities. Not only is, say, Vienna different from Paris, Melbourne different from Vancouver, and Hanoi different from Kuala Lumpur, but they are also located in different regions and countries with their own economic conditions, legislations, etc., influencing the organization and administration of the cities. Yet the Anholt City Ranking presents a league table of the "World's most attractive cities." Such league tables based on the commensuration of what is inherently heterogeneous serves to "transform cognition," Espeland and Sauder (2007: 16) say. By creating a ranking list, relations among the entities examined are simultaneously created and obscured thus directing attention to new factors. "Commensuration is meant for organizing, integrating, and eliminating information," Espeland and Sauder (2007: 17) suggest.

For outsiders, having only limited understanding of how, e.g., universities are assessed and how academic credibility is constituted, league tables are convenient tools inasmuch as some expert panel makes a systematic assessment of universities' performance and presents a neat list of universities, clearly demonstrating what university is at the very top this year, but also reporting the changes from previous years. Immense sources of data and information are thus aggregated and transformed through calculative practices into an instrument that purports to put on display an unambiguous and straightforward evaluation. Critics contend, however, that rankings and league tables, despite their pedagogic features and their communicative merits, easily mislead the outsider and tend to obscure the very assessment procedures that have been used to construct the league table (Pusser and Marginson, 2013; Gruber, 2014). Despite such concerns, league tables are today popular and used in a wide variety of contexts. In addition, in the second instance, league tables impose additional costs that affect other actors in the system being subject to ranking.[6]

The Case of Law School Ranking

Sauder and Espeland (2009) examine how American law schools are subject to intense ranking activities, and how this specific form of performance assessment affects the way law schools are organized and how they allocate their resources (for a study of business school ranking, see Wedlin, 2006). In Sauder and Espeland's (2009) view, the rankings serve to "create a single norm for excellence in legal education," leading what was initially an imposed model to gradually become a shared, de facto standard. Over time, the pressure to conform to this performance standard is internalized, and the behaviour of law school professors and decision makers changes accordingly. As commensuration both overlooks or marginalizes contingencies to lower the assessment costs, and is based on the promise to provide a more transparent and easy-to-understand mapping of entities in a particular field—that is, rankings paradoxically obscure in order to enlighten—the information provided is nevertheless always subject to disputes and discussions. Furthermore, rankings is "a zero-sum technology," wherein one school's success comes "at the expense of others," and wherein "small differences matter" (Sauder and Espeland, 2009: 73). That is, one law school may invest more resources and may perform better than the previous year, but if other schools invest *even more* and perform *even better*, the first school will lose positions in the league table nonetheless. The long-term effects are not entirely favourable for either faculty and university decision makers, or students: "[These] properties transform rankings into a zero-sum affair that encourages meticulous scrutiny, distrust, innovation in gaming techniques [i.e., how to manipulate the system], and pressure for conformity" (Sauder and Espeland, 2009: 79).

Khurana (2007: 335–345), addressing the ranking of business schools, speaks about "the tyranny of the rankings," and academics often express harsh critique of the influence of rankings and how they compromise academic objectives and virtues. Sauder and Espeland (2009) also emphasize that rankings purport to enter a "natural state of things" and are able to account for factual conditions, while, in real life, university representatives are acutely aware of the role and influence of these rankings and consequently adjust their activities and behaviours to comply with what the rankings measure and value.

Sauder and Lancaster (2006) provide first hand data from the *U.S. News & World Report* (USN) rankings and student application data to empirically test whether the rankings have an immediate effect on the organization of law schools in the U.S. By and large, law schools deans and professors see some value in being subject to external ratings, but believe the negative effects of the rankings outweigh the positive benefits (Sauder and Lancaster, 2006: 109). Sauder and Lancaster (2006) emphasize that the methodology used in the USN ranking tends to confuse *statistical* and *practical* significance (a widespread mistake also in quite informed, scholarly circles, a condition Ziliak and McCloskey, 2008, examine in detail). The consequence is that minor statistical differences may lead to large movements in the ranking as diminutive statistical deviations are amplified beyond its practical relevance: "[T]here is a lot of fluctuation in the ranks of schools due to very small and statistically insignificant changes in their scores or the scores of the schools near them in the rankings" (Sauder and Lancaster, 2006: 114). This phenomenon is also observed in the statistical methods used in the two major world university rankings *Academic Ranking of World Universities* (ARWU) and *Times Higher Education Supplement* (THES) (Saisana, d'Hombres, and Saltelli, 2011). As small differences (defined in technical terms as being statistically insignificant) are amplified, it is inadequate to speak of "differences in quality" outside of the top ten list of these universities, Saisana, d'Hombres, and Saltelli (2011) argue:

> Apart from the top 10 universities, neither the ARWU not the THES should be used to compare the performance of individual universities. Equally deceptive can be the interpretations of changes in rank for a given university, as indulged in by the media. The position of the majority of the universities is highly sensitive to the underlying statistical methodology chosen by the rankers ... The ranks of 43 universities in the ARWU's top 100 fall outside the confidence interval ... as do 61 universities in the THES's top 100. (Saisana, d'Hombres, and Saltelli, 2011: 175)

For this reason, outsiders with no detailed statistical know-how (e.g., journalists eager to tell engaging stories of heroic accomplishments or tragic declines in academic prestige) draw conclusions from the rankings beyond their practical significance. One of the principal effects of the amplification of minor statistical differences is that rankings and league tables are characterized by dynamic movements as law schools and universities find themselves in new places in the rankings, more or less every single year:

> Overall, in each year roughly 68 percent of schools experience a change in rank from the previous year. This is largely because USN [*U.S. News & World Report*] makes very fine distinctions among the top 50 schools even though the quality measures of these schools from a continuous normal distribution where schools at the center of distribution have very similar scores: in other words, the scores of these schools—especially those close to the center of

distribution—are very similar, so very small changes in their scores can have disproportionate effects on their ranks. (Sauder and Lancaster, 2006: 114)

In the case of the ARWU and THES rankings, there was a similar activity observed: "Almost half of the universities in the top 100 shifts more than 20 positions on the academic performance indicator compared to the overall rank" (Saisana, d'Hombres, and Saltelli, 2011: 168). In Sauder and Lancaster's (2006: 116) view, it is unfortunate that "normal statistical fluctuations" are viewed by external audiences as "real changes in quality" for two reasons. First, such conclusions are in many cases not justified on the basis of sound and widely agreed upon statistical methods. Second, which is more of a social consequence of the widespread trust in numeracy, this belief (rather than the facts) per se makes it strategically wise for law school decision makers to try to counteract a loss in ranking. In some cases, such activities transfer resources from the actual law school training and research activities to mere impression management and symbolic work engagements that influence the ranking per se more than the quality of the education as such, which the ranking purports to mirror. Drawing on student application data and the USN rankings, Sauder and Lancaster (2006: 128) conclude that the USN rankings, regardless of their statistical accuracy, "[h]ave a significant impact on the admission process in law schools." Given such evidence, it makes sense that law schools start to play what Sauder and Lancaster (2006: 117) refer to as the "the reputation game."

The Questions of Reactivity, Validity, and the Robustness of Analytical Models

Sauder and Espeland (2009) refer to strategic and tactical activities to counteract the negative effects of ranking procedures as *reactivity*, being a combination of the subject's internalization of certain norms and virtues, and the practical (some would even say cynical) uses of the rankings to one's own benefit. While reactivity is a rational response to new governance practices, it is also precisely what undermines the naturalistic view of rankings, their assumed or proposed ability to provide an undistorted view of a particular field or activity. If everyone in law schools or elsewhere is busy acting in accordance with a prescribed analytical framework—e.g., pursuing a "teach to the test" strategy—then it becomes complicated to know, in the end, *what* the league table actually represents. Ultimately, rankings become self-fulfilling prophecies at the point where they merely measure how effectively universities adapt to the demands imposed by external evaluators.

Bermis, Zajac, and King (2014) examine how the business periodical Fortune's ranking of American companies' reputation leads to forms of reactivity when playing the reputation game. Bermis, Zajac, and King (2014: 591) open their paper by emphasizing that given the influence of rankings such as Forbes' *Best Managed Companies in America* or the Fortune ranking, there is "[s]urprisingly little research [that] has focused on the antecedent processes that generate these rankings." Examining the connections between the use of certain financial performance measures and the firm's reputation, Bermis, Zajac, and King (2014: 604) identified evidence of reactivity: "As a particular measure becomes more prevalently used, market actors begin 'playing to the numbers,' which in turn alter the ability of the measure, such as firm revenue, to truly gauge firm performance." For instance, while firm earnings may be a legitimate and relatively easy-to-understand performance measure for individuals without detailed finance market expertise, empirical studies of public companies' reported earnings have demonstrated that "more firms make or exceed their earnings projections", i.e., they almost always perform as predicted or slightly better, which would be, Bermis, Zajac, and King (2014: 604) suggest, "a probabilistically unlikely outcome." That is, public companies are today planning their earnings reported to satisfy finance market actors' expectations. CEOs and directors know that finance markets punish "missed earning projection" at an unproportional rate in terms of lowered share price evaluations, and thus they carefully ensure that earnings reported converge with predictions or slightly exceed them. In terms of reputation ranking, in the case where an increasing number of public firms "[d]emonstrate relatively equal levels of earnings growth," this measure loses its role as a "differentiating measure" in the construction of the reputation league tables (Bermis, Zajac, and King, 2014: 604). Bermis, Zajac, and King (2014) thus propose that reputation ranking is not a stable framework for measuring reputation over time, but instead the methodology used to determine "reputation" is dynamically adjusted to the process wherein "financial measures fall in and out of favor with the market" (Bermis, Zajac, and King, 2014: 605). In other words, reputation is no longer an independent variable that the ranking commensurates, but instead the concept of reputation is "subject to the changing perceptions of evaluators" (Bermis, Zajac, and King, 2014: 605).

Rather than being a *cause* as predicted from a common sense standpoint, wherein reputation has a market value as firms with good reputation perform better than firms with less advantageous reputation—i.e., the very *raison d'être* for the ranking as such—reputation is instead the ability to comply with for-the-time-being favoured finance market performance measures. For instance, the recognition of Corporate Social Responsibility (CSR), a heavily debated and contested managerial concept and portfolio of practices, indisputably motivated by the firm's willingness to contribute to the wider society, and thus, being an issue of reputation rather than a hard bottom-of-the-line measure, is one example of how "performance" is a moving target open for negotiation in the face of changing conditions. While the concerns for CSR may be of relevance for a reputation ranking, Bermis, Zajac, and King (2014: 591) found that "[f]irms are not receiving reputational benefits from proactively pursuing socially responsible activities, but instead receive a reputational discount if they fail to live up to the minimum standard of social responsibility." That is, if firms ignore CSR issues altogether, they may be punished for this negligence, but investing beyond this minimum level does not provide any benefits either. That is, a "diminishing return on reputation investment" can be observed in the case of CSR, especially in the case where finance market actors no longer regard CSR policies as co-produced or associated with performance metrics but start to treat it as prominent management fad.

In summary, the study of Bermis, Zajac, and King (2014) demonstrates that the Fortune reputation ranking is not so much based on a robust theoretical model, including the parameters companies need to consider to maintain their legitimacy and status in society, as it is a measurement of these very same firms' ability to adjust their strategies and policies to finance market actors' transient performance variables. "Reputation" is therefore released from its conventional semantic meaning and instead serves as an indicator of the firm and industry's capacity to adjust to finance market changes and demands. Just like in the case of law school rankings and the ARWU and THES university rankings, the league tables produced and disseminated are not so much resting on a solid and immutable research design or on statistically robust data, but are constructed to accommodate changes and novelty in the market to also be able to transform quite weak signals into significant change in rankings. In addition, there is strong evidence of reactivity in terms of the significant actors "playing to the numbers" (Bermis, Zajac, and King, 2014: 604) to achieve more favourable rankings.

Taken together, the ranking of both academic institutions and companies does not of necessity capture what they purport to measure, but instead they tend to distort the underlying activity they claim to mirror. Adler and Harzing (2009: 80) list a long series of measuring problems and externalities pertaining to the use of university rankings, examining the specific field of research in international business, and propose that while rankings purport to measure universities' productivity, they are "[a]ctually false aggregations from the individual to the institutional level, rather than a measure of the university's current or future ability to contribute to the discipline or society." Furthermore, De Mesnard's (2012: 498) analysis reveals a series of elementary statistical errors that are present in many ranking procedures, including "problems of nomenclature, double affiliation, and aggregation of very large research institutions purely for the purpose of being more prominent in the ranking systems." Data with such "extreme variability" therefore cannot reliably be used to "meaningfully rank anything and certainly should not be used to assess the worth, or lack thereof, of one university relative to another" (Adler and Harzing, 2009: 80). Drawing on the functionalist sociology framework of Niklas Luhmann (1995, 2000), we can say that rather than representing two distinctly separated social systems, that of the evaluator and the domain being subject to evaluation, there is an autopoetic production of statistical data and ranking procedures wherein the two systems are entangled in an ongoing process of communication, and where it is no longer practically possible to fully separate the inside from the outside. In this view of rankings, there are reasons to welcome what Sauder and Lancaster (2006: 132) speak about as a "[m]ore careful consideration of the unintended, and sometimes unnoticed, consequences that these evaluations produce."

In addition to the reactivity of the inside actors, Kornberger and Carter (2010) emphasize (just like, e.g., Mirowski, 2011) that, today, many of the companies that generate these rankings and league tables are private companies, and not government agencies, that treat these procedures and reports as commercial products. As a consequence, rankings and league tables cannot be too static or inert but there needs to "be some action" to attract attention from paying clients and the wider public. "I only look at the movements," Søren Kierkegaard announced. The same goes for the producers of league tables: unless there is some drama in the way, e.g., law schools are either losing positions or working their way up the list, the league tables themselves appear dull and uneventful, possibly being themselves too conservative in their measurements and thus at risk of being suspected of curbing initiatives and entrepreneurial action. That is, as a commercial product or at least a product that demands media attention to make sense and to play a role in society, rankings need to be dynamic. At the same time, when the THES global university rankings arrive every year, it presents basically the same English-speaking universities as usual at the top, slightly modified vis-à-vis the previous year. This ranking in particular indicates that unless a university is located in an English-speaking country, there is little use in even trying to compete over the top positions. Moreover, the list of universities seems to be very weakly correlated with other rankings of different countries' economic performance and "quality of life" more broadly. Major economies like Germany and renowned welfare states such as Norway or Switzerland are for instance not very well represented on the THES list. Such intuitively weak connections between social welfare and the rating of the university system[7] is yet another legitimate objection to the exalted interest in the ranking of heterogeneous universities, all being in their own particular ways rooted in their local social and economic conditions.

In some cases, factors being entirely independent of what is subject to ranking are brought into the analysis as relevant factors to consider, as in the case of Collett and Vives (2013) making the claim that because MBA graduates with diplomas from European and Asian universities earn relatively more money today vis-à-vis MBA graduates with diplomas from American universities, the ranking of American MBAs is affected unfavourably. But how the surrounding society determines the value of an MBA diploma is separate from the quality of the MBA programme per se (at least in the short term), making such factual evidence deceiving. In Scandinavian countries and other countries with relatively even distribution of income, being part of the welfare state tradition and a consequence of union-based wage bargaining, no MBA education programme would ever be treated as being competitive if such measures were given considerable weight in the ranking. At the same time, countries like Sweden are frequently in the top ten or even top five positions when the economy or industry is ranked in terms of its competitiveness or capacity to innovate. In this case, there is clearly a premium on sidelining welfare state policies and a concern regarding a compressed income structure in the economy.[8] In such cases, certain ideologies are inscribed already into the fabric of the auditing and ranking industry, making economic equality not so much an accomplishment as a liability. The consequence is that such rankings are of interest only for a more limited number of actors, as they provide a skewed image of actual performance. If nothing else, such concerns would entice the reader to learn more about the underlying calculative practices that generate the rankings. In many cases, it is unfortunately very complicated to lay hands on such information, Free, Salterio, and Shearer (2009) suggest, examining the *Financial Times'* ranking of MBA education:

> What emerges ... from the field data is a view of auditing as a collection of negotiated and highly adapted pragmatic routines which may add credibility to the rankings, but in a way that cannot be easily communicated to users. Audit procedures, like the statistical underpinnings of the rankings themselves, are opaque enough that very few users outside of the *FT* [Financial

Times] can figure out how they work, yet clear enough to convey legitimacy. (Free, Salterio, and Shearer, 2009: 137)

Like Power (1996, 1997) and Kipnis (2008), Free, Salterio, and Shearer (2009) stress that audit is not so much about assessing "what is out there," as it is a self-recursive procedure wherein the audit process itself constructs its object of analysis, in this case, the "qualified MBA education":

> Where organizations do not have clear measures of productivity which relate their inputs to their outputs, the audit efficiency and effectiveness is in fact a process of defining and operationalizing measures of performance for the audited entity. That is, the efficiency and effectiveness of organizations are not so much verified as constructed around the audit process itself. (Free, Salterio, and Shearer, 2009: 138)

To summarize, in the present governance regime, universities are increasingly subject to external control wherein auditors are assessing the performance of university professors on the basis of shared standards. This very idea of "shared standards" is of central importance here: as "standards" indicate a relatively stable and mature environment and the ability of central actors to negotiate and define robust and reliable standards, the expression "shared standards" is explicitly in opposition to change and renewal that characterize dynamic and innovative environments. The university is developed to conduct research and to teach, and while teaching normally draws on past accomplishments (i.e., after the research findings have been verified or corroborated through the peer-review procedure that remains, despite its limitations, the principal control mechanism for the production of truth-claims in the sciences), the research activities are constructed to advance novel ideas and to generate new research findings. New thinking always presupposes risk-taking, a long-term commitment to a specific issue, and the hard-nosed attitude that there must someplace be more things to be said about an object matter. When there is a continuous monitoring and assessment of academic performances, on university, department, research group, and individual levels, the incentives to embark on such explorative projects examining unchartered territories are downplayed.

UNIVERSITY GOVERNANCE AND OPPORTUNISTIC BEHAVIOUR

It is widely agreed that the lists-and-algorithm based governance of universities generates considerable externalities, not least the soaring costs to acquire a university education that is caused by universities passing on the bill for their investment in activities conducive to better ranking to future students. In addition, there is evidence of opportunistic behaviour and fraud that coincides with the struggle over academic prestige. Such behaviour puts the entire institution of academic know-ledge production at risk and should therefore be subject to scholarly attention.

It is widely agreed that scientific fraud "distorts scholarly knowledge, thereby hampering and misleading scientific progress," Necker (2014: 1747) argues, and yet the predominant university governance regime has actively promoted and justified, she continues, "a winner-takes-all market in which rewards are only granted to those first to make a discovery and therefore obtain recognition from peers" (Necker, 2014: 1747). Necker (2014: 1747) suggests that this new governance regime has led to a situation wherein, e.g., economists engage in forms of "scientific mis-behavior," including data fabrication and plagiarism. In the web-based survey material reported by Necker (2014), collected anonymously through the European Economic Association's (EEA) home page in the autumn of 2010, it is reported that 83.2% of the respondents claimed that the "perceived level of publication pressure" was "high" or "very high." In addition, the "perceived change in publication pressure" was reported to be "high" or "very high" by 79.2% of the respondents. Further adding to the pressure to publish, 46.6% of the respondents reported a "high" or "very high" "perceived level of pressure to raise external funds"; 68.3% also reported that this pressure had increased over the last period of time (Necker, 2014: 1747, Figure 2). Among the community of economists, in a typical year, "a case of plagiarism is experienced by 29% of all responding editors," Necker (2014: 1748) writes. In a follow-up survey of rank-and-file economists, "almost one quarter report that they have been plagiarized" (Necker, 2014: 1748). In the empirical material collected by Necker (2014), there are many cases of scientific misconduct that indicate that economists are willing to cut ethical corners and to let odd be even to be able to compete in the "publish or perish game" of their scholarly field. Needless-to-say, the surveyed economists "strongly agree" that "high publication pressure exists," and consequently, "the most frequently cited cause for scientific misbehavior is publication pressure" (Necker, 2014: 1759). Such empirical data throw a shadow over the predominant university governance regime's assumption that the most efficient way to measure scientific quality is to count and measure the quality of publications through citation rates. This strong emphasis on bibliometric calculations and monitoring, ultimately based on an actuarial science methodology, may in fact undermine scientific progress, critics have claimed.

Ghostwriting

In some cases, external observers may be utterly surprised by the sheer nerve some scholars demonstrate in their pursuit for academic prestige and influence. One such practice is the evidence of ghost-written academic papers, penned by professional writers employed by, e.g., major pharmaceutical companies, and thereafter sent out to leading academic researchers in the field for them to endorse and sign before they are sent off to academic journals (Sismondi, 2011). While this procedure may sound like an urban myth, several researchers account for such practices. In order to have new drugs approved by regulatory authorities, pharmaceutical companies need to conduct clinical trials where a group of patients are consuming the candidate drug and are compared with a test group given a placebo. When the data is collected, analysed, and presented in a report, the data is submitted to regulatory authorities. While data may be complicated to assess, the clinical data can be published in academic papers that confirm the significance of the clinical results, and that testify to the robustness of the underlying research design of the study. If such academic papers accompany the new drug application, the pharmaceutical company submitting the application can build a stronger case around their candidate drug, potentially tipping the scale in their favour. That is, as being part of their R&D procedure, cash-rich pharmaceutical companies have been reported to hire skilled academic writers, writing academic papers presenting the clinical data favourably, and thereafter asking leading academics in the field to agree to serve as co-authors or even corresponding authors of such papers. For the pharmaceutical companies that to-date may have ploughed down something like a billion US dollars in the new drug development work, the signed academic journal paper provides a licence for the clinical data and benefits from the scientific credibility of an authority in the field. For the individual researcher, yet another publication adds to the stock of academic accomplishments, conducive to attractive status positions and privileges. For the university, finally, a leading academic contributor one more time confirms his or her scholarly authority within a specific field. The downside of this win–win–win agreement is that the general public may be misled, and that the long-term credibility of scholarly knowledge production is compromised. If academic researchers are to be trusted, they need to submit to widely recognized methodological frameworks and procedures for verification, regardless of who is paying for the research work—be it a state fund or a privately owned company.

As reported by Clarke et al. (2003: 169), a study in the U.S. reveals that "industry-sponsored research" is 3.6 times more likely to produce "results favourable to the sponsoring company" than research funded by a regular independent financier (e.g., state-controlled research funds). The shift from the state funding research work to private companies, most noteworthy in the life sciences and biomedicine, implies that there is a new pressure on researchers to provide commendatory results and practically useful data. In the 1970s and 1980s, the role of industry-funded research increased further and, in the new millennium, academic research work is almost exclusively defined as what is practically relevant and financially attractive. In this new world where the universities are not only treated as a repository of knowledge but are advanced as a vehicle for economic growth and innovation, opportunistic behaviour such as ghost-written journal papers are not too far away.

Mirowski and van Horn (2005: 528–529) claim that the presence of ghostwriting has grown in virtually all types of journals, and that there is evidence of different data being reported to regulatory authorities such as the Food and Drug Administration (FDA) from that to the journals, clearly indicating that the data has been selected to serve the interests of the authors. Mirowski and van Horn (2005) here distinguishes between "honorary authors" (in the case of the leading scientific authority being explicitly addressed as not being the leading author) and "ghost authors" (where such information is not disclosed to the reader) and found that these two types of texts were quite prevalent in academic journals:

> In the aggregate, 19% of the papers had evidence of honorary authors, 11% had evidence of ghost authors, and 2% seemed to possess both ... [in another study] 39% of the reviews had evidence of honorary authorship, while 9% had evidence of ghost authorship. (Mirowski and van Horn, 2005: 528)

This daunting view is shared by Healy (2006), a psychologist who has had experience of being approached by a pharmaceutical company to sign a journal paper penned on his behalf:

> [G]hostwriting is no longer occurring only in peripheral journals and affecting only review articles. It happens in the most prestigious journals in therapeutics, and it probably happens preferentially for papers reporting randomized trials and other data-driven papers. (Healy, 2006: 72)

Brody (2007: Chapter 7), in turn, dedicates an entire chapter of his critique of the multinational pharmaceutical industry to the issue of ghostwriting in medical research.

Taken together, the race to acquire prestigious positions in the academic field imposes new norms and values upon academic researchers, and encourages them to abandon inherited scholarly traditions and norms. In some cases, new university governance practices have led to higher degrees of transparency and a closer connection between academic knowledge production and societal needs and interests, but, in many cases, such accomplishments are accompanied by unintended consequences and externalities including forms of opportunistic behaviour and fraud. The strong emphasis on the short-term economic value generated in academic research work is also a factor to consider, which not only undermines the attractiveness of academic careers more generally, but also threatens to undermine the legitimacy of research programmes that target complex scientific problems. In the following, these two concerns will be examined.

GOVERNANCE AND THE WANING INSTITUTION LOCUS: THE CASE OF UNIVERSITY GOVERNANCE

Before addressing the implications of new university governance regimes in more detail, the question of *meaning*, a non-economic concept, is introduced. Several governance researchers emphasize how the term meaning has shifted in the new governance regime, no longer seated within professional and occupational communities but taking on other individualist connotations: "In general, governance signifies the moving away from the legalistic, bureaucratic, centralized top-down configuration of authority to a reflexive, self-regulatory and horizontal 'market-like' configuration," Shamir (2008: 3–4) argues. At the same time, Johns (2016: 130) adds, the term governance as such implies "the regularization and authoritative patterning of conduct, knowledge, and sense." Governance is thus what combines an understanding of how human action, forms of knowledge, and meaning are mutually constitutive and thus need to be understood within the horizon of meaning of the governed subject. However, within the new regime of indicator culture and list-plus-algorithm governance, rooted in economic theory and calculative practices, social theory terms such as meaning are not easily bankable but are at times considered unnecessary theoretical complications that are difficult to operationalize into robust measures. In fact, one of the principal features of the post-New Public Management governance regime is to overcome and transcend, even undo, claims made by social scientists that humans are meaning-seeking and meaning-constructing beings, whose practices and activities cannot be fully understood outside elusive or fuzzy, yet solidly sensible terms such as meaning. A paternalist tradition of governance actively shuns such terms, as it easily undermines the scientific aura of the models and methodologies advocated, making economic conditions and preferences the exclusive input variables in the analytical models.

Disappointment with Present Institutions and their Rituals: Flight from the Institution Locus

Turner (1976) makes a distinction between the "institution locus" and the "impulse locus" as two generic mechanisms in the construction of a meaningful image of the self. Under the institution locus, "[t]he real self is revealed when an individual adheres to a high standard, especially in the face of serious temptation to fall away. A person shows his true mettle under fire" (Turner, 1976: 992). The real self is thus essentially a product of the institutional setting wherein the individual acts, and therefore the real self is revealed *only* when the individual is "in full control of his faculties and behaviors" (Turner, 1976: 993). The contrasting locus is based on *impulse*, and enacts the real self as consisting of "deep, unsocialized, inner impulses" (Turner, 1976: 992); in the impulse view, "the true self is something to be discovered" (Turner, 1976: 992). This enactment of the real self is refuted by the institution locus, which renders the "waiting around for self-discovery" to occur as being untenable. In contrast, under the institution locus, the self is something "attained, created, achieved, not something discovered" (Turner, 1976: 992).

Even though the institutional self is self-disciplined, socialized, well mannered, and based on the individual's willingness to submit to abstract rules and traditional beliefs that may no longer seem to justify their relevance from afar, also the institutional self accommodates frustration and disappointment that surfaces when institutions fail or appear devoid of meaning. Turner (1976: 1004) argues that a meaningful image of the self is dependent on institutional conditions that incorporate "distinctive privileges, responsibilities, and skills." When institutional conditions such as rites of passage lead to disappointment, the individual experiences a "generalized sense of unreality"—a sense of loss of meaning; "When the institutional framework is characterized by disorder and undependability, when it fails as an avenue to expanded opportunity for gratification, the true self cannot be found in institutional participation," Turner (1976: 1005) says. In other words, when, e.g., governance practices being implemented are officially declared to contribute to the overall social welfare generated within an organization, an industry, or field, while in fact they are perceived by relevant actors as being little more than a thinly veiled mechanism of control or a vehicle for securing competitive games in every instance of a line of work, a sense of "unreality," a rift between perceived and officially declared realities, emerges. This sense of unreality is also experienced when action and consequence are separated, as in the case of political rhetoric promising that, e.g., a reform will eventually, if waiting patiently, generate wellbeing benefit for all (as in the case of, e.g., free trade agreements being allegedly "good in all parts" according to commentators and pundits, while commonly leading to job loss and faltering economic welfare for specific groups, thus being excluded from the anticipated net benefits). "The institutional order may still be relatively efficient and predictable, but the increasing time span between action and consequence and the increasing dependence on extrinsic rewards may contribute to a sense of unreality in institutional activities," Turner (1976: 1005) summarizes.

The Case of Life Science Research

Turner's generalized model can be applied to university governance and waning professional jurisdiction in, e.g., the life sciences, today re-modelled on the basis of what Gittelman (2016) calls the "Silicon Valley model of entrepreneurship," structured around venturing and the capitalization of abstract scientific know-how, and being less concerned with the joint contributions of the community of academic researchers. As Sapir and Oliver (2017: 48) remark, "universities are traditionally associated with the norms of 'open science' and the free dissemination of knowledge." At the same time, Sapir and Oliver (2017) continue, universities are also "notorious for their lack of transparency and tendency to conceal information in order to avoid scandals." When, e.g., intellectual property rights, the foundational legal device of the Silicon Valley model of entrepreneurship, become an overarching concern for universities, a new normative system that enacts the legal protection of scientific inventions as "a necessary, beneficial and inseparable part of the current public mission of research universities" is established, and the traditional professional norms of academic scientists (e.g., Merton, 1973) are marginalized (Sapir and Oliver, 2017: 34). As a consequence, Sapir and Oliver (2017: 34) continue, there are "deep tensions" and "contra-dictory pressures" related to the commercialization of academic research, including the "increasing secrecy" at the expense of "cooperation and information sharing" (Sapir and Oliver, 2017:48), two major pillars of traditional academic research. Evans (2010) reports empirical evidence supporting Sapir and Oliver's prediction that commercialization leads to lower degree of knowledge sharing:

> Insofar as citations to an article proxy engagement with its ideas, industry funding reduces the distance that ideas travel from industry-sponsored labs ... Industry sponsorship deflects the dissemination of ideas away from their natural path to new authors, institutions, and regions. In the idiom of actor–network theory, by enrolling companies in their research, scientists appear less able to enroll other academics. (Evans, 2010: 779)

In addition and outside the domain of the commercialization of academic science, there is evidence of a general decline in the propensity to participate in knowledge sharing (Leahey, 2016; Haas and Park, 2010). Not only do commercialization activities pose a threat to traditional academic virtues, but a university must also learn to decouple its various objectives and activities, and yet uphold a façade supportive of its legitimacy, grounded in the public view that the university is an institution that generate a public good, not yet subjected to enterprising activities. As Sapir and Oliver (2017: 34) write, this double act of decoupling various research activities (commercial, tax-funded, etc.) and maintaining a pre-commercial tradition is a precarious balancing of interests and sources of legitimacy:

> While universities and scientists are increasingly encouraged to become entrepreneurial, to engage in technology transfer activities and to generate revenues, at the same time they must exercise constant "damage control" to protect their public image against accusations of greediness, of "double taxation" of the public, and of betrayal of their public mission. (Sapir and Oliver, 2017: 34)

As, e.g., Turco (2012) has demonstrated, in practice, this decoupling is not always easily accomplished as inherited professional norms may undermine the decoupling strategies imposed from the apex of a corporation.

Fochler's (2016a, 2016b) study of Austrian life scientists is indicative of the decline of meaningful institutional conditions that animate academic scientists with a sense of commitment and community, as scientists see little more than fierce competition and a ceaseless struggle over financial resources and status positions:

> Changes in the governance of academic careers in recent years have been quite successful in turning both faculty and junior researchers into

entrepreneurs—not necessarily entrepreneurs interested in commercializing their research, but entrepreneurial managers of their own careers, publications, and grant portfolios. (Fochler, 2016b: 924)

These changes have not been implemented overnight, but a series of articles has highlighted the deconstruction of traditional academic virtues (Czarnitzki, Grimpe, and Toole, 2015; Mirowski, 2011; Anderson, 2008; Smith Hughes, 2001). In the new regime of university governance, King (2000: 411) argues, "a new economic motivation is driving states to redefine relationships by pressing institutions to become more account-able, more efficient, and more productive in the use of publicly generated resources." This economic motivation has in turn engendered the devel-opment of an entirely new performance measurement apparatus, moni-toring the efficiency of the operations in detail:

> Performance-based planning and funding has also become a convenient means for governments to compare and rank the productivity of one institution against the productivity of another. League tables, scorecards, national rankings, and report cards are some of the popular devices developed by governing officials to compare institutional performance measurements. (King, 2000: 9)

The researchers in Fochler's (2016a: 269) study favoured small-sized biotechnology companies as their employers, and they appreciated having the possibility to "work on a team"—particularly those with an academic background. The biotechnology companies, despite being under constant pressure to raise more venture capital to finance their development activities, apparently offered an attractive alternative to the more com-petitive academic milieu, or the major corporations, stricken by endless political turf wars. One interviewee argued that the biotechnology company offered the possibility of concentrating on "one big thing" rather than keeping up with a variety of career targets:

> In a company, you move big things, things a single person could never do. In academia, you always have to be wary: ... where am I on the author list? First, last? If not, then your contribution is not worth anything, really. You have to look after yourself in academia much more than in companies. And that's a great thing about companies. You don't have to work at building ten individual careers – you can work together on one big thing. (Life science company scientist, cited in Fochler, 2016a: 271)

In Fochler's (2016a: 276) account, the biotechnology companies offered an institutional platform that allowed them "to plan, conduct and retain control over their research work along a long-term trajectory." In contrast, academia and large corporations (e.g., big pharma) fail to provide researchers with "sufficient agency to conduct non-mainstream research with a long-term perspective." In academia, funding problems and "topical hype cycles" serve as obstacles to continuous epistemic work on a specific topic (Fochler, 2016a: 276); in larger companies, "risk-averse management decisions may terminate entire lines of research" (Fochler, 2016a: 276).

The work of Vallas and Kleinman (2008) provides evidence supportive of Fochler's (2016a) findings. The academy is no longer, if it ever was, a safe haven wherein "blue sky research" was conducted to benefit mankind at large. Today, academic researchers work under the pressure to make the best use of the tax-payers' money: "[N]owadays I think it's absolutely critical that we justify the use of taxpayer money based upon the fact that it has some potential to have impact on people," one academic scientist said (cited in Vallas and Kleinman, 2008: 292). In the U.S. tenure track system for career advancement, untenured researchers are put under pressure to deliver credible research results and an accompanying publication track record within a defined period of time, and can thereafter, if successful, anticipate a reasonably predictable scholarly career and life style. Today, this implicit contract is undermined by commercial pressures, many of Vallas and Kleinman's (2008) inter-viewees argued:

> Even if you have tenure, in order to keep your lab functional, you have to keep the publications and grants coming in, so it's never completely free. And to get the grants you have to work on stuff which is considered fundable. (Academic scientist, cited in Vallas and Kleinman, 2008: 293)

In addition, as the new rules of the game are increasingly geared towards commercial ends, as dictated by the Silicon Valley model of entre-preneurship, the academy is at risk of losing one of its primary features, the mechanisms for intra-professional knowledge sharing, conducive to more valid and robust research work, some of the interviewees argued:

> That's becoming an increasingly serious problem in science that, that people are really not sharing things the way they used to, and it's becoming more competitive … It's mostly self-protective and it doesn't have to do with financial interests. It has to do with credit, advancement, grants, prestige, all those things and that's why I think the simple answer is that the field has become highly competitive. (Academic scientist, cited in Vallas and Klein-man, 2008: 296–297)

When the academy is choosing the commercialization path, Vallas and Kleinman (2008) found a comparable change and in some ways a contradictory tendency in the bioscience industry, wherein venture capital-backed firms mimicked the traditional academic model for knowledge production (e.g., research journal publishing). As scientific legitimacy is one valued component of the Silicon Valley model, bioscience companies provided opportunities for life science researchers to pursue their scholarly careers within market-based companies:

> [S]everal of our industrial scientists, who had grown disenchanted with the pressure to generate revenue and elected to leave desirable academic positions in favour of commercial employment. These scientists felt compelled to work for corporations—ironically enough, precisely to escape the entrepreneurial pressures they encountered within the academy. (Vallas and Kleinman, 2008: 293)

One of the interviewees, working in a bioscience company, commended the employer's willingness to recognize the value of academic research work: "I think it's sort of the dual nature of [this] company that they both want to produce drugs and want to be recognized as a first-rate research place" (Bioscience company scientist, cited in Vallas and Kleinman, 2008: 301). By and large, Vallas and Kleinman's (2008) study supported Fochler's (2016a, 2016b) more recent study, suggesting that the university is no longer unrivalled by industry and companies, imitating an academic mode of knowledge production. Such findings cast doubt on the resilience of the research university as social institution, historically rooted in the belief that it is a site generating a public good, but today demonstrating substantial degrees of hybridity in its mixing of commercial and non-commercial objectives and incentive systems derived therefrom.

Speaking in Turner's (1976) terms, the academy and large corporations have failed to substantiate and fill the official recognition of research liberties with meaning, yet been unable to provide life science researchers with the agency needed to excel in their domain of scientific expertise. These two settings are characterized by governance practices that emphasize market relations and market assessment on a short-term basis, leading to the disappointment on the part of the academic scientists. It is thus a paradox that the field of scientific inquiry, closest to the finance market valuation of scientific expertise and performance, and most dependent on venture capital has become a sanctuary for academic liberties. When academic science is today governed on the basis of the alleged virtues of ceaseless competition and the struggle over financial resources and status, the academy loses some of its attraction, and life science spin-outs are deemed to provide better and more inspiring working conditions.

As Holloway (2015: 745) remarks, "market relations are expanded into traditionally public arenas, such as universities, and national science policies are created to encourage private investment in science and university–industry partnerships by strengthening intellectual property (IP) rights and decreasing public funding." Beverungen, Hoedemaekers, and Veldman (2014: 62) add that this market logic, now well entrenched in the university system, correlates with declining state funding and increased demands for financial accountability, i.e., the changes are imposed on what befalls the university system rather than being driven by academic researchers' interests and preferences. Thus it comes as no surprise that Vallas and Kleinman's (2008: 305) study of life scientists abandoning the university to seek employment in start-up bioscience firms reveals that "university administrators are far more supportive of the commercial ethos than are the faculty members they oversee." In the end, the institutional and cultural *Überbau* of the university system renders academic researchers, and researchers in the sciences in particular, as the salt of the earth and the primus motor of human knowledge and understanding on the surface level, while in fact providing few possibilities for actively fulfilling such a role. When such an institutional framework fails to offer little more than detailed monitoring of performance and a persistent emphasis on ceaseless competition over academic influence and positions, what Turner (1976) calls the "unreality" of the institution locus emerges; the deviation between formally stated goals and actual accomplishments become untenable. As a consequence, the institutional self wanes to the point where the institution (e.g., the university) is abandoned altogether.

UNIVERSITY GOVERNANCE REGIMES AND THE CONCEPT OF MEANING

The British philosopher Alfred North Whitehead (1925) introduced the term *the fallacy of misplaced concreteness* in an attempt to criticize the Cartesian–Newtonain worldview wherein all mechanisms can be carefully separated into distinct and independent entities being part of a clockwork-like system. In Whitehead's view, the "simple location" of clear-cut entities represents an intellectualist and analytical fallacy. Drawing on such an analytical model, governance is increasingly structured on the basis of the capacity of indicators and other performance measurements to "stand in for" and to "represent" underlying continuous processes; the use of indicators and similar governance techniques are thus not so much capable of apprehending underlying practices "as they are," as they actively construct the social world they purport to represent (Power, 2015). That is, governance practices have *performative capacities* (and therefore agency, see, e.g., Svetlova, 2012; MacKenzie, 2004; MacKenzie and Millo, 2003) and they institute reactivity (Espeland and Saunder, 2007) as a predictable response.

Examining the project to construct "universal" governance standards that indicate "governance quality" on a common scale, Bhagat, Bolton, and Romano (2008: 1807–1808) argue that such a project is unable to overcome its internal theoretical inconsistencies. For instance, *governance* and *performance*, the two key variables subject to monitoring, are plausibly *endogenous*, meaning that "their relationship is bidirectional rather than unidirectional" (Bhagat, Bolton, and Romano, 2008: 1807–1808). This implies that there is no "one best way" to measure corporate governance, but this assumption is precisely what is the guiding principle for the development of a "good governance index." More specifically, the "exogenous relationship" stipulated between governance and performance is per se indicative of the presence of a simple location fallacy of the Whiteheadian type. No matter how hard the kitten chases its tail, the two parts of the body (say, claw and tail) are inextricably bound up; when the one moves the other will follow, to the chagrin of the kitten. Similarly, governance regimes that purport to operate from some neutral vantage point (Thomas Nagel's, 1986, "view from nowhere"), always of necessity already from the outset assumes a series of political, practical, and theoretical interests. Proponents of novel governance practices easily overlook that their operative models and rhetoric commonly succumb to the fallacy of misplaced concreteness, failing to recognize that actors being subject to governance practices respond to such changes, and may even respond more profoundly than the proponents of the governance practice anticipate, as in, e.g., the case of the waning of the institutional self. Therefore, not only are the politics of measuring and the short stretch between the new governance practices and paternalism concerns that deserve to be the subject of scholarly attention, but also the very epistemological basis for governance regimes needs to be examined.

The increased pressure on, e.g., academic life science researchers, rooted in the norm of the cleansing purity of competitive games, and materialized into a university governance regime that stresses publication track records, the practical utility of research findings, and the financial valuation of individual research results, justifies and enforces an operative governance model that allegedly works *in abstracto*, in a world devoid of intelligent human actors who actively respond to threats of loss of jurisdictional discretion, status, and privileges. In a real-life setting, in contrast, such a governance regime may in fact undermine such highly stated goals and their anticipated social welfare effects. That is, relying exclusively on self-interest and "rationality" (in the neoclassical economic theory view as the consistent adherence to the ordinal ordering of temporally stable preferences) as the primary driver for performance and social welfare is arguably simplistic and possibly mistaken. Governance regimes that fail to enact human actors as responsive, institutional selves (Turner, 1976), most anxious to "do good" and to actively respond to changes in performance measurement practices, easily undermine their own intentions. Politics and the struggle over various resources are always of necessity part of any governance regime, but to be able to generate socially beneficial outcomes, such politics must be at least temporarily buried or tolerated upfront. However, when such political embedding of governance regimes is consistently downplayed or trivialized, the consequence may be an undermining of the institution locus, with disappointment, cynicism, and other unintended consequences following (e.g., academic researchers choosing to leave the university). These challenges involved in fashioning governance practices that benefit a variety of interest should be examined in broad daylight. For instance, the market logic and its various materializations such as the Silicon Valley life science venturing model need to be examined not only as being based on sound governance principles but also advancing ulterior motives, that is, to render basic research findings amenable to private venture capital investment, or to simply discipline academic scientists. In every instance, a scholarship on governance is supportive of such an analytical project. Governance matters, but it matters in ways that are far more complicated and manifold than may be recognized officially; the misplaced concreteness of extant governance regimes shuns such a recognition.

SUMMARY AND CONCLUSION

In a world not exclusively governed by reason and where trust is in short supply, various governance practices are implemented to monitor or counteract opportunistic or illicit behaviour. Traditional governance regimes have emphasized, e.g., bureaucratic control and self-disciplining professional norms, but with the emergence of digital media, new forms of calculation-based and numerical measures are implemented. In such governance regimes, commensuration across heterogeneous organizations and professional communities are accomplished on the basis of increasingly aggregated performance measures. In the new indicator culture and its algorithmic governance, aggregated and induced quanta and ratios serve to mute political controversies and to impose an aura of scientific objectivity and respectability that bestows governance regimes with an infrastructural quality, i.e., they become taken for granted and cease to inspire debates or trigger resistance (Star, 1999). Unfortunately, the emphasis on short-term utility and the use of venture capital investment attractiveness as standards for assessing academic performance undermine inherited scholarly and professionals norms, and academic researchers may eventually lose their faith in governing agencies including university management and its board of directors, whose ability to fully understand the nature of scientific work and discovery may be doubted. In such situations, the decline of the institution locus leads to academic researchers seeking employment elsewhere. In this new situation, governance regimes need to better accommodate and respond to actual, real-life demands as being perceived by governed subjects, or else governance regimes are at risk of undermining their own best intentions on the basis of the fallacies they embody (i.e., the overstatement of simple location as epistemological principle).

NOTES

1. "In the works of Lucretius," primarily in his *On the nature of things* (written in the first century BC), Berressem (2005: 53) writes, "the clinamen designates 'the smallest possible angle' by which the atom deviates from the straight line of the fall of atoms through a laminar void; an 'infinitely small deviation' that marks the beginning of the world as atomic turbulence."
2. Williams and Cook (2016: 718), examining the increased use of econometric methods in law enforcement and regulatory activities after the enactment of the Dodd–Frank Act, suggest that a new "regulatory rationality" is being established. "[R]egulators have sought to bolster their investments in economic expertise, dramatically expanding their capacities for economic analysis and according economists a much more prominent role in the rulemaking process," Williams and Cook (2016: 702) claim. While commonly being advanced as instrumental, mathematized rationality in its purest form, econometric methods frequently include modification of data and statistical methods to fit the purpose of the activities: "Most econometricians will readily admit to 'cleaning', 'smoothing', or 'pre-whitening' their data so that it is easier to work with and is more 'user-friendly,'" Williams and Cook (2016: 711) write. Still, such "cleaning" is not simply made for the sake of "convenience" or the benefits of "better-looking data," but these are "essential steps in the construction of statistically viable models" (Williams and Cook, 2016: 711). To that extent, the *bon mot* of the British statistician George E.P. Box, "all models are wrong, but some are useful" (cited in Williams and Cook, 2016: 716), captures an essential feature of algorithm governance: its political roots can be concealed by mathematical and statistical operations, in most cases inaccessible for lay audiences and functionaries not being trained in relevant disciplines. Furthermore, Williams and Cook (2016: 717) argue, "as a data-driven rather than a theory-driven approach," econometrics is also "expedient," i.e., it needs to add *ad hoc*

hypotheses to explain the data at hand (see e.g., Styhre, 2016), which implies that governance regimes relying on econometrics data and modelling is at risk of amplifying the is-ought fallacy, wherein empirical data—regardless of its robustness and accuracy—entices the analyst to make normative statements.

3. Credit scoring is an oligopolistic business in the U.S., with the "big three" consumer rating agencies Experian, Equifax, and TransUnion accounting for over 90 percent of the market, Rona-Tas and Hiss (2010: 118) report. In addition, there is evidence of vertical integration in the credit rating industry, as in the case of Equifax acquiring a little known company named TALX in May 2007 (Rona-Tas, 2017: 69). TALX is the largest payroll outsourcing firm in the U.S., and claims to have "payroll data of 190 million employee records, covering a third of the US workforce, from about 2,000 large employers that include the US Postal Service, the Federal and State governments, most universities and colleges, all car manufacturers, McDonald's and all the major fast food companies just to name a few" (Rona-Tas, 2017: 69). Being able to combine an oligopolistic position in credit rating with the access to such data creates strategic advantages vis-à-vis other credit raters. In addition, the secrecy of credit rating poorly sides with vertical integration, as it raises concerns regarding the risks of moral hazard and the possibility of extracting monopolistic rents, an externality that befalls other constituencies.

4. Karger (2005: 46–47) offer some details regarding the calculation of FICO scores, including the five categories of (1) payment history (with a 35 percent weight in the algorithm) (2) amounts owed (30 percent), (3), length of credit history (15 percent), (4) the amount of new credit (10 percent), and (5) types of credit used (10 percent).

5. Kroll et al. (2017: 704) defend such legal protection of algorithms and related data management practices, and suggest that "There are strong policy justifications for holding back information in the case of automated decisionmaking." Revealing software source code and input data can "expose trade secrets, violate privacy, hamper law enforcement, or lead to gaming of the decisionmaking process," Kroll et al. (2017: 704) argue. At the same time, Kroll et al. (2017: 636) admit that the "accountability mechanisms and legal standards" that govern decision processes "have not kept pace with technology." They continue: "The tools currently available to policymakers, legislators, and courts were developed primarily to oversee human decisionmakers." The legal issue to determine the accountability of digital or mathematical objects such as algorithms is a formidable challenge for all jurisdictions.

6. Such actors include students and future generations of students. Gordon (2015: 57) writes that the cost of a university education has risen, using 1972 as the benchmark year, at "more than triple the overall rate of inflation." On balance, the current level of American college completion is dependent on "a dramatic rise in student borrowing" (Gordon, 2015: 57). Furthermore, income statistics demonstrate that the college-to-high-school wage premium has been stable since around year 2000 (Kochan and Riordan, 2016: 423). Consequently, Americans today owe $1.2 trillion in college debt, and future generations may be deterred from entering college programmes as they are "[p]riced out of the market for higher education" (Gordon, 2015: 57). The consequences of such waning interest in college education are considerable.

7. Münch (2014) remarks that so-called elite universities do not of necessity provide any societal benefits beyond their immediate benefactors (e.g., employees and graduates capitalizing on status positions); France, Münch (2014: 173) writes, "has been home to elite schools for over three hundred years," and yet international comparisons suggest that this has provided "neither an academic, nor economic gain for the country." In the U.K., Oxford University and Cambridge University have operated within the same elitist structure for centuries but with similar limited societal and economic effects. In the U.S., indisputably the leading academic nation, the academic prowess is not derived from the splendour of elite universities such as Harvard, Princeton, and Yale as such, Münch (2014: 173) argues, but because of "the sufficient number of competitors and the overall competitive structure of the field." In contrast, elite universities simultaneously embody and help to perpetuate a social structure "characterized by great inequality and enormous disintegration," Münch (2014: 173) proposes (see, e.g., Stevens, 2009; Schleef, 2006). Phipps and Young (2015:

314) further stress this feature of the "marketized university," which today "[e]xist within (and perpetuate) a culture based on 'having' or 'getting' (grades and/or jobs), which develops a sense of entitlement and in which education becomes a transactional exchange." As a consequence of this new understanding of university education, Phipps and Young (2015: 314) add, "students' lives are directed towards economic self-interest and credential acquisition rather than connection." Therefore, the pursuit of excellence that now sweeps over the globalized academic landscape, Münch (2014: 173) forebodingly declares, "marks the beginning of a journey into a future that will be of benefit for neither to science nor to society."

8. In addition, the fact that 19 of the THES top 100 universities are situated in the UK, while "only 2 and 3 universities respectively are located in France and Germany" (Saisana, d'Hombres, and Saltelli, 2011: 168), indicates a bias towards favouring English-speaking universities. In addition, regardless of the analytical model underlying the ranking, the correlation between country-level economic performance and the presence of top universities seems feeble, as, e.g., the German economy and the German welfare state appear to work quite well on the basis of limited access to "world class universities." As universities are commonly believed to play a key role in socio-economic systems, there are reasons to question both the relevance and the accuracy of, e.g., the THES ranking, as it fails to take into account wider socio-economic conditions and changes. Such argument underlines that rankings and similar governance devices are primarily aimed at monitoring scholarly work in isolation from the wider social consequences of such practices.

4. Governance and market regulation as market making: stated ambitions, episodic success, and shortcomings and failures in finance market regulation

INTRODUCTION

Levitin (2014: 2042) states that the financial regulation problem is, at its core, "a governance problem." That is, rather than markets being produced by the blind forces of nature and being beyond the interests of influence of human beings and their agencies, markets and their regulatory monitoring and control is a deeply political process wherein defined actors need to handle a variety of trade-offs and to select from choice alternatives. Still, as Thiemann and Lepoutre (2017: 1812) remark, the extant literature on regulation, a major component of governance, "assign[s] unequivocally negative impacts to intensive links between regulators and the regulated." That is, regulation is by and large perceived as a negative intervention by economic actors, according to this regulation literature. In addition, institutional theorists, taking a more affirmative view of regulation and regulators, tend to consider the work of regulators and regulation as operating "outside" markets (Thiemann and Lepoutre, 2017: 1776). Regardless of the view taken, in both perspectives, Thiemann and Lepoutre (2017: 1776) argue, the relationship between the regulator and the regulated become an "adversarial interactive and iterative process, [leading to] a perpetual cat and mouse cycle of regulation–rule avoidance–reregulation, where market actors innovate with financial instruments to evade regulatory control and regulators then seek to expand regulation to recapture control." For instance, one of the most important features of finance market regulation, Levitin (2014) argues, is to determine the balance between economic growth and the stability of the economic system: "[H]igher costs of capital will result in less growth. Thus, the trade-off that needs to be considered is one of growth versus stability" (Levitin, 2014: 2036). By implication, favouring the one economic parameter comes at the loss of the other, and therefore, Levitin (2014: 2036) continues, "[W]e should seek to have the *correct* level of credit and growth, rather than simply *more* credit and growth. Yet, this just begs the question of whether we prefer volatile growth to stability."[1]

In regulating finance markets and global finance markets in particular, "the regulator's choice of policy depends on its own preferences vis-à-vis the trade-off between stability and competitiveness," Singer (2007: 23) argues. As market competition has been proposed as an almost universally applicable remedy to all sorts of economic and social shortcomings and malaises in the free market doctrine that has dominated since the early 1980s, the competitiveness alternative has been selected by policy makers in many cases. This is at the bottom line a political choice, yet supported by economic theory doctrines that inscribe price-setting mechanisms and free market competition with efficiency-inducing qualities, allegedly widely outpacing any other economic or political mechanism. Furthermore, in addition to the choice of economic growth and competition over finance market stability, policy makers have favoured a regulatory model that emphasizes that markets should be monitored by market actors, not some external government agency (even though such agencies remain in operation to date). As La Porta et al. (2000: 22) notice, the Securities and Exchange Commission (SEC), the authority monitoring the U.S. finance industry (and thus, by implication, the global finance industry as financial assets such as securities issued by U.S. finance institutions are traded globally), emphasizes "self-regulation by the intermediaries." Coffee (2006) includes auditors, attorneys, securities analysts, and rating agencies in the category of market intermediaries. In practice, three major private firms, the credit rating agencies of Moody's, Standard and Poor's, and Fitch, rose to prominence and created de facto monopolies in the 1980s and 1990s. Such authoritative positions were the outcome of political decisions and mirrored both the polity and the finance industry's own preference for regulation by market actors rather than external government agencies, potentially being concerned about other socio-economic interests than sheer finance market efficiency and growth. In fact, the Big Three rating agencies were all "protected from competition by a Securities and Exchange Commission regulation dating back to 1975" (Friedman and Kraus, 2012: 2).

This new world of finance industry expansion was thus not a haphazard or unintended outcome but was firmly based on free market thinking, part economic theories, part political doctrines (and notoriously complicated to separate into discrete categories), Friedman and Kraus (2012: 2) write: "[Financial regulators] were ignorant of the legal oligopoly of the 'rating agencies,' and … they were blinded by 'economism,' or the belief that markets are, in the default position, perfect, such that market participants are, in effect, omniscient." Even in the event where market actors proved to be fraudulent or to act opportunistically, as in the much-debated and spectacular failure of the energy commodities company Enron, free market protagonists manage to maintain and further expand the market-based regulatory doctrine. The Sarbanes–Oxley Act, the immediate political response to the Enron debacle, did not, for instance, lead to "state-led regulations" but to "more market-based solutions" (Soederberg, 2008: 666).[2] Unlike the scientists responding to new empirical data and modifying the underlying theoretical model accordingly, the free market protagonists protected their core idea, that of self-regulating and self-correcting efficient markets, from any evidence that would compromise the doctrine.

As a practical matter, in this governance regime, finance market regulation became not so much a matter of monitoring and regulating markets on the basis of objectives and goals enacted by democratically elected bodies as it is a technocratic domain of expertise centred on calculating, estimating, and commensurating financial risks. Williams (2013: 547) for instance, identifies two technologies in finance market regulation: "(1) surveillance and detection technologies, (2) datamining and risk profiling applications." In this governance regime, structured around "risk management" as its core concept and practice (Power, 2005; Kalthoff, 2005; Spira and Page, 2002), the political foundation of all regulatory practices is buried, and the governance of finance markets becomes a technocratic pursuit, a form of engineering practice that is excluded from the public gaze and widely overlooked because of its allegedly dull and uneventful routines. Such strategies to conceal political objectives under the veil of uninspiring technocratic practices seem to work well during upward shifts in the economic cycle, or when market actors do act with prudence, but when there is turbulence in the system (as in the 2006–2009 period) considerable problems surface.

Hacker and Pierson (2010: 195) notice that the de-regulation of "bank branching," no longer separating banking and commerce and commercial and investment banking, occurred gradually and step-wise, as in the case of the Glass–Steagall Act, the New Deal legislation that regulated banking for almost seven decades, which was relaxed in 1987, 1989, and 1997, before finally being repealed by the Gramm–Leach–Bliley Act of 1999. To accomplish these reforms, the finance industry lobbied fiercely and piped considerable financial resources into the American political system (Topham, 2010: 133; Wilmarth, 2013: 1293). There is no surprise that authoritative commentators such as Princeton economist Alan

Blinder (2013: 345) regards the 2008 finance industry collapse as an effect of "*too little* regulation, not *too much*." Critics of the influence of the Chicago school of economics' free market doctrine, beginning with Nixon's presidency, have persistently used terms such as "market fundamentalism" to denote the naivety of the benevolent view of markets as being self-correcting on the basis of their price system and the risks of reputational penalties ("shaming"). In Centeno and Cohen's account (2012: 331), for instance, the proposition that the market is "the institutionalized solution to practically every human problem," represents a Panglossian position wherein "the market could resolve all conflicts and provide optimal distribution without external regulation." This dream of the market (and the finance market in particular) as an economic *perpetuum mobile*, totally self-enclosed and yet optimally functional, has not yet materialized. Instead, many commentators have emphasized the deficiencies of this received model, the thin empirical support for its underlying assumptions, and, not least, the political simplifications such a model presupposes and implies. For instance, speaking about the latter, Fraser (2014) questions how a "market society," intended to maximize what free market protagonists such as Friedrich von Hayek spoke of as "economic freedom," could be sustained on the basis of the sole principle that all societal assets should be subject to market pricing and the accompanying commodification:

> Efforts to create a "market society," composed of commodities all the way down, necessarily trigger crisis. Destabilizing nature, finance, and social reproduction, such efforts are bound to undermine both the constitutive elements of social life and the presuppositions of commodity production and exchange. (Fraser, 2014: 546)

Against this background, the rise of the free market model and its first major systemic meltdown, i.e., the 2008 finance industry crisis and the subsequent "Great Recession," now entering its second decade, this chapter examines the attempts to strike a viable balance between economic growth and competition on the one hand (whereof the latter is widely assumed among card-carrying economists to be the precursor of economic growth—a proposition that should be tested against empirical evidence), and stability on the other. As already stated, the tendency has been to favour economic growth and competition, not least because that is what leading market actors, having pockets deep enough to pay for lobbyism and to donate to political campaign funds, opt for. On the other hand, it would be a misrepresentation to say that this choice of economic growth and a competition-oriented governance regime has been able to provide benefits, including growing social welfare, as its proponents have claimed since the mid-1970s. Instead, the story told in this chapter is filled with unanticipated opportunistic behaviour and regulatory capture on the part of significant market actors, leading to a market system that is considerably less efficient than that being modelled in theoretical treatises. That is, what works in textbooks and on paper proves to work less well in real-world economies, wherein speculative behaviour is not an anomaly but a constitutive feature of finance markets.

FINANCE MARKET EXPANSION I: SECURITIES MARKETS AND THE "DEMOCRATIZATION OF CREDIT"

Finance Innovations and the "Democratization of Credit"

In the economic regime of competitive capitalism, wherein "all that is solid melts into air" as Karl Marx and Friedrich Engels characterized the new economic order in their *Communist Manifesto*, and later characterized by Joseph Schumpeter (an avid but concerned reader of Marx's work) as what is propelled by processes of "creative destruction," wherein new innovations undermine previously dominant technologies, innovation is a sacred concept. Founded on advances in scientific practices, promoted by reforms in the university system in the first half of the nineteenth century in Germany and France, and propelled by increasingly sophisticated scientific expertise and engineering skills, and other relevant know-how, innovations are at the very heart of the modern experience. During the lifetime of the modern man or woman, a seemingly endless flow of novel innovations materializes and these are introduced to the wider public. In a way, the Western tradition of thinking and its Enlightenment ideals are manifested in the very production of new technologies, pharmaceuticals, and infrastructure systems that help humans live longer, more comfortable, and more rewarding lives. Innovation is, in short, part of the experience of living in the late modern era.

When it comes to financial innovations, it is important, Murdock (2012: 530) writes, to recognize that "[t]here are substantial differences between financial innovation and technological innovation." For instance, while technological innovation holds the promise of solving some practical problem, financial innovations are primarily developed to secure the return of the finance institute issuing the new financial assets. Such ulterior motive has limited auxiliary benefits, even though the finance industry representatives and their agents point at "increased market efficiencies" and campaigns that initiate the "democratization of credit." Such arguments and stories are still primarily euphemisms as, e.g., the democratization of credit is at best a secondary objective, subsumed by the profit motives of the finance innovation originator. Frame and White (2004), otherwise positive towards finance industry innovations, argue convincingly that one of the main reasons for finance industry actors participating in financial innovations is to either circumvent existing regulation, or to create financial instruments that by their sheer presence in the market will justify legislative or regulatory reforms in line with industry interests. Pistor (2013: 320) also recognizes this view and says that "financial innovation plays an important role in managing the elasticity of contractual commitments as well as legal constraints." More specifically, Pistor (2013: 320) continues, an important purpose of financial innovation is "to alleviate the costs of regulation by, for example, freeing capital from reserve requirements and making it available for lending purposes." Seen in this view, financial innovation is of necessity conducive to neither finance market stability, nor economic growth, but should be seen as the outcome from a rent-seeking activity that may or may not generate positive welfare effects.

In addition, just as in the case of the software company that releases "beta-versions" of its software products to defined clients so that they can help the company discover undetected "bugs" in the system, so too are financial innovations commonly accompanied by problems that do not reveal themselves until they are entering real-world economies and are exposed to market pricing mechanisms. For instance, one significant concern is how specific financial assets should be priced over the economic cycle (e.g., Alp, 2013; Bluhm and Wagner, 2011). As downturns in the economic cycle, crises, panics, and bank runs all affect the pricing of financial assets, novel financial assets such as derivative instruments (e.g., securities) demonstrate a volatility in pricing; what is worth X in the economic upsurge phase may be worth (i.e., is priced) at only a fraction of X in the downward phase.

In addition, and just as important, whenever there are possibilities for turning illiquid holdings (say, a portfolio of home mortgage loans with a duration of, say, 30 years) into a liquid asset, the possibilities for securitizing underlying assets may create incentives to enrol more market actors (e.g., home mortgage debtors) to maintain the expansion of the derivative market (Shin, 2009). When the pool of high-quality clients is exhausted, a speculative phase begins wherein lower quality clients are engaged (e.g., the sub-prime market borrowers in the case of mortgage-backed securities (MBSs)). This is therefore the moment wherein the tail begins to wag the dog, when the derivatives market becomes a more central concern than the underlying, original market. This continuation of the expansion of the securities trade, propelled by the introduction of low-quality clients, also increases the risk of mortgage holders defaulting, which in turn inflates systemic risks. Whenever the finance industry crosses the Rubicon and, e.g., lowers credit rating standards (as in the case of the 2002–2006 sub-prime home mortgage market), speculation is bound to leverage risks to unbearable levels. In the following, the case of the MBS market will be discussed as one domain where finance market regulation failed in a predictable manner, and with the costs of the resolution work being passed onto tax-payers and to the original home mortgage holders in particular. As the story contains non-trivial technical details, it is divided into a number of sections.

The Securitization of Illiquid Assets

Securities is a class of derivative instrument that enables the holder of a financial asset, say a home mortgage loan contract, to spread the risks of the mortgage holder defaulting across a number of finance industry actors. In addition, the securitization of the original, financial assets turns an essentially *illiquid* asset, e.g., a contract with a defined return and with a duration of 30 years, into a *liquid* asset that can be traded. In Bluhm and Wagner's (2011: 194) technical terms, "securitization turns asset cash flows into marketable securities by applying derivative technology and financial modeling to allow leveraged investment in rated but also unrated forms." While this sounds like an elementary repackaging of actual contracts held by the securities originator, the issuer of the security, this class of derivative instruments is based on a series of agreements between market actors, and between market actors and regulators, and with assumptions shared across the spectrum of finance industry actors. Shin (2009: 310) argues that securitization may facilitate greater credit supply, which benefits borrowers, but the choice to increase the credit supply is taken by the "constituents of the banking system taken as a whole." As the return on equity (i.e., the original home mortgage loan) is magnified by leverage, the risk is distributed in the financial system as soon as an asset is securitized. Once securitization has become an established practice, the issuance of securities leverages the return on the stock of financial assets at the same time as systemic risk grows when large amounts of securities are sold to a large variety of finance market actors. To further exploit the economies of scale in the finance industry (Coffee, 2011b: 815), the balance sheet of the securities issuer needs to expand. This means in practice that new borrowers must be found and enrolled (Shin, 2009: 310). For instance, in the case of the home mortgage market and the use of MBSs to securitize such loans, when all "prime borrowers" already hold a mortgage loan, the banks have to "lower their lending standards in order to lend to subprime borrowers" in the next stage (Shin, 2009: 310). This in turn, by definition, leverages the risks of mortgage holders defaulting, and therefore, Shin (2009: 310) argues, "the seeds of the subsequent downturn in the credit cycle are thus sown."

While proponents of securitization have persistently argued that this class of financial derivative instruments serves to stabilize the finance industry as risks are distributed and thus buffered by more actors, and that securitization also offers the social welfare benefit of "democratizing the supply of credit" (which is only partially true or true by default, as such benefits are not justified by the project to materialize democratic objectives, but to leverage the return on equity of finance market actors), the former assumption is based on the premise that finance market actors—and not the least credit raters—act with prudence and are capable of monitoring, assessing, and not least pricing assets correctly. Following the 2008 crisis and the subsequent Great Recession, securitization is today seen in a less optimistic view, and the apparently cynical attitude of securities traders, captured by the motto that "there is always a greater fool in the chain who will buy the bad loan" (Shin, 2009: 312), sides poorly with the idea of the finance industry as a "confidence-based industry." Moreover, as a practical matter, much of the outstanding securities were lifted off the books and located in the so-called special purpose vehicles within the shadow banking system that served to leverage finance market risk to unprecedented levels. This means that many of the risks were located outside of the formal banking system that is protected from defaulting on the basis of access to a central bank as a lender-of-last-resort. The expanding shadow banking system was thus yet another practice that undermined the possibilities for making securities a class of financial asset that rendered the finance industry more resilient.

Shadow Banking and the Expansion of the Capital Base

Fernandez and Wigger (2016: 408) define shadow banking as "[b]orrowing and lending by non-depository financial institutions—so-called non-banks or quasi-banks." More specifically, the shadow banking system is a term that denotes an extensive and elaborate network of firms and activities, jointly generating credit:

Shadow banking comprises a system of non-banks, such as non-depository or investment banks, asset management firms, hedge and private equity funds or financial holding corporations that interconnect across various jurisdictions, making use of a broad range of products and markets. Shadow banking involves maturity or liquidity transformations without having to comply with regulatory requirements such as capital reserves and other (trading) rules. (Fernandez and Wigger, 2016: 413)

Greenwood and Scharfstein (2013: 21) define shadow banking as "financial intermediaries that conduct maturity, credit, and liquidity transformation without explicit access to central bank liquidity or public sector credit guarantees." Shadow banking is thus finance industry activities that are undertaken outside of the lender-of-last-resort system, i.e., it is "not formally backed by government liquidity facilities or insurance" (Levitin, 2016: 361). The magnitude of shadow banking is considerable, calculated by the U.S. Financial Stability Board (FSB) to have risen from US$26 trillion in 2002 to US$71 trillion in 2012; this 2012 figure "is equivalent to almost half of the size of the regular banking system" (Fernandez and Wigger, 2016: 408). In Martin's (2014: 246) account, the size of the shadow banking system is even larger: by 2008, the shadow banking system stood at US$25 trillion, "more than twice the size of the traditional banking system."

While the shadow banking system is widely portrayed as being what adds to the aggregated risk in the global financial system, Fernandez and Wigger (2016) deny, despite its elusive and nocturnal name, that the shadow banking system is in any way "illegitimate," or operates outside the legal and regulatory framework determined by sovereign states and transnational regulatory agencies. Instead, the shadow banking is (1) an outgrowth from the regulated finance industry, being subsidized and protected by the sovereign state and transnational agencies, and (2) sanctioned by legislation and the operative regulatory frameworks: "Large systemic banks in advanced economies operate as powerful nodes by sponsoring or owning non-banks in order to exploit leverage opportunities beyond domestic deposit or liquidity requirements" (Fernandez and Wigger, 2016: 413). Being designed in such a manner, the shadow banking system is serving as a functional solution to handle what Fernandez and Wigger (2016: 409) refer to as "the recurring structural problem of overaccumulation"; in an economy that favours liquidity over illiquidity, there is a "lack of attractive possibilities to reinvest past profits in the production sphere" (Fernandez and Wigger, 2016: 409). Investment in land or nature, real estate, or mergers and acquisitions, being other investment options, are also comparably unattractive, as "investments in the financial circuit" are more profitable than investments in these domains (Fernandez and Wigger, 2016: 412).[3] This tendency to re-invest surplus finance capital in the finance industry is running counter to the frequently stated *raison d'être* of the finance industry, the work to transfer finance capital from mature and stagnating but cash-rich industries to high growth sectors of the economy. Shadow banking instead demands that the concept of credit is re-defined: credit is not denoting an actual physical resource, but is the creation of an IOU (pronounced "I owe you"), a contractual relation that stipulates that a certain amount of finance money should be repaid on a specific date in the future. While this elementary contractual nature of credit is reasonably simple, this licence to create credit has a variety of implications:

> Credit (and its flipside, debt) as a circulating form of fictitious capital is not rooted in what has already been produced but lays a claim to the appropriation of a portion of the production of future surplus value, thereby linking the present to the future. Claims to future surplus production can be made infinitely in theory, particularly if the issuance of credit/debt is unregulated or if there are hardly any constraints. Finance capital thrives, however, not only on extracting (future) surplus created in the sphere of economic production— the primary circuit of capital—but it can also attain ephemeral value through mere circulation and thus appear seemingly unrelated to productive activity. (Fernandez and Wigger, 2016: 411)

The challenge or problem is that while credit can be issued on the basis of general expectations and risk management predictions on the part of the issuer of credit (e.g., a licensed bank, operating under the regulatory framework of the sovereign state), based on a rational estimate that the debtor will be able to terminate the contract, this creation of credit *de novo* and *ex nihilo* cannot operate in total isolation from the "real economy," the non-financial sector wherein illiquid production capital (e.g., machinery and human resources) are employed to generate finance capital, i.e., liquid capital. Under normal conditions, when the economic cycle is in an upward movement and with no crisis or finance market instabilities in sight, credit is issued as a form of "fictitious capital" on the borrower's account at almost no cost for the creditor. In this case, licensed private institutional creditors, such as banks, are not only transforming already existing money as credit (as in the case of bank deposits, representing money earned through, e.g., salaried work), but these institutional creditors fabricate new money in isolation from other economic activities. When credit is issued within the shadow banking system, the leverage of the financial system increases, and, as various finance instruments such as debt instruments can be "re-used multiple times as collateral," the shadow banking system inflates (Fernandez and Wigger, 2016: 409).

Again, when the economy is in an upward movement and when finance institutions serve high-quality clients, i.e., clients with good solidity capable of terminating their contracts, the growth of the shadow banking system per se is not a problem: "As long as the economy is capable of taking on and honouring increasing levels of debt, shadow banking will continue to prosper" (Fernandez and Wigger, 2016: 412). However, as Shin (2009) shows, the finance system continuously seeks to attract new clients to keep the system going, expanding the issuance of credit to enrol low-quality clients, more likely to default or otherwise being unable to terminate their contracts. In the long run, this credit expansion becomes unsustainable: "[w]henever the accumulation of capital and the accumulation of debt get too out of sync, a capitalist crisis emerges," Fernandez and Wigger (2016: 412) say. The expansion of credit, in the regulated finance industry or in the shadow banking system, separated from real-economy growth conducive to the clients' capacity to repay loans, can then only be maintained if the sovereign state serves as the lender-of-last-resort, i.e., if a bailout is politically ensured, explicitly or implicitly:

> In the current context of lingering scarcity of high-quality collaterals as a ground for the issuance of new debt, shadow banking is likely to expand further in the future. This is immensely problematic as the current pace of debt creation cannot be maintained endlessly, and a similar recapitalization of so-called banks of systemic importance ("too big to fail") with taxpayers' money will not only be politically unfeasible but also de facto impossible. (Fernandez and Wigger, 2016: 410)

By and large, the expansion of the shadow banking system, entangled with the introduction of sophisticated financial innovations such as securitization on a large scale during an historical period of de-regulatory pressures, coincides with the global and pervasive expansion of debt, also in the Great Recession period: overall debt, including public, private and corporate debt, increased from U$142 trillion in 2007 (corresponding to 269 percent of world gross domestic product (GDP)), to US$199 trillion in 2015 (corresponding to 286 percent of world GDP) (Fernandez and Wigger, 2016: 423). Furthermore, the finance industry itself, today dependent on over-leveraging and borrowing from other financial institutions as a way to raise the return on equity, is "more indebted than any other economic sector," Fernandez and Wigger (2016: 423) remark. They continue:

> Seen from a broader perspective, the rise of shadow banking epitomizes the
> transformation from the macroeconomic demand management of regulated
> capitalism of the Keynesian era to the supply-side-oriented debt-led accumu-
> lation regime of the neoliberal era in the Western industrialized world.
> (Fernandez and Wigger, 2016: 422)

In the medium- to long-term perspective, this expansion of credit
separated from real GDP growth is unsustainable. During more than three
decades, financial markets expanded, over-leveraged and "grew out of
proportion relative to the real economy" (Fernandez and Wigger, 2016:
423). Even the most conservative estimates suggest, Fernandez and
Wigger (2016: 423) continue, more than a "threefold expansion of the
ratio of global financial assets to global GDP." The aggregated financial
risks do not only outgrow the capacity of sovereign states to bail out
failing finance institutions, but the ability of legal and political institutions to secure ownership claims and contractual rights are also
weakened, no longer able to contain the totality of credit issuance within
extant legislation (Fernandez and Wigger, 2016: 425). In that situation,
contractual credit relations expand beyond the realm of the sovereign
state (as in the case of Iceland in 2008, hosting no less than three
distressed mega-banks), historically being the lender-of-last-resort.

In this context, it is important to notice that securities as a theoretical
construct, supported by prudential and risk-calculating financial traders
and with credit raters having both the competence to calculate parametric
risks and the integrity needed to downgrade assets at risk, and security
issuance in a real-world economy are two entirely different things.
Deteriorating credit score standards making sub-prime borrowers eligible
for home mortgage loans, less disciplined credit rating, the expansion of
shadow banking spreadsheets, and not least an incentive structure that
rewarded leveraged returns on equity while imposing no penalties on
downside risk, was a brew that paved the way for the 2008 crisis. In the
next section, what Shin (2009: 331) metaphorically compares to a
balloon inflating (i.e., the securities market) with an increasing proportion of sub-prime home mortgage loans over time, will be examined in
more detail.

Securitization and the Residential Home Market Expansion: Predatory Lending and the Sub-prime Lending Expansion

Time and again, it is repeated that in the 1950s and 1960s, banking and
financial services was an uneventful, somewhat dull but comfortable
career choice for graduates from elite universities that anticipated a

career where they could hit the golf course by three o'clock and did not have to endure any major commotion. The same is claimed regarding the real estate market and home mortgage lending. Prior to the turn of the millennium, real estate was considered a relatively safe investment, but with the birth of securitization and the issuance of MBSs on an industrial scale in the 2000–2005 period, all this would change. In the five-year period, the number of sub-prime loans "jumped from 456,631 in 2000 to 2,284,420 in 2005" (Murdock, 2012: 525). In addition, in terms of the percentage of all MBSs issued, this new MBS market was increasingly dominated by private-label securitization, rising from "less than 20 to over 50 percent from 2002 to 2006" (Mian and Sufi, 2014: 97). This indicated that it was smaller, frequently fly-by-night finance institutions that propelled the MBS market. The sharp growth of the MBS market was an indication of the housing bubble that affected certain regions in the U.S., with Florida and California as outstanding examples of the sub-prime mortgage market expansion.

Speaking before Congress in October 2005, Ben Bernanke (cited in Mian and Sufi, 2014: 78), by then chairman of Council of Economic Advisers, and soon nominated as the chairman of Federal Reserve, the most prominent of the regulatory agencies in the U.S. finance system, asserted that the soaring housing prices were no more no less than an indication of a healthy and vigorous economy, whose various actors could now take advantage of the munificent credit supply: "Housing prices have risen by nearly 25 percent in the past two years. Although speculative activity has increased in some areas, at a national level these price increases largely reflect strong economic fundamentals." Such declaration *ex cathedra* belied other evidence of the condition of the housing market. Mian and Sufi (2009: 1453) show that the 2002–2005 period was the *only* period in an 18-year period wherein mortgage growth and income growth were negatively correlated. Under "normal conditions," declining income on an aggregated level serves to cool off the housing market as presumptive house buyers make rational calculations on the basis of the economic means they access. Furthermore, data from the 2002–2005 period indicates an expansion of sub-prime mortgage securitization (Mian and Sufi, 2009: 1453). In brief, despite presumptive house buyers not making sufficient money to buy their own homes, they were offered sub-prime mortgage loans to fulfil their dream (this being an explicit political objective in Washington). As the housing market had been, as a matter of fact, relatively stable and with slowly but stable growing housing prices prior to 2000, these loan takers were possibly also convinced that the conditions stated in their contracts were reasonable. More importantly, this new category of sub-prime borrowers cannot be assumed to be able to oversee, nor fully understand, the new financial architecture they were now part of, and to assess its medium- to long-term consequences, as not even leading authorities, the economics professors and economic advisors speaking from the highest office, were able to make a moderate and tempered analysis.

Mian and Sufi's (2009: 1453–1454) detailed data, collected at the level of ZIP code areas (used in the U.S. postal code system), indicate that the rate of securitization was much stronger in "subprime ZIP codes" in comparison to "prime ZIP codes" during the period. This suggests that securitization per se was the primus motor of the expansion of the sub-prime home mortgage market. Using Shin's (2009) metaphor, the balloon of the home mortgage loan market was increasingly filled with loan borrowers with low so-called FICO-scores (the industry standard to assess the risk of the loan taker defaulting within two years; Rona-Tas and Hiss, 2010: Keys et al., 2009), which on the one hand served to continue to fuel the securities market but also, on the other hand, leveraged the risk of systemic failure as the "quality" (e.g., the solvency of the client) of the underlying loans was gradually deteriorating, i.e., the calculated parametric risk of the loan taker failing to terminate the contract and to repay the loans was increasing considerably. In the end, the systemic risk reached proportions that could no longer be buffered by the at this time globalized MBS/collateralized debt obligation (CDO) market, and when default rates increased in the 2005–2007 period, especially in ZIP code areas with a high degree of sub-prime borrowers and private-company securities originators, the global financial system became unstable. Mian and Sufi (2009: 1454) suggest moral hazard on behalf of the MBS originators, indicating that they were possibly aware of the fragility of the sub-prime market and its accompanying securities market. Despite not sharing the positive prospects of the housing market prices, MBS originators continued to to issue securities, ultimately resulting in the collapse of the sub-prime market. This suspicion points at two explanations for the expansion of the primary sub-prime market and the secondary MBS/CDO market, both unflattering for finance industry actors: either the finance industry actors believed the house market prices would continue to grow as a fundamental economic phenomenon, possibly separate from the expansion of the finance industry per se, which in turn rendered many loan originators, who actively ignored substandard FICO-scores when making loan decisions, overtly naïve; or, alternatively, the loan originators were cynically exploiting the sub-prime market borrowers to make money in the secondary MBS/CDO market.

While Mian and Sufi (2009: 1454) are agnostic about the rationale and beliefs of loan originators, while hinting at the former explanation as credible,[4] e.g., Engel and McCoy (2001, 2007) and McCoy, Pavlov, and Wachter (2009) explicitly speak about "predatory lending" as being the driver of the sub-prime and MBS/CDO market expansions in the first years of the new millennium.

Predatory Lending as Market Making

The securitization of sub-prime mortgage loans, in MBS, CDOs, and other mortgage-related securities, provided an "important incentive for subprime lending, which made such lending a source of profit, rather than of risk, for mortgage originators," White (2009: 394) argues (see also Eggert, 2002; Peterson, 2007). While the term *predatory lending* has "no consensus legal definition" (Fligstein and Roehrkasse, 2016: 621), the Federal Deposit Insurance Corporation (cited by Fligstein and Roehrkasse, 2016: 621) characterizes the behaviour as "imposing unfair and abusive loan terms on borrowers, often through aggressive sales tactics; taking advantage of borrowers' lack of understanding of complicated transactions; and outright deception." Engel and McCoy (2001: 1260) define predatory lending as a "a syndrome of abusive loan terms or practices" that involve one or more of the following five problems:

1. loans structured to result in seriously disproportionate net harm to borrowers,
2. harmful rent seeking,
3. loans involving fraud or deceptive practices,
4. other forms of lack of transparency in loans that are not actionable as fraud, and
5. loans that require borrowers to waive meaningful legal redress.

(Engel and McCoy, 2001: 1260)

Expressed more to the point, Engel and McCoy (2007: 2043) say that predatory lending is a syndrome of loan abuses that "benefit mortgage brokers, lenders, and securitizers to the serious detriment of borrowers." Unlike high-quality lenders, being concerned with their reputation and therefore assuring that a borrower's risk of default is within a defined tolerable statistical probability to justify a mortgage loan, predatory lenders are speculators that demonstrate less concern for the interest and economic welfare of borrowers. More importantly, predatory lending is made both possible and attractive because predatory lenders, Engel and McCoy (2001: 1293) write, "can engage in an array of possible deceptions and then unload their loans on the secondary market." Even in the case where secondary-market institutions may attempt to shift the loss back to lenders when borrowers default, predatory lenders, being thinly capitalized as part of their business model, can avoid liabilities by simply dissolving or declaring bankruptcy.

One major concern from a legal scholar's point of view is that Wall Street firms securitize sub-prime home loans "without determining if loan pools contain predatory loans" (Engel and McCoy, 2007: 2040). This in turn creates what George Akerlof (1970) refers to as a "lemon problem" wherein the buyers of securities (e.g., MBSs) are not aware of the fact that the pool of securitized loans contains unattractive and overtly risky low-quality loans. In the worst case scenario, Wall Street's lack of routines for sifting out the bad, predatory lending seeds facilitates opportunistic or illicit behaviours in home mortgage loan markets, i.e., predatory lending is de facto tolerated despite its contribution to lever-aged systemic risks. An additional concern is that securitization, which was introduced as a means to stabilize finance markets through the distribu-tion of risk and to increase the supply of credit to benefit economic growth, has unintended negative consequences for home mortgage borrowers; "securitization inflicts negative externalities on sub-prime borrowers in at least four ways," Engel and McCoy (2007: 2041) say (for an overview of the consequences of securitization of "low-documentation loans," i.e., sub-prime mortgage loans, see Rajan, Seru, and Vig, 2015).

First, securitization provides possibilities for funding small, thinly capitalized lenders and brokers (which, it is important to note, was potentially one of the main political ideas justifying legal reforms in the first place, to promote entrepreneurial activities and venturing), thus enabling them to enter the housing market (Engel and McCoy, 2007: 2041). While this argument is not per se deviating from the legislator's intentions, securitization invites home mortgage loan market actors who demonstrate less prudence than policy makers may have wished. Second, securitization "dilutes" the incentives of lenders and brokers to "avoid making loans with excessive default risk," as they are able to pass on risk to a secondary market, which, in turn "has other ways to protect itself" (Engel and McCoy, 2007: 2041). Thinly capitalized lenders and brokers are thus able to benefit from very risky positions as they can secure a free rider position at low cost when they include their loans in larger pools of mortgage contracts being securitized on the secondary MBS market. The lenders' and brokers' "pricing of risk" is therefore considerably lower than it would be in the case where they themselves would have needed to account for such risks. The securities market thus provides possibilities for free riding, a position that competitive markets, neoclassical eco-nomic theory stipulates, should eliminate through the pricing mechanism by imposing a penalty of excessive risk taking.

Third, securitization denies injured borrowers many legal rights because the present legislation undermines the agreements that define the traditional lender–borrower relation (Engel and McCoy, 2007: 2041). This argument is highly complex in its details and applies to a varying degree to different U.S. states, but emphasizes how finance market independence tends to neutralize inherited legal traditions. Fourth and lastly, over time securitization inflates the costs of sub-prime burrowing because "investors demand a lemons premium for investing in subprime mortgage-backed securities" (Engel and McCoy, 2007: 2041). This argument runs counter to the argument that securitization increases the supply of credit, and the first argument that Wall Street tends to "white-wash" thinly capitalized lenders and brokers' loans. Yet the argument points at the "lemon problem" (the costs involved in separating "bad" and "good" loans), wherein not all sub-prime loans are of necessity defaulting, but with those borrowers capable of terminating their contracts now carrying a larger burden than they would if the lemon problem did not materialize. Expressed differently, the predatory lender's win is the prudent lender's loss, de facto being a premium paid and sanctioned by the policy makers to financial speculators at the expense of primarily American households located in the lower-income brackets (Baumer et al., 2017). Therefore, taken together, predatory lending was one of the key features of the sub-prime market expansion, carefully accounted for by, e.g., Mian and Sufi (2009). Moreover, the capacity to securitize sub-prime loans provided ample opportunities for thinly capitalized lenders and brokers, entering the home mortgage market to make a return on speculation, to pass on the financial risks to the global MBS market, thus forcing high-quality lenders acting with prudence to absorb and account for such risks. Ultimately, the sub-prime borrowers had to bear the brunt of the costs, either in the case they fulfilled their contracts or if they defaulted. In the end, the democratization of credit through the means of securitization proved to be illusory, and a political objective complicated to fulfil within the present finance industry structure.

The Consequences of Predatory Lending

Writing in hindsight is something completely different from predicting outcomes, but when the dust had settled, it was apparent that the entire home mortgage loan market and the finance industry practices were far from perfect, jointly generating the 2008 finance industry meltdown. When the floor went out of the housing market, very much a diametrically opposed scenario of Ben Bernanke's sanguine view outlined only three years earlier, a considerable proportion of borrowers found themselves in a position where their houses were "below the waterline," i.e., they had acquired their homes at an inflated market price and now had to live with the consequences: "[b]y the end of 2008, every sixth borrower owed more than his or her home was worth" (McCoy, Pavlov, and Wachter, 2009: 1332). Now, suddenly, finance industry executives were cognizant of the risks of securitization. Ken Thompson, Wachovia's former chairman and chief executive officer, testified to the conditions created in the 2000–2007 period:

> The financial engineering [securitization] … was in fact among the primary contributors to the risky lending practices that led to home price bubbles in many markets … Home prices were buoyed by the willingness of institutional investors across the world to buy these subprime loans in the form of complex securities created by investment banks. (Ken Thompson, cited in McCoy, Pavlov, and Wachter, 2009: 1329)

The Howl of Minerva takes flight only at nightfall, was Hegel's concern: we tend to learn a lesson only when it is getting late, and at times *too* late, and this was apparently the case in the home mortgage lending market.

A number of lessons can be learned on the basis of the sub-prime mortgage industry case. First of all, market actors were apparently incapable of pricing risk correctly, which in turn cast a doubt on the efficacy of the price-mechanism that is commonly invoked to justify de-regulatory reform. In the home mortgage loan market, "default risk for subprime mortgages was neither calibrated, reserved for, nor priced," McCoy, Pavlov, and Wachter (2009: 1332–1333) write. Instead, the risks were socialized and in the end the finance industry was bailed out by the federal government. McCoy, Pavlov, and Wachter (2009: 1335) argue that "the initial deregulation" of the market, a new pro-business, free market policy developed throughout the 1989s and 1990s, was a "necessary condition" for the emergence of "a critical mass of imprudent mortgages." Yet the reforms were not generating the "race to the bottom" on its own: "The mortgage industry itself was undergoing structural change in its financing mechanism that made it possible for mortgage professionals to sell products with heightened risk and to 'disperse that risk among investors at large'" (McCoy, Pavlov, and Wachter, 2009: 1335). In addition, in a case of "exceptionally poor timing," federal banking regulators changed the risk-based capital rules in December 2007 to let finance institutions "compute their minimum capital requirements themselves," using a statistical model known as "Value-at-Risk" (VaR; Conti-Brown, 2009: 1461; McCoy, Pavlov, and

Wachter, 2009: 1349–1450). The new VaR standard did little to anticipate or counteract the finance crisis on the way. Ultimately, finance
market actors, with wind in their sails as their activities were praised by
leading authorities such as Ben Bernanke and being left alone by
regulators, suffered from overconfidence—an endemic cognitive bias
during all bubbles (Gerding, 2005; Paredes, 2003): "[L]enders believed
their ability to assess risk of loans was so good that they created ever
more complicated mortgage instruments with different and complicated
metrics of default risk pricing" (McCoy, Pavlov, and Wachter, 2009:
1337). In the end, perceived upside risks served to marginalize downside
risks, which were never fully anticipated in the calculative practices.
Perhaps, if finance industry actors cynically believed they were operating under the protection of the sovereign state as a lender-of-last-resort,
socializing the risks, downside risks were never factually a matter of
joint concern.

Second, the "markets-regulate-themselves-better-than-any-central-
agency-does" argument, the leitmotif of decades of de-regulation of
finance markets, proved to be unsubstantiated by empirical evidence. On
the contrary, the credit rating agencies, the disciplinary mechanism *par
préférence* in the finance industry, failed to demonstrate a minimal degree
of integrity and concern for the wider socio-economic consequences of
their ratings: the credit rating agencies kept rating most securities being
issued at the highest AAA level until the bitter end when the whole
finance market came to a halt. One class of derivative instruments, the
credit default swaps (CDS), which could in theory serve to cool off the
risk appetite if being rated in accordance with the risks they contain,
were in fact undermined on the basis of inadequate, overoptimistic
ratings. This led to aggressive CDS issuers being granted the possibility
of "underpricing of risk in the entire market very quickly" (McCoy,
Pavlov, and Wachter, 2009: 1370). Augustin et al. (2016: 178) adds that
there is "sufficient anecdotal evidence to suggest that CDS affect the
prices of the underlying securities," that is, CDS issuance affects
the economic incentives of key agents in the financial system and alter
the behaviour of investors, firms, and regulators. However, such evidence,
surfacing in the event of the unfolding and rapidly escalating crisis, was
running counter to the conventional wisdom that CDS and other securities served to stabilize finance markets. Augustin et al. (2016: 178) thus
argue that such claims, unaccompanied by factual evidence, "[w]ould
have met with considerable skepticism, if not scorn, among financial
economists even two decades ago." In short, finance theorists and finance
market actors had a firm belief in new finance innovations having an

innate capacity to price risks correctly, but such an affirmative view of the rationality of man-made finance instruments proved to be overoptimistic.

Another class of derivative instruments, CDOs, were equally complicated to rate for the credit rating agencies. As has been emphasized in the finance theory literature, pricing CDOs demands both substantial skills and access to market data series including the entire economic cycle:

> CDOs are highly complex and need a certain repertoire that includes valuation teams, booking capabilities, monitoring facilities, etc. if such a repertoire is not in place and fully functional—as could be the case for smaller institutions—then it is not recommended to invest in CDOs. (Bluhm and Wagner, 2011: 217)

MacKenzie and Spears (2014: 424) add that two different CDOs can be "hard to compare," and it can be complicated to judge whether "the spreads offered by the tranches of the one are more or less attractive than those offered by the tranches of the other." Lysandrou and Nesvetailova (2015: 273) agree with this assessment, and argue that CDOs may only be "second floor securities," but add that "the jump in complexity going from ABS [Asset-Backed Securities, e.g., MBSs] to CDOs is many times greater than the jump going from the 'ground floor' government and corporate debt securities to the 'first floor' asset backed securities." For instance, the CDO asset class contains heterogeneous instruments, designed to serve specific clients' needs, which makes them essentially illiquid:

> Asset-backed securities have a transparent conformity in that each type has a single asset class as collateral (residential mortgage loans, credit card loans, commercial property loans, and so on). By contrast, no two individual CDOs were alike because of the large variety of ways in which different asset classes (subprime backed securities, other nonconforming loan backed securities, prime ABS, and so on) could be mixed together as the backing collateral. CDOs could still be sold, but only as unique, customised products tailored to suit the specific needs of specific investors. (Lysandrou and Nesvetailova, 2015: 273)

Such difficulties arguably make CDOs unsuitable as a security being marketed and issued on a large scale, simply because the sheer difficulty of pricing them: "[I]t takes a lot to be successful in the CDO investor space," Bluhm and Wagner (2011: 218) say: "There are countless examples of investors whose CDO investment got them into trouble in the course of the crisis."[5] More specifically, The Gaussian Copula correlation model, a risk model developed by David Li (MacKenzie and

Spears, 2014), promoted as being the analytical model taming chance in CDO trade in a way similar to the Black–Scholes model in options trade, failed to live up to its hype; seemingly, the Gaussian Copula correlation model "[a]llowed a precise mathematical computation of the risks posed by these instruments. In fact, the Gaussian Copula models were simply not designed to forecast such an event" (Markham, 2009: 1126). In the end, the extant risk assessment models failed to predict the sub-prime crisis and to accommodate its systemic consequences for the globalized finance market.

A study reported by Coffee (2011a), examining 916 CDOs issued between January 1997 and December 2007, found that the credit rating agencies "[d]id not follow a consistent policy or valuation model with respect to subordination, but rather regularly made 'adjustments' on subjective grounds." Such findings indicate that pricing CDOs is a far from trivial operation. Consequently, when the crisis struck in the autumn of 2008, the market value of CDOs plummeted: "[a]s of June 30, 2009, 90% of the collateralized debt obligations (CDOs) that were issued between 2005 and 2007 and were rated AAA by S&P had been downgraded, with 80% graded below investment grade" (White, 2013: 105). For individual firms, this caused substantial losses. For instance, in 2008, Merrill Lynch wrote down US$5.7 billion due to exposure to the Super-Senior CDOs (Markham, 2009: 1126). More easy-to-price assets such as MBSs that were issued during the previous years and rated AAA were now similarly downgraded (63 percent of all outstanding securities), whereof 52 percent were downgraded below investment grade (White, 2013: 105). This is overwhelming evidence of the failure of the credit rating model, the governance model endorsed by finance market actors and their sponsors and agents.

Third and finally, the sub-prime home mortgage market debacle provides a strong case in favour of government-led regulatory control, i.e., the state does in fact play a legitimate and necessary role as a market maker. For instance, data reveals that the lowest default rates during the crisis and its aftermath were at state banks and thrifts which are "subject both to state and federal regulation" (McCoy, Pavlov, and Wachter, 2009: 1357). When the state plays an active role, there is less systemic risk derived from the default of key market actors, which reduces the costs and consequences for the wider economy, including tax-payers. At the same time, McCoy, Pavlov, and Wachter (2009: 1357) point at evidence of "regulatory capture" as the Federal Securities and Exchange Commission initiated reforms that transferred authority from regulatory agencies to defined market actors. In 2004, the Securities and Exchange Commission in 2004 allowed "the five top investment banks to reduce their capital to miniscule levels and become dangerously leveraged" (McCoy, Pavlov, and Wachter, 2009: 1357). Almost all of those banks "took outsize risks in subprime securitizations," and, in 2008, "all five underwent near-collapse in 2008" (McCoy, Pavlov, and Wachter, 2009: 1357–1358):

> In March of that year, Bear Steams was saved only through a $29 billion infusion of cash from the Federal Reserve Board and a shotgun wedding to JPMorgan Chase. Almost six months later to the day, the federal government allowed Lehman Brothers to fail. In the maelstrom that ensued, Merrill Lynch hastily brokered its sale to Bank of America. The last two leading independent Wall Street firms, Goldman Sachs and Morgan Stanley, filed rush applications to become bank holding companies in order to assure permanent access to the Fed's discount window. (McCoy, Pavlov, and Wachter, 2009: 1358)

This episode of inadequate regulatory control on the part of the SEC is not conducive to median voters' reasonable interests. However, a political solution to the economic problem of regulatory control seems to be the only viable and legitimate solution in a period where the finance industry has expanded in size and scope, and today is impossible to disentangle from the wider real economy. "Efficient markets do not self-organize: they need to be cued and maintained by regulatory oversight," McCoy, Pavlov, and Wachter (2009: 1374) summarize their argument.

The finance industry collapse of 2008 was neither simply a "bump in the road," nor the "perfect storm" hitting an otherwise sound and well-managed industry, devoid of culpability. Instead, the magnitude of the crisis and the degree of opportunistic behaviour shed light on an industry that operates according to other agendas than were officially stated, i.e., to supply finance capital to non-financial businesses and to participate in prudent deposit holding and lending. The finance industry is today a money machine being sponsored and subsidized by the state, and, as will be discussed in the next section, the case of the home mortgage loan market and its collapse is by no means the end of the story. When one market is exhausted or overrun by speculators and minor actors (now being the site where what Warren Buffet, cited in Cohan, 2011: 446, referred to as "the three I's of new markets—Innovators, Imitators, and Idiots" —participated, or was, in the case of the first of the three, in the stage of leaving), the large finance conglomerates move their activities elsewhere.

FINANCE MARKET EXPANSION II: THE MERCHANTS OF WALL STREET AND THE DE-REGULATION OF COMMODITIES TRADE

Commodities Market Speculation and its Consequences

In theory, securitization was supposed to serve as a market-based mechanism that stabilized the finance market through the ability of such finance assets to value and price risk more adequately than other finance instruments are capable of doing. This was the argument put forth for decades by free market protagonists, as well as from the highest office (e.g., Alan Greenspan, chairman of the Federal Reserve), but the theory did not hold much water when accompanied by declining credit rating prudence and when the finance industry was globalized so poorly rated securities could contaminate substantial shares of the global financial system. That is, to paraphrase Ronald Reagan's famous anti-government declaration, "securitization is not the solution, it is the problem." Worse still, the repeal of the Glass–Steagall Act in 1999 and 2000, at the end of the Clinton presidency, provided finance industry actors with the right to participate in non-financial trade in, e.g., the global commodities markets. When the floor went out of the sub-prime mortgage market, finance industry actors moved their finance capital from the real estate market to the commodities market (Omarova, 2013). The consequences were immediate and lasting. This section of the chapter will account for how finance institutions penetrated the commodities market and sketch some of the consequences, whereof many remain obscure to this day.

A small but significant literature indicates that commodities prices have become more volatile since the commodities trade has been de-regulated (for an authoritative overview, see Clayton, 2016). "There is growing evidence that the unprecedented magnitude of swings and excessive volatility in commodity prices over the past decade can be seen as a reflection of the ever increasing linkages between activities in commodity and financial markets," Nissanke (2012: 733) writes. For instance, in the 1999–2001 period, commodity price developments were relatively smooth and financial investments in commodity markets were insignificant (Mayer, 2012: 759). In 2002, commodity prices and index trader investments started to increase and peaked in mid-2008, at the height of the finance industry crisis. In the first half of 2008, the steepest price increases were observed for crude petroleum (52 percent) and food (51 percent)—two "politically sensitive consumer goods" (Nissanke, 2012: 734). Oil prices peaked at over US$140 a barrel in early July 2008 but plummeted below US$50 in November–December 2008, thereafter reaching a trough at US$35–$45 in February 2009 (Nissanke, 2012: 734). The oil price volatility has continued during the Great Recession, being higher between 2007 and 2012 than during the "oil shocks" following the 1973 Organization of Petroleum Exporting Countries' oil embargo, the 1979 Iranian Revolution, and the 1990–1991 Persian Gulf War (Greenberger, 2013: 709). According to commentators, speculation in oil prices is a "fact," not some hypothesis or conjecture: "Oil prices are high because of speculation, pure and simple. That's not an assertion, that's a fact. Yet rather than attack the speculation and rid ourselves of the problem, we flail away at the symptoms," economist Mike Norman argues (cited in Greenberger, 2013: 722). The speculation in oil prices has also led to political disputes as certain industries have been forced to carry the economic burden of raising oil prices; in an "Open Letter to All Airline Customers" published in 2008, the CEOs of 12 U.S. airline companies stated that "normal market forces are being dangerously amplified by poorly regulated market speculation" (cited in Greenberger, 2013: 722). In March 2011, when the crude oil market price stood at US$100 per barrel, the CEO of ExxonMobil testified to the United States Senate Finance Committee that "market fundamentals only justified a price of $60 to $70 per barrel" (Greenberger, 2013: 721).

The concern is that traditional traders, what Nissanke (2012: 743) refers to as *informed traders*, who "use derivatives instruments mainly for risk-hedging purposes and [who] try to base trading decisions on the market fundamentals of a particular commodity," are now competing with financial traders who make a return on taking positions in commodity-specific markets but without actually trading the commodities as such, and who therefore affect supply–demand balances and commodity prices (Mayer, 2012: 765). This class of traders include two types of traders: (1) *Noise traders*, "who take positions on commodity trade in relation to the development of other asset markets as part of investors' portfolio allocations such as index traders" (Nissanke, 2012: 743), and (2) *Uninformed traders*, "who typically apply statistical techniques such as chartist analysis or momentum trading on price trends, instead of basing decisions on information about the market fundamentals of physical commodities" (Nissanke, 2012: 743). Noise traders make a return on the basis of arbitrage, price fluctuations within and between markets, and uninformed traders basically serve the same role in biasing commodity prices (i.e., prices are no longer set on the basis of economic fundamentals) as they cannot, on the basis of their trading methods, distinguish between price changes induced by informed traders on the basis of "shifts in market fundamentals" (e.g., changes in supply and demand of the commodity), and the price changes triggered by noise traders. Whenever money managers (i.e., noise traders and uninformed traders) enter the markets, using, e.g., futures commodities as a financial asset vehicle in their trade, price levels are changing, "more often than not," Mayer (2012: 753) says.

In a free market theory model, all kinds of traders, regardless of their underlying interests and motivations, are trading under the influence of the efficient market hypothesis, stipulating that all available public information is included in the market price at every single point in time. The empirical basis for this hypothesis is questioned in studies of commodity market price fluctuation, indicating that the flow of "speculative investments" into commodities markets has in fact led to "higher and increasingly volatile commodities prices" (Williams and Cook, 2016: 702). Mayer's (2012) empirical data also undermines the efficient market hypothesis:

> Taken together, these results suggest a significant impact of financial investment on price developments in a wide range of commodities over the period July 2006–June 2009. This significant impact of index trader positions on price developments, combined with the absence of reverse causality, and the fact that index traders do not take positions based on commodity market fundamentals, may also be interpreted as indicating that the efficient market hypothesis fails in relation to commodity markets. (Mayer, 2012: 763)

Nissanke (2012: 746) argues that empirical evidence shows that "unregulated derivatives markets and dealings," overpopulated by financial investors "with little interest in physical commodities," have increased the likelihood of generating "excessive volatility." When commodities prices, now susceptible to the effects of noise traders' and uninformed traders' arbitrage, can no longer serve their intended function, to signal market fundamentals such as the demand for certain commodities, market actors can no longer make "informed decisions affecting demand and supply, including investment decisions for the substitution and conservation of resources" (Nissanke, 2012: 746). "Under such conditions," Nissanke (2012: 746) continues, "futures markets would cease to perform their intended function—that of price discovery and risk hedging for physical stakeholders." The long-term consequence is that a few finance industry actors are granted the licence to trade and speculate in politically sensitive commodities, whose prices affect the everyday life of billions of people, in many cases some of the poorest and most vulnerable people on the planet:

> While excessive volatilities can provide traders and investors with attractive short-term gains, the long-term consequences from an asset price bubble-bust

are now widely acknowledged as being extremely harmful, entailing a heavy collateral damage to world trade and real economies as well as high social costs worldwide. The recent global crisis is a clear testimony to the presence of an enormous wedge between private and social returns from activities in asset markets. (Nissanke, 2012: 747)

Rapidly increasing prices of food and fuel and price shocks have already "sparked off social and political unrest across the globe," Nissanke (2012: 732) says. The downside of financial speculation, permitted by national and transnational political entities and their defined agencies, translates into rising costs that "hit particularly hard the livelihood of the urban and rural poor in developing countries" (Nissanke, 2012: 732). Commodities trade is therefore a highly politically charged issue (Williams, 2014).

Tang and Xiong (2012) examine how finance institutions have increasingly participated in commodities market trade. After 2004, Tang and Xiong (2012: 54) argue, there is "[a] salient empirical pattern of greatly increased price co-movements between various commodities." In addition, before the early 2000s (i.e., just after the substantial legislative reforms were enacted and implemented), evidence suggests that "commodity markets were partly segmented from outside financial markets and from each other" (Tang and Xiong, 2012: 56). After 2000, many finance institutions have started to consider commodities "a new asset class" worthy of exploring. As a result of this awakened interest, billions of investment dollars flowed into commodity markets from financial institutions, insurance companies, pension funds, foundations, hedge funds, and wealthy individuals (Tang and Xiong, 2012: 56–57). This in turn led to new empirical phenomenon being observed in the pricing data, i.e., "[p]rices of non-energy commodities have become increasingly correlated with oil prices" (Tang and Xiong, 2012: 72). In Tang and Xiong's (2012) analysis, such empirical evidence is indicative of "[a] fundamental process of financialization among commodity markets, through which commodity prices have become more correlated with each other." By implication, speculation in commodities leads to a modification of the entire market pricing function—the mechanism that per se enables efficient and allocatively optimal markets in the orthodox economic theory doctrine—so that "[t]he price of an individual commodity is no longer determined solely by its supply and demand" (Tang and Xiong, 2012: 72). Instead, commodities prices are increasingly determined, Tang and Xiong (2012: 72) argue, "by the aggregate risk appetite for financial assets and the investment behavior of diversified commodity index investors."

Henderson, Pearson, and Wang (2014) provide further evidence of the extended role played by finance institutions in global commodities markets. In their study, so-called CLNs (Commodity-Linked Notes), a financial instrument, impact commodity spot prices in ways that make the price mechanism complicated to relate to the underlying supply and demand of the actual commodity. As a consequence, Henderson, Pearson, and Wang (2014) suggest that finance institutions and their speculative investments affect commodities pricing activities in ways that are conducive neither to market efficiency nor increased social welfare:

> [T]he trades of financial institutions play an important role in price formation in the commodities futures markets ... [i]nformational frictions prevent commodity market participants from observing fundamentals, causing them to misinterpret demand for commodity positions that is not based on information or related to macroeconomic fundamentals as conveying information about future macroeconomic growth, impacting market prices. (Henderson, Pearson, and Wang, 2014: 1309).

To further substantiate the thesis that finance institutions and their interests in generating finance capital on the basis of its equity investment now cast a long shadow over commodities markets and the pricing of commodities, Sockin and Xiong (2015: 2063) argue that, e.g., the crude oil and copper markets are today globalized, and that this in turn "[e]xposes market participants to heightened informational frictions regarding the global supply, demand, and inventory of these commodities." In such markets, the so-called market for commodity futures (where "futures" are the defined financial asset being traded) may influence the pricing of commodities in considerable ways. As Sockin and Xiong (2015: 2078) argue, proponents of futures trade claim that this trade is separated from the pricing of commodities (i.e., the underlying asset), but Sockin and Xiong (2015) are less sanguine about this separation of futures trade and pricing, simply because the information needed to trade a future is considerably lower than in the case of the trading of the commodity per se: "In practice, the lower cost of trading futures contracts compared with trading physical commodities encourages greater participation and facilitates aggregation of dispersed information among market participants" (Sockin and Xiong, 2015: 2078).

Providing empirical data to substantiate their propositions (futures trade does affect commodity pricing in predictable ways), Sockin and Xiong (2015: 2085) report that the "commodity price boom of 2007 to 2008" was not caused by a speculative bubble but was derived from "the large inflow of investment capital" from the faltering home mortgage market, leading to "distorted signals" regarding commodity prices. In the next stage, creating confusion among market participants about "the strength of emerging economies," including China and India, whose demand for commodities was generally thought to be the driver of commodities prices in the period. Therefore, as factual evidence, noise in futures market trading seems to interfere with "goods producers' expectation," which affects their "commodity demand" (Sockin and Xiong, 2015: 2086). Expressed differently, finance industry actors' speculation in commodities markets does lead to additional information collection costs and thus impairs the commodity markets' pricing; the interests of the few put the interests of the many at risk and increase the costs of the entire market. "Our analysis," Sockin and Xiong (2015: 2086) argue, provides "a coherent argument for how the large inflow of investment capital to commodity futures markets, by jamming commodity price signals and leading to confusion about the strength of emerging economies, might have amplified the boom and bust of commodity prices in the 2007 to 2008 period."

Such studies and evidence indicate either a poorly functioning regulation of the finance industry, leaving it to market-based actors themselves to monitor, e.g., the whereabouts of paying clients, or a regulatory framework and a policy that turn a blind eye to speculative, deficient, or even fraudulent market pricing activities, wherein market prices no longer represent the nexus between supply and demand (as stipulated by Economics 101 textbooks, following the Marshallian tradition of economic theory), but instead become an index of the risk appetite among major finance industry actors at a given point in time. Whether these two scenarios in turn indicate a regulatory failure, or a successful case of enforcing free market pricing demands a widening of the horizon of the theoretical understanding and meaning within which such empirical conditions can be explained. We thus turn to Omarova's (2013) analysis of the "Merchants of Wall Street" to examine the wider economic, legal, and political consequences of the expansion of finance institutions' activities in commodities markets.

The Merchants of Wall Street

In the American post-New Deal economic policy, there has been a careful separation of banking and commerce, protected by legislation and enforced by regulatory oversight and court ruling, Omarova (2013) declares:

The separation of banking and commerce is one of the fundamental principles underlying the U.S. system of bank regulation. State and federal banking statutes impose a complex web of restrictions and prohibitions on the business activities and investments of U.S. commercial banks and their affiliates. (Omarova, 2013: 273)

Just as indicated by the studies reported by Sockin and Xiong (2015), Henderson, Pearson, and Wang (2014), and Tang and Xiong (2012), Omarova (2013: 300) also points at changes in global commodities markets pricing in the early 2000s, now suddenly "[e]xperiencing a sharp and sustained rise in prices, building up to a major commodity boom." According to a World Bank report (cited in Omarova, 2013: 300), "[a]verage commodity prices doubled in U.S. dollar terms (in part boosted by dollar depreciation), making this boom longer and stronger than any boom in the 20th century." More importantly, Omarova (2013: 300) continues, "the beginning of this unprecedented commodity price boom coincided with the increased push by large U.S. financial institutions to establish large-scale physical commodity trading operations."

Another factor that should be considered in this setting is the role played by Enron, by the time of its bankruptcy not only being the seventh largest company in the U.S., but also being a business press and popular management writing phenomenon and the free market protagonist's exemplary case (see, e.g., Hamel's, 2000, praise of Enron's "risk management competencies") of how finance market innovations, including the use of derivative instruments, could "revolutionalize the energy market" and lead to "spectacular success" (Hamel, 2000: 219). While the much-debated Enron case left much of the free market model in ashes, being an embarrassing case for a long series of defined or self-declared economic authorities, Enron was still "the pioneer in financializing commodity and energy markets" (Omarova, 2013: 309). Enron's model blending commodities trade with finance instruments and finance trading became the new blueprint for the commodities trade market. When Enron failed, independent investment banks such as Goldman Sachs (hereafter Goldman) and Morgan Stanley were invited by U.S. regulatory authorities to become key players in the global markets for physical commodities and energy (Omarova, 2013: 309); the preeminence of Goldman, Morgan Stanley, and J.P. Morgan Chase (JPMC) as commodity derivatives dealers and their access to cheap credit and liquidity gave Goldman and Morgan Stanley "key advantage over large energy companies that attempted to replicate Enron's initial success" (Omarova, 2013: 309). The regulatory authorities approved Goldman, Morgan Stanley, and JPMC's applications to become so-called Bank Holding Companies (BHC) in

2008, "almost literally overnight, without putting them through its normal, lengthy and detailed review process," Omarova (2013: 310) argues. Prior to this licence being issued in September 2008, at the midst of a global finance industry meltdown, Goldman and Morgan Stanley were "independent investment banks with extensive equity investments in various commercial businesses" (Omarova, 2013: 311–312), but since September 2008, the two firms "[h]ave established themselves as the key players in the production, processing, transportation, storage, and trading of a wide range of physical commodities" (Omarova, 2013: 311–312). The legislation raising a firewall between banking and commerce, being a predominant political doctrine in U.S. industrial policy, was thus abandoned at short notice during the most turbulent period of Western capitalism in seven decades. This is arguably a remarkable policy of great significance.

Under all conditions, there is no doubt why this licence to trade commodities is attractive to Goldman and Morgan Stanley. Omarova (2013) point at two distinct benefits:

> There are two main reasons for this expansion. First, direct participation in the production and marketing of physical commodities yields crucial informational advantages for these firms' derivatives trading business. Continuous access to inside information on current price trends in the commodity spot markets enhances their ability to price and trade commodity-linked derivatives in the most profitable ways ... Second, the steady upward trend in global commodities prices since the early 2000s, going hand in hand with the increasing flow of financial investors' money into the sector, made physical commodity trading potentially a lucrative business in its own right. Buying, selling, storing, and moving commodities can generate handsome profits in a world that depends on the flow of these commodities for its very survival. (Omarova, 2013: 312)

Derivatives market actors benefit from access to information and the build-up of information collecting and processing competencies, and the licence to participate in lucrative markets is a benefit in its own right. If nothing else, Goldman's financial statements—not always so easy to lay hands on—indicate that the firm values such financial possibilities:

> Goldman's filings show more fluctuations in the gross fair value of physical commodities in the firm's inventory during the same three-year period. Specifically, as of March 31, 2009, Goldman reported $1.2 billion in this line item. At the end of the next quarter, the number fell to $682 million. It peaked at the end of 2010 at over $13 billion. As of March 31, 2012, Goldman reported the gross fair value of its physical commodities inventory at

$9.5 billion. At the end of 2012, Goldman's number rose to $11.7 billion. (Omarova, 2013: 273)

Goldman, the iconic Wall Street investment bank, not untarnished by rumours of self-serving behaviour at risk of generating wider socio-economic externalities, is thus a de facto key player in the American and global commodities market. In Omarova's (2013) view, this deviation from the received U.S. policy should be subject to extensive analysis, not least from the view of jurisprudence. First of all, Omarova (2013: 269–270) points at the concentration of power this model begets, merging banking and commerce: "When the same banking organizations that control access to money and credit also control access to such universal production inputs as raw materials and energy, they are in a position to exercise disproportionate control over the entire economic—and, by extension, political—system." The wider consequences of this key objection will be further discussed shortly, but Omarova (2013) also points to legal and risk management implications, including a series of difficult questions that need to be asked.

The legal objection is that the main reasons for not mixing banking with general commerce are (1) the need to preserve "the safety and soundness" of the federally insured U.S. banking system, and (2) the need to ensure "a fair and efficient flow of credit to productive economic enterprise" (i.e., commerce proper), and these are deemed to be two distinctively separated and separable political goals and policy objectives (Omarova, 2013: 343). In addition, as an auxiliary policy benefit, when separating the world of banking from the world of commerce, an "excessive concentration of financial and economic power" is avoided (Omarova, 2013: 343). Unfortunately, Omarova (2013: 333) argues, "Even a cursory overview of publicly available information shows that the current commodity operations of Morgan Stanley, Goldman, and JPMC … effectively nullify the principle of separating banking from commerce" (Omarova, 2013: 333). With the new policy, banking and commerce are two sides of the same coin, with significant consequences following. Omarova (2013: 338) here expresses her impatience with the tardiness of the implementation of the Dodd–Frank Act, the principal political response to the 2008 finance market collapse and "the most wide-ranging financial sector reform law since the Great Depression" (see also Wilmarth, 2013: 1289; Coffee, 2011b: 815; Tillman, 2012).[6] As Omarova (2013: 338) stresses, the "practical efficacy" of the Dodd–Frank Act depends on the "final outcomes of the long and complicated implementation process." Today, unfortunately, the subjects of the Dodd–Frank Act have been most successful in being able to postpone and neutralize the act's key component. Therefore, it is important, Omarova (2013: 340) warns, "not to underestimate financial institutions' proven ability to engage in successful regulatory arbitrage to avoid constraints on their profit-making activities." Finance institutions that have proved to be "too big to fail," may now also be "too big to regulate at all."

In terms of being a question of risk management policy making, Omarova (2013) finds few arguments justifying the policy reforms. Omarova addresses the case of Morgan Stanley, investing heavily in the energy commodities market, both lucrative in its own right and further capitalized on through the firm's issuing of securities and other derivative instruments, yet exposing the firm to considerable non-parametric risks, i.e., risks that are not possible to apprehend by present risk management calculations and methods:[7]

> [a] direct and active involvement in the business of oil and gas processing, storage, and transportation creates significant risks for Morgan Stanley. Global energy prices are notoriously volatile and depend on a complex interplay of various factors, including geopolitical ones. More importantly, however, these activities expose the firm to potential legal liability, financial loss, and reputational damage in the event of industrial accidents, oil spills, explosions, terrorist acts, or other catastrophic events that cause serious environmental harms. It is difficult to quantify the extent of this risk, especially in the case of potential large-scale environmental disaster, but it is not difficult to imagine that it may be potentially fatal even for a large company with a formidable balance sheet. For a financial institution whose main business depends greatly on its reputation and market perceptions of the quality of its credit, even a remote risk of such an event may be too much to live with. (Omarova, 2013: 317)

Even though Morgan Stanley per se is "too big to fail and to jail" (in the present day suggestive vocabulary), a major disaster falling upon the firm would have considerable consequences for the global finance system. Still, Omarova (2013) indicates risks on a high magnitude:

> Let us imagine, for example, that an accident or explosion on board an oil tanker owned and operated by one of Morgan Stanley's subsidiaries causes a large oil spill in an environmentally fragile area of the ocean. As the shocking news of the disaster spreads, it may lead Morgan Stanley's counterparties in the financial markets to worry about the firm's financial strength and creditworthiness. Because the full extent of Morgan Stanley's clean-up costs and legal liabilities would be difficult to estimate upfront, it would be reasonable for the firm's counterparties to seek to reduce their financial exposure to it. In effect, it could trigger a run on the firm's assets and bring Morgan Stanley to the verge of liquidity crisis or collapse. (Omarova, 2013: 344)

Taking legislative and regulatory reforms and the overbearing risks of the new governance regime aside, ultimately the question of whether financial oligopolies should be able to participate in the production and distribution of commodities is a wider political issue including the risks (and benefits, possibly) of the concentration of economic and political power in the hands of a small group of finance industry actors, historically being unhesitant to use their resources to inform policy making processes to their own advantage.

Concentration of Power and the Economic Subsidies of Large Banks

Omarova (2013: 345) emphasizes that banks perform a "special" public service and therefore enjoy a "special public subsidy through access to federal deposit insurance, special liquidity facilities, and other forms of implicit government guarantees." These unique packages of subsidies and exemptions create possibilities for "huge balance sheets, high credit ratings, and access to plentiful and relatively cheap financing," which in turn create sustainable competitive advantages for the banks that they can exploit if they compete with other firms that are not granted such privileges. As a consequence, finance industry actors represent not just *any* business charter, but a *specific* form of business charter of vital importance for the economic system of competitive capitalism. This in turn makes the regulation of the finance industry actors a key democratic concern: "The choice of moving into the physical commodities business does not belong solely to bank executives—the choice ultimately belongs to the taxpaying, bank-subsidizing public," Omarova (2013: 346) suggests. Omarova (2013: 350) argues that banks, already being too big to fail—and thus simply being "too big," in Alan Greenspan's account—should not be given "an additional source of leverage over the economy," as such a policy would elevate the risks of "cross-sector concentration of economic power" to an entirely new level. Needless to say, this concentration of economic power in the hands of the few is already at a significant level:

> In 1970, the five largest banks held 17% of banking assets, the next ninety-five banks had 37% of assets, and the 12,500 smallest banks had 48% of assets. By 2010, the share of the five largest banks had increased to 52% the share of the next ninety-five had dropped to 32%, and the share of the 5,700 smallest banks had plummeted to 16%. (Murdock, 2012: 541–542)

After the 2008 events, the finance industry was even further oligopolized as "the Big 14" were consolidated into even fewer megabanks (Blinder,

2013: 166–167, Table. 6.1; see also Bell and Hindmoor, 2015) as a consequence of deliberative political action: "Bank of America acquired Countrywide [Financial Corporation] and Merrill Lynch, and grew 138%; J.P Morgan Chase acquired Bear Stearns and Washington Mutual, and grew 51%; and Wells Fargo acquired Wachovia, and grew 43%" (Dallas, 2011: 280).

If finance institutions that already control and monitor the flow of finance capital in the economy are also capable of governing the supply of, e.g., raw materials and energy, especially if they can do so on the basis of the specific privileges they have received to accomplish the original former task, economic concentration becomes an economic and political issue (Omarova, 2013: 350). To address more technical details, still of great importance for policy making, when bundling the right to issue derivative instruments and to hold energy asset (say, in crude oil) contracts, firms with such licences may in fact benefit from the volatility of energy prices. If the price of the underlying asset were stable (or at least predictable on the basis of existing price-estimation models), there would be no reason for hedgers and speculators to enter into derivative contracts tied to that price. Conversely, if the price volatility is significant to the extent that fluctuating energy prices are deemed a systematic risk for key market actors, the higher demand for derivatives instruments enables a transfer of the underlying risk to other market actors (Omarova, 2013: 348). Therefore, Omarova (2013: 348) deduces, "this basic fact reveals the fundamental incentive for a derivatives dealer with sufficient market power in the underlying physical commodity markets to maintain price volatility in such markets, regardless of the fundamentals of supply and demand, as the necessary condition of continuing viability and profitability of its commodity derivatives business." Granting finance institutions the licence to simultaneously trade commodities and to issue derivative instruments tied to commodities prices thus invites speculation and permits moral hazard, which ultimately increases the cost of living for "ordinary Americans," Omarova (2013: 349) summarizes. While Goldman and Morgan Stanley predictably make the argument that such licences enhance their ability to predict derivative market asset price changes and therefore are conducive to overall market efficiency, that stipulated benefit comes at the cost of unprecedented concentration of economic power and a leverage of systemic risk. Moreover, the standard argument that what is "good for Goldman Sachs is good for the economy" rings hollow, especially after the debacle of 2008. The finance industry oligopolies have proven time and again that they are more concerned with the financial performance of their own industry than with socio-economic welfare, at best being tangential to or a side-effect of their operations.

The Consequences of Regulatory Failure: The Socialization of Risks and Losses, the Privatization of Benefits

The cases presented above, that of the securitization of home mortgage loans and the expansion of sub-prime markets, and the subsequent expansion of finance institute engagement in commodities trade, are two examples of consequences of less-than-perfect governance regimes. The "too big to fail" and "too big to jail" narratives have circulated in media and in scholarly quarters for more than a decade now, and there seems to be some apathy or cynicism regarding the democratically elected bodies'—the U.S. House of Representatives and the Senate and their defined regulatory agencies—abilities to tame the unruly and increasingly oligarchic finance industry. One of the key concerns is how the oligarchic finance industry is capable of privatizing profits while passing on the bill to the tax-payers in the case of losses. The de facto policy to bail out finance institutions in the event of default has a long but somewhat concealed tradition in U.S. politics, beginning with Paul Volcker's Federal Reserve chairmanship and being prolonged by Ben Bernanke during the 2008 events. In Conti-Brown's (2016: 57) account, Volcker, named chairman of Federal Reserve by President Jimmy Carter, "brought the [bail-out] doctrine into modern practice and provided the antecedents for its continued shelf life." Giving a speech in 1982 (cited by Panitch and Gindin, 2012: 179, original emphasis omitted), Volcker opened up for the "too big to fail" policy: "We are not here to see the economy destroyed in the interest of not bailing somebody out." The next Fed chairman that had to face economic realities as grim as Volcker was Ben Bernanke, a conservative Princeton economist, heavily influenced by Chicago economics school monetarism (Levitin, 2014: 1996), who followed the Volcker doctrine closely:

> "I think we did the right thing to try to preserve financial stability," [Ben Bernanke] said of the Bear [Steans] interventions. "That's our job. Yes, it's moral hazard-inducing, but the right way to address this question is not to let institutions fail and have a financial meltdown." (Ben Bernanke, former Fed Chairman, in an interview with Cassidy, 2009: 320)

Apparently, the alleged Social Darwinist features of the unforgiving market, separating the viable economic actors from the weak and faltering, otherwise praised by free market protagonists, is thus mysteriously overlooked when it comes to the most powerful and financially influential actors. "The survival of the fittest" here simply means "the survival of those with political clout," but as the free market model advocacy is based on the pricing mechanism, and politics otherwise being dismissed as an illegitimate intervention into supposedly self-regulating and self-correcting free markets, the Volcker doctrine is a puzzling component in the free market model. In what is otherwise claimed to be a robust model of economic price-setting and transactions, suddenly, when strong incentives to deviate from the otherwise pre-scribed model emerge, a resolution system that guarantees full operative security for actors at the apex of the finance system is introduced (Pistor, 2013).

The bailout of the U.S. finance industry in the autumn of 2008 is a prime example of how the Volcker doctrine is translated into practical action. Facing resistance in Congress, Secretary of Treasury Hank Paulson's "three-page proposal" named the Troubled-Assets Relief Program (TARP) was voted down on Monday September 29, but as the crisis deepened, the Congress passed the bill on Friday, October 3, 2008 (Blinder, 2013: 161). In order to fulfil its purpose, TARP stated few conditions to be fulfilled to "avoid stigma," a doctrine, Blinder (2013: 202) argued, that dominated the TARP design. In other words, the finance industry that would squander billions or even trillions of U.S. dollars, and that would create the recession that lasted for more than a decade, was treated with great leniency to enable a restoration of the faith in the global finance system. The credit system being at the core of the global capitalist economy, despite its mind-boggling complexity and labyrinthine features, was thus in the end dependent on the sovereign state and its political support and economic assistance: "[T]he decision to infuse banks with capital under the 2008 Troubled Asset Relief Program was made in part to encourage banks to continue lending and to refrain from dramatically reducing their lending capacity" (Peek and Rosengren, 2016: 85).

In the quite extensive post-2008 literature, there are many explanations of the causes of the events, but there is a consistency in recognizing that the market-based regulatory system, with credit rating agencies serving as the watchdogs that failed to serve this role, does not work as well in real-world economies as it does in the free market protagonist's textbook market model. In addition, few, with the exception of a handful of libertarians whose knee-jerk reaction is to dismiss anything the state and the government do as cost-inducing and efficiency-reducing interventions, saw any alternatives to the bailout. In the worst case scenario, commentators claimed, the entire global capitalist economic system would be brought to a standstill, with devastating consequences for the proverbial "man on the street." Levitin (2016: 409) argues persuasively that bailout as a standardized ex-post resolution policy is here to stay as the global finance industry reveals a complexity and entanglement with the "real economy" to the point where it is no longer possible to separate the two in meaningful ways: "Despite the post-2008 'never again' rhetoric, the bailouts of 2008 are a stark reminder that 'too big to fail' markets are implicitly guaranteed." If bailouts are separated from their economic connotations and are instead treated as a governance device, bailouts can assume the role of a mechanism that kicks in "[w]henever the market's failure threatens politically unbearable social consequences," Levitin (2016: 449) suggests.

Levitin, a legal scholar, is no free market protagonist, and nor is he turning a blind eye to already considerable finance industry privileges and subsidies, but to assume that bailouts will not be part of the arsenal of governance devices that democratically elected institutions access is naïve, Levitin (2016) claims. Rather than being "exceptional," "a singular event," or "a unique occurrence," Levitin (2014: 2030) argues elsewhere, the financial crisis of 2008 showed that "[t]he entire financial system is guaranteed by the federal government, either explicitly or implicitly" (see also Pistor, 2013). In the present economic system of competitive capitalism, characterized by "a highly leveraged financial system" being granted the political privilege and the concession to "privatize gains and socialize losses," "the only thing preventing bailouts is a more robustly capitalized financial system" (Levitin, 2014: 2030). However, the increased costs for higher capitalization (i.e., the equity-to-outstanding-liabilities ratio is lowered to reduce default risks) will be externalized to clients, and therefore the aggregated cost of "economic stability" may still be higher in the increased capitalization scenario than in the bailout scenario. The privilege to be bailed out by the sovereign state, i.e., to socialize losses, may therefore, despite its political costs and consequences—finance industry millionaire professionals enjoying levels of operative security that no other group can dream of, especially in the market theory model—have social welfare benefits competing models cannot surpass. In addition, this seems to be—unsurprisingly—a model that also the finance industry actors themselves endorse. For instance, Murdock (2012: 541) cites a Standard & Poor's statement from 2011, wherein the firm representative argued that "[G]iven the import-ance of confidence sensitivity in the effective functioning of banks, we believe that under certain circumstances and with selected systemically important financial institutions ... future extraordinary government support is still possible." This reads quite clearly as a willingness to pass on the bill to tax-payers whenever the industry ends up in a situation where the "confidence" in the industry is at stake, i.e., during episodes of self-inflicted crises. For Standard & Poor's, the option to have the federal state as a standing reserve is apparently an attractive scenario. It is likely that many other actors bestowed with such extraordinary privileges would agree on this statement.

After the Crisis: Regulatory Capture and the Inertia of Political Bodies

The post-2008 literature is quite detailed on the aggregated costs of the entire finance industry collapse. Blyth (2013: 45) argues that the 2008 bailout cost US$1.75 trillion, or 12.1% of the U.S. GDP; in the UK, the same figure accounted for 12.8% of the GDP (Blyth, 2013: 45). Other commentators has calculated substantially higher economic costs when the wider economic consequences are included: "[T]he $700 billion was only the tip of the iceberg in terms of the financial assistance provided to the big banks. Bloomberg reported that the federal government pledged over $12.8 trillion to avoid a financial meltdown" (Murdock, 2012: 507). That is quite a bit of money and the transfer of this finance capital primarily resulted in people at the bottom of the income pyramid suffering the losses and the wider socio-economic consequences. Yet, if finance regulation is a governance problem at the core, then it is of great interest to examine how the most devastating economic crisis in generations materialized into novel legislation and policies. For those who hoped for the 2008 finance industry meltdown to serve as an epiphany or a turning point for how economic affairs are being governed and regulated, the outcomes were excruciatingly disappointing, Pontusson and Raess's (2012) review of the literature indicates:

> One thing seems clear: in none of our five countries [examined] did governments articulate structural reform of the financial sector as a policy goal during the bailouts of financial institutions in 2008–2009. To the extent that policy makers recognized the need for structural reform, they were willing to postpone any legislation in this realm for the sake of rapidly implementing short-term measures they considered essential to restoring the provision of credit to households and companies. (Pontusson and Raess, 2012: 27)

Similarly, Münnich (2016: 284), examining the political responses in the U.K. and Germany, argues that the changes in legislation and regulatory oversight have been only marginal: "[W]e have seen only a modest adjustment of capital market regulation, marked by the new Basel III capitalization rules and a gradual reform of banking oversight in the EU."

Münnich (2016) argues that politicians and policy makers in two dominant European states, hosting finance industries closely bound up with the global, U.S.-led finance industry, invoked various normative and moral ideas to make sense out of the events of 2008. Claiming that a minority of finance traders participated in harmful "speculation," and that an otherwise sound national finance industry was "contaminated from the outside," were two of the normative ideas circulating in political quarters, serving to prevent or postpone legislative action and regulatory reform. In other words, the finance industry has been most successful in selling the image of itself as a socio-economic welfare generating industry that fares best when being left on its own, but still occasionally suffering from the opportunistic behaviour of a small group of actors succumbing to illicit behaviour when being put under pressure to compete:[8]

> Facing uncertainty at the onset of the crisis, policymakers oriented their crisis perception along the assumption that it had been caused by financial actors pursuing illegitimate, immoral forms of profit. Policymakers and public commentators from all camps in Germany agreed that the crisis had been caused by bankers engaging with speculative activities rather than providing real economy investment. In the British debate, a major cause of the crisis was seen in traders gaining profits without being able to secure an effective management of economic risks. This moral filtering of the public debates left policymakers blind for the domestic structural and organizational dimensions of the crisis in both countries. The core problem of the boom years was the explosion of leverage and a growing interdependence of all financial corporations. For both countries, this meant that the largest parts of their financial sectors had been fully engaged in or even driven the international securitization process. (Münnich, 2016: 303)

In a similar manner, in the U.S., Paul Krugman has argued (cited in Crotty, 2009: 578), leading politicians such as Tim Geithner, President Obama's Secretary of Treasury, "have made clear that they still have faith in the people who created the financial crisis." Moreover, Geithner stated that the private finance system model is still to be trusted, as "governments do a bad job in running banks"—"as opposed, presumably, to the wonderful jobs the private bankers have done," Krugman remarks—and that bailouts and other guarantees and privileges would continue to come with no strings attached. Even at the height of the most brutal, devastating economic crisis in generations, there is little evidence of any second thoughts about the power concentration and risks in the finance industry. To explain this political inertia and conceptual blindfolding, the term regulatory capture is useful.

Regulatory capture

As a legal and practical matter, in the U.S., "most financial regulatory policy is carried out by independent agencies" (Levitin, 2014: 2037). Such agencies can be government-sponsored or private companies, but they operate with an arms'-length's distance from the democratically elected political bodies that pass legislation. This distance is institutionalized to insulate regulatory agencies from political turf games and short-termism: "The purpose of agency independence is to free policy-making from political interests, allow it to be set in reliance on objective scientific facts, and avoid the delays and distortions of politics" (Levitin, 2014: 2037). Unfortunately, the finance industry crisis of 2008 served to discredit the ideal of a "politically insulated, technocratic administrative agency," Levitin (2014: 2038) argues: "A regulatory system created under years of technocratic oversight collapsed in spectacular fashion, leaving technocrats bewildered and even panicked" (Levitin, 2014: 2038). The claim of technocratic or scientific expertise, justifying regulatory licences and accompanying privileges (i.e., the autonomy from political institutions), were thus undermined by evidence of incompetence and failure (Levitin, 2014: 2038). If Levitin's (2014) assessment of the political climate after 2008 is correct, the question is then why is there such an alarming tardiness in the response to the overbearing risks derived from what is now an even more concentrated and oligopolistic finance industry? Levitin (2014) points at a number of conditions.

First of all, corporate power and the capacity to orchestrate what is called *regulatory capture* matters. Regulatory capture means that corporations and industries are capable of influencing legislation, law enforcement, and the accompanying regulatory practices in ways that are inconsistent with constitutional statutes and/or stated political goals. "Regulatory capture may take the form of regulatory forbearance, the acceptance by the regulator of deviant behavior by the regulated," Thiemann and Lepoutre (2017: 1779–1780) argue. Regulatory capture is in short industry having a say and an influence in areas it should not, *de jure* and de facto, be able to inform.

Second, *agency capture* means that corporations or industries are capable of informing or influencing the work of regulatory agencies in ways that are inconsistent with constitutional statutes and/or stated political goals. Levitin (2014: 2042) lists a long series of mechanisms that are conducive to agency capture, including agencies that rely on regulated industries to access information, revolving-door employment, and groupthink. Agency capture can also happen on the basis of "[r]egulators all approaching problems with similar methodology, training, and experience, and through social chumminess between regulators and regulated entities" (Levitin, 2014: 2042). Agency capture is thus essentially a concern derived from human nature being what it is, and on the grounds that relevant and useful information is costly to collect and process, two conditions which in turn put pressure on regulatory agencies to act with prudence, and to carefully monitor agents' relations with the regulated industries.

Third, in addition to regulatory and agency capture, Levitin (2014: 2042–2043) addresses *ideological capture*, wherein regulators "[b]ecome enthralled by a particular ideological view of how the world operates (or should operate)," as an issue to consider. Levitin's (2014) ideological capture is thus tangential to what Thiemann and Lepoutre (2017: 1780) refer to as *cognitive capture*, the tendency that the frequent interaction between regulators and the regulated leads to joint ways of thinking and perceiving the world, no longer imposing meaningful and functional discriminatory demarcation lines between the two parties. For instance, if both market actors and regulators share the conviction that markets are most efficient when left on their own to self-correct and restore themselves in the event of economic crises—a textbook case of a free market theory position—as was the case of the Federal Reserve chairmanship of Alan Greenspan and his successor Ben Bernanke, regulative practices are easily shaped by such ideological beliefs. Despite being concerned about the consequences of cognitive capture, Thiemann and Lepoutre (2017: 1780) still tone down the risk of collaborative interactions: "While regulators, by the nature of their profession, may have to interact closely with the regulated ... it has been shown that cognitive capture does not necessarily result from such interactions."

Fourth, Levitin (2014: 2044) speaks about *legislative capture*, which means that corporations or industries, either directly or through their defined agents, are capable of influencing and informing legislative processes in ways that benefit their interests. In the case of the finance industry, there is ample evidence of legislative capture (e.g., Mian, Sufi, and Trebbi, 2010; Thornburg and Roberts, 2008). Such capacities are essentially a function of the access to finance capital that can be transferred to policy making bodies for the benefit of industry interests: "The financial services industry exercises considerable political clout, in large part through massive political campaign donations and lobbying" (Levitin, 2014: 2044). For instance, in the 2012 election cycle only, the financial services sector, including individuals, "gave over $670 million in campaign contributions" (Levitin, 2014: 2044). Wilmarth (2013: 1293) reports that the finance industry spent more than US$8.6 billion on "political contributions and lobbying between 1998 and 2012," whereof US$5.34 billion was committed to lobbying (a sum in parity with the lobbying expenses of "Miscellaneous Business" and "Health," with US$5.42 billion and US$5.35 billion spent on lobbying in the period, respectively). This tendency to influence the political system on the basis of economic incentives and direct campaign contributions is an over-arching tendency in the American political system, coinciding (or being co-produced, some might say) with growing economic inequality, expanding the pool of political contributors. "Campaign contributions by individuals have grown over time, with 3,138,564 individuals making itemized contributions in 2012 compared to 224,322 in 1980," Bonica et al. (2013: 111) write. More specifically, it is the top 0.01 percent of the income earners who make around 40 percent of the campaign contributions, Bonica et al. (2013: 111) show: "[T]he share of total income received by the top 0.01 percent of households is about 5 percent but that the share of campaign contributions made by the top 0.01 percent of the voting age population is now over 40 percent." Such evidence indicates that the political system is exposed to economic power in ways that may undermine the legitimacy of democratic institutions, many commentators have warned time and again. Not the least Barack Obama (cited in Mayer, 2016: 321) has remarked that "inequality distorts our democracy": "It gives an outsized voice to the few who can afford high-priced lobbyists and unlimited campaign contributions, and it runs the risk of selling out our democracy to the highest bidder."

In addition to the "revolving door practices" in Washington and other political centres (Vidal, Draca, and Fons-Rosen, 2010), creating systemic risks derived from various forms of regulatory capture, Thiemann and Lepoutre (2017) add that the sheer complexity of what is being regulated, especially in transnational governance wherein local, federal, regional, and international legislation and regulatory frameworks may create ambiguities, or, on the contrary, "regulatory holes" that may create possibilities for arbitrage, needs to be considered when monitoring regulatory practices. The "increasing complexity of the systems regula-tors have to supervise" include not only "myriad products and activities being regulated," but also involves the condition that "several competing regulators arguably have simultaneous jurisdictions over any given prod-uct or activity" (Thiemann and Lepoutre, 2017: 1780). In the finance industry, the ambiguities generated in this regulatory regime, including transnational rules and "the transient nature of these regulations," create a space for national regulators to "exercise their discretion and choose how and when to engage regulated banks and intermediate gatekeepers in the rule-making and rule-enforcement process" (Thiemann and Lepoutre, 2017: 1795). In this view, regulation unfolds as a form of legal-practical field that has a hard time moving in lock-step with, e.g., the underlying high-paced trade in the finance industry, being at best partial and incomplete and thus providing opportunities for rule evasion and to act with impunity.

Taken together, the four categories of capture (regulatory, agency, ideological, and legislative capture) all contribute to a situation wherein the finance industry is capable of shaping the legislative and regulatory framework to their own advantage. This is arguably the reason why the finance industry has been so remarkably successful in privatizing profits and socializing losses, a de facto policy that tax-payers with only limited direct interest in the finance industry may find puzzling, and that suffers from democratic deficit. In the extreme position, such activities can be seen as the mechanism through which the finance industry is hi-jacking the economic system of competitive capitalism and takes the tax-payers as hostages. More puzzling still, democratically elected institutions have apparently little interest in amending the situation, Levitin (2014) suggests. The short-term orientation of political actors and the lack of incentives to re-regulate what no one notices as long as it works thus undermine solid finance industry regulation, conducive to median voter interests.

At the same time as these conditions are repeated in the literature, "the reasons for the lack of interest in a more democratically responsive financial system in the United States are not clear," Levitin (2014: 2052) argues. More generally, the inability of democratic institutions to successfully fight economic inequality has been a source of scholarly inquiry (Jacobs and Dirlam, 2016; Bonica et al., 2013; Gilens, 2012). Still, there is evidence of regulatory efforts that are successful, especially when regulators are "embedded in the interpretive communities" of the regulated actors, so that regulators are cognizant of "rule-bending behavior" that better equips them with the capacity to re-regulate when needed:

> We show that when the regulator is both central in the network of actors that determine the meaning of compliance and linked to both the regulated and semiprivate gatekeepers, creative compliance will less likely go undetected and provide regulators with the capabilities to constrain such behavior. In contrast, the more peripheral regulators are to these networks, or the more they lack diversity of perspectives in their network by being connected only to the regulated, the more markets will evolve in ways that reflect creative compliance of the regulated. (Thiemann and Lepoutre, 2017: 1778)

Such evidence suggests that effective market regulation "requires more, not less, interaction between regulators, the regulated, and the gate-keepers" (Thiemann and Lepoutre, 2017: 1814); to regulate means to be in the "middle of things," yet to maintain the integrity to uphold meaningful lines of demarcation between the regulator and the regulated.

Furthermore, Levitin (2014) argues that there is a trade-off between finance market stability and economic growth, and that policy makers thus need to determine a tolerable level of instability (resulting in a larger supply of cheap finance capital that can be invested in, e.g., entrepreneurial ventures) to maximize the economic growth enabled by a defined stock of capital. Even though stable growth may be preferable to volatile growth over the long term, the political system and its mediatized communication with voters and other relevant actors tend to make short-term outcomes what matters politically. The short-termism is ultimately a form of temporal tragedy and a social dilemma of democratic societies, wherein individually elected politicians need to demonstrate their wins-to-losses ratio to their constituencies to be able to secure campaign funding and to earn political support. Therefore, Levitin (2014: 2037) continues, "growth is more alluring than stability as it offers immediate distributional and hence political benefits, as long as the costs of volatility can be pushed into the future." Therefore, as factual matter, the "time inconsistency" of political preferences between growth and stability "shades any discussion of bank capital requirements" (Levitin, 2014: 2037); politicians may know or intuitively understand that a too lax political–legislative system sub-optimizes the net economic welfare of the finance industry system, but their own individual incentives prevent them from overcoming institutional inertia. Politicians are thus incentivized to demonstrate what can be referred to as a "rational passivity," which in turn justifies lenient regulation and generous resolution systems.

Still, the original question remains, surfacing time and again during recurrent financial crises, of how politicians' lack of incentives to embark on the project to institute more robust regulatory frameworks should be handled; "there is little upside for politicians in pursuing better financial regulation. No one notices financial regulation when it works. There is no reward for doing a good job" (Levitin, 2014: 2053). Such a lack of incentives is accentuated when the risks of regulatory capture looms, especially in industries with both deep pockets and whose run-of-the-mill practices are non-transparent for "everyday people"—in fact, even in the event of the largest crisis in seven decades unfolding, few people beyond a few experts, functionaries, and scholars are informed about its causes and consequences. One of the reasons why the renowned Princeton economist and former Federal Reserve director Alan Blinder invested time and effort to write his authoritative overview of the 2008 events was to enlighten the American public of the risks they are now exposed to on an everyday basis: *"The American people still don't quite know what hit them*, and why it happened, or what the authorities did about it—especially why government officials took so many and unusual and controversial actions," Blinder claims (2013: xvi, emphasis in the original). In the end, too many people, whereof some should arguably be more informed than they have proven themselves to be in the trial of fire, are left in the dark regarding the wheeling and dealing of the global finance industry. It is advisable that this situation is amended.

SUMMARY AND CONCLUSION

As in all "good governance" (see e.g. Aguilera and Cuervo-Cazurra, 2004), it is most complicated to strike a balance between regulatory oversight and control, and mechanisms that benefit innovation and venturing in finance industry governance. Financial innovations such as securities and junk bonds in many cases do contribute to a more efficient allocation of capital as also high-risk assets may have a market value for certain market actors. Unfortunately, financial innovations are also at risk of being abused in, e.g., predatory lending campaigns that serve to privatize economic rents, while passing on the costs for the systemic risks to the broader community of finance market actors and the lender-of-last-resort, the sovereign state and its tax-payers. As has been emphasized in the literature on finance market crises, in the upward movement phase, there is little concern regarding the expansion of credit and debt and the leverage of risk, but in the downward movement phase, commentators, pundits, policy makers, and the wider public quickly lose patience with finance industry activities. The over-confident belief in the robustness of the finance industry in the upward phase and the at times close to hysterical reactions to the lost ground in the downward phase is per se an intriguing social and economic phenomenon, certainly worthy of more detailed scholarly inquiry. Instead of singlehandedly praising the finance industry in the good times and demonizing it when things turn bleak, the underlying incentives, performance–reward, and compensation systems being implemented should be examined in detail to better understand the collective, yet uncoordinated action of finance market actors. Such an analysis indicates that the finance industry incentive systems are not of necessity conducive to net economic welfare; the benefits of the few in, e.g., commodities market speculation generate costs that are carried by the many. In a democratic political system, there are consequently strong incentives to actually govern the finance industry to better align individual and collective interests, but without eliminating the possibilities for innovation and venturing. Needless to say, the design, implementation, and enforcement of such a governance system is a far from trivial assignment.

NOTES

1. The Dodd–Frank Act in the U.S. and the Basel III regulatory framework, two immediate political responses to the finance industry crisis, are frequently cited as "causes for the ostensibly worsening liquidity" (Adrian et al., 2017: 44). "All major US dealers are now subject to the Federal Reserve's stress tests and enhanced capital and liquidity requirements, as well as the more stringent Basel III rules," Adrian et al. (2017: 48) write. Liquidity, and more specifically *asset liquidity*, is here defined as "the cost of exchanging assets for cash," and is an important indicator of economic fitness as asset illiquidity "deters trade and hence investment, impeding the efficient allocation of risk and capital in the economy" (Adrian et al., 2017: 44). In mainstream economics theory, regulations and other market restrictions reduce liquidity and impose additional costs on market actors. Nevertheless, Adrian et al.'s (2017) review of the literature on liquidity in finance markets (in turn related to the supply of credit and the cost of finance capital) reveals no major decline in liquidity: "Despite the many factors affecting dealer business models, we do not uncover clear evidence of a widespread worsening of liquidity in two markets in which dealers remain important market makers (Adrian et al., 2017: 48). Such evidence is of relevance for the substantiation of the "growth versus stability" proposition that Levitin (2014: 2036) stipulates. The shift from "volatile growth" to increased stability in finance markets may in fact not have the draconian effects on growth, credit supply, liquidity, and other economic fundamentals as critics of regulatory control predict.
2. Pernell, Jung, and Dobbin (2017) argue that the Sarbanes–Oxley Act (commonly abbreviated as SOX) generated new risk management practices that were harmful for long-term economic stability. One of the implications of SOX was that "CEOs were particularly keen to signal they were serious about compliance because SOX made them personally responsible for risk control," Pernell, Jung, and Dobbin (2017: 513) argue. A new category of "risk experts" argued that "they could keep executives out of jail" (Pernell, Jung, and Dobbin, 2017: 513), and were thus successful in advancing their professional jurisdiction under the SOX statutes. Whereas previous risk experts thought their duty was to "minimize costs, prevent major losses, and avoid catastrophe," i.e., represented a more conservative view of the term "risk," the new generation of risk experts no longer saw as their goal to "avoid risk" but to "optimize risk," given certain levels of returns stipulated (Pernell, Jung, and Dobbin, 2017: 515). To pursue their goal of "maximizing risk-adjusted returns," the new generation of risk experts enacted derivatives as the primary tool to enable "quick, precise, and efficient adjustments to mortgage, bond, and currency exposures" (Pernell, Jung, and Dobbin, 2017: 512). While the use of derivatives has been closely associated with "speculation," and, by implication, "gambling" (Lynch, 2011)—every finance trader's demon—the new risk experts, so-called Chief Risk Officers (CROs), served a wider symbolic function in the finance industry, namely to provide a "moral licence" to trade derivatives on an industrial basis. This moral licence in turn justified a series of activities that arguably was not intended by the Sarbanes–Oxley legislators:

   > We suggest that a form of organization-level moral licensing was at work in this case: in appointing CROs, banks signaled to trading-desk managers that they worked at a "risk aware" firm, and that risk management was someone else's job. This, we propose, reduced desk managers' self-monitoring of risky behavior. Creating a new office to manage compliance can lull managers into a false sense of security, promoting exactly the behavior that regulation was intended to prevent. (Pernell, Jung, and Dobbin, 2017: 512)

The empirical material reported by Pernell, Jung, and Dobbin (2017: 525) demonstrates an association between the presence of CROs and "greater holdings of over-the-counter options, swaps, and credit derivatives." At the same time, the role of the CRO and the degree of derivatives holdings more specifically are determined by the interests, incentives, and performance–reward systems, wherein top executives with an interest in "boosting short-term returns" may approve derivatives trade, whereas institutional investors or CEOs being more risk averse may "restrain CRO promotion of new derivatives" (Pernell, Jung, and Dobbin, 2017: 525). The Sarbanes–Oxley Act was thus intentionally leaving it to the market actors such as corporations to monitor and assess their exposure to market risk, but the unintended consequences of the legislative reform was that CROs hired by corporations to signal compliance with the new, more risk-averse regulatory framework, served to redefine the idea of risk and provided moral licences to expose the firm to even higher non-parametric risk, i.e., uncertainty. Seen in this light, the critical view of the market-based self-regulation mandated by SOX taken by, e.g., Soederberg (2008) are worthy of more detailed scholarly attention.

3. It is telling, Brennan (2014: 251) remarks, that the change in trading behaviour in the 1980s, 1990s, and 2000s turned finance markets from being the sites where non-financial businesses supplied initial public offerings of shares into sites wherein these corporations on net were purchasing more equity than they raised capital. The finance market is thus no longer primarily serving the role of allocating capital on the basis of finance market actors' uncoordinated and dispersed investment decisions—which had typically been the case before the 1980s, and which serves as the axiomatic first principle in free market theory advocacy—but as an external market providing various mechanisms, operations, and devices (e.g., stock repurchase programmes, derivatives trade, securitization at various levels) supportive of the corporations' maximization of returns on equity at stipulated levels of risk.

4. "The expectations-based hypothesis that high price expectations by lenders are responsible for the expansion in sub-prime mortgage credit from 2002 to 2005" is credible, Mian and Sufi (2009: 1454) argue.

5. Given the difficulty in pricing CDOs and assessing their market risks, it is unsurprisingly hedge funds, leading a new wave of shareholder activism, which are both potent and controversial inasmuch as they prompt debates about whether activism "creates, captures, or destroys corporate value" (Goranova and Ryan, 2014: 1241), that are the foremost investors in CDOs. As opposed to more "governance-oriented activism," seeking to gain the political control over corporations, hedge fund managers target "more profitable and financially healthy firms" (Goranova and Ryan, 2014: 1243) to extract economic value on behalf of their clients. As a consequence of this investment strategy, Coffee and Palia (2016: 550) write, hedge fund activism is associated with (1) "increased leverage," i.e., higher levels of debt in targeted firms, (2) "increased shareholder payout (through either dividends or stock buybacks)," and (3) "reduced long-term investment in research and development (R&D)." While other fund managers, e.g., in pension funds or mutual funds, can be expected to demonstrate "rational apathy," which is characteristic for "more diversified and even indexed investors," hedge fund managers actively coordinate their activism to increase their return. Being incentivized to expose themselves to high risks, hedge fund managers have a considerably higher risk-appetite than most market actors (Kahan and Rock, 2007).

    The estimated worth of outstanding CDOs at the end of 2006 was US$3 trillion, a class of finance assets based on the pooling of mortgage-backed securities, "mainly comprising those backed by subprime and other non-conforming mortgage loans, with other asset-backed securities as collateral" (Lysandrou, 2011: 325). While hedge funds held only 1 percent of the world's "total stock of securities" at the time, valued at US$122 trillion, the hedge funds held *nearly half* of all outstanding CDOs (Lysandrou, 2011: 336). As the hedge fund instrument is designed to generate above-average returns for their clients (a service for which they get paid above-average fees), hedge fund managers are pushed into investment in increasingly risky assets, also being more complicated to price and to handle through the risk management routines being implemented, either voluntarily on the basis of perceived market risks or as a consequence of regulatory reform. In Lysandrou's (2011: 326) account, it was "the unexpectedly rapid collapse of the CDO market" that led to the "breakdown in trust between the large commercial banks," in the next stage leading to the cardiac arrest of the global finance industry in the autumn of 2008.

This story has been told several times and with great detail and precision, but the question remains, why was there such a demand for high-risk finance assets in the 2002–2007 period? In Lysandrou's (2011: 335) view, the excessive demand for finance market investments, especially high-yield products, propelled the sub-prime home mortgage loan market, in turn generating mortgage-backed securities and, on the "second floor level," high-risk/high-yield products such as CDOs: "[I]n the search for yield, investors pressured the investment banks to supply structured credit products in ever greater quantities and, to do this, these banks needed the mortgage originators to take whatever steps were necessary to induce as many subprime borrowers as was possible to take out mortgage loans." This market demand was in turn derived from the liquidity preference of finance market actors, translated into an excessive extraction of economic value from non-financial companies, generating a surplus finance capital problem and having its source in policies and corporate governance practices conducive to economic inequality: "Just as wage earners typically faced the problem of how to make up the shortfall between current income and consumption, so did immensely wealthy individuals typically face the opposite problem of where to store their wealth," Lysandrou (2011: 324) summarizes.

6.   More specifically, Section 737 of the Dodd–Frank Act was written with "the clear goal" of returning to the kind of "hard position limits" for noncommercial financial institutions that prevailed before the Commodity Futures Trading Commission (CFTC) granted "stealth staff exemptions from the position limits requirements" of the Commodity Exchange Act of 1936 (CEA), Greenberger (2013: 709) argues. That is, under the strictures of Section 737, CFTC should no longer be able to issue trade licences to financial institutions, granting them the right to participate in, e.g., commodities trade.

7.   For an extended analysis of risk management theory and its practical applications, see e.g., Hardy and Magire (2016), Ellul (2015), Millo and Mackenzie (2009), and Spira and Page (2002).

8.   In fact, the belief in the behaviour of a "small, deviant group" explaining a system-wide collapse is untenable on scientific grounds. Mishina et al. (2010) demonstrate that the risks of "corporate illegality," defined as "an illegal act primarily meant to benefit a firm by potentially increasing revenues or decreasing costs" (Mishina et al., 2010: 702), is a systemic concept that can be explained on the basis of corporate and industry characteristics. The risks of corporate illegality are higher when three distinct conditions exist: (1) when firms are historically successful and where "high social aspirations" are encouraged (as in the case of most "elite firms"; see, e.g., Rivera and Tilcsik, 2016; Rivera, 2015); (2) when the high social aspirations are challenged by prospects of "poor future relative performance"; and (3) when, e.g., shareholders and other external stakeholders put pressure on organizations "to meet or exceed the expectations." This third factor only applies to "prominent firms," Mishina et al. (2010: 716) add. Kilduff et al. (2016: 1509) demonstrate that rivalry, a "relationship between a focal actor and a target actor that is characterized by the experience of heightened psychological stakes of competition by the focal actor when competing against the target actor," is a key factor to consider when explaining opportunistic behaviour: "[A]ctors who feel rivalry towards their opponents are more likely to engage in the kind of behavior that defines the ugly side of competition, including deception, cheating, and sabotage," Kilduff et al. (2016: 1529) summarize.

As the finance industry is characterized by harsh competition and fierce rivalry (see, e.g., Ho, 2009), the thesis regarding individuals' deviations from the protocol seem both incredible on theoretical grounds and empirically unsubstantiated. In their conclusion, Mishina et al. (2010: 717) suggest that corporate illegality is partially explained by leadership practices and the governance function of corporations, especially in firms where executives are constantly pressured to achieve "better and better relative performance" and where, e.g., directors are "unforgiving of any slips." Intense competition, the prestige of the firm, and the pressures of stakeholders, most notably active shareholders, are thus systemic conditions that predict corporate illegality more accurately than the folk psychology idea of individuals failing to live up to highly stated ethical norms; corporate illegality is a group phenomenon rather than the individual's deplorable failure.

Furthermore, this evidence casts doubt on the virtues and socio-economic benefits of competition more generally, being, as Charness, Masclet, and Villeval (2014: 38) discuss, widely seen as the gateway to optimal use of economic and social resources in economic theory:

> It is traditionally assumed in standard economic theory that competition is desirable for several different reasons. Competition leads to an efficient allocation of productive resources on the market, giving consumers better products of a lower price. It promotes innovation by increasing the cost of failing to invest in research and development. Competition also enhances overall performance within firms by inducing employees to exert higher work effort. (Charness, Masclet, and Villeval, 2014: 38)

Reporting a study of how ranking and the introduction of a flat wage setting in a defined community affects the behaviour of the experimental subjects, Charness, Masclet, and Villeval (2014) show that increased competition leads to higher levels of sabotage, which in turn induces economic and social costs. When wages are fixed, the experimental data shows, "many individuals exhibit competitive behavior," but when ranking is introduced, which de facto creates additional incentives, "unethical behavior" becomes more common as "some individuals are willing to pay to improve their rank by sabotaging others' work or by increasing artificially their own relative performance" (Charness, Masclet, and Villeval, 2014: 41). One of the managerial implications is that it is unclear *a priori* whether sabotage and opportunistic behaviour more generally are more widespread under a flat-wage scheme compared with a performance-based scheme (Charness, Masclet, and Villeval, 2014: 53), i.e., the increased competition introduced on the basis of "rank feedback" (Charness, Masclet, and Villeval, 2014: 50) is not per se conducive to firm-specific advantages or socio-economic benefits. In theoretical terms, competition may do good or it may be harmful, and the outcome is dependent on wider social norms and practices, the studies of Mishina et al. (2010), Kilduff et al. (2016), and Charness, Masclet, and Villeval (2014) demonstrate.

PART III

Theoretical and practical implications

5. The unfinished business of governance: towards new governance regimes

INTRODUCTION

As the three previous chapters have indicated, there is a trade-off between stability and efficiency in the economic system. Expressed differently, when the balance of power favours market efficiency, this translates into a political accountability problem, as the claim that the overarching goal of economic policy is to maximize economic efficiency implies lenient regulatory activities, which by implication undermine the active role of democratically elected political entities. Coffee (2011b) points at this tension in the field of finance market regulation:

> [F]inancial institutions are a special case. Given the natural tension between the social interest in prudent bank regulation and the shareholder interest in profit maximization through higher leverage, corporate governance reforms that enhance shareholder power may at the same time weaken regulatory control over financial institutions. (Coffee, 2011b: 814)

What Coffee (2011b: 815) calls the "fundamental mismatch" between the banks' short-term character of their liabilities and the longer-term character of their assets, wherein depositors "expect and receive high liquidity," whereas borrowers "expect to repay their loans over a multi-year period," is a key concern for both industry actors and regulators as the stability/efficiency trade-off surfaces and needs to be handled. "Capitalism works only when institutions are forced to absorb the consequences of the risks that they take on. When banks can pocket the upside while spreading the cost of their failures, failure is almost certain," Mallaby (2010: 13) remarks. When the finance industry is left to regulate itself as it wishes, the efficiency criteria will dominate, historical records prove (Gerding, 2005). The preference for liquidity over illiquidity, and efficiency over stability, is justified by the incentives systems in the finance industry, which tend to underprice risk and thus to undermine prudential decision making. However, what still needs to be explained is "the deregulatory snowball" (Hammond and Knott, 1988) or deregulation processes and mechanisms more widely (Kroszner and Strahan, 1999) that have dominated, e.g., the finance industry over the last three decades, i.e., the shift in governance regime from one based on state-controlled agencies to one relying on market-based agencies (e.g., auditors and credit rating agencies).

To explain this shift in governance, a series of theories and empirical conditions at hand should be examined. First of all, the growth of lobbyism and "the activities of organized interest groups" (Bebchuk and Neeman, 2010: 1090) has arguably played an active role in shaping the new governance regime. For some commentators, lobbying is a perfectly legitimate mechanism in competitive industries (e.g., Hall and Deardorff, 2006), dependent on political influence to advance specific interests: "We view lobbying on investor protection as important because, in the ordinary course of events, most corporate issues are intensely followed by the interest group with sufficient stake and expertise but are not sufficiently understood and salient to most citizens," Bebchuk and Neeman (2010: 1090) write. Other commentators are more sceptical towards lobbying, primarily not because of its rent-seeking motivations, but because lobbying tends to tilt the balance of power between various stakeholders and interests, as certain market actors command financial resources that enable them to influence the political system in substantial ways. "Between 1998 and 2010, the amount of money all corporations reported spending on their own lobbyists increased by 85 percent, going from $1.13 billion in 1998 to $2.09 billion in 2010 (in constant 2012 dollars)," Drutman (2015: 12) reports. Translated into a business interest vis-à-vis nonbusiness and social interests ratio, in 2012 this ratio was 34-to-1, up from 22-to-1 in 1998 (Drutman, 2015: 13); that is, for every dollar spent on advocating nonbusiness and social interests, 34 dollars are at the same time spent on promoting business interests. Furthermore, Drutman (2015: 78) demonstrates, "[c]orporate lobbying is largely pro-active" (accounting for about 70 percent of all lobbyism spending) and 60 percent of all lobbying focus on "industry level" concerns, rather, the interests of specific firms (Drutman, 2015: 78, Table 4.3). This means that lobbying is essentially targeting policy making activities that shape the future of industries.

Another concern pertaining to lobbyism is the lack of discrimination between the political system and the lobbyism industry, with "revolving door lobbyists" (Vidal, Draca, and Fons-Rosen, 2010) moving back and forth between political entities and lobbyist firms in Washington, DC and elsewhere. As a condition that compromises the political accountability of democratically elected institutions, lobbyism is not the clear-cut information provider service it purports to be, but is now closely entangled with the political bodies being served. Like in the mathematical model of the Moebius-strip, it is impossible to determine what is the inside and the outside of these activities.

A second condition paving the way for de-regulatory reform in the finance industry is the increased output of finance asset innovations (Funk and Hirschman, 2014). Examining the repeal of the Glass–Steagall Act in 1999 and 2000, the eminent New Deal legislation that served as the principal framework for the regulation of the finance industry for more than six decades, Funk and Hirschman (2014: 692) argue that the emergence of the market for credit default swaps (CDS) in combination with favourable regulatory interpretations of existing rules served to change the balance of power in the finance industry. This new balance of power was used to forge political coalitions that shared the goal of retiring the Glass–Steagall (Funk and Hirschman, 2014: 692). In this case, new financial innovations, increasingly complex in their design and thus more complicated to price and to trade (i.e., the new financial assets were essentially illiquid, especially as there were no market pricing data available over the entire economic cycle), served to encircle and to render the extant legislation irrelevant. The repeal of the Glass–Steagall Act was therefore not originally accomplished on the basis of a widespread belief in its inefficacy, but because finance industry actors actively developed and traded financial assets that the existing legislation could no longer handle in meaningful ways. The performativity of new financial assets translated into substantive political action, which enabled increased finance industry autonomy and discretion.

Third and finally, political ideology has actively contributed to a new political climate wherein de-regulation is (or was for long periods of time) *à la mode*. As Horwitz (1986: 144) remarks, "the stated intent of deregulation is to foster competition and efficiency." For free market theorists, competition is a virtue, conducive to self-discipline and rational decision making, in turn maximizing the efficiency of economic activities, and therefore competition is a principal virtue and objective in *all domains* of human organization and societies. This acclaim of competition and, by implication, market making was advanced by selected scholarly communities, funded by wealthy donors and activists with a commitment to the "pro-business cause" in the 1960s, 1970s, and 1980s. From the 1970s, the new species of think tank economists and legal scholars also entered the scene. Think tank scholars advocated what McLevey (2015) refers to as "utilitarian epistemic cultures," wherein policy-relevant and action-oriented social research was conducted by and communicated within targeted political bodies, mainstream and niche media, and lobbyist firms. Think tank scholarship (a hybrid rhetorical term advanced to mimic universities and their elaborate, largely respected, and long-standing model for peer-review control of research output and truth-claims) is thus serving to bridge scholarly communities and "non-specialized audiences" (McLevey, 2015: 276). When acting in this intermediary role, think tank scholars take pride in their ability to "get things done," i.e., to actively shape and inform the conversation in and the conventional wisdom of political communities, in industry, and in the wider public, McLevey (2015) argues:

> There is an almost Habermasian (1989)[1] ethical and political imagery when some think tanks describe the space of opinions—or the public sphere more generally—as a democratic, intellectual arena where a diversity of experts and advocates talk through the issues of the day. (McLevey, 2015: 286)

As a majority of think tanks in the U.S. are today financed by pro-business interests, the ideological basis for de-regulatory reforms has been strengthened, which has served to shift the balance of power to benefit business interests at the expense of nonbusiness and social interests. In many cases, there is suspicion that policy making has occurred on grounds that are similar to what Cabantous and Gond (2011: 583) refer to as a "performative praxis," i.e., "rational decision making" unfolds as a process where social actors reconstruct their decisions through "reorganizing and reconstructing data to fit with their a priori definition of 'decision process.'" That is, "rational decision making" does not proceed from preferences and choice alternatives through empirical data available to reach the final decision, but starts with preferred outcomes (i.e., a specific decision) and mobilizes a patchwork of arguments in favour of that decision, making what is supposedly the endpoint of the decision making process ("the rational decision") in fact its starting point. In such garbage-can decision processes (Cohen, March, and Olsen, 1972), "rationality" does not so much denote a *modus tollens*-type procedure ("If A, then B," etc.) as it is a form of rhetorical justification of the stated objectives to be enshrined by the decision at hand. A solid ideological foundation, indubitable to its followers and thus serving as an indisputably true core set of propositions, provides justification for a revised concept of rationality on stipulated moral and ethical grounds, i.e., when one believes oneself to be right, the end occasionally justifies the means.

These various conditions and factors have all contributed to a situation wherein de-regulatory reforms and policies have become part of the conventional wisdom regarding governance regimes. Increased investment in activities that create political influence that benefits industry interest, and the active work to create innovations that render legislation and regulatory control outmoded, are arguably today factors that strongly shape governance regimes. This in turn generates a situation wherein "governance in books" and "governance in a real-world economy" diverges. In this real-world economy of continuous lobbying and ceaseless ideological work to advance, e.g., the efficiency criterion as a foremost political objective, policy making processes and legislative action deviate in considerable ways from sleek and parsimonious theoretical models and textbook cases. Governance policies therefore encounter more severe difficulties in realizing the benefits that protagonists of specific governance regimes and de-regulatory programmes anticipate, which ultimately leads to, when positive effects are not materializing, the demand for more detailed monitoring and/or reforms, or new legislation. In other words, governance is not so much a desired state of immaculate perfection as it is a ceaseless process to balance and mediate various interests within the horizon of economic possibilities, the political conditions at hand, and jointly stated socio-economic goals. This also makes the concept of "the unfinished business of governance" an oxymoron as governance is by definition, in these terms, "unfinishable"—it is what is continuous and ongoing, only temporarily being stabilized into transient states of operational functionality. For instance, this is why what Block (2010) calls "precommitment devices" such as bailouts are of great importance when it comes to finance market regulation. The sheer complexity of the global finance industry cannot simply be contained and neutralized on the basis of predefined regulatory practices. When an economic crisis hits the economy, the state and transnational governance bodies just cannot leave it to the finance market actors themselves to re-stabilize the confidence in the market, as the aggregated social costs of this option overshadow the costs of a bailout. Expressed differently, the costs of the moral hazard, generated by the lender-of-last-resort's precommitment devices and additional costs induced, are still dwarfed in comparison to a full-scale finance industry collapse. "Pretending that there will never be another bailout simply leaves us less prepared when the next severe crisis hits. The challenge is to develop a procedure that leaves the government prepared, without creating any additional moral hazard," Block (2010: 227) summarizes.

In this final chapter, some of the difficulties involved in translating "textbook governance models" into actual, "real-world economy governance" will be attended to. For instance, rather than assuming that governance is devoid of politics and interests, an idea captured by the belief in efficiency as some kind of disinterested and neutral performance criterion, governance is always already political in nature, never separated from the wider institutional conditions of the socio-economic system. Governance regimes thus need to be understood as what is in a process of ceaseless change and adaptation, attending to a manifold of interests and serving various stakeholders, themselves in many cases articulating heterogeneous interests and beliefs.

GOVERNANCE AS A POLITICIZED FIELD: THE CASE OF THE FINANCE INDUSTRY

If we assume that governance remains an unfinished business and that the efficiency criterion is neither a legitimate, nor an advisable standard for governance regimes, how should governance be framed in the new millennium? Economic theory certainly has a role to play but it must not dictate how other disciplines and regulatory models should be designed, unless being supported by empirical evidence that substantiates certain propositions and normative models. In all too many cases, empirical studies have demonstrated that economic propositions, lifted out of academic papers, poorly predicts behaviour and outcomes, which makes them marginal in developing robust governance systems conducive to regulatory transparency and, on the next level, socio-economic welfare.

Levitin's (2014) calls for democratically elected institutions' control over the economy (in substantive terms, a control over the finance industry) and Levitin's (2011) and Omarova's (2011) proposals for regulatory reforms reinforce political accountability and insulate taxpayers from the overbearing consequences of the "too big to fail" finance conglomerates are some examples of legal theorists taking a lead in advocating new governance regimes. Apparently, political accountability, a term that reintroduces political issues in economic affairs and governance regimes, is now in fashion. For free market theorists, staunchly defending the market as an economic mechanism *sui generis* since at least the publication of Walter Lippmann's *An inquiry into the principles of the good society* in 1937, this is an intolerable return of politics in the domain of economic affairs. At the same time, as will be discussed below, the critique of the sovereign state as a market maker has only been a lip service of free market protagonists, as partisan politics and political turf wars have always been an irreducible component of the free market model (a term that as such belies its own content, as "economic freedom" never means "freedom from politics," but only "freedom from politics that does not serve the free market cause"; see, e.g., Mirowski, 2013;

Harcourt, 2011; Vogel, 1996). Under all conditions, the new governance regimes being implemented in corporations, in industries, and in public sector or quasi-public sector organizations such as universities need to rehabilitate the concept of accountability. As in many other cases, it is the finance industry, the one industry to determine and master all other industries in contemporary competitive capitalism on the basis of its finance capital-supplying function and the accompanying subsidies exemptions, that is the most illustrative case when it comes to the need to reform the governance regime.

The Concentration of Economic Power

Table 5.1 indicates that the U.S. finance sector has grown substantially in nominal and relative terms since the early 1990s. Moreover, the four largest American banks (JPMorgan Chase, Bank of America, Citigroup, Wells Fargo) held assets worth a 9 percent share of American GDP in 1990; in 2011, 21 years later, this figure was 50 percent (Wilmarth, 2013: 1406).

Table 5.1   The growth of American finance industry in nominal value as a share of U.S. GDP

Year	Total assets ($ trillion)	Share of US GDP (%)	Level of debt (%)
1991	15.06	254	40
2002	37.71	360	70
2006	55.62	420	120

Source: Adapted from Wilmarth (2013: 1406).

Despite their sheer size, outnumbering many national economies, these financial conglomerates receive federal subsidies, which creates funding cost advantages. Such subsidies amounted to $4 billion per year before the financial crisis of 2008, but rose sharply in the 2007–2009 period to $60 billion annually, peaking at $88 billion in 2008 (Wilmarth, 2013: 1313, note 112). Moreover, it is questionable to what extent these megabanks contribute to economic growth (the overarching goal in neoclassical economic theory), or to social welfare more generally.[2] Several studies indicate that the growth of financial conglomerates have contributed only very little to economic growth, and some studies, like

Cetorelli and Gambera's study (2001), even find a negative correlation between banking sector concentration and economic growth:

> We find that concentration in the banking sector determines a general deadweight loss that depresses growth. However, we also find evidence that bank concentration promotes the growth of those industries that are more in need of external finance by facilitating credit access to firms, especially younger ones. (Cetorelli and Gambera, 2001: 618)

Wilmarth (2013: 1427) argues that most studies show that banks "larger than $100 billion" in holdings no longer generate "favorable economies of scale or scope" (after eliminating state subsidies), which suggests that large financial conglomerates do not add to economic wellbeing. More specifically, a Federal Reserve study shows that larger banks (with assets over US$250 billion) allocated only 14 percent of their assets to business lending in 2007, and, by 2012, the share had further declined to 12 percent. In contrast, smaller banks (with assets under US$10 billion) devoted 30 percent of their assets to business lending in both 2007 and 2012. Such data cast doubt over the socio-economic role of large-scale finance industry actors and their agents' repeated argument that de-regulation is necessary to maintain the international competitiveness of large American banks, and the finance industry more widely. In fact, Wilmarth (2013: 1427) argues, "there is no reason to believe that multinational corporations would fail to obtain adequate financial services in the absence of trillion-dollar financial conglomerates." Large corporations have long relied on syndicates of banks and securities firms to supply the finance capital needed; large corporations do not need single institutions to access finance capital.

Moreover, the concentration of economic power in a handful of finance conglomerates—fewer today than before the financial crisis—also leads to a decline of diversity in the U.S. finance industry: between 1979 and 1994, a period of intense de-regulatory activity, over 4,500 independent banks, representing 36 percent of all banks, closed (Panitch and Gindin, 2012: 173). Tregenna (2012) questions the alleged benefits for the real economy of financial oligopolies, generated on the basis of policy making and propelled by close-knit ties between Wall Street and Washington on the basis of various lobbying and campaign funding activities:

> [T]he effects of bank concentration on bank profitability come at the expense of non-bank entities (as opposed to smaller banks). This is a significant finding, particularly in the context of the result that operational efficiency is not particularly important in explaining bank profitability. It suggests that high levels of bank concentration in the banking sector could be detrimental

to the "real economy." The "net rents" arising from concentration in the banking sector would essentially come at a cost to the non-banking sector as of the economy, through lower rates on deposits and/or higher lending rates and/or higher fees and exchanges. This could thus be expected to have negative effects on the "real economy," in terms of investment and growth. (Tregenna, 2012: 627)

Tregenna's (2012) account, the growth of financial oligopolies comes at the expense of non-financial sectors of the economy; the argument that the finance industry is the *primus motor* of economic growth, advanced to justify further de-regulatory reform, needs to be substantiated. In fact, the opposite seems to be the case (Cetorelli and Gambera, 2001). Such evidence seems to gain little traction in policy making quarters, possibly because finance industry interests, and the interest of the megabanks in particular, wield a substantial influence within democratically elected entities.

Politics All The Way Down: Blending Political Activism and Governance in Finance Industry Regulation

After the 2008 finance industry collapse, there was the customary and predictable call for re-regulatory reform and a tighter control over the finance industry following all bubbles and financial crises (Gerding, 2005), a pattern that Coffee (2011b: 815) refers to as the "regulatory sine curve." Despite considerable evidence of excessive risk taking, opportunistic behaviour, and corporate crime (while most Wall Street representatives acted with impunity), and not least a socialization of downside risk, the finance industry has been most active in slowing down and undermining the primary legislative reform, the Dodd–Frank Act. Omarova (2011: 414) describes the Dodd–Frank Act as "the most comprehensive and far-reaching financial reform legislation in the United States since the New Deal" (see e.g., Tillman, 2012; Coffee, 2011b), but the significance of the legislation is dependent on its implementation and law enforcement. To date, Wilmarth (2013: 1289) argues, the finance industry has obstructed its implementation on the basis of three campaigns:

[T]he financial industry has pursued a three-front campaign that has blocked the fulfillment of many of Dodd–Frank core reforms. First, the industry's aggressive lobbying efforts have persuaded regulatory agencies to delay or water down regulations mandated by Dodd–Frank. Second, industry trade groups have filed lawsuits to strike down completed rules. Third, the industry helped to elect a Republican majority in the House of Representatives in 2010 and again in 2012, and Republican leaders have introduced numerous bills to repeal or weaken key provisions of Dodd–Frank. (Wilmarth, 2013: 1289)

For the lay observer, such campaigns signal a remarkable attitude on the part of the finance industry actors and their agents, arguably rooted in the belief that the industry has enough political clout to resist or neutralize even the legislative procedures of democratically elected political entities. The close and intimate connections between Wall Street and Washington arguably promote such self-confidence, always making finance industry interest a foremost political concern. For instance, Wilmarth (2013: 1359) argues that both the George W. Bush and Obama Administrations—which took over the political leadership in the midst of the crisis—assigned a "much lower priority to solving the home foreclosure crisis than it did to shoring up the largest banks (which bore significant responsibility for causing the crisis in the first place)." Barofsky (2012), serving within one of the federal agencies, reports that at the zenith of the crisis, when politicians and state functionaries were up to their neck in work to re-stabilize the finance industry, Treasury Department officials expressed their concern that homeowners, now being evicted on mass scale as their home mortgage loans were foreclosed, would take advantage of federal subsidies. To these officials, this was an intolerable moral hazard. To Barofsky, this response from the political system was "beyond ironic":

> Though some home owners might try to take advantage of the program by intentionally not making mortgage payments in order to qualify—that risk paled in comparison to that created by Treasury by the way it had rescued the too-big-to-fail banks. Rather than requiring those executives to suffer the consequences of their failures, Treasury had handsomely rewarded those who had failed to do their jobs, saving the banks and making sure that almost all of them kept their jobs and the enormous bonuses they had taken home before the crisis stuck. (Barofsky, 2012: 197)

During the entire bailout and rescue activities, the Department of Justice (DOJ) made no decisions to indict leading banks or their senior executives (Wilmarth, 2013: 1374), a rational passivity (at best) justified on the basis that finance industry stability should be re-established at all economic and political costs, or as an act of a paid-for-service within a clientelism governance regime, rooted in a crony capitalism tradition (at worst). Moreover, federal agencies have not brought any criminal charges against finance industry actors, and only a handful of civil claims against senior officers of finance companies for "falsely certifying their companies' public reports" have been filed. This indolence is noteworthy as Sections 302 and 906 of the Sarbanes–Oxley Act, the principal legislative piece that followed the Enron bankruptcy in December 2001, "impose civil and criminal penalties on senior officers for false certifications of annual and quarterly reports" (Wilmarth, 2013: 1374). That is, the finance industry actors and their agents were granted the licence by the political system to act with impunity, despite the fine-grained regulatory framework enacted by democratically elected entities.

This political immunity has not always been assumed in the U.S.; Coffee (2007: 275) identifies "697 enforcement actions" initiated by the Securities and Exchange Commission and DOJ between 1978 and 2004, leading to substantial evidence of law enforcement still being functional in the period:

> Finally, some 755 individuals and 40 firms were indicted; 543 of the individuals pleaded or were found guilty while only 10 were acquitted. A total of 1230.7 years of incarceration and 397.5 years of probation were imposed (with the average sentence being 4.2 years). (Coffee, 2007: 276)

Based on this empirical evidence, Coffee (2007: 276) is optimistically affirming the legal system's capacity to enforce its own legislation: "In short, financial fraud by issuers, their agents, and their employees is both heavily punished in the United States and punished by multiple and overlapping enforcers." Critics argue that such optimistic views of law enforcement efficacy are undermined by what Wilmarth calls the "revolving door" model that defines the relationship between Wall Street and Washington:

> [T]he financial sector's lobbying expenditures and campaign contributions increased dramatically after 1990. Wall Street's ability to wield great political influence and to offer highly-compensated employment also created powerful incentives for a rapidly spinning "revolving door" between leadership positions in financial regulatory agencies and senior positions at Wall Street firms and their law firms, accounting firms and trade associations. (Wilmarth, 2013: 1408)

In terms of sheer body count, measuring the number of individuals that cross the line between finance and politics, there is substantial evidence of exchanges. In only 2009 and 2010, "(i) the financial industry hired more than 1,400 lobbyists who were former federal employees, including 73 former members of Congress and two former Comptrollers of the Currency, and (ii) the six largest U.S. banks employed more than 240 lobbyists who were former government insiders" (Wilmarth, 2013: 1408). Specific finance firms such as Goldman Sachs (at times granted the moniker "Government Sachs" on the basis of its close connections to Congress and the White House; Mandis, 2013; Cohan, 2011) are widely regarded as the recruitment ground for political officials, not the least for the highest offices:

The White House has often looked to Wall Street experts for advice, and Goldman partners have advised several presidents and cabinet members, leading to an incestuous web between government and Goldman—hence the nickname Government Sachs. At the highest levels within Goldman, there was, and is a conscious effort to build and maintain relationships with important people. (Mandis, 2013: 237)

The Secretary of Treasury of both the Clinton administration, Robert Rubin (1995–1999), and the Bush Jr. Administration, Henry "Hank" Paulson (2006–2009), were chairmen of Goldman Sachs before their public service, and Henry Fowler, ending his term as Secretary of Treasury in 1968, joined Goldman Sachs. Furthermore, Wilmarth (2013: 1410) writes, "both Rubin and Paulson appointed several of their Goldman colleagues to senior Treasury posts during their respective tenures as Treasury Secretary."

Such close connections between political and legislative power and finance industry actors put political accountability at risk; when systemic risk rises to unprecedented levels, calling for the federal state to bail out banks to restore the confidence in a robust finance industry to continue its lending to non-financial firms, an absolute and unnegotiable demand for the capitalist circulation of capital to continue, there should be no shadow of a doubt that politicians and state officials can ensure the stability of the economic system. Levitin (2011) outlines the mechanisms at work during a finance industry crisis. First of all, a finance industry crisis is caused by uncertainty regarding the various market actors' ability to fulfil their contracts. This uncertainty, caused by excessive risk taking and equity leverage, leads creditors to protect their loans, either by calling them or demanding more collateral. This rush to call loans or demand more collateral is "the phenomenon of the run," Levitin (2011: 469) writes; when debtors are "suddenly pinched for capital and may suffer liquidity problems," Levitin (2011: 469) continues, they in turn limit their ability to "satisfy the claims of all their creditors." Furthermore, the larger the equity leverage, the more severe the crisis. At the same time, leverage is a key temptation for bank managers, willing to take risks to outperform competitors: "Only banks that employ high leverage can realize the full economies of scale that are inherent to the banking business" (Coffee, 2011b: 815).[3] This means that one or a few highly leveraged finance institutions, finding themselves in a precarious situation, may contaminate the entire finance industry. When such idiosyncratic risks are soaring, they may "snowball into full-blown financial crises with serious costs to society, which means that there are strong welfare arguments for avoiding them" (Frieden, 2016: 36). This uncertainty and the action taken on such grounds leads to the related phenomenon, namely that new credit expansion stops in the situation where credit risk cannot be "comfortably gauged and priced" (Levitin, 2011: 469). This brings credit lending to a standstill, and this second mechanism also exacerbates the first problem, as liquidity problems can no longer be solved on the basis of new borrowing. "Extraordinary levels of uncertainty made it difficult or impossible even for the largest financial institutions to borrow on the interbank market, which is necessary for them to carry on everyday business," Frieden (2016: 36) argues. The finance industry thus ceases to function as intended, as uncertainty regarding solvency spread, all over the industry, which makes solvent institutions victims because it is complicated for outsiders to discriminate between firms at risk and solvent firms (Levitin, 2011: 469). At this stage, which occurred in 2008, the only way to restore the faith in the finance market and to overcome the rational but self-interested behaviour of market actors escalating the crisis is that a non-market agent (e.g., the sovereign state and its agencies such as the central bank) steps in and guarantees the solidity of finance industry actors:

> [V]irtually every government has agreed, in one way or another, to act as an implicit or explicit lender of last resort. This means that it stands ready to provide liquidity to the financial market to keep otherwise solvent financial institutions from being bankrupted by a contagious loss of confidence. (Frieden, 2016: 36)

This activity—the bailout—restores the confidence in the finance system, but only when it becomes clear to outsiders which firms are healthy and which are not (Levitin, 2011: 469). This also means that poorly managed and well-managed firms are at risk of being treated the same (Coffee, 1986: 36). This, de facto, is a form of penalty imposed on well-managed firms, which now suffer from the so-called "lemon problem" (Akerlof, 1970) wherein insiders know more than outsiders, and where prudential firms are put in the same basket as poorly managed firms and thus carry some of the cost low-quality firms should have carried themselves. The resolution system of the bailout thus operates through less-than-perfect mechanisms that generate moral hazard and offer possibilities for free riding.

Levitin (2011: 481) argues that each bailout campaign is unique, being a "system unto itself" (see e.g., Sjostrom, 2009, on the AIG bailout).[4] The statutory resolution system, i.e., the bailout organization, has the merit of "depoliticizing" financial resolution inasmuch as the statutory system makes individual firms' resolutions a legal, rather than political, matter, Levitin (2011: 481) argues. This, in turn, eliminates or mutes "the uncertainty and unpredictability of politics," which understandably is the last thing the hyper-nervous finance industry needs at the moment when it balances on the edge of the abyss and has been brought to a standstill (Levitin, 2011: 481). At the same time, Levitin (2011: 481) continues, politics is not entirely excluded from the statutory resolution system as the rescue activities create "repayment waterfalls": "the highest priority creditors are repaid first, and the lower priority ones are repaid only to the extent there are funds available" (Levitin, 2011: 481), consistent with the propositions of Pistor's (2013) legal theory of finance (discussed shortly). The decision regarding *who* should get repaid first, *who* second, and so on, "involves political choices" (Levitin, 2011: 481). Unfortunately, the bailout mechanism also creates moral hazard because "firms that expect to be bailed out will be incentivized to engage in overly risky behavior because the downside risk is socialized, while the upside is retained" (Levitin, 2011: 481–482). The political and ethical costs of the bailout as the statutory resolution system *par préférence* are therefore considerable, but this mechanism is still politically palatable because it can effectively handle the systemic risk of the integrated finance industry. The bankruptcy resolution, for instance, forcing inefficient and poorly managed firms out of the market thus avoids moral hazards (and therefore, institutes prudence, as "what one sows, one must reap," to paraphrase the Bible), do not always "address the distributional concerns" when "too-big-to-fail firms" are at risk, and there may be socially unacceptable consequences that the bankruptcy option cannot prevent, Levitin (2011: 485) argues. For instance, in the case of the AIG bailout, a *Wall Street Journal* commentator pointed out the immense and essentially unpredictable systemic risks (and, by implication, the considerable political consequences) involved in enforcing a bankruptcy:

> AIG's size and complexity meant that its tentacles were spread throughout the financial system, making it almost impossible to be certain about the impact of a collapse—other than to know it was potentially catastrophic. (Monica Langley et al., "Bad Bets and Cash Crunch Pushed Ailing AIG to Brink," *Wall Street Journal*, September 18, 2008, cited in Sjostrand, 2009: 978)

For instance, the AIG stock was one of the top ten most popular holdings in so-called 401(k) retirement plans, the *New York Times* noticed, and a collapse of AIG would therefore "cause an enormous run on mutual funds" (Eric Dash and Andrew Ross Sorkin, "Throwing a Lifeline to a Troubled Giant," *New York Times*, September 18, 2008, cited in Sjostrand, 2009: 978), a "rational response" from pension fund savers that would cause the situation to deteriorate further. Therefore, rather than restoring confidence in the finance industry, "bankruptcy can exacerbate systemic risk" (Levitin, 2011: 485). This makes forced bankruptcies on a broad scale a poorly functioning resolution mechanism, unable to compete with bailouts. As a consequence, policy makers and regulation agency directors need to swallow the bitter pill of sanctioning moral hazard among politically influential finance industry actors to save the economic system and restore its functionality: "Governments need to stand ready to intervene in an emergency to supply funds to financial markets to avoid a descent into panic" (Frieden, 2016: 36). As the Clinton Administration Secretary of Treasury, Robert Rubin (cited in Wilmarth, 2013: 1425), remarked in an interview, "Too big to fail isn't a problem with the system. It *is* the system."

A former Washington-based senior legislative aide and lawyer-lobbyist (cited in Wilmarth, 2013: 1408) confirmed this view:

> Money is the basis of almost all relationships in [Washington] DC ... [O]ur political campaign system and [Washington] DC's mushrooming Permanent Class—who alternate between government jobs and lawyering, influence-peddling and finance—mean Wall Street always wins.

Such testimonies do not indicate that accountability is always placed in the first room in politically elected entities and their defined agencies. Furthermore, there are behavioural mechanisms that affect policy makers, anxious to get favourable recognition for their work from voters and in the media, Rizzo and Whitman (2009b: 693) argue: "Policymakers may be affected by the improved political position of an interest group that has a victory under its belt." As politicians are interested in signalling victories in the future, they want to hear "winning ideas" so they can claim to have made legislative accomplishments in campaign speeches and in the communication with voters. This means, by implication, Rizzo and Whitman (2009b: 693) say, that interest groups with "recent victories will be more likely to be 'persuasive.'" Policy making thus becomes path-dependent ("success breeds success," generating a certain "Matthew effect"—"For unto every one that hath shall be given" [Matt. 25: 29]—in policy making), and those commanding the economic resources to access policy makers and to inform their agendas and political programmes are likely to exclude more diverse views and interests (Bonica et al., 2013; Hacker and Pierson, 2010, 2002). Taken together, there is substantial evidence that suggests that the finance industry has been given the authority to dictate how the industry is regulated, possibly on the basis of the recurrent argument that "What is good for Wall Street is good for the U.S. economy"—an argument that rings hollow when considering economic fundamentals and available statistical data.

Polymorphous Politics and Governance Regimes

Based on this evidence and these testimonies, some conclusions can be stated. First, finance industry regulation has always been politicized "all the way down," complete with "revolving doors" between Wall Street and Washington that mix up and blend interest and political responsibilities in ways that make political accountability a hard-to-accomplish feature within the existing governance regime. Second, if "efficiency" is no longer a legitimate, nor practically useful guiding principle within governance regimes, there is a need for precise reforms that emphasize the political accountability of governance regimes. The substantial issue at hand is therefore: how can a governance regime be developed in a milieu where the distinction between regulator and regulated entities, a *sine qua non* for a robust legal-regulatory model, is porous and continuously transgressed? Levitin (2011), discussed shortly, advocates a combination of *ex ante* and *ex post* regulation, with the bailout option as an explicit and legitimate political governance device; Omarova (2011), in contrast, calls for increased self-regulation (making the nuclear energy and chemistry industries meaningful role-model industries), in combination with reduced subsidies and exemptions that would insulate taxpayers against the effects of imprudent and illicit behaviour in industry. In both cases, improved political accountability and the ambition to avoid a widespread externalization of downside risks in the finance industry are guiding principles and stated objectives. In order to handle the unfinished business of finance industry regulation, the political system must, like Baron von Münchhausen, "lift itself by its hair" and at least temporarily separate itself from the political responsibilities towards its munificent sponsors and campaign-contributors on Wall Street. Needless to say, the challenge is formidable, authoritative commentators make clear:

> [F]inancial institutions remain frustratingly inscrutable. Despite nearly a century of concerted research and periodic financial crises, the connections between the governance of banks, their individual performance, and the long-run stability of the financial system are not well understood. Many questions remain unanswered about the causes of the crisis. (Mehran and Mollineaux, 2012: 216)

The historical record suggests this is a non-trivial operation, putting existing partnerships and collaborations at stake. But that is on the other hand the very nature of politics—to accomplish stated goals on the basis of incomplete resources and the difficulties involved in surveying the entire political field and to predict the consequences of purposeful action. There are no reasons to abandon the hope that this is doable within the existing political system; expressed differently, the alternatives are few.

TWO PRACTICAL PROPOSALS: THE POLITICAL ACCOUNTABILITY AND GOVERNANCE RE-UNITED IN GLOBAL FINANCE REGULATION

Following the global finance industry collapse in 2008, many commentators and scholars have expressed their concern regarding the failure of the market-based regulation of the finance industry, making credit rating agencies the watchdogs of the finance trade and recognizing few other governance mechanisms. Unfortunately, just like in the classic Sherlock Holmes story "Silver Blaze," the dog *did not* bark, possibly because it was dependent on paying clients expecting favourable ratings to continue participating in the expansion of securities markets under the so-called "the issuer pays principle" (Alp, 2013; Cornaggia and Cornaggia, 2013; White, 2009).[5] As this new regime was unsustainable, a new governance regime needs to take its place to actually fill all the political exclaims of "Never again!" with some substance. As detailed by, e.g., Barofsky (2012), Sorkin (2009), and many others, the 2008 events ended with the federal government, the tax-payers' agency, picking up the bill and bailing out the finance industry. The bailout money has been repaid to the American tax-payers, and in the end the question is whether the bailout model, de facto being in place since the early 1980s, is a good or a bad policy, and if the political system can offer better *ex post* resolution systems?

To start, the concept of bailout demands some further explanation. "I define 'bank rescue' or 'bank bailout' as any government-sponsored delay in the exit of insolvent banks that is explicitly or implicitly funded by public resources," Rosas (2006: 176) writes. In short, a bank is being bailed out if it "continues to operate after insolvency" (Rosas, 2006: 176). Block (2010: 156) defines a bailout as "[a] form of government assistance or intervention specifically designed or intended to assist enterprises facing financial distress and to prevent enterprise failure." A bailout is thus a form of industry subsidy that is immediate, an emergency effort to prevent imminent collapse, or a "backward-looking attempt" to rescue private entities from "economic damage that has already occurred." A bailout is therefore an *ex post* resolution mechanism being part of a wider governance regime. As opposed to bailouts, Block (2010: 160) argues, *stimulus* is a complementary state-funded subsidy that is "forward looking," designed to "spark economic growth or redevelopment." As being an *ex ante* regulation mechanism, stimulus oftentimes operates on the basis of the incentives of a third party (e.g., consumers) and is more indirect and thus generates outcomes more complicated to predict from the policy makers' view:

> By institutional design, stimulus legislation relies heavily on incentives to taxpayers, provided through special tax deductions and credits. The total actual cost of such legislation to the government, in terms of revenue foregone, will depend upon how much taxpayers choose to use the incentives. To some, this is the beauty of tax incentives: taxpayers effectively "vote" on how much will be spent by either taking advantage of the incentive or not. Difficulties in determining in advance the extent to which taxpayers will take advantage of particular incentives make long-term budgeting for such incentives difficult. (Block, 2010: 163)

In practice, therefore, in the event of an imminent economic crisis, the bailout mechanism offers considerable advantages in comparison to stimulus: a bailout can restore confidence in the market by making the sovereign state act as the lender-of-last-resort.

It is noteworthy that a bailout does not of necessity need to imply any transfer of e.g., tax-money, but a bailout occurs as soon as a government "alter[s] bank regulation in order to change the legal definition of insolvency" (Rosas, 2006: 176); in the face of a bank insolvency crisis, the predefined regulatory framework and its enforcement may be relaxed, or the state may serve and announce its role as a lender-of-last-resort to avoid bank runs that would render banks insolvent. Bailouts are in essence an event where the state steps into the market to provide support for failing industries or companies; the bailout is thus the indisputable moment where "politics" enters "the economy."

In addition to bailouts, Rosas (2006) argues, governments can follow the "Bagehot rule,"[6] that is, to "force the exit of insolvent institutions" (Rosas, 2006: 176). The Bagehot rule is the choice of governments concerned with "upholding the market mechanism and diminishing moral hazard incentives in the banking sector" (Rosas, 2006: 176), who at the same time can anticipate and contain the wider financial and economic consequences of this policy choice, i.e., the policy makers need to be convinced they are not creating a system-wide collapse on the basis of their decision. The benefits of the Bagehot rule are that it "avoids socialization of bank losses" and "eventually strengthens the financial system by eliminating weak banks" (Rosas, 2006: 176). An additional benefit is that it creates possibilities for economic and political account-ability, where the moral hazard[7] implied by the bailout model is eliminated. The bailout model, wherein insolvent banks are allowed to continue their operations, in effect subsidizes the losses of bankers and depositors and shifts "the burden of bank insolvency to taxpayers" (Rosas, 2006: 175). Needless to say, that is not of necessity an attractive option for policy makers, but when the risk of a system-wide collapse looms, the bailout option may be chosen on the basis of the lack of credible alternatives.

The literature provides both positive and negative cases of the two policy choice alternatives. For instance, Murdock (2012: 545) examines the Swedish bank crisis in the early 1990s wherein the Swedish govern-ment opted for the Bagehot rule in Rosas' terms (2006). Rather than letting banks "slowly write off bad assets in the hope that earnings, over time, would return them to solvency," the government "forced the banks to recognize their losses and nationalized one-fifth of the banking system" (Murdock, 2012: 545). As a result, the Swedish economy "turned around in two years" (Murdock, 2012: 545). When facing a seemingly overwhelming banking crisis in the Icelandic economy in 2008–2009, the government followed the Swedish model with great success, protecting the Icelandic tax-payers from carrying costs that would neither be possible to handle, nor would be morally justifiable to pass on to the Icelandic population. The Irish government, in contrast, fearing that a capital flight would leave what was in the 1990s referred to as the "Celtic tiger economy" (alluding to the so-called Asian tigers, the high-growth economies of Hong Kong, South Korea, Taiwan, and Singapore), opted for the bailout model, unfortunately with less favourable outcomes: "the sovereign debt of Ireland increased to the point where Ireland's solvency became questionable, and interest rates on the Irish debt shot up" (Murdock, 2012: 545–546). In the end, German banks and others who had extended credit to the Irish banks "were bailed out by the Irish taxpayers, while the Irish people bore the brunt of an austerity program that has kept the country in recession" (Murdock, 2012: 545–546). The Icelandic population benefitted from a staid and determined economic policy executed by the government, while the Irish government decided to pass on the costs to the Irish tax-payers.

Such evidence and stories do not of necessity make bailout politically unattractive, Levitin (2011) argues. On the contrary, if the bailout mechanism is connected to political accountability, it is an economically sound and politically legitimate *ex post* resolution device, Levitin (2011) claims. In Levitin's account, the global finance industry is today so deeply entangled with the real economy and with the day-to-day lives of billions of citizens that it is analytically as well as politically complicated to separate "finance" from the rest of the economy. This view is consistent with what Pistor (2013) calls a "legal theory of finance." Pistor (2013: 315) argues that finance is "legally constructed"; it does not stand "outside the law" inasmuch as financial assets are "contracts the value of which depends in large part on their legal vindication." This view is consistent with Lang's (2013: 156) claim that markets "should not be imagined as existing prior to law, but are in part constituted by law." That is, Lang (2013: 156) emphasizes, "law's relationship to economic life is both regulative *and* constitutive."[8] At the same time as law and finance are "locked into a dynamic process," the relation between these two entities is "paradoxical," Pistor (2013: 323) argues:

> [L]aw and finance stand in an uneasy, paradoxical relation to one another. Law lends credibility to financial instruments by casting the benevolent glow of coercive enforceability over them. But the actual enforcement of all legal commitments made in the past irrespective of changes in circumstances would inevitably bring down the financial system. If, however, the full force of law is relaxed or suspended to take account of such change, the credibility law lends to finance in the first place is undermined. (Pistor, 2013: 323)

Seen in this view, much of the epistemological assumptions made in finance theory and in common sense thinking become undone, e.g., the separation between the state and the market, private or public, no longer makes sense, as finance markets are "always and necessarily both" (Pistor, 2013: 322). That is, describing finance as a system of private contracting subject to some external constraints, imposed by state-governed or licensed regulatory bodies, "misses much of what is unique to contemporary finance," Pistor (2013: 323) argues: Finance is based on money as "the legal tender," relies on "the legal enforceability of private/private commitments," and in the last instance depends "on backstopping by a sovereign."

Stout's (2011) critical assessment of the role of the Commodity Futures Modernization Act (CFMA), passed by Congress in late 2000 (for details, see Maney, 2016, Chapter 8; Topham, 2010), in generating the 2008 finance industry crisis is illustrative of Pistor's (2013) theoretical model, and how legal reforms re-shape markets. Blinder (2013: 279), a respected Princeton economics professor and a former Federal Reserve vice chairman (1994–1996), describes CFMA as "an outrageous piece of legislation that actually *banned* the regulation of derivatives," leaving it to market actors to regulate themselves. In Stout's (2011: 37) account, "[t]he 2000 CFMA directly caused the 2008 credit crisis." Stout says that this claim is "[c]onsistent with the evidence, including the timing, scope, and facts of the crisis as it actually unfolded. No empirical evidence refutes the hypothesis." CFMA unleashed an unprecedented wave of finance market speculation (Stout, 2011: 24–26), well catalogued in the literature, but the new piece of legislation offered few of the benefits its advocates claimed would materialize, including better liquidity in finance markets and better pooled risks, serving to stabilize the economy:

> [T]he economic value of providing greater marginal liquidity in the spot market for equities has not been empirically established and is easily exaggerated ... The economic benefits of more accurate ("efficient") equity prices are similarly theoretical and easily exaggerated. Unless a company is actually selling stock to raise capital for some investment, the benefits of ensuring new information gets reflected into stock prices hours or minutes faster than it would otherwise may be modest at best. (Stout, 2011: 30)

More importantly, the disastrous effects of CFMA, which the world economy still recovers from, close to two decades after the legislation was passed in the last hours of the Clinton presidency and being largely unnoticed by mainstream media (Topham, 2010), "were not the result of changes or 'innovations' in financial markets. They were the result of *changes in the law*" (Stout, 2011: 31). "[The] lesson is that law matters. All significant markets, including financial markets, must be built on some underlying legal infrastructure," Stout (2011: 37) contends: "Without a deep understanding of the nature and importance of the legal rules that organize financial markets it is impossible either to understand the markets, or to predict their behavior" (Stout, 2011: 37).[9] The finance market is a creation of the sovereign state through its legislative procedures, as stipulated by Pistor's (2013) legal theory of finance. Consequently, assumptions regarding a neat separation between, e.g., the state and private actors needs to be retired, and empirical conditions call for a revisionist view of regulation: there is no such thing as "unregulated" financial markets, and the term *de-regulation* is a misnomer, Pistor (2013: 321) announces.[10] In this view, de-regulation instead denotes the "implicit delegation of rule-making to different, typically non-state actors, with the understanding that in all other respects they enjoy the full protection of the law" (Pistor, 2013: 321).

The legal theory of finance also emphasizes the flexibility of law and how such flexibilities primarily benefit the interests of actors at the apex of the finance system: "[T]he binding nature of legal and contractual commitments tends to be inversely related to the hierarchy of finance: Law tends to be binding on the periphery and relatively more elastic at the apex of the financial system" (Pistor, 2013: 317). Pistor thus suggests that the legal principle of equality before the law, also guiding contract law and otherwise cherished in legal theory and judiciary practice, is sidelined in the legal theory of finance. Pistor explains:

> A legal system committed to the rule of law is meant to apply law irrespective of status or identity. Contracts are designed to create credible commitments that are enforceable as written. Yet, closer inspection of contractual relations, laws and regulations in finance suggests that law is not quite as evenly designed or applied throughout the system. Instead, it is elastic. The elasticity of law can be defined as the probability that ex ante legal commitments will be relaxed or suspended in the future; the higher that probability the more elastic the law. In general, law tends to be relatively elastic at the system's apex, but inelastic on its periphery. (Pistor, 2013: 320)

For instance, in a period of financial crisis (such as in the autumn of 2008), the flexibility of law and its prioritizing of actors at the strategic apex is made manifest in political and legal decisions, leading to, e.g., homeowners, being the foremost victims of the decline of the sub-prime mortgage market,[11] finding themselves in the periphery of the federal rescue activities: "Homeowners in the US may be on the periphery of the US financial system … While major financial intermediaries received emergency liquidity support from the Fed or government bailouts, homeowners faced personal bankruptcy and foreclosure in accordance with the law" (Pistor, 2013: 320: See also Mian and Sufi, 2014; Piskorski, Seru, and Vig, 2010; Gelpern and Levitin, 2009). Therefore, the question on what legal, economic, and political grounds bailout decisions and, more generally, the creation of standardized resolution systems should be justified needs to take into account the irreducible fact of the legal theory of finance, that is, that actors at the very apex of the system "exercise discretionary powers in times of crisis over whether to intervene and whom to rescue" (Pistor, 2013: 321). This means, in practice, whether it is politically attractive or not, that "those sufficiently close to the apex are more likely to benefit from the relaxation or suspension of ex ante legal commitments than those on the periphery" (Pistor, 2013: 321). Political entities and actors may express their willingness to enact fair resolution systems, beneficial for all stake-holders and not only already privileged actors at the apex of the finance system, but in practice such stated ambitions rhymes poorly with actual conditions and the problems at hand. There is a long record of legislation and regulatory policies aimed at taming the finance industry to bring down its systemic risks and to create incentives to act with prudence in day-to-day finance trading. Therefore, consistent with Pistor's (2013) theory, Levitin (2011) argues it is naïve to assume that finance crises and finance industry meltdowns can be handled on the basis of *ex ante* regulation; in fact, the sharp growth in finance industry crises coincides with increased *ex ante* regulatory control (Calomiris and Haber, 2014).

In this context, the concept of *systemic risk* needs to be examined in some detail. Systemic risk cannot be understood as an analytical and practical term with a "precise, generally accepted definition," Levitin (2011: 443) writes. Yet, Levitin (2011: 444) continues, existing definitions are "at once too narrow and too vague and fail to account for the political nature of systemic risk responses." The conventional definition renders systemic risk as the risk of "[a] single firm's failure having substantial negative effects on the broader economy" (Levitin, 2011: 444); but one single firm's failure cannot be a "systemic" risk unless the wider industry or the entire economic system is bound up with similar contracts and liabilities to the failing firm; thus systemic risk is a more deep-seated and politically nested term than this baseline definition suggests. The two arguments advanced above, that (1) the finance industry cannot be examined and regulated per se, but is always already being bound up with wider financial, economic, and social interests, and (2) *ex ante* regulation is an insufficient response to governance demands, leads Levitin (2011: 438) to redefine systemic risk as a *political* rather than an *economic* matter: "[S]ystemic risk must be conceived in terms of political accountability and legitimacy. Systemic risk is ultimately a political, rather than an economic, matter." This is a key proposition in Levitin's governance model, as it makes political accountability a key component of the proposed governance regime:

> Accordingly, discussions of systemic risk cannot be restricted to financial firms, and attempts to gauge whether a risk is truly systemic must look to social norms, such as those expressed by the median voter. Existing definitions of systemic risk are either too narrow, as they relate solely to the banking system, or fail to grapple with the level of broader impact that makes a risk systemic, and none account for the political economy of bailouts. (Levitin, 2011: 438)

Based on the two propositions listed above, Levitin (2011) claims that it is, as a legal and political means, impossible to "create a standardized resolution system" that will be "rigidly adhered to in a crisis." When policy makers and regulators encounter a severe situation like in 2008, they are not likely to just stick to the protocol, but they will deploy all resources at hand. That is, in Rosas' (2006) terms, the Bagehot rule assumes a significant degree of *sang froid* on the part of a series of interconnected regulators and market actors, and that can perhaps no longer be stipulated in the era of globalized finance. Therefore, Levitin (2011: 439) contends, when the "the results of an *ex ante* loss allocation are socially unacceptable" and when all other choice alternatives are exhausted, "bailouts are inevitable" (Levitin, 2011: 439); that is, "when staring into the abyss of a financial collapse, politicians like bureaucrats may opt for rescue rather than self-destruction," Pistor (2013: 328) says. Levitin (2011) continues:

> The financial Ulysses cannot be bound to the mast. Although we may want Ulysses to be bound to the mast when the sailing is smooth to avoid the sirens' call of politically directed state intervention in the market, the situation changes once the ship has hit the rocks. Once the ship is foundering, we do not want Ulysses to be bound to the mast, lest go down with the ship and drown. Instead we want to be sure his hands are free—to bail. (Levitin, 2011: 439)

As Levitin makes systemic risk a *political concept*, this pro-bailout stance does not mean that Levitin (2011) advocates a *carte blanche* for finance industry actors to act at will and to continue to privatize gains and socialize losses. On the contrary, the agencies assigned the role to monitor the finance industry and to command significant resources within their *ex post* regulation, including the bailout option as a lender-of-last-resort activity, need to be more closely connected to democratically elected political entities, Levitin (2011: 440) claims. This means, in turn, that for instance the Federal Reserve Board is "a particularly poor candidate for resolution authority because of its exceptional insulation from political accountability" (Levitin, 2011: 440). In other words, what Levitin proposes is a decisive break with the free market model, prescribing apoliticized governance regimes and self-regulation, and the Washington consensus governance doctrine, relying on technocratic discretion and execution. Levitin argues that if the 2008 events showed something in brutal clarity, it is that the technocratic governance model does not live up to its expectations and therefore the technocratic jurisdiction needs to be strengthened by closer links to politically accountable institutions (Levitin, 2011: 442): "Bailouts are an inevitable fact of modern economic life, but they require a standardized, transparent, and politically accountable process that includes a haircut mechanism[12] to maintain political legitimacy, which is essential for their ultimate efficacy" (Levitin, 2011: 443).

More specifically, Levitin (2011) advocates a governance regime wherein the creditors are supported in pricing risks more accurately. This means in practice that creditors should carry a larger burden of the losses impaired by imprudent finance traders, which in turn would reduce the undesirable influence of moral hazard and systemic risk:

> [H]aircuts on creditors are essential for limiting government losses, reducing moral hazard (and thus systemic risk in the first place), and particularly for ensuring bailouts' political legitimacy. If a firm's creditors believe that they will incur haircuts upon the failure of the firm, they will raise their prices to reflect that risk; therefore, the riskier the firm's behavior, the more costly it will be for the firm. A credible threat of haircuts thus reduces moral hazard. (Levitin, 2011: 440)

Levitin's article abounds with technical legal details, whereof many are specific for the U.S. legal system, but the main message of relevance for governance theory is that Levitin (2011) retires the apolitical governance regime that has been in fashion since the 1970s. The bailout option may seem politically unattractive but in today's finance-led economy, it is politically unavoidable in Levitin's (2011) account. What needs to be strengthened though, is the political accountability of the governance regime, which calls for *more* involvement of democratically elected political bodies, not *less*, as argued previously. In Levitin's (2011) terms, finance industry governance remains an unfinished business, and it is an unfinished business that needs to recognize systemic risk as a political concept whose solutions are to be found within polity.

The Self-regulation Governance Regime

Omarova (2011) presents an alternative model of finance industry regulation that is based on self-regulation. Omarova (2011: 415) admits that in the Great Recession era, the idea of financial industry self-regulation "is not politically popular." To promote industry's right to "run their own affairs" in this political climate, characterized by a scepticism towards banks' and other financial institutions' ability to act in a "socially responsible or publicly minded manner," is counterintuitive, Omarova (2011: 416) says. Still, Omarova (2011) argues that the present governance regime, structured around government regulation, works poorly.[13] First of all, regulated financial institutions, and the large finance industry conglomerates in particular, have proved time and again that they have the capacity to by-pass regulators and to engage in "sophisticated and effective regulatory arbitrage and lobbying" (Omarova, 2011: 463): "Regulatory agencies in charge of the financial services sector often display strong signs of industry 'capture' and increasingly engage in nontransparent and highly informal rulemaking that falls outside public scrutiny and tends to favor the industry" (Omarova, 2011: 463). Second, the so-called "revolving door" between the finance industry and its leading conglomerates and the political entities in Washington seriously impairs the possibilities for creating a firewall between the finance industry and the political system:

> The incestuous relationship between the industry and its government watch-dogs is further exemplified by the existence of a "revolving door" policy, where agency officials move to lucrative private sector positions and prominent industry executives are appointed to top regulatory posts. (Omarova, 2011: 463–464)

In this environment of regulatory capture and the significant political clout on the part of the finance industry, Omarova (2011: 413) argues, "[t]he financial services industry currently lacks meaningful incentives to develop this new type of more publicly minded and socially responsible self-regulation." Instead of instituting even *more* regulation along the well-trodden paths, a political response that is likely to lead to "the familiar pattern of intense industry lobbying to stall the reforms or to secure sufficient loopholes in the proposed rules to enable regulatory arbitrage" (Omarova, 2011: 464), new approaches need to be tested in the industry—a "self-regulation model."

Omarova (2011: 421) defines self-regulation as "[a] regime of collective rulemaking, whereby an industry-level entity develops and enforces rules and standards governing behavior of all industry members." As she (2011: 422) continues, in academic and policy discourse, "self-regulation" is frequently used as "a proxy for complete freedom of market actors from any government regulation," but, in this case, it does not denote the adherence to such a free market protocol. In the new model of self-regulation, the power to create regulatory rules belongs no longer exclusively to the sovereign state and its agencies, but a new more flexible governance model, in which "power to set and enforce the rules is increasingly diffused among a variety of societal actors working alongside the governments" (Omarova, 2011: 416), replaces the traditional top-down, centre-to-periphery regulation model. In Omarova's view (2011: 418), private industry actors are likely to be in the best position to "[i]dentify and understand underlying trends in the increasingly complex financial markets and to gather and analyze, in real time, information most relevant to systemic risk management."

The burden to determine, e.g., prudential risk management practices are thus shifted from public regulators to private actors operating in the market. As a consequence, much of the subsidies and legal benefits that, e.g., the finance industry takes advantage of become obsolete, which in turn serves to separate the regulatory agencies and finance industry. In Omarova's (2011) self-regulation model, there is no room for the bailout mechanism (that Levitin, 2011, advocates) as that would be part of a crony capitalism model wherein tight links between politicians and industry leaders are a constitutional mechanism in the economic model at hand. That is, the self-regulation model means that the finance industry loses some of its inherited privileges, subsidies, and exemptions from the state, but gains the full right to regulate itself. This insulates tax-payers from managerial malfeasance and serves to purify a more clearly market-based system.

One of the major challenges for the self-regulation model is to establish what Omarova (2011) calls a "community of fate mentality," a sense of sharing a commitment to socially and economically defined joint causes. This sounds like an unsurmountable challenge for an industry that has made "greed" (Omarova, 2011: 490) and personal gain the dominant driving force of the operations for decades, but Omarova (2011: 420) points at the nuclear power industry and chemical manufacturing as two credible role-model industries. Following the Three Miles Island and Bhopal disasters, these two industries started to develop an entirely new attitude towards systemic risks and accepted that industry actors—and not only regulators—had a key role to play to avoid similar disasters in the future. To Omarova (2011), such an extended, public view of the industry is needed to amend the present situation:

> [M]odern financial institutions do not have meaningful incentives to create a system of embedded self-regulation. This absence of incentives to self-regulate is due to a variety of factors, including regulatory fragmentation and heterogeneity of interests throughout the industry, little direct public involvement in monitoring the industry's performance, and insufficient political pressure on the industry to self-monitor for systemic risk. Perhaps the most important obstacle to self-regulation is the lack of a "community of fate" mentality within the financial industry, which currently enjoys extraordinary security through its access to an extensive public safety net and the near certainty of government bailouts in the event of a crisis. (Omarova, 2011: 420)

As already stated, granting the finance industry the licence to regulate itself as it believes is the most attractive balance between efficiency and stability needs to be accompanied by an elimination of, e.g., federal deposit insurance and other forms of public subsidy to create incentives to act in accordance with "a community of fate mentality." That is, Omarova's (2011: 439) self-regulation model seeks to "embed" financial practices in "broader social values and regulatory principles," as opposed to the previous "top-down model," separating the industry from public interest and yet accompanied by various subsidies and privileges.

This new regulatory model and new governance regime is absolutely necessary to implement as finance industry conglomerates are today behemoths that embody a disproportionate amount of economic and political power, now "effectively holding the governments and the public, whose tax payments finance those governments, hostage" (Omarova, 2011: 470). As we can learn from history, Omarova (2011: 490) argues, "it is at best naive and at worst hypocritical to claim that financial firms and their managers will be willing or able to control their greed for the sake of the public good." That is, what policy makers, regulators, and the wider public learn from history is that "[n]o amount of institutional reform will be able to 'nudge' the financial services industry toward greater responsibility and effective self-regulation," Omarova (2011: 490) claims.

Summary and Conclusion

In both Levitin's (2011) and Omarova's (2011) advocacy of regulatory reform, the question of political accountability is brought to the forefront. What Omarova (2011) calls the "traditional top down" regulation model, where finance industry actors are given the right to pursue self-interested strategies to undermine the effects of regulatory control, is not effective in an environment where contestants for the highest positions in Washington (e.g., the Secretary of Treasury, the chair of the Securities and Exchange Commission, etc.) are recruited from within the finance industry, and where lobbyism and campaign donations are part of the political architecture. Furthermore, the competitive struggles between the U.K. and London and the U.S. and New York ("NYLON") over finance industry activities and investment have served as a strong motivator for the industry's by-passing of regulatory control (Wilmarth, 2013: 1394–1395). This "race to the bottom" in terms of permissive regulatory oversight has continued outside of the political and legal limelight, and has in many cases been tolerated by democratically elected entities. The work of, e.g., Levitin (2011) and Omarova (2011) indicate that the patience of certain politicians and the wider public is running short, and political accountability is on the agenda anew. The unfinished business of governance is thus a question of how to balance efficiency and stability in ways that reduce the risk exposure of the tax-payers and the voters. Politics and political accountability is of necessity part of this model.

SUMMARY AND CONCLUSION: THE UNFINISHED BUSINESS OF GOVERNANCE

The principal idea advanced in this volume is that governance is in many complex and convoluted ways related to the sharp growth in economic inequality being observed and reported in a substantial scholarly literature. It has been a popular doctrine among political scientists, political advisors, and policy makers to assume that democratic states are of necessity capable of establishing mechanisms that insulate themselves from their own ossification and decline. Not least have many disastrous military operations overseas been initiated on the basis of this belief in the superiority of the democratic political system. The belief in democracy remains solid in the political mainstream in most developed and industrial states—and for good reasons—but democratic polity is by no means infallible or vaccinated against illiberal political forces. Many democratic states, including not least the U.S., otherwise taking pride in the world's oldest and most revered constitution, have initiated many reforms to counteract, e.g., economic inequality (see, e.g., Hinton, 2016) but have failed as other political objectives (e.g., the securing of free market pricing in an expanding number of industries and social services) have marginalized this issue (Bonica et al., 2013). Democratic states are, therefore, seemingly paradoxical, able to accommodate activities and programmes undermining the innermost essence of democratic politics to generate the largest possible social and economic welfare for the largest possible proportion of the population. In a market-based society, the question of governance is a key issue to target to fully understand underlying mechanisms that generate economic inequality, e.g., the deviation between productivity growth and real-wage growth after 1970. Market society advocacy is based on the chimera that it is anonymous market actors who make decisions on the basis of their uncoordinated processing of public information—not so much "voting with their feet" as through their purchasing decisions (Fourcade and Healy, 2017). This is the master-narrative of orthodox neoclassical economic theory, distributing decisions across all market participants. Outside speculative economic thinking, decisions are not always made in such a manner: instead it is qualified men and women, mostly highly educated, intelligent, and with the best intentions, that make decisions pertaining to governance issues. These men and women—CEOs, directors, policy makers, regulators operating on governmental licences, etc.—may not at all share an uncritical belief in market pricing, or may not actively support political decisions conducive to economic inequality, but to-date, such decisions made have generated the mostly unintended (but in some cases, strategically pursued) consequence of economic inequality. Governance practices are therefore not something that simply surface or emerge *ex nihilo*, but are the outcome from conscious political actions and economic decision making; it is a man-made system, yet shrouded in substantial uncertainty and at times even mystery.

Much governance literature, especially in corporate governance, suffers from its own disciplinary and ideological blindfolds, where minor details are scrutinized in detail ad nauseam and with diminishing return on investment (e.g., the tripartite model including CEOs, directors, and shareholders), while the larger issues are left in the dark (Coffee, 2006). For instance, regardless of whether the analyst endorses shareholder primacy governance or not, the fact remains that the corporation is a team production effort, and therefore the overwhelming emphasis on how corporate governance decisions affect shareholder wealth is simply overstated vis-à-vis other concerns. For instance, the shareholder primacy hegemony correlates with the decline of the public corporation and with lower degrees on Initial Public Offerings (IPOs) in the American economy (Schneider, 2015: 194), a fact that can be interpreted as that it is becoming increasingly unattractive to have shareholders, and firms are therefore held in private equity. This interpretation of a factual condition is by no means far-fetched or otherwise undermines the recognition of the corporation as principal vehicle for economic enterprising, or the market as the favoured site for economic transaction. But what are the wider socio-economic consequences if the corporation, widely endorsed as a primary mechanism for the production of economic value, is excluded from the public sphere and is increasingly closely held? As Blair and Stout (2001: 1795) remark, "the boardroom is a notoriously opaque environment. Even in large firms, only the most public and bitter battles are reported in the press." In the future, corporate governance decisions may be even further removed from the public sphere and even more veiled in secrecy, making essentially competitive capitalism emerge as a form of closed society or a subterranean fraternity protected from the public gaze and largely inaccessible for the median voter. How would such a scenario in turn affect the century-long tradition of enacting competitive capitalism as a popular concern, ranging from investment clubs (Harrington, 2008) and campaigns to enrol more citizens in stock-trading (Ailon, 2015; Hochfelder, 2006) to political slogans such as "the ownership society" (a catch-phrase introduced by the Bush Jr. administration)? The transformation, in Melman's (1997) terms, of private capitalism into state capitalism in the New Deal era is being undermined, and scholars, pundits, and policy makers ponder alternative "future capitalisms" (Harcourt, 2014; Wallerstein et al., 2013).

Governance and corporate governance in particular do have a decisive effect on, e.g., economic equality, and therefore governance is and will remain an important mechanism in democratic, industrialized, and differentiated economies. The enigma that needs to be approached is: why does, e.g., the corporate governance literature basically ignore this condition? "The champions of truth are hardest to find, not when it is dangerous to tell it, but rather when it is boring," Nietzsche (1876/1994: 237) remarks. Economic inequality is for many orthodox economists a non-issue, being more a consequence of poor and uninformed choices of certain market actors than a systemic feature of the economic system economists purport to both understand and to be in the position to govern. This takes us to an alternative explanation for the ignorance of governance's wider socio-economic consequence, the "learned ignorance" (with Nicholas of Cusa's theological concept; Koyré, 1959: 8) of certain actors, i.e., their inability to see what is in front of them in broad daylight on the basis of the doctrines and conventional wisdom blindfolding the professional actor. "Some of the most crucial properties of the world are not regarded as concealed beneath a mask of deceptive appearances, things inferred from pale suggestions or riddled out of equivocal signs," Geertz (1975: 22) writes in his acclaimed essay on common sense as a culture; "the most crucial properties of the world" are "just there," "invisible only to the clever." The failure to anticipate or to even recognize events as they unfold in front of an audience or a professional community has been observed time and again (e.g., Fligstein, Brundage, and Schultz, 2017), being a most puzzling concern for, e.g., psychologists or historians, making the question of culpability and blame a key issue in post-hoc resolution processes (see e.g., Kenny, 2015; Hood, 2011; Hargie, Stapleton, and Tourish, 2010; Vaughan, 1996; Gephart, 1993). Intelligence and integrity are oftentimes seen as individual and collective resources that insulate the actor and communities against illicit behaviour, but also highly intelligent and cultivated individuals may fall prey to delusions and participate in criminal and immoral activities, we learn time and again from history. In fact, ample evidence suggests that groups that count themselves among "the best and the brightest" are the ones most susceptible to group think, cognitive dissonance, positive asymmetry, etc. Intelligence, defined in functional terms as information-processing capacities, can do good and do harm.

As this volume has hopefully demonstrated, governance is a manifold and complex, situated and contingent activity, ceaselessly being adjusted to new conditions and emerging information that could not be reasonably expected to be included in the original decision making point. To govern means to balance legislation, regulatory frameworks, political objectives and interest, inherited traditions, beliefs, and doctrines, and all this under the influence of cognitive limitations and restricted and mostly insuffi-cient time frames. In other words, governance is of necessity an unfinished business, always in the making and never completed once and for all. Furthermore, as unintended consequences of purposeful action are all policy makers' demons, the will to do good may easily lead astray or generate new issues and concerns underway. The data and information collected to inform governance decisions may be incomplete, ambiguous, or disputed, which further complicates the decision making. At the same time, an integrated theory about the nature of governance on various levels, ranging from the macro-scale (in transnational governance) to the meso-scale (the state, region, or industry level), and the micro-scale (corporate governance) enables an understanding of how various forms of governance practices and decisions contribute to social and economic welfare. This volume has been written with this ambition in mind, to release governance from the tripartite CEO–director–shareholder model, and to recognize a wider scope of issues and concerns, which are of relevance also for the economic system of competitive capitalism. The unfinished business of governance is therefore the starting point for a renewal of at least the research on corporate governance.

NOTES

1. McLevey (2015) here refers to the German social theorist Jürgen Habermas' theory of communicative rationality, presented in his major two-volume work *The Theory of Communicative Action* (Habermas, 1984, 1987). In Habermas' view, communication contains and conveys a specific rationality that is conducive to joint understanding and agreements. It may be noted that Habermas' affirmative view of the virtues of communi-cation has been disputed on both theoretical and substantial grounds by e.g., Niklas Luhmann (1995).
2. For instance, despite the size and influence of the finance industry, approximately 70 million Americans do not have a bank account or access traditional financial services (Baradaran, 2015: 139). The poorer share of the population therefore has to pay considerable fees to be part of the monetary economy; "the average unbanked family," Baradaran (2015: 94) writes, spends "almost 10 percent of its income" on financial transactions.

3. When assessing the leverage of financial institutions and the risk they are exposed to, it is important to keep in mind that the shadow banking system adds to the burden of banks in distress (Adrian and Ashcraft, 2012). The de-regulation of the securities market in 1999 and 2000 in the U.S. was one of the primary drivers of the shadow banking system expansion (Greenwood and Scharfstein, 2013: 21); as securities were endorsed by federal agency representatives and representatives of regulatory agencies as a finance market device that served to distribute risks across several market actors, the finance industry institutions were eager to take on more risk. Unfortunately, the issuance of credit in "nondepository financial intermediaries" made banks more susceptible to "liquidity shocks, runs on liabilities, and fire sales of assets" during downturns in the economic cycle (Peek and Rosengren, 2016: 94). The developer of the shadow banking system thus underrated the inherent instability of the finance market, in the end leading to the Federal Reserve having no choice but to take action to restore the confidence in the finance industry to make it operable:

    > The extensive borrowing from the Federal Reserve facilities illustrates just how impaired financing was at many nondepository financial institutions. Although these institutions had received relatively little academic scrutiny, they had become critical infrastructure for the continuing movement to more market-centric financing. However, unlike banks, for which financial regulation had been designed to mitigate the impact of liquidity and capital shocks, broker–dealers were not well positioned by regulations for either type of shock. (Peek and Rosengren, 2016: 93-94)

    In the end, the combination of securitization and the shadow banking system facilitated the expansion of, e.g., the sub-prime home mortgage market, leading to a contamination of the entire finance industry and eventually leading to its stalemate in the fall of 2008, where no more credit could be issued. This outcome runs counter to the conventional wisdom of finance theorists and free market protagonists, suggesting that "a primary function of the financial sector is to dampen the effects of risk by reallocating it efficiently to parties that can bear risks the most easily" (Greenwood and Scharfstein, 2013: 26); rather than reducing systemic risks, securitization and the shadow-banking system amplified systemic risk to unprecedented levels. Stricter capital rules and stress tests, Peek and Rosengren (2016: 93–94) argue, would have been able to ensure that banks had far larger "capital cushions" protecting them from emerging problems. That is, *more*, not *less* regulatory oversight would possibly have maintained the functionality of the system.

4. The case of AIG (American International Group), was one of the of the most controversial bailout decisions being part of the Bush Administration's bank rescue program TARP. At the time of the rescue, the insurance company AIG reported more than US$2.7 trillion notational derivatives exposure, whereof US$1 trillion was "with only twelve financial firms" (Helleiner, 2011: 71). Similar to the even more spectacular but more ill-fated energy company Enron, also an "innovator" in the era of finance market expansion, AIG had used financial markets to "transform itself from a traditional insurance company to a bank-like firm" (McDonald and Paulson, 2015: 102). AIG participated in securities lending to transform insurance company assets into residential mortgage-backed securities and collateralized debt obligations, "ultimately losing US$21 billion and threatening the solvency of its life insurance subsidiaries" (McDonald and Paulson, 2015: 102).

    Prior to the 2008 bailout, AIG had paid more than US$1.6 billion in fines for misreporting its books between 2000 and 2005 (Freeman, 2010: 168), and in many cases the "risk management" routines seemed underdeveloped at best: "Despite its reliance on fragile sources of funding, AIG had no specialized liquidity risk committee until 2007," McDonald and Paulson (2015: 103) write, suggesting that AIG's senior management had a solid but unsubstantiated belief in real estate-related investments as being safe bets. Despite the lost court cases, AIG was still treated as "one of the great financial institutions in the world" by the regulators (Freeman, 2010: 168). AIG Financial Products Division, with CEO Joseph Cassano having a background from the junk bond pioneers Drexel Burnham Lambert, the "junk-bond king" Michael Milken's home base, rewarded his 400 employees with individual annual compensations exceeding US$1 million on average

(Eichengreen, 2015: 204). Taken together, "salaries and bonuses accounted for a third of the unit's total revenues," Eichengreen (2015: 204) reports. In 2008, AIG Financial Products Division lost US$40.4 billion. Even though the U.S. Government now owned 80 percent of the AIG shares as part of the resolution activities, and had invested US$180 billion of tax money to rescue the firm (US$170 billion in Barofsky's (2012: 138) account), AIG nevertheless announced on March 14, 2009, that it would pay 377 members of the division "a total of $220 million in bonuses for 2008, an average of over $500,000 per employee" (Crotty, 2009: 565). Seven employees were lucky to receive more than US$2 million each, all this despite the remarkable US$40.4 billion loss during the preceding year. The AIG bonus announcement created an outrage in Washington, DC among politicians and officials, who widely regarded this as an unprecedented case of managerial malfeasance, shamelessly defying all description (Suárez, 2014: 86). In the end, when AIG had been safely brought into the harbour by the government agencies and faith in the financial markets had been restored, the story about AIG took an expected turn and "reality outpaced satire" (as Mirowski, 2013: 9, puts it), when the former CEO of AIG, Hank Greenberg, "brought a suit against the U.S. government for not bailing out AIG at a sufficient munificent rate." McDonald and Paulson's (2015: 102) claim that AIG's transformation into a "bank-like firm," "ultimately proved disastrous" rests not only on financial and economic but also moral and ethical grounds.

5. "[W]e conclude that Moody's relatively uninformative ratings result from conflicts of interest in the issuer-pays model," Cornaggia and Cornaggia (2013: 2265) summarize in their study of one of the "Big Three" credit rating agencies. "First-time issuers create a flow of revenues for rating agencies. Hence, rating agencies have incentives to provide more issuer-friendly ratings in order to attract further business in this fast growing asset class," Alp (2013: 2455) explains in an attempt to theoretically substantiate his finding that credit rating quality has deteriorated over time.

6. The Bagehot rule is named after the British journalist Walter Bagehot (1826–1877), who famously claimed that "money does not manage itself" (cited in Mehrling, 2011: 8), indicating the need for the state to serve as the lender-of-last-resort and therefore being able to claim the legitimate role as a regulator of e.g., the finance industry.

7. The concept of moral hazard, frequently used in passing in the governance literature, deserves some explication. Baker (1996: 239) argues that the term, derived from the emerging nineteenth-century insurance industry, originally denoted the risk (or "temptation") that the client, provided with a contract (the insurance) that could turn an unattractive or under-valued asset into monetary compensation for losses in the event of, say, a fire in a real estate, would act opportunistically to liquidify his or her assets. Despite the formulation of what Baker (1996) refers to as the "economics of moral hazard," moral hazard has "never been a straightforward, purely logical or scientific concept," Baker (1996: 239) argues. For instance, economists such as Kenneth Arrow have used the insurance industry terminology and substituted its key terms with neoclassical economic theory concepts such as "incentives." This in turn has served to understate the institutional embedding of the term moral hazard, Baker (1996: 243) argues: "On purely technical grounds, the economics of moral hazard are incomplete because by assuming that individuals are in control of their situations, the economics of moral hazard ignore institutional control over what people do to prevent or minimize the cost of loss." In other words, in Baker's (1996) view, economics of moral hazard are capable of formulating propositions regarding the incentives that various types of private and social insurances generate (say the proclivity to "increase the consumption of health care," or benefit from "paid time off from work"), but it does not of necessity follow from such propositions that social policy should reduce the benefits derived from such insurances, simply because the social benefits from welfare policies outweigh the social costs. As the economics of moral hazard ignores the institutional set-up wherein such "moral hazards" are potentially generated (a consequence of the rational choice theory model being applied, eliminating supra-individual factors), economists systematically undervalue the efforts of, e.g., the welfare state or private insurance companies to protect the injured, the sick, and the poor

from economic hardship and social exclusion. Worse still, by advancing a theory of moral hazard that purports to strictly operate on the basis of economic incentives and market prices, while in fact being based on an "ethics of self-sufficiency," economists have encouraged policy makers, tax-payers, and voters to assume that the injured, the sick, and the poor are "in control of themselves and their situation." This, in turn, Baker (1996: 244) argues, has served to "absolve the rest of us of our responsibility for that situation." Ultimately, the economics of moral hazard advance and advocate on theoretical grounds the idea that "social responsibility is a bad thing" (Baker, 1996: 244). Therefore, the ignorance of how the wider institutional framework serves to evade and neutralize incentives leading to opportunistic behaviour, and that the socio-economic benefits of various insurance systems are larger than the costs, economic theory uses the term of moral hazard in an idiosyncratic way and under the auspices of the orthodox neoclassical economic theory model.

8. As it is the state and the government that enact laws, markets and governments should not be viewed as "polar opposites," Jacobides (2005: 488) says; "there is a direct need for governmental support to facilitate the emergence of markets" (Jacobides, 2005: 488). In the end, a market is co-developed by industry participants, the government, and regulators, as these market makers create an "[i]nstitutional backbone for exchange, including but not limited to information standards and norms of collaboration," without which markets cannot operate, Jacobides (2005: 491) proposes.

9. Stout (2011: 37) notes that the members of the President's Working Group who advocated a de-regulation of the Over-The-Counter (OTC) derivatives trade were economists and bureaucrats "without legal training," whereas the most prominent critic of the legislation-in-the-making, Brooksley Born, the chairman of the Commodity Futures Trading Commission (CFTC) (1996–1999), was a lawyer.

This inability to recognize the role of legal reform and to examine its empirical consequences for market practices is more widespread than may be intuitively believed. Smith and Gai's (2017) study of changes in the hedge fund market is one exemplary case of how market actors' voluntaristic practices are examined both in isolation from legislative practices and treated as being the primus motor of market changes. After 1999, Smith and Gai (2017: 1042) note that the hedge fund industry "began an abrupt and dramatic shift toward increased product differentiation." For instance, between 2000 and 2008, so-called funds of funds investment tripled (Smith and Gai, 2017: 1052, Figure 3) and acquired considerable attention in news media (Smith and Gai, 2017: 1054, Figure 4). In Smith and Gai's (2017: 1051) analysis, enacting market actors as the key actors in orchestrating the change, such structural changes in the hedge fund industry were caused by a financial crisis unfolding in Russia in 1998, and the bailout of the Long Term Capital Management (LTCM), demanding a US$3.63 billion capital infusion, orchestrated by the Federal Reserve Bank of New York. "As a result of the 1998 crisis ... funds of funds seized the opportunity to capitalize on heightened investor anxiety and the increasing need for due diligence. We argue it was at this point that funds of funds began to alter their approach to brokerage" (Smith and Gai, 2017: 1053). That these changes were triggered by the considerable legal reforms of 1999 and 2000, the Gramm–Leach–Bliley Act of 1999 (officially named the Financial Services Modernization Act (FSMA)) and Commodity Futures Modernization Act (CFMA) of 2000, do not occur to Smith and Gai (2017), who fail to address or even mention any legislative activities in the period whatsoever to substantiate the empirical phenomenon being examined. Instead, Smith and Gai (2017) maintain their voluntaristic view of fund managers, being in the positon to autonomously pursue new, more risky strategies: "Individual hedge fund managers, long stymied by knowledge asymmetries between themselves and end capital investors, were more than willing to push innovative, idiosyncratic products onto the market" (Smith and Gai, 2017: 1054). To substantiate this interpretation, Smith and Gai (2017) cite funds of funds managers, offering highly technocratic and technical explanations for their activities (including finance market staple terms such as *diversification* and *volatility*), statements that Smith and Gai (2017) candidly accept at face value, i.e., as devoid of any legal underpinnings:

> The big chunk of what funds of funds need to do is look for diversification. The typical fund of funds wants to deliver pretty low volatility return streams to investors. The best way to do that is to have a very diversified portfolio so the funds of funds will naturally look for different strategies and the market will supply that. (Interview, Funds of Funds manager, February 25, 2009, London, cited in Smith and Gai, 2017: 1054)

Smith and Gai's (2017) overstating of finance industry actors' ability to act independently within the industry is indicative of what can be referred to as "legal amnesia," the tendency to overlook, ignore, and marginalize law and legislative practice when explaining social practices, and market practices in particular. Dobbin and Sutton (1998: 472) suggest that this tendency is rooted in a neglect of the key role of the sovereign state and its agencies in creating and monitoring markets:

> Americans develop collective amnesia about the state's role in shaping private enterprises … Americans subscribe to the theory that firms operate in a Hobbesian economic state of nature, in which behavior depends very much on managerial initiative and markets and very little on political initiative and law. (Dobbin and Sutton, 1998: 472)

10. Krippner (2017) suggests that the creation of credit is an "indispensable tool of statecraft," enabling economic citizenship for a larger share of the population. Consequently, there is evidence of community-based activism to secure credit supply for defined and historically disadvantaged groups such as women or people of colour, treating the access to credit as an elementary citizen right (Krippner, 2017). Unfortunately, Quinn's (2017) study of the creation of the federal home mortgage loan institute Fannie Mae under the Lyndon B. Johnson Administration reveals that government officials may embrace finance industry solutions and techniques to handle perceived budget problems, only to learn that these solutions are difficult to control later on, and thus contribute to later fiscal or financial crises. "[N]ational budgets link the fates of fiscal institutions and financial markets," Quinn (2017: 79) summarizes. In this legal view of finance, the sovereign state, its associated entities, and the finance industry develop close ties that are complicated to disentangle during, e.g., the resolution work that follows financial crises.

11. As Pistor (2013: 320) notes, not only are homeowners, whose interests are recognized only after most of the key actors' interests have been secured, expected to carry significant proportions of the systemic risk in the finance system, either directly as the holders of home mortgage loan contracts or indirectly as tax-payers, but they are also exposed to currency risk as their underlying contracts are translated into securities being sold on a global financial market.

12. A "haircut" is a finance industry shorthand term denoting the difference between the market value of an asset used as loan collateral (say, the market value of a real estate) and the amount of the loan, i.e., the credit issued. "To take a haircut" means that the creditor is willing to accept a loss if there are other benefits accruing either directly or indirectly to the creditor from this breach of the contract.

13. In 2013, *The Economist* published data from a survey including 400 financial executives, and over 50 percent of the respondents admitted they were "at least in part being 'flexible' over ethical standards" (Gordon and Zaring, 2017: 566). In addition, numerous polls have suggested that "[b]ankers are among the least trusted of all the professions," Gordon and Zaring (2017: 567) write. Consistent with Omarova's (2011) proposal, Gordon and Zaring (2017: 562) advocate what they refer to as "ethical banking," a concept that "mimic[s] the root values adopted by professional responsibility codes."

Bibliography

Abdelal, Rawi (2007), *Capital rules: The construction of the global finance*, Cambridge, MA: Harvard University Press.

Adelstein, Richard P. (1991), "The nation as an economic unit": Keynes, Roosevelt, and the managerial ideal, *Journal of American History*, 78(1): 160–187.

Adler, Nancy, and Harzing, Anne-Wil (2009), When knowledge wins: Transcending the sense and nonsense of academic rankings, *Academy of Management Learning & Education*, 8(1): 72–95.

Adrian, Tobias, and Ashcraft, Adam B. (2012), Shadow banking regulation, *Annual Review of Financial Economics*, 4: 99–140.

Adrian, Tobias, Fleming, Michael, Shachar, Or, and Vogt, Erik (2017), Market liquidity after the financial crisis, *Annual Review of Financial Economics*, 9: 43–83.

Aghion, Philippe, and Holden, Richard (2011), Incomplete contracts and the theory of the firm: What have we learned over the past 25 years? *The Journal of Economic Perspectives*, 25(2): 181–197.

Aguilera, Ruth V., and Cuervo-Cazurra, Alvaro (2004), Codes of good governance worldwide: What is the trigger? *Organization Studies*, 25(3): 415–443.

Ailon, Galit (2015), Rethinking calculation: The popularization of financial trading outside the global centres of finance, *Economy and Society*, 44(4): 592–615.

Akerlof, George (1970), The market for "lemons": Quality uncertainty and the market mechanism, *Quarterly Journal of Economics*, 84(3): 488–500.

Alchian, Armen A. (1965), The basis of some recent advances in the theory of management of the firm, *Journal of Industrial Economics*, 7: 30–41.

Alderson, Arthur S., and Nielsen, François (2002), Globalization and the great u-turn: Income inequality trends in 16 OECD countries, *American Journal of Sociology*, 107(5): 1244–1299.

Alp, Aysun (2013), Structural shifts in credit rating standards. *The Journal of Finance*, 68(6), 2435–2470.

Amadae, Sonja Michelle (2003), *Rationalizing capitalist democracy: The Cold War origins of rational choice liberalism*, Chicago & London: The University of Chicago Press.

Amadae, Sonja M. (2016), *Prisoners of reason: Game theory and neoliberal political economy*, Cambridge: Cambridge University Press.

Anderson, Gina (2008), Mapping academic resistance in the managerial university, *Organization*, 15(2): 251–270.

Arnoldi, Jakob (2016), Computer algorithms, market manipulation and the institutionalization of high frequency trading, *Theory, Culture & Society*, 33(1): 29–52.

Arrow, Kenneth J. (1974), *The limits of organization*, New York: W.W. Norton.

Augustin, Patrick, Subrahmanyam, Marti G., Tang, Dragon Y., and Wang, Sarah Q. (2016), Credit default swaps: Past, present, and future, *Annual Review of Financial Economics*, 8: 175–196.

Aven, Brandy L. (2015), The paradox of corrupt networks: An analysis of organizational crime at Enron, *Organization Science*, 26(4): 980–996.

Babb, Sarah (2013), The Washington Consensus as transnational policy paradigm: Its origins, trajectory and likely successor, *Review of International Political Economy*, 20(2): 268–297.

Baker, Tom (1996), On the genealogy of moral hazard, *Texas Law Review*, 75(2): 237–292.

Baradaran, Mehrsa (2015), *How the other half banks: Exclusion, exploitation, and the threat to democracy*, Cambridge, MA: Harvard University Press.

Barker, Richard, and Schulte Sebastian (2016), Representing the market perspective: Fair value measurement for non-financial assets, *Accounting, Organizations, and Society*, 56: 55–67.

Barofsky, Neil M. (2012), *Bailout: An inside account of how Washington abandoned main street while rescuing Wall Street*, New York: Free Press.

Bartley, Tim (2007), Institutional emergence in an era of globalization: The rise of transnational private regulation of labor and environmental conditions, *American Journal of Sociology*, 113(2): 297–351.

Bartolini, Stefano, Bonatti, Luigi, and Sarracino Francesco (2014), The Great Recession and the bulimia of US consumers: Deep causes and possible ways out, *Cambridge Journal of Economics*, 38(5): 1015–1042.

Baumer, Eric P., Ranson, J.W. Andrew, Arnio, Ashley N., Fulmer, Ann, and De Zilwa Shane (2017), Illuminating a dark side of the American dream: Assessing the prevalence and predictors of mortgage fraud across U.S. counties, *American Journal of Sociology*, 123(2): 549–603.

Baumol, William J. (1959), *Business behavior, value and growth*, New York: Macmillan.

Bebchuk, Lucian A., and Neeman, Zvika (2010), Investor protection and interest group politics, *Review of Financial Studies*, 23(3): 1089–1119.

Becker, M.C. (2004), Organizational routines; A review of the literature, *Industrial and Corporate Change*, 13(4): 643–677.

Bell, Stephen, and Hindmoor, Andrew (2015) *Masters of the universe, slaves of the market*, Cambridge, MA: Harvard University Press.

Benton, Richard A. (2016), Corporate governance and nested authority: Cohesive network structure, actor-driven mechanisms, and the balance of power in American corporations, *American Journal of Sociology*, 122(3): 661–713.

Bergstrand, Kelly (2014), Cognitive shocks: Scientific discovery and mobilization, *Science as Culture*, 23(3): 320–343.

Berle, Adolf A., Jr (1932), For whom corporate managers are trustees: A note, *Harvard Law Review*, 45(8): 1365–1372.

Berle, Adolf A., and Means, Gardiner C. (1932/1991), *The modern corporation & private property*, New Brunswick: Transaction Publishers.

Berlin, Isaiah (1958), *Two concepts of liberty: An inaugural lecture, delivered before the University of Oxford on 31 October 1958*, Oxford: Clarendon Press.

Berman, Elizabeth Popp (2012), *Creating the market university: How academic science became an economic engine*, Princeton & Oxford: Princeton University Press.

Bermiss, Y. Sekou, and Greenbaum Bruce E. (2016), Loyal to whom? The effect of relational embeddedness and managers' mobility on market tie dissolution, *Administrative Science Quarterly*, 61(2): 254-290.

Bernhardt, Annette (2012), The role of labor market regulation in rebuilding economic opportunity in the United States, *Work and Occupations*, 39(4): 354–375.

Bernstein, Lisa (1992), Opting out of the legal system: Extralegal contractual relations in the diamond industry, *Journal of Legal Studies*, 21(1): 115–157.

Berressem, Hanjo (2005), "Incerto tempore incertisque locis": The logic of the clinamen and the birth of physics, in Abbas, Niran, ed., *Mapping Michel Serres*, Ann Arbor: The University of Michigan Press, (pp. 51–71).

Bertrand, Marianne, and Mullainathan, Sendhil (2003), Enjoying the quiet life? Corporate governance and managerial preferences, *Journal of Political Economy*, 111(5): 1043–1075.

Beverungen, Armin, Hoedemaekers, Casper, and Veldman, Jeroen (2014), Charity and finance in the university, *Critical Perspectives on Accounting*, 25(19): 58–66.

Bevir, Mark (2009), *Key concepts in governance*, Thousand Oaks & London: Sage.

Bevir, Mark (2012), *Governance: A very short introduction*, Oxford & New York: Oxford University Press.

Bhagat, Sanjai, Bolton, Brian, and Romano, Roberta (2008), The promise and peril of corporate governance indices, *Columbia Law Review*, 108(8): 1803–1882.

Bidwell, Matthew J. (2013), What happened to long-term employment? The role of worker power and environmental turbulence in explaining declines in worker tenure, *Organization Science*, 24(4): 1061–1082.

Bidwell, Matthew, Briscoe, Forrest, Fernandez-Mateo, Isabel, and Sterling, Adina (2013), The employment relationship and inequality: How and why changes in employment practices are reshaping rewards in organizations, *Academy of Management Annals*, 7: 61–121.

Bignami, Francesca (2005), Transgovernmental networks vs. democracy: The case of the European information privacy network. *Michigan Journal of International Law*, 26: 807–868.

Biondi, Yuri (2013), The governance and disclosure of the firm as an enterprise entity, *Seattle University Law Review*, 36(2): 391–416.

Biven, Josh, and Shierholz, Heidi (2013), The great recession's impact on jobs, wages, and incomes, in Wolfson, Martin H., and Epstein, Gerald, A. eds. (2013), *Handbook of the political economy of financial crises*, New York & Oxford: Oxford University Press (pp. 61–94).

Blair, Margaret M. (2003), Locking in capital: What corporate law achieved for business organizers in the nineteenth century, *UCLA Law Review*, 51(2), 387–455.

Blair, Margaret M., and Stout, Lynn A. (1999), A team production theory of corporate law. *Virginia Law Review*, 85(2), 247–328.

Blair, Margaret M., and Stout, Lynn A. (2001), Director accountability and the mediating role of the corporate board. *Washington University Law Review*, 79(2): 403–449.

Blinder, Alan S. (2013), *When the music stopped: The financial crisis, the response, and the work ahead*, New York: Penguin.

Block, Cheryl (2010), Measuring the true cost of government bailout, *Washington University Law Review*, 88: 149–228.

Bluestone, Harry, and Harrison, Bennett (1982), *Deindustrialization of America: Plant closings, community abandonment, and the dismantling of basic industry*, New York: Basic Books.

Bluhm, Christian, and Wagner, Christoph (2011), Valuation and risk management of collateralized debt obligations and related securities, *Annual Review in Financial Economics*, 3: 193–222.

Blyth, Mark (2013), *Austerity: The history of a dangerous idea*, Oxford & New York: Oxford University Press.

Boatright, John R. (1994), Fiduciary duties and the shareholder-management relation: Or, what's so special about shareholders? *Business Ethics Quarterly*, 4(4): 393–407.

Bolton, Patrick, Freixas, Xavier, and Shapiro, Joel (2012), The credit ratings game, *Journal of Finance*, 67(1): 85–112.

Bonica, Adam, McCarty, Nolan, Poole, Keith T., and Rosenthal, Howard (2013), Why hasn't democracy slowed rising inequality? *Journal of Economic Perspectives*, 27(3): 103–124.

Bork, Robert H. (1978), *The antitrust paradox: A policy at war with itself*, New York: Free Press.

Boudon, Raymond (2003), Beyond rational choice theory, *Annual Review of Sociology*, 29: 1–21.

Bougen, Philip D., and Young, Joni J. (2012), Fair value accounting: Simulacra and simulation, *Critical Perspectives on Accounting*, 23(4): 390–402.

Brady, David, Baker Regina S., and Finnigan, Ryan (2013), When unionization disappears: State-level unionization and working poverty in the United States, *American Sociological Review*, 78(5): 872–896.

Brandeis, Louis D. (1914/1967), *Other people's money and how the bankers use it*, New York: Harper Torchbooks.

Braudel, Ferdnand (1980), *On history*, Chicago & London: The University of Chicago Press.

Brav, Alon, Jiang, Wei, and Kim, Hyunseob (2015), The real effects of hedge fund activism: Productivity, asset allocation, and labor outcomes. *Review of Financial Studies*, 28(10): 2723–2769.

Brennan, David M. (2014), "Too bright for comfort": A Kaleckian view of profit realisation in the USA, 1964–2009, *Cambridge Journal of Economics*, 38(1): 239–255.

Brighenti, Andrea Mubi (2018), The social life of measures: Conceptualizing measure–value environments, *Theory, Culture & Society*, 35(1): 23–44.

Brody, Howard (2007), *Hooked: Ethics, the medical profession, and the pharmaceutical industry*, Lanham: Rowman & Littlefield.

Brudney, Victor (1997), Contract and fiduciary duty in corporate law, *Boston College Law Review*, 4(4): 595–665.

Budros, Art (1999), A conceptual framework for analyzing why organizations downsize, *Organization Science*, 10(1): 69–82.

Büthe, Tim, and Mattli, Walter (2011), *The new global rulers: The privatization of regulation in the world economy*, Princeton: Princeton University Press.

Buturovic, Zeljka and Tasic, Slavisa (2015) Kahneman's failed revolution against economic orthodoxy, *Critical Review*, 27(2): 127–145.

Cabantous, Laure, and Gond, Jean-Pascal (2011), Rational decision making as performative praxis: Explaining rationality's *Éternel Retour*, *Organization Science*, 22(3): 573–586.

Calomiris, Charles W., and Haber, Stephen H. (2014), *Fragile by design: The political origins of banking crises and scarce credit*, Princeton & Oxford: Princeton University Press.

Camerer, Colin F., and Fehr, Ernst (2006), When does "economic man" dominate social behavior? *Science*, 311(5757): 47–52.

Campbell, John L., and Lindberg, Leon N. (1990), Property rights and the organization of economic activity by the state, *American Sociological Review*, 55(5): 634–647.

Camus, Albert, (1951/2000), *The rebel*, trans. by Anthony Bower, London: Penguin.

Carnes, Nicholas (2013), *White-collar government: The hidden role of class in economic policy making*, Chicago & London: The University of Chicago Press.

Cary, William L. (1974), Federalism and corporate law: Reflections upon Delaware, *Yale Law Journal*, 83(4): 663–705.

Cassidy, John (2009), *How markets fail: The logic of economic calamities*, New York: Picador.

Centeno Miguel A., and Cohen Joseph N. (2012), The arc of neoliberalism, *Annual Review of Sociology*, 38: 317–340.

Cetorelli, Nicola, and Gambera, Michele (2001), Banking market structure, financial dependence and growth: International evidence from industry data, *Journal of Finance*, 56(2): 617–648.

Charness, G., Masclet, D., and Villeval, M.C. (2014), The dark side of competition for status, *Management Science*, 60(1): 38–55.

Charny, David (1990), Nonlegal sanctions in commercial relationships, *Harvard Law Review*, 104(2): 393–467.

Cheng, Ing-Haw, and Xiong, Wei (2014), Why Do hedgers trade so much? *Journal of Legal Studies*, 43(S2): S183–S207.

Chong, Kimberly, and Tuckett, David (2015), Constructing conviction through action and narrative: How money managers manage uncertainty and the consequence for financial market functioning, *Socio-Economic Review*, 13(2): 309–330.

Chu, Johan S.G., and Davis, Gerald F. (2016), Who killed the inner circle? The decline of the American corporate interlock network, *American Journal of Sociology*, 122(3): 714–754.

Citron, Danielle Keats, and Pasquale, Frank A. (2014), The scored society: Due process for automated predictions, *Washington Law Review*, 89(1): 1–33.

Clark, Robert C. (1989), Contracts, elites, and traditions in the making of corporate law, *Columbia Law Review*, 89(7): 1703–1747.

Clarke, Adele E., Mamo, Laura, Fishman, Jennifer R., Shim, Janet K., and Fosket, Jennifer Ruth (2003), Biomedicalization: Technoscientific transformations of health, illness, and U.S. biomedicine, *American Sociological Review*, 68: 161–194.

Clayton, Blake C. (2016), *Commodity markets and the global economy*, New York: Cambridge University Press.

Coffee, John C. (1984), Regulating the market for corporate control: A critical assessment of the tender offer's role in corporate governance, *Columbia Law Review*, 84(5): 1145–1296.

Coffee, John C. (1986), Shareholders versus managers: The strain in the corporate web, *Michigan Law Review*, 85(1): 1–109.

Coffee, John C. (2003), What caused Enron? A capsule social and economic history of the 1990s, *Cornell Law Review*, 89: 269–309.

Coffee John C. (2006), *Gatekeepers: The professions and corporate governance*, New York & Oxford: Oxford University Press.

Coffee, John C. (2007), Law and the market; The impact of enforcement, *University of Pennsylvania Law Review*, 156(2): 229–311.

Coffee, John C. (2011a), Ratings reform: The good, the bad, and the ugly, *Harvard Business Law Review*, 1: 231–278.

Coffee, John C. (2011b), Systemic risk after Frank–Dodd; Contingent capital and the need for regulatory strategies beyond oversight, *Columbia Law Review*, 111(4): 795–847.

Coffee, John C., and Palia, Darius (2016), The wolf at the door: The impact of hedge fund activism on corporate governance, *Journal of Corporation Law*, 41(3): 545–607.

Cohan, William D. (2011), *Money and power: How Goldman Sachs came to rule the world*, London: Allen Lane & New York: Anchor Books.

Cohen, Michael D., March, James G., and Olsen, Johan P. (1972), A garbage can model of organizational choice, *Administrative Science Quarterly*, 17: 1–25.

Collett, François, and Vives, Luis (2013), From preeminence to prominence: The fall of U.S. business schools and the rise of European and Asian business schools in the Financial Times Global MBA Rankings, *Academy of Management Learning & Education*, 12(4): 540–563.

Conti-Brown, Peter (2009), Proposed fat-tail risk metric: Disclosures, derivatives, and the measurement of financial risk, *Washington University Law Review*, 87: 1461.

Conti-Brown, Peter (2016), *The power and independence of the Federal Reserve*, Princeton: Princeton University Press.

Coombs, Nathan (2016), What is an algorithm? Financial regulation in the era of high-frequency trading, *Economy and Society*, 45(2): 278–302.

Cooper, Christine, Graham, Cameron, and Himick, Darlene (2016), Social impact bonds: The securitization of the homeless, *Accounting, Organizations and Society*, 55: 63–82.

Cornaggia, Jess, and Cornaggia, Kimberly J. (2013), Estimating the costs of issuer-paid credit ratings, *Review of Financial Studies*, 26(9): 2229–2269.

Cremers, K.J. Martijn, and Sepe, Simone M. (2016), The shareholder value of empowered boards, *Stanford Law Review*, 68(1): 67–148.

Crotty, James (2009), Structural causes of the global financial crisis: A critical assessment of the "new financial architecture," *Cambridge Journal of Economics*, 33(4): 563–580.

Czarnitzki, Dirk, Grimpe, Christoph, and Toole, Andrew A. (2015), Delay and secrecy: Does industry sponsorship jeopardize disclosure of academic research? *Industrial and Corporate Change*, 24(1): 251–279.

Dacin, M. Tina, Munir, Kamal and Tracey, Paul, (2010), Formal dining at Cambridge colleges: Linking ritual performance and institutional maintenance, *Academy of Management Journal*, 53(6): 1393–1418.

Daily, Catherine M., Dalton, Dan R., and Cannella, Albert A., Jr (2003), Corporate governance: Decades of dialogue and data, *The Academy of Management Review*, 28(3): 371–382.

Dallas, Lynne L. (2011), Short-termism, the financial crisis, and corporate governance. *Journal of Corporation Law*, 37: 264–364.

Daston, Lorraine (2015), Simon and the sirens: A commentary, *Isis*, 106(3): 669–676.

Davidson, Paul (2014), Income inequality and hollowing out the middle class, *Journal of Post Keynesian Economics*, 36(2): 381–384.

Davis, Gerald F. (2009), *Managed by the markets: How finance reshaped America*, Oxford University Press.

Davis, Gerald F. (2015), The twilight of the Berle and Means corporation, in Maria Goranova and Verstegen Ryan, Lori, eds. (2015), *Shareholder empowerment: A new era in corporate governance*, New York: Palgrave Macmillan (pp. 155–168).

Davis, Gerald F., and Greve, Henrich R. (1997), Corporate elite networks and governance changes in the 1980s, *American Journal of Sociology*, 103(1): 1–37.

Davis, Gerald F., and Kim, Suntae (2015), Financialization of the economy, *Annual Review of Sociology*, 41: 203–221.

Davis, Gerald F., and Stout, Suzanne K. (1992), Organization theory and the market for corporate control: A dynamic analysis of the characteristics of large takeover targets, 1980–1990, *Administrative Science Quarterly*, 37(4): 605–633.

Day, Ronald E. (2014), *Indexing it all: The subject in the age of documentation, information, and data*, Cambridge, MA: The MIT Press.

De Araujo, M. (2009), Hugo Grotius, contractualism, and the concept of private property: An institutionalist interpretation. *History of Philosophy Quarterly*, 26(4): 353–371.

De Mesnard, Louis, (2012), On some flaws of university rankings: The example of the SCImago report, *Journal of Socio-Economics*, 41(5): 495–499.

Deleuze, Gilles (1995), *Negotiations*, New York: Columbia University Press.

Dembinski, Paul H., Lager, Carole, Cornford, Andrew, and Bonvin, Jean-Michel, eds. (2006), *Enron and world finance: A case study in ethics*, New York & Houndmills: Palgrave Macmillan.

Demsetz, Harold (1969), Information and efficiency: another viewpoint, *Journal of Law & Economics*, 12(1): 1–22.

Dencker, John C., and Fang, Chichun (2016), Rent seeking and the transformation of employment relationships: The effect of corporate restructuring on wage patterns, determinants, and inequality, *American Sociological Review*, 81(3): 467–487.

Desan, Christine (2005), The market as a matter of money: Denaturalizing economic currency in American constitutional history, *Law & Social Inquiry*, 30(1): 1–60.

DiMaggio, Paul and Powell, Walter W. (1983), The iron cage revisited: Institutional isomorphism and collective rationality in organizational fields. *American Sociological Review*, 48(2): 147–160.

Dobbin, Frank (1994), *Forging industrial policy*, Cambridge: Cambridge University Press.

Dobbin, Frank, and Jung, Jiwook (2010), The misapplication of Mr. Michael Jensen: How agency theory brought down the economy and why it might again, *Research in the Sociology of Organizations*, 30B: 29–64.

Dobbin, Frank, and Sutton, John R. (1998), The strength of a weak state: The rights revolution and the rise of human resources management divisions, *American Journal of Sociology*, 104(2): 441–476.

Dodd, E. Merrick, Jr (1932), For whom are corporate managers trustees? *Harvard Law Review*, 45(7): 1145–1163.

Downer John (2011), "737-Cabriolet": The limits of knowledge and the sociology of inevitable failure, *American Journal of Sociology*, 117(3): 725–762.

Drucker, Peter F. (1955), *The practice of management*, Melbourne, London & Toronto: Heineman.

Drutman Lee (2015), *The business of America is lobbying: How corporations became politicized and politics became more corporate*, Oxford: Oxford University Press.

Du Gay, Paul, Millo, Yuval, and Tuck, Penelope (2012), Making government liquid: Shifts in governance using financialisation as a political device, *Environment and Planning C: Government and Policy*, 30(6): 1083–1099.

Duggan, Lisa (2003), *The twilight of equality? Neoliberalism, cultural politics, and the attack on democracy*, Boston, MA: Beacon Press.

Duménil, Gérard, and Lévy, Dominique (2004), *Capital resurgent: Roots of the neoliberal revolution*, trans. by Derek Jeffer, Cambirdge: Harvard University Press.

Düppe, Till, and Weintraub, E. Roy (2014), Siting the new economic science: The Cowles Commission's activity analysis conference of June 1949. *Science in Context*, 27(3): 453–483.

Easterbrook, Frank H., and Fischel, Daniel R. (1981), The proper role of a target's management in responding to a tender offer, *Harvard Law Review*, 94(6): 1161–1204.

Easterbrook, Frank H., and Fischel, Daniel R. (1993), Contract and fiduciary duty. *Journal of Law and Economics*, 36(1): 425–446.

Ebenstein, Lanny (2015), *Chicagonomics: The evolution of Chicago free market economics*, London: St. Martin's Press.

Edelman, Lauren B., Fuller, Sally Riggs, and Mara-Drita, Iona (2001), Diversity rhetoric and the managerialization of law, *American Journal of Sociology*, 106(6): 1589–1641.

Eggert, Kurt (2002), Held up in due course: Codification and the victory of form over intent in negotiable instrument law, *Creighton Law Review*, 35: 503–640.

Eichengreen, Barry (2015), *Hall of mirrors: The Great Depression, the Great Recession, and the uses—and misuses—of history*, New York & Oxford: Oxford University Press.

Eisenberg, Melvin Aron (1969), Legal roles of shareholders and management in modern corporate decisionmaking, *California Law Review*, 57(1): 1–181.

Eisenberg, Melvin A. (1990), Contractarianism without contracts: A response to Professor McChesney, *Columbia Law Review*, 90, 1321–1331.

Ellul, Andrew (2015), The role of risk management in corporate governance, *Annual Review of Financial Economics*, 7: 279–299.

Elzinga, Kenneth G. (1977), The goals of antitrust: Other than competition and efficiency, What else counts? *University of Pennsylvania Law Review*, 125(6), 1191–1213.

Engel, Kathleen C., and McCoy, Patricia A (2001), A tale of three markets: The law and economics of predatory lending, *Texas Law Review*, 80(6): 1255–1381.

Engel, Kathleen C., and McCoy, Patricia, A. (2007), Turning a blind eye: Wall Street finance of predatory lending. *Fordham Law Review*, 75(4): 2039–2103.

Erickson, Paul (2010), Mathematical models, rational choice, and the search for Cold War culture, *Isis*, 101(2): 386–392.

Erickson, Paul, Klein, Judy L., Daston, Lorraine, Lemov, Rebecca, Sturm, Thomas and Gordin, Michael D. (2013), *How reason almost lost its mind: The strange career of Cold War rationality*, Chicago & London: The University of Chicago Press.

Ertimur, Yonca, Ferri, Fabrizio, and Stubben, Stephen R. (2010), Board of directors' responsiveness to shareholders: Evidence from shareholder proposals, *Journal of Corporate Finance* 16(1): 53–72.

Espeland, Wendy N., and Saunder, M. (2007), Ranking and reactivity: How public measures recreate social worlds, *American Journal of Sociology*, 113(1): 1–40.

Evans, James A. (2010), Industry collaboration, scientific sharing, and the dissemination of knowledge, *Social Studies of Science*, 40(5): 747–791.

Evans, Peter (1995), *Embedded autonomy*, Princeton & London: Princeton University Press.

Fama, Eugene F., and Jensen, Michael (1983), Separation of ownership and control, *Journal of Law and Economics*, 26(2): 301–325.

Fang, Lily, Ivashina, Victoria, and Lerner, Josh (2015), The disintermediation of financial markets: Direct investing in private equity, *Journal of Financial Economics*, 116(1): 160–178.

Feldman, Martha S. (2000), Organization routines as a source of continuous change, *Organization Science*, 11(6): 611–629.

Feldman, Martha S., and March, James G. (1981), Information in organizations as signal and symbol, *Administrative Science Quarterly*, 26: 171–186.

Fernandez, Rodrigo, and Wigger, Angela (2016), Lehman Brothers in the Dutch offshore financial centre: The role of shadow banking in increasing leverage and facilitating debt, *Economy and Society*, 45(3–4): 407–430.

Fisch, Jill E. (2010), The overstated promise of corporate governance, *The University of Chicago Law Review*, 77(3): 923–958.

Fischel, Daniel R. (1978), Efficient capital market theory, the market for corporate control, and the regulation of cash tender offers, *Texas Law Review*, 57(1): 1–46.

Fligstein, Neil (1990), *The transformation of corporate control*, Cambridge & London: Harvard University Press.

Fligstein, Neil, and Roehrkasse, Alexander F. (2016), The causes of fraud in the financial crisis of 2007 to 2009: Evidence from the mortgage-backed securities industry, *American Sociological Review*, 81(4): 617–643.

Fligstein, Neil, Brundage, Jonah Stuart, and Schultz, Michael (2017), Seeing like the Fed: Culture, cognition, and framing in the failure to anticipate the financial crisis of 2008, *American Sociological Review*, 82(5): 879–909.

Fochler, Maximilian (2016a), Beyond and between academia and business: How Austrian biotechnology researchers describe high-tech start-up companies as spaces of knowledge production, *Social Studies of Science*, 46(2): 259–281. doi:10.1177/0306312716629831.

Fochler, Maximilian (2016b), Variants of epistemic capitalism: Knowledge production and the accumulation of worth in commercial biotechnology and the academic life sciences, *Science, Technology & Human Values*, 41: 922–948. doi:10.1177/0162243916652224.

Fourcade, Marion, and Healy, Kieran (2013), Classification situations: Life-chances in the neoliberal era, *Accounting, Organizations and Society*, 38(8): 559–572.

Fourcade, Marion, and Healy, Kieran (2017), Seeing like a market, *Socio-Economic Review*, 15(1): 9–29.

Fox, Edward G., Fox, Merritt B., and Gilson, Ronald J. (2016), Economic crisis and the integration of law and finance: The impact of volatility spikes, *Columbia Law Review*, 116(2): 325–407.

Frame, W. Scott, and White, Lawrence J. (2004), Empirical studies of financial innovation: Lots of talk, little action? *Journal of Economic Literature*, 42(1): 116–144.

Frank, Robert H. (2007), *Falling behind: How rising inequality harms the middle class*, Berkeley: University of California Press.

Frankfurt, Harry (1987), Equality as a moral ideal, *Ethics*, 98(1), 21–43.

Franks, Julian, and Mayer, Colin (1996), Hostile takeovers and the correction of managerial failure, *Journal of Financial Economics*, 40: 163–181.

Fraser, Nancy (2014), Can society be commodities all the way down? Post-Polanyian reflections on capitalist crisis, *Economy and Society*, 43(4): 541–558.

Fraser, Steve, and Gerstle, Gary, eds. (1989), *The rise and fall of the New Deal order, 1930–1980*, Princeton: Princeton University Press.

Free, Clinton, Salterio, Steven E., and Shearer, Teri (2009), The construction of auditability: MBA rankings and assurance in practice, *Accounting, Organizations and Society*, 34(1): 119–140.

Freeman, Richard B. (2010), Its Financialization! *International Labour Review*, 149(2): 163–183.

Frieden, Jeffry (2016), The governance of international finance, *Annual Review of Political Science*, 19: 33–48.

Friedman, Jeffrey, and Kraus, Wladimir (2012), *Engineering the financial crisis: Systemic risk and the failure of regulation*, Philadelphia: University of Pennsylvania Press.

Friedman, Milton, and Friedman, Rose (1979), *Free to choose: A personal statement*, New York & London: Harcourt Brace Jovanovich.

Froot, Kenneth A., Scharfstein, David S., and Stein, Jeremy C. (1992), Herd on the street: Informational inefficiencies in a market with short-term speculation, *The Journal of Finance*, 47(4): 1461–1484.

Frydman, Roman, and Goldberg, Michael D. (2011), *Beyond mechanical markets: Asset price swings, risk, and the role of the state*, Princeton: Princeton University Press.

Fujimura, Joan H. (1996), *Crafting science: A sociohistory of the quest for the genetics of cancer*, Cambridge: Harvard University Press.

Fukuyama, Francis (2016), Governance: What do we know, and how do we know it? *Annual Review of Political Science*, 19: 89–105.

Fuller, Gregory W. (2016), *The great debt transformation: Households, financialization, and policy responses*, New York & Houndmills: Palgrave Macmillan.

Funk, Russell J., and Hirschman, Daniel (2014), Derivatives and deregulation: Financial innovation and the demise of Glass–Steagall, *Administrative Science Quarterly*, 59(4): 669–704.

Galbraith, James K. (2002), A perfect crime: Inequality in the age of globalization, *Daedalus*, 134(1): 11–25.

Garvey, Gerald T., and Swan, Peter L. (1994), The economics of corporate governance: Beyond the Marshallian firm, *Journal of Corporate Finance*, 1(2): 139–174.

Geertz, Clifford (1975), Common sense as a cultural system. *The Antioch Review*, 33(1): 5–25.

Gelpern, Anna, and Levitin, Adam J. (2009), Rewriting Frankenstein contracts: The workout prohibition in residential mortgage-backed securities, *Southern California Law Review*, 82: 1077–1152.

Gephart, Robert P., Jr (1993), The textual approach: Risk and blame in disaster sensemaking, *Academy of Management Journal*, 36(6): 1465–1514.

Gerding, Erik F. (2005), Next epidemic: Bubbles and the growth and decay of securities regulation, *Connecticut Law Review*, 38: 393–453.

Gilens, Martin (2012), *Affluence and influence: Economic inequality and political power in America*, Princeton & Oxford: Princeton University Press.

Gilson, Ronald J., and Gordon, Jeffrey N. (2013), The agency costs of agency capitalism: Activist investors and the revaluation of governance rights, *Columbia Law Review*, 113: 863–927.

Gittelman, Michelle (2016), The revolution re-visited: Clinical and genetics research paradigms and the productivity paradox in drug discovery, *Research Policy*, 45: 1570–1585.

Goldberg, Victor P. (1976), Toward an expanded economic theory of contract, *Journal of Economic Issues*, 10(1): 45–61.

Goldstein, Adam (2012), Revenge of the managers: Labor cost-cutting and the paradoxical resurgence of managerialism in the shareholder value era, 1984 to 2001, *American Sociological Review*, 77(2): 268–294.

Goranova, Maria, and Ryan, Lori Verstegen (2014), Shareholder activism: A multidisciplinary review, *Journal of Management*, 40(5): 1230–1268.

Gordon, David (1996), *Fat and mean: The corporate squeeze of working Americans and the myth of managerial downsizing*, New York: Free Press.

Gordon, Gwendolyn, and Zaring David (2017), Ethical bankers, *Journal of Corporation Law*, 42: 559–596.

Gordon, Jeffrey N. (2003), What Enron means for the management and control of the modern business corporation: Some initial reflections, *The University of Chicago Law Review*, 69: 1233–1250.

Gordon, Robert J. (2015), *The rise and fall of American growth: The U.S. standard of living since the Civil War*, Princeton: Princeton University Press.

Green, Donald P., and Shapiro, Ian (1994), *Pathologies of rational choice theory: A critique of applications in political science*, New Haven & London: Yale University Press.

Greenberger, Michael (2013), Closing Wall Street's commodity and swaps betting parlors, *George Washington Law Review*, 81(3): 707–748.

Greenwood, Robin, and Scharfstein, David (2013), The growth of finance, *Journal of Economic Perspectives*, 27(2): 3–28.

Greve, Henrich R., Kim, Ji-Yub (Jay), and Teh, Daphne (2016), Ripples of fear: The diffusion of a bank panic, *American Sociological Review*, 81(2): 396–420.

Gruber, Thorsten (2014), Academic sell-out: How an obsession with metrics and rankings is damaging academia, *Journal of Marketing for Higher Education*, 24(2): 165–177.

Haakonssen, Knud (1985), Hugo Grotius and the history of political thought, *Political Theory*, 13(2): 239–265.

Haakonssen, Knud (1996), *Natural law and moral philosophy: From Grotius to the Scottish enlightenment*, Cambridge: Cambridge University Press.

Haas, M.R., and Park, S. (2010), To share or not to share? Professional norms, reference groups, and information withholding among life scientists, *Organization Science*, 21(4): 873–891.

Habermas, Jürgen (1984), *The theory of communicative action: Vol 1: Reason and the rationalization of society*, London: Heineman.

Habermas, Jürgen (1987), *The theory of communicative action: Vol 2: Life world and system: A critique of functionalist reason*, Cambridge: Polity Press.

Hacker, Jacob S., and Pierson, Paul (2002), Business power and social policy: Employers and the formation of the American welfare state, *Politics & Society*, 30(2), 277–325.

Hacker, Jacob S., and Pierson, Paul (2010), *Winner-take-all politics: How Washington made the rich richer and turned its back on the middle class*, New York: Simon and Schuster.

Hacker, Jacob S., Rehm, Philipp, and Schlesinger, Mark (2013), The insecure American: Economic experiences, financial worries, and policy attitudes, *Perspectives on Politics*, 11(1): 23–49.

Hall, Richard L., and Deardorff, Alan V. (2006), Lobbying as legislative subsidy, *American Political Science Review*, 100(1): 69–84.

Hamel, Gary (2000), *Leading the revolution*, Boston, MA: Harvard Business School.

Hammond, Thomas H., and Knott, Jack H. (1988), The deregulatory snowball: Explaining deregulation in the financial industry, *The Journal of Politics*, 50(01): 3–30.

Harcourt, Bernard E. (2011), *The illusion of free markets*, Cambridge & London: Harvard University Press.

Harcourt, Wendy (2014), The future of capitalism: A consideration of alternatives, *Cambridge Journal of Economics,* 38: 1307–1328. doi:10.1093/cje/bet048.

Hardy, Cynthia, and Magire, Steve (2016), Organizing risk: Discourse, power and "riskification," *Academy of Management Review*, 41(1): 80–108.

Hargie, Owen, Stapleton, Karyn, and Tourish, Dennis (2010), Interpretations of CEO public apologies for the banking crisis: Attributions of blame and avoidance of responsibility, *Organization*, 17(6): 721–742.

Harrington, Brooke (2008), *Pop finance: Investment clubs and the new investor populism*, Princeton & Oxford: Princeton University Press.

Hart, Oliver D. (1988), Incomplete contracts and the theory of the firm, *Journal of Law, Economics, & Organization*, 4(1), 119–139.

Haskel, Jonathan, Lawrence, Robert Z., Learner, Edward E., and Slaughter, Matthew J. (2012), Globalization and US wages: Modifying classic theory to explain recent facts, *The Journal of Economic Perspectives*, 26(2), 119–139.

Hausman, Daniel M., and Welch, Brynn (2010), Debate: To nudge or not to nudge, *Journal of Political Philosophy*, 18(1): 123–136.

Hawley, Ellis (1966), *The New Deal and the problem of monopoly*, Princeton: Princeton University Press.

Healy, Kieran (2006), *Last best gifts: Altruism and the market for human blood and organs*, Chicago & London: The University of Chicago Press.

Hegel, George Wilhelm Friedrich (1820/1981), *Hegel's philosophy of rights*, trans. by T.M. Knox, London: Oxford University Press.

Hegel, George Wilhelm Friedrich (1999), *The Hegel Reader*, Steven Houlgate, ed., Oxford: Blackwell.

Helleiner, Eric (2011), Understanding the 2007–2008 global financial crisis: Lessons for scholars of international political economy, *Annual Review of Political Science*, 14: 67–87.

Henderson, Brian J., Pearson, Neil D., and Wang, Li (2014), New evidence on the financialization of commodity markets. *Review of Financial Studies*, 28(5): 1285–1311.

Hill, Claire, and Painter, Richard (2009), Berle's vision beyond shareholder interests: Why investment bankers should have (some) personal liability, *Seattle University Law Review,* 33: 1173–1199.

Hinton, Elizabeth (2016), *From the war on poverty to the war on crime: The making of mass incarceration in America*, Cambridge, MA: Harvard University Press.

Hirschman, Daniel, and Berman, Elizabeth Popp (2014), Do economists make policies? On the political effects of economics, *Socio-Economic Review*, 12(4): 779–811.

Ho, Karen (2009), *Liquidated. An ethnography of Wall Street*, Durham & London: Duke University Press.

Hochfelder, David (2006), "Where the common people could speculate": The ticker, bucket shops, and the origins of popular participation in financial markets, 1880–1920, *Journal of American History*, 93(2): 335–358.

Holloway, Kelly Joslin (2015), Normalizing complaint: Scientists and the challenge of commercialization, *Science, Technology, & Human Values*, 40(5): 744–765.

Hood, Christopher (2011), *The blame game: Spin, bureaucracy, and self-preservation in government*, Princeton & Oxford: Princeton University Press.

Horwitz, Robert B. (1986), Understanding deregulation, *Theory & Society*, 15(1&2): 139–174.

Hovenkamp, Herbert (1985), Antitrust policy after Chicago, *Michigan Law Review*, 84(2): 213–284.

Hung, Ho-fung, and Thompson, Daniel (2016), Money supply, class power, and inflation: Monetarism reassessed, *American Sociological Review*, 81(3): 447–466. doi:10.1177/0003122416639609.

Hunt, John Patrick (2009), Credit rating agencies and the worldwide credit crisis: The limits of reputation, the insufficiency of reform, and a proposal for improvement, *Columbia Business Law Review*, 109(1): 109–209.

Hyman, Louis (2011), *Debtor nation: The history of America in red ink*, Princeton: Princeton University Press.

Ivanova, Maria N. (2017), Profit growth in boom and bust: The Great Recession and the Great Depression in comparative perspective, *Industrial and Corporate Change*, 26(1): 1–20.

Jacobides, Michael G. (2005), Industry change through vertical disintegration: How and why markets emerged in mortgage banking, *Academy of Management Journal*, 48(3): 465–498.

Jacobs, David, and Dirlam, Jonathan C. (2016), Politics and economic stratification: Power resources and income inequality in the United States, *American Journal of Sociology*, 122(2): 469–500.

Jacobs, David, and Myers, Lindsey (2014), Union strength, neoliberalism, and inequality: Contingent political analyses of U.S. income differences since 1950, *American Sociological Review*, 79(4): 752–774.

Jain, Sanjay, George, Gerhard, and Maltarich, Mark (2009), Academics or entrepreneurs? Invstigating role identify modification of university scientists involved in commercialization activity, *Research Policy*, 39: 922–935.

Jencks, Christopher (2002), Does inequality matter? *Daedalus*, 134(1): 49–65.

Jensen, Michael C., and Meckling, William H. (1976), Theory of the firm: Managerial behavior, agency costs and ownership structure, *Journal of Financial Economics*, 3(4): 305–360.

Johns, Fleur (2016), Global governance through the pairing of list and algorithm, *Environment and Planning D: Society and Space*, 34(1): 126–149.

Johnson, Ericka (2007), Surgical simulations and simulated surgeons: Reconstituting medical practice and practitioners in simulations, *Social Studies of Science*, 37: 585–608.

Jolls, Christine, Sunstein, Cass R., and Thaler, Richard R. (1998), A behavioral approach to law and economics. *Stanford Law Review*, 1471–1550.

Jones, Owen (2011), *Chavs: The demonization of the working class*, London: Verso.

Jung, Jiwook (2016), Through the contested terrain: Implementation of downsizing announcements by large U.S. firms, 1984 to 2005, *American Sociological Review*, 81(2): 347–373.

Kahan, Marcel, and Rock, Edward B. (2007), Hedge funds in corporate governance and corporate control, *University of Pennsylvania Law Review*, 155(5): 1021–1093.

Kahneman, Daniel (2011), *Thinking, fast and slow*, New York: Farrar, Straus, and Giroux.

Kaldor, Nicholas (1972), The irrelevance of equilibrium economics, *The Economic Journal*, 82(328): 1237–1255.

Kalleberg, Arne L. (2015), Financialization, private equity, and employment relations in the United States, *Work and Occupations*, 42(2) 216–224.

Kalthoff, Herbert (2005), Practices of calculation. Economic representation and risk management, *Theory, Culture & Society*, 22(2): 69–97.

Kamenica, Emir (2012), Behavioral economics and psychology of incentives, *Annual Review of Economics*, 4: 427–452.

Kar, Robin (2016), Contract as empowerment, *The University of Chicago Law Review*, 83(2): 759–834.

Karabarbounis, Loukas, and Neiman, Brent (2014), The global decline of the labor share, *The Quarterly Journal of Economics*, 129(1): 61–103.

Karger, Howard (2005), *Shortchanged: Life and debt in the fringe economy*, Oakland: Berrett-Koehler.

Karlsen, Mads Peter, and Villadsen, Kaspar (2016), Health promotion, governmentality and the challenges of theorizing pleasure and desire, *Body & Society*, 22(3): 3–30.

Kaufman, Jason (2008), Corporate law and the sovereignty of states, *American Sociological Review*, 73(3): 402–425.

Kear, Mark (2017), Playing the credit score game: Algorithms, "positive" data and the personification of financial objects, *Economy and Society*, 46(3–4): 346–368.

Kennedy, David (2016), *A world of struggle: How power, law, and expertise shape global political economy*, Princeton: Princeton University Press.

Kenny, Katherine Elizabeth (2015), Blaming deadmen: Causes, culprits, and chaos in accounting for technological accidents, *Science, Technology, & Human Values*, 40(4): 539–563.

Keys, Benjamin J., Mukherjee, T., Seru A., and Vig, V. (2009), Did securitization lead to lax screening? Evidence from subprime loans, *Quarterly Journal of Economics*, 125: 307–362.

Khurana, Rakesh (2002), *Searching for a corporate savior: The irrational quest for a charismatic CEO*, Princeton: Princeton University Press.

Khurana, Rakesh (2007), *From higher aims to hired hands: The social transformation of American business schools and the unfulfilled promise of management as a profession*, Princeton: Princeton University Press.

Kilduff, Gavin, Galinksy, Adam D., Gallo, Edoardo, and Reade, J. James (2016), Whatever it takes to win: Rivalry increases unethical behavior, *Academy of Management Journal*, 59(5): 1508–1534.

King, Alexander, F. (2000), The changing face of accountability: Monitoring and assessing institutional performance in higher education, *Journal of Higher Education*, 71(4): 411–431.

King, Mervyn (2016), *End of alchemy: Money, banking and future of global economy*, London: Little, Brown.

Kipnis, Andrew (2008), Audit cultures: Neoliberal governmentality, socialist legacy, or technological governing, *American Ethnologist*, 35(2): 275–289.

Klamer, Arjo, and McCloskey, Donald (1992), Accounting as the master metaphor of economics, *European Accounting Review*, 1(1): 145–160.

Klausner, Michael (2013), Fact and fiction in corporate law and governance, *Stanford Law Review*, 65(6): 1325–1370.

Klein, April, and Emanuel Zur (2009), Entrepreneurial shareholder activism: Hedge funds and other private investors, *Journal of Finance*, 64(1), 187–229.

Kleinman, Daniel Lee, and Vallas, Steven P. (2001), Science, capitalism, and the rise of the "knowledge worker": The changing structure of knowledge production in the United States. *Theory and Society*, 30(4), 451–492.

Klick, Jonathan, and Mitchell, Gregory (2006), Government regulation of irrationality: Moral and cognitive hazards, *Minnesota Law Review*, 90: 1620–1664.

Kochan, Thomas A., and Riordan, Christine A. (2016), Employment relations and growing income inequality: Causes and potential options for its reversal, *Journal of Industrial Relations*, 58(3): 419–440.

Kogut, Bruce M. (2012), *The small worlds of corporate governance*, Cambridge & London: MIT Press.

Kohler, Robert (1994), *Lords of the fly: Drosophila genetics and experience of life*, Chicago & London: The University of Chicago Press.

Kornberger, Martin, and Carter, Chris, (2010), Manufacturing competition: How accounting practices shape strategy making in cities, *Accounting, Auditing & Accountability Journal*, 23(3): 325–349.

Koyré, Alexandre (1959), *From the closed world to the infinite universe*, New York: Harper Torchbooks.

Krippner, Greta R. (2011), *Capitalizing on crisis: The political origins of the rise of finance*, Cambridge, MA & London: Harvard University Press.

Krippner, Greta R. (2017), Democracy of credit: Ownership and the politics of credit access in late twentieth-century America, *American Journal of Sociology*, 123(1): 1–47.

Kristal, Tali (2013), The capitalist machine: Computerization, workers' power, and the decline in labor's share within U.S. industries, *American Sociological Review*, 78(3): 361–389.

Kroll, Joshua A., Huey, Joanna, Barocas, Solon, Felten, Edward W., Reidenberg, Joel R., Robinson, David G., and Yu, Harlan (2017), Accountable algorithms, *University of Pennsylvania Law Review*, 165(3): 633–705.

Kroszner, Randall S., and Strahan, Philip E. (1999), What drives deregulation? Economics and politics of the relaxation of bank branching restrictions, *Quarterly Journal of Economics*, 114(4): 1437–1467.

Kuhn, Thomas S. (1962), *The structure of scientific revolutions*, Chicago: University of Chicago Press.

Kus, Basak (2012), Financialisation and income inequality in OECD nations: 1995–2007, *Economic and Social Review*, 43(4): 477–495.

La Porta, Rafael, Lopez-de-Silanes, Florencio, Shleifer, Andrei, and Vishny, Robert W. (1998), Law and finance. *Journal of Political Economy*, 106(6): 1113–1155.

La Porta, Rafael, Lopez-de-Silanes, Florencio, Shleifer, Andrei, and Vishny, Robert (2000), Investor protection and corporate governance, *Journal of Financial Economics*, 58(1–2): 3–27.

Lamoreaux, Naomi R. (1998), Partnerships, corporations, and the theory of the firm. *American Economic Review*, 88(2): 66–71.

Lane, Jan-Erik (2000), *New public management*, London & New York: Routledge.

Lang, Andrew T.F. (2013), The legal construction of economic rationalities, *Journal of Law and Society*, 40(1): 155–171.

Lange, Ann-Christina, Lenglet, Marc, and Seyfert, Robert (2016), Cultures of high-frequency trading: mapping the landscape of algorithmic developments in contemporary financial markets, *Economy and Society*, 45(2): 149–165.

Latour, Bruno (2005), *Assembling the social: An introduction to actor–network theory*, Oxford & New York: Oxford University Press.

Laux, Christian, and Leuz, Christian (2009), The crisis of fair-value accounting: Making sense of the recent debate, *Accounting, Organizations and Society*, 34: 826–834.

Lave, Jean (1988), *Cognition in practice: Mind, mathematics, and culture in everyday life*, Cambridge: Cambridge University Press.

Laverty, Kevin J. (1996), Economic "short-termism": The debate, the unresolved issues, and the implications for management practice and research, *Academic Management Review*, 21: 825–860.

Lazonick, William (2010), Innovative business models and varieties of capitalism: Financialization of the U.S. corporation, *Business History Review*, 84: 675–702.

Leahey, E. (2016), From sole investigator to team scientist: Trends in the practice and study of research collaboration, *Annual Review of Sociology*, 42: 81–100.

Leeson, Peter T., Ryan, Matt E., and Williamson, Claudia R. (2012), Think tanks, *Journal of Comparative Economics*, 40: 62–77.

Leibenstein, Harvey (1966), Allocative efficiency vs. "X-efficiency." *The American Economic Review*, 56(3): 392–415.

Lenglet, Marc (2011), Conflicting codes and codings: How algorithmic trading is reshaping financial regulation, *Theory, Culture & Society*, 28(6): 44–66.

Levitin, Adam J. (2011), In defense of bailouts, *Georgetown University Law Review*, 99: 435–514.

Levitin, Adam J. (2014), The politics of financial regulation and the regulation of financial politics: A review essay, *Harvard Law Review*, 127(7): 1991–2068.

Levitin, Adam J. (2016), Safe banking: Finance and democracy, *The University of Chicago Law Review*, 83(1): 357–455.

Lewis, Jamie, Atkinson, Paul, Harrington, Jean, and Featherstone, Katie (2013), Representation and practical accomplishment in the laboratory: When is an animal model good-enough? *Sociology*, 47(4): 776–792.

Leys, Simon (2012), *The hall of uselessness: Collected essays*, Collingwood: Black Inc.

Lin, Ken-Hou (2016), The rise of finance and firm employment dynamics, *Organization Science*, 27(4): 972–988.

Lin, Ken-Hou, and Tomaskovic-Devey, Donald (2013), Financialization and U.S. income inequality, 1970–2008, *American Journal of Sociology*, 118(5): 1284–1329.

Lippmann Walter (1937), *An inquiry into the principles of the good society*, Boston, MA: Little, Brown.

Lobel, Orly (2004), The renew deal: The fall of regulation and the rise of governance in contemporary legal thought. *Minneapolis Law Review*, 89: 342–470.

Lorenz, Chris (2012), If you're so smart, why are you under surveillance? Universities, neoliberalism, and new public management, *Critical Inquiry*, 38: 599–629.

Lucretius (2001), *On the nature of things*, Indianapolis: Hackett.

Luhmann, Niklas (1995), *Social Systems*, Stanford: Stanford University Press.

Luhmann, Niklas (2000), *Art as a social system*, trans. Eva M. Knodt, Stanford: Stanford University Press.

Lydenberg, Steve (2014), Reason, rationality, and fiduciary duty, *Journal of Business Ethics*, 119: 365–380.

Lynch, Timothy E. (2011), Gambling by another name: The challenge of purely speculative derivatives, *Stanford Journal of Law, Business & Finance*, 17(1): 67–130.

Lysandrou, Photis (2011), Global inequality as one of the root causes of the financial crisis: A suggested explanation, *Economy and Society*, 40(3): 323–344.

Lysandrou, Photis, and Nesvetailova, Anastasia. (2015), The role of shadow banking entities in the financial crisis: A disaggregated view, *Review of International Political Economy*, 22(2): 257–279.

Macaulay, Stewart (1963), Non-contractual relations in business: A preliminary study, *American Sociological Review*, 28(1): 55–67.

Macey, Jonathan (2008), *Corporate governance: Promises kept, promises broken*, Princeton: Princeton University Press.

MacKenzie, Donald (2004), The big, bad wolf and the rational market: Portfolio investment, the 1987 crash and the performativity of economics, *Economy and Society*, 33(3): 303–334.

MacKenzie, Donald, and Millo, Yuval (2003), Constructing a market, performing a theory: A historical sociology of a financial market derivatives exchange, *American Jounal of Sociology*, 109(1): 107–145.

MacKenzie, Donald, and Spears, Taylor (2014), "A device for being able to book P&L": The organizational embedding of the Gaussian copula, *Social Studies of Science*, 44(3): 418–440.

Madrian, Brigitte C. (2014), Applying insights from behavioral economics to policy design, *Annual Review of Economics*, 6: 663–688.

Major, Aaron (2014), *Architects of austerity: International finance and the politics of growth*, Stanford: Stanford University Press.

Mallaby, Sebastian (2010), *More money than God: Hedge funds and the making of a new elite*, New York: Penguin.

Mandis, Steven G. (2013), *What happened to Goldman Sachs: An insider's story of organizational drift and its unintended consequences*, Boston, MA & London: Harvard Business Review Press.

Maney, Patrick J. (2016), *Bill Clinton: New gilded age president*, Lawrence: University Press of Kansas.

Manne, Henry G. (1962), The "higher criticism" of the modern corporation. *Columbia Law Review*, 62(3): 399–432.

Manne, Henry G. (1965), Mergers and the market for corporate control, *Journal of Political Economy*, 73(2): 110–120.

Manne, Henry G. (1967), Our two corporation systems: Law and economics, *Virginia Law Review*, 53(2): 259–284.

Maravelias, Christian (2009), Health promotion and flexibility: Extending and obscuring power in organizations, *British Journal of Management*, 20: S194–S203.

Markham, Jerry W. (2009), The subprime crisis—a test match for the bankers: Glass–Steagall vs. Gramm–Leach–Bliley, *University of Pennsylvania Journal of Business Law*, 12: 1081–1134.

Marris, Robin (1964), *The economic theory of "managerial" capitalism*, London: Macmillan

Martin, Felix (2014), *Money: The unauthorized biography*, London: Vintage.

Martinez-Moyano, Ignacio J., McCaffrey, David P., and Oliva, Rogelio (2014), Drift and adjustment in organizational rule compliance: Explaining the "regulatory pendulum" in financial markets, *Organization Science*, 25(2): 321–338.

Mayer, Jane (2012), The growing financialization of commodity markets: Divergences between index investors and money managers, *Journal of Development Studies*, 48(6): 751–767.

Mayer, Jane (2016), *Dark money: The hidden history of the billionaires behind the rise of the radical right*, New York: Doubleday.

Mayer-Schönberger, Victor, and Cukier, Kenneth (2013), *Big data: A revolution that will transform how we live, work, and think*, Boston, MA: Houghton Mifflin Harcourt.

McCoy, Patricia A., Pavlov, Andrey D., and Wachter, Susan M. (2009), Systemic risk through securitization: The result of deregulation and regulatory failure. *Connecticut Law Review*, 41(4): 1327–1375.

McDonald, Robert, and Paulson, Anna (2015), AIG in hindsight, *Journal of Economic Perspectives*, 29(2): 81–105.

McLevey, John (2015), Understanding policy research in liminal spaces: Think tank responses to diverging principles of legitimacy, *Social Studies of Science*, 45(2): 270–293.

Medvetz, Thomas (2010), "Public policy is like having a Vaudeville act": Languages of duty and difference among think tank-affiliated policy experts, *Qualitative Sociology*, 33: 549–562.

Mehran, Hamid, and Mollineaux, Lindsay (2012), Corporate governance of financial institutions, *Annual Review of Financial Economics*, 4: 215–232.

Mehrling, Perry (2011), *The new Lombard Street: How the Fed became the dealer of last resort*, Princeton & Oxford: Princeton University Press.

Melman, Seymour (1997), From private to state capitalism: How the permanent war economy transformed the institutions of American capitalism, *Journal of Economic Issues*, 31(2): 311–330.

Mengis, Jeanne, and Eppler, Martin J. (2008), Understanding and managing conversations from a knowledge perspective: An analysis of the roles and rules of face-to-face conversations in organizations, *Organization Studies*, 29(10): 1287–1313.

Merry, Sally Engle (2011), Measuring the world: Indicators, human rights, and global governance, *Current Anthropology*, 52(S3): S83–S95.

Merry, Sally Engle (2016), *The seductions of quantification: Measuring human rights, gender violence, and sex trafficking*, Chicago & London: The University of Chicago Press.

Merton, Robert K. (1973), *The sociology of science: Theoretical and empirical investigations*, Norman W. Storer, ed., Chicago: The University of Chicago Press.

Mian, Atif and Sufi, Amir (2009), The consequences of mortgage credit expansion: Evidence from the U.S. mortgage default crisis, *The Quarterly Journal of Economics*, 124(4): 1449–1496.

Mian Atif, and Sufi, Amir (2010), The great recession: Lessons from microeconomic data, *The American Economic Review*, 100(2): 51–56.

Mian, Atif, and Sufi, Amir (2014), *House of debt*, Chicago & London: The University of Chicago Press.

Mian, Atif, Sufi, Amir, and Trebbi, Francesco (2010), The political economy of the US mortgage default crisis, *The American Economic Review*, 100(5): 1967–1998.

Miller, P., and O'Leary, T. (1987), Accounting and the construction of the governable person, *Accounting, Organization, and Society*, 12(3): 235–265.

Millo, Yuval, and Mackenzie, Donald (2009), The usefulness of inaccurate models: Towards an understanding of the emergence of financial risk management, *Accounting, Organization and Society*, 34: 638–653.

Mirowski, Philip (2011), *Science-Mart: Privatizing American science*, Cambridge & London: Harvard University Press.

Mirowski, Philip (2013), *Never let a serious crisis go to waste: How neoliberalism survived the financial meltdown*, London & New York: Verso.

Mirowski, Philip, and Van Horn, Robert, (2005), The contract research organization and the commercialization of scientific research, *Social Studies of Science*, 35(4): 503–548.

Mishina, Yuri, Dykes, Bernadine J., Block, Emily S., and Pollock, Timothy G. (2010), Why "good" firms do bad things: The effects of high aspirations, high expectations, and prominence on the incidence of corporate illegality, *Academy of Management Journal*, 53(4): 701–722.

Mitchell, Gregory (2005), Libertarian paternalism is an oxymoron, *Northwestern University Law Review*, 99(3): 1245–1278.

Mizruchi, Mark (2004), Berle and Means revisited: The governance and politics of large U.S. corporations, *Theory and Society*, 33: 519–617.

Mizruchi, Mark S. (2010), The American corporate elite and the historical roots of the financial crisis of 2008, *Research in the Sociology of Organizations*, 30B: 103–139.

Mizruchi, Mark S. (2013), *The fracturing of the American corporate elite*, Cambridge, MA: Harvard University Press.

Mizruchi, Mark S. (2017), *The Power Elite* in historical context: A reevaluation of Mills's thesis, then and now, *Theory & Society*, 46(2): 95–116.

Mizruchi, Mark S., and Marshall, Linroy J., II (2016), Corporate CEOs, 1890–2015: Titans, bureaucrats, and saviors, *Annual Review of Sociology*, 42: 143–163.

Monaghan, Lee F., Hollands, Robert, and Pritchard, Gary (2010), Obesity epidemic entrepreneurs: Types, practices and interests, *Body & Society*, 16(2): 13–71.

Moore, Marc T., and Rebérioux, Antoine (2011), Revitalizing the institutional roots of Anglo-American corporate governance, *Economy and Society*, 40(1): 84–111.

Morgan, Glenn (2016), New actors and old solidarities: Institutional change and inequality under a neo-liberal international order, *Socio-economic Review*, 14(1): 201–225.

Münch, Richard (2014), *Academic capitalism: Universities in the global struggle for excellence*, New York: Routledge.

Münnich, Sascha (2016), Readjusting imagined markets: Morality and institutional resilience in the German and British bank bailout of 2008, *Socio-Economic Review*, 14(2): 283–307.

Murdock, Charles W. (2012), The big banks: Background, deregulation, financial innovation, and "too big to fail," *Denver University Law Review*, 90: 505–558.

Myers, Stewart C., and Rajan, Raghuram G. (1998), The paradox of liquidity, *Quarterly Journal of Economics*, 113(3): 733–771.

Naciri, Ahmed (2015), *Credit rating governance: Global credit gatekeepers*, Abingdon & New York: Routledge.

Nagel, Thomas (1986), *The view from nowhere*, Oxford and New York: Oxford University Press.

Necker, Sarah (2014), Scientific misbehavior in economics, *Research Policy*, 43(10): 1747–1759.

Nelson, Nicole C. (2013), Modeling mouse, human, and discipline: Epistemic scaffolds in animal behavior genetics, *Social Studies of Science*, 43(1): 3–29.

Nietzsche, Friedrich (1876/1994), *Human, all too human*, London: Penguin.

Nissanke, M. (2012), Commodity market linkages in the global financial crisis: Excess volatility and development impacts, *Journal of Development Studies*, 48(6): 732–750.

Nussbaum, Martha C. (2010), *Not for profit: Why democracy needs the humanities*, Princeton: Princeton University Press.

Offer, Avner, and Söderberg, Gabriel (2016), *The Nobel factor: The prize in economics, social democracy, and the market turn*, Princeton & London: Princeton University Press.

Olson, Mancur (1965), *The logic of collective action*, Cambridge, MA: Harvard University Press.

Omarova, Saule T. (2011), Wall Street as community of fate: Toward financial industry self-regulation. *University of Pennsylvania Law Review*, 159(2): 411–492.

Omarova, Saule T. (2013), The merchants of Wall Street: Banking, commerce, and commodities. *Minnesota Law Review*, 98: 265–355.

O'Neil, Cathy (2016), *Weapons of math destruction: How big data increases inequality and threatens democracy*, London: Allen Lane.

Osberg, L., and Smeeding, T.M. (2006), Fair inequality? An international comparison of attitudes to pay differentials, *American Sociological Review*, 71: 450–471.

O'Sullivan, Mary (2000), *Contests for corporate control: Corporate governance and economic performance in the United States and Germany*, New York & Oxford: Oxford University Press.

Owen-Smith, Jason (2006), Commercial imbroglios: Proprietary science the contemporary university, in Frickell, Scott, and Moore, Kelly, eds. (2006), *The new political sociology of science: Institutions, networks and power*, Madison: The University of Wisconsin Press, pp. 63–90.

Palan, Ronen, Murphy, Richard, and Chavagneux, Christian (2010), *Tax havens: How globalization really works*, Ithaca: Cornell University Press.

Palley, Thomas I. (2013), *Financialization: The economics of finance capital domination*, New York and Houndmills: Palgrave Macmillan.

Panitch, Leo, and Gindin, Sam (2012), *The making of global capitalism: The political economy of American empire*, London & New York: Verso.

Paredes, Troy A. (2003), Blinded by the light: Information overload and its consequences for securities regulation, *Washington University Law Quarterly*, 81: 417–485.

Pargendler, Mariana (2016), The corporate governance obsession, *Journal of Corporation Law*, 42(2): 359–403.

Pasquale, Frank (2015), *The black box society: The secret algorithms that control money and information*, Cambridge, MA: Harvard University Press.

Peek, Joe, and Rosengren, Eric (2016), Credit supply disruptions: From credit crunches to financial crisis, *Annual Review of Financial Economics*, 8: 81–95.

Peñaloza, Lisa, and Barnhart, Michelle (2011), Living U.S. capitalism: The normalization of credit/debt, *Journal of Consumer Research*, 38(4): S111–S130.

Pentland, Brian T., and Rueter, Henry H. (1994), Organization routines as grammars of action, *Administrative Science Quarterly*, 39(3): 484–510.

Pernell, Kim, Jung, Jiwook, and Dobbin, Frank (2017), The hazards of expert control: Chief risk officers and risky derivatives, *American Sociological Review*, 82(3): 511–541.

Perugini, Cristiano, Hölscher, Jens, and Collie, Simon (2016), Inequality, credit and financial crises, *Cambridge Journal of Economics*, 40(1): 227–257.

Peterson, Christopher L. (2007), Predatory structured finance, *Cardozo Law Review*, 28(5): 2185–2282.

Philips-Fein, Kim (2009), *Invisible hands: The making of the conservative movement from the New Deal to Reagan*, New York: W.W. Norton & Co.

Phipps, Alison, and Young, Isabel (2015), Neoliberalisation and "lad cultures" in higher education, *Sociology*, 49(2): 305–322.

Piketty, Thomas (2014), *Capital in the Twenty-First Century*, Cambridge, MA: Harvard University Press.

Piskorski, Tomasz, Seru, Amit, and Vig, Vikrant (2010), Securitization and distressed loan renegotiation: Evidence from the subprime mortgage crisis. *Journal of Financial Economics*, 97(3): 369–397.

Pistor, Katharina (2013), A legal theory of finance, *Journal of Comparative Economics*, 41(2), 315–330.

Pitofsky, Robert (1979), The political content of antitrust, *University of Pennsylvania Law Review*, 127(4): 1051–1075.

Polillo, Simone (2011), Money, moral authority, and the politics of creditworthiness, *American Sociological Review*, 76(3): 437–464.

Polillo, Simone, and Guillén, Mauro F. (2005), Globalization pressures and the state: The worldwide spread of central bank independence, *American Journal of Sociology*, 110(6): 1764–1802.

Pontusson, Jonas, and Raess, Damian (2012), How (and why) is this time different? The politics of economic crisis in western Europe and the United States, *Annual Review of Political Science*, 15: 13–33.

Poon, Martha (2007), Scorecards as devices for consumer credit: The case of Fair, Isaac & Company Incorporated, *The Sociological Review*, 55(s2): 284–306.

Porter, Theodore M. (1995), *Trust in numbers: The pursuit of objectivity in science and public life*, Princeton: Princeton University Press.

Porter, Theodore M. (2012), Surface and depth in science and science studies, *Osiris*, 27(1): 209–226.

Power, Michael (1996), Making things auditable, *Accounting, Organization, and Society*, 21(2–3): 289–315.

Power, Michael (1997), *The audit society: Rituals of verification*, Oxford & New York: Oxford University Press.

Power, Michael (2005), Enterprise risk management and the organization of uncertainty in financial institutions, in Knorr Cetina, Karin, and Preda, Alex, eds. (2005), *The sociology of financial markets*, Oxford & New York: Oxford University Press (pp. 250–268).

Power, Michael (2010), Fair value accounting, financial economics and the transformation of reliability, *Accounting and Business Research*, 40(3): 197–210.

Power, Michael, (2015), How accounting begins: Object formation and the accretion of infrastructure, *Accounting, Organizations, and Society*, 47: 43–55.

Prasad, Monica (2012), *The land of too much: American abundance and the paradox of poverty*, Cambridge & London: Harvard University Press.

Pusser, Brian, and Marginson, Simon (2013), University rankings in critical perspective, *Journal of Higher Education*, 84(4): 544–568.

Quinn, Sarah (2017), "The miracles of bookkeeping": How budget politics link fiscal policies and financial markets, *American Journal of Sociology*, 123(1): 48–85.

Rader, Karen Ann (2004), *Making mice: Standardizing animals for American biomedical research*, Princeton: Princeton University Press.

Rajan, Raghuram G. (2006), Has finance made the world riskier? *European Financial Management*, 12(4): 499–533.

Rajan, Uday, Seru, Amit, and Vig, Vikrant (2015), The failure of models that predict failure: Distance, incentives, and defaults, *Journal of Financial Economics*, 115: 237–260.

Reay, Michael J. (2012), The flexible unity of economics, *American Journal of Sociology*, 118(1): 45–87.

Redbird, Beth, and Grusky, David B. (2016), Distributional effects of the Great Recession: Where has all the sociology gone? *Annual Review of Sociology*, 42: 185–215.

Reisch, George A. (2005), *How the cold war transformed philosophy of science: To the icy slopes of logic*, Cambridge & New York: Cambridge University Press.

Reynaud, Bénédicte (2006), The void at the heart of rules: Routines in the context of rule-following, *Industrial Corporate Change*, 14(5): 847–871.

Reynaud, Bénédicte (2017), Forms of trust and conditions for their stability, *Cambridge Journal of Economics*, 41(1): 127–145.

Rheinberger, Hans-Jörg, (1997), *On historicizing epistemology: An essay*, trans. David Fernbach, Stanford: Stanford University Press.

Richards, Neil M., and King, Jonathan H. (2013), Three paradoxes of big data, *Stanford Law Review. Online*, 66: 41–46.

Riker, William H. (1995), The political psychology of rational choice theory, *Political Psychology*, 16(1): 23–44.

Riles, Annelise (2011), *Collateral knowledge: Legal reasoning in the global financial markets*, Chicago: The University of Chicago Press.

Rivera, Lauren A. (2015), *Pedigree: How elite students get elite jobs*, Princeton and Oxford: Princeton University Press.

Rivera, Lauren A., and Tilcsik, András (2016), Class advantage, commitment penalty: The gendered effect of social class signals in an elite labor market, *American Sociological Review*, 81(6): 1097–1131.

Rizzo, Mario J. (1980), The mirage of efficiency, *Hofstra Law Review*, 8(3): 641–658.

Rizzo, Mario J., and Whitman, Douglas Glen (2009a), The knowledge problem of new paternalism, *Brigham Young University Law Review*, 905(4): 905–968.

Rizzo, Mario J., and Whitman, Douglas Glen (2009b), Little brother is watching you: New paternalism on the slippery slopes, *Arizona Law Review*, 51: 687–739.

Roberts, John (2009), No one is perfect: The limits of transparency and an ethic for "intelligent" accountability, *Accounting, Organisations and Society*, 34: 957–970.

Rock, Edward B., and Wachter, Michael L. (2001), Islands of conscious power: Law, norms, and the self-governing corporation, *University of Pennsylvania Law Review*, 149(6): 1619–1700.

Roe, Mark J. (1994), *Strong managers, weak owners: The political roots of American corporate finance*, Princeton: Princeton University Press.

Romano, Roberta (1984), Metapolitics and corporate law reform, *Stanford Law Review*, 36: 923–1016.

Romano, Roberta (1985), Law as a product: Some pieces of the incorporation puzzle, *Journal of Law, Economics, & Organization*, 1(2): 225–283.

Rona-Tas, Akos (2017), The off-label use of consumer credit ratings, *Historical Social Research*, 42(1), 52–76.

Rona-Tas, Akos, and Hiss, Stefanie (2010), The role of ratings in the subprime mortgage crisis: The art of corporate and the science of consumer credit rating, *Research in the Sociology of Organizations*, 30A: 115–155.

Rosas, Guillermo (2006), Bagehot or bailout? An analysis of government responses to banking crises, *American Journal of Political Science*, 50(1): 175–191.

Rosett, Joshua G. (1990), Do union wealth concessions explain takeover premiums? The evidence on contract wages, *Journal of Financial Economics*, 27(1): 263–282.

Roth, Wolff-Michael (2009), Radical uncertainty in scientific discovery work, *Science, Technology & Human Values*, 34(3): 313–336.

Rowe, Frederick M. (1984), The decline of antitrust and the delusions of models: The Faustian pact of law and economics, *Georgetown Law Journal*, 72: 1511–1570.

Roy, William G. (1997), *Socializing capital: The rise of the large industrial corporation in America*, Princeton: Princeton University Press.

Rueda, David and Pontusson, Jonas (2000), Wage inequality and varieties of capitalism, *World Politics*, 52(3): 350–383.

Saisana, Michaela, d'Hombres, Béatrice, and Saltelli, Andrea (2011), Rickety numbers: Volatility of university rankings and policy implications, *Research Policy*, 40(1): 165–177.

Sapir, Adi, and Oliver, Amalya L. (2017), From academic laboratory to the market: Disclosed and undisclosed narratives of commercialization, *Social Studies of Science*, 47(1): 33–52.

Sassen, Saskia (2014), *Expulsions: Brutality and complexity in the global economy*, Cambridge: The Belknap Press.

Sauder, Michael, and Espeland, Wendy Nelson (2009), The discipline of rankings: Tight coupling and organization change, *American Sociological Review*, 74: 63–82.

Sauder, Michael, and Lancaster, Ryon (2006), Do rankings matter? The effects of U.S. News & World Report rankings on the admissions process of law schools, *Law & Society Review*, 40(1): 105–134.

Scheidel, Walter (2017), *The great leveler: Violence and the history of inequality from the Stone Age to the twenty-first century*, Princeton: Princeton University Press.

Schleef, Debra J. (2006), *Managing elites: Professional socialization in law and business schools*, Lanham, MD: Rowman & Littlefield.

Schneider, Marguerite (2015), Managerialism versus shareholderism: An examination of hedge fund activism, in Goranova, Maria, and Verstegen Ryan, Lori, eds. (2015), *Shareholder empowerment: A new era in corporate governance*, New York: Palgrave Macmillan (pp. 171–199).

Schneper, William D., and Guillén, Mauro F. (2004), Stakeholder rights and corporate governance: A cross-national study of hostile takeovers, *Administrative Science Quarterly*, 49(2): 263–295.

Selznick, Philip (1959), The sociology of law, *Journal of Legal Education*, 12: 521–531.

Sen, Amartya K. (1977), Rational fools: A critique of the behavioral foundations of economic theory, *Philosophy & Public Affairs*, 6(4): 317–344.

Shamir, Ronen (2008), The age of responsibilization: On market embedded morality, *Economy and Society*, 37: 1–19.

Sheppard, Eric, and Leitner, Helga (2010), Quo vadis neoliberalism? The remaking of global capitalist governance after the Washington Consensus, *Geoforum*, 41(2): 185–194.

Shiller, Robert J. (2003), *The new financial order: Risk in the 21st century*, Princeton: Princeton University Press.

Shin, Hyun Song (2009), Securitization and financial stability, *The Economic Journal*, 119(536): 309–332.

Shin, Taekjin (2013), The shareholder value principle: The governance and control of corporations in the United States, *Sociology Compass*, 7(10): 829–40.

Sikka, Prem (2009), Financial crisis and the silence of the auditors, *Accounting, Organizations and Society*, 34(6–7): 868–873.

Simmel, George (1978), *The philosophy of money*, London: Routledge and Kegan Paul.

Simmons, Omari Scott (2015), Delaware's global threat, *Journal of Corporation Law*, 41(1): 217–264.

Simon, Herbert A. (1955), A behavioral model of rational choice, *Quarterly Journal of Economics*, 69(1): 99–118.

Singer, David Andrew (2007), *Regulating capital: Setting standards for the international financial system*, Ithaca and London: Cornell University Press.

Sismondi, Sergio (2011), Corporate disguise in medical science: Dodging the interest repertoire, *Bulletin of Science, Technology and Society*, 31(6): 482–492.

Sjostrom, William K. (2009), The AIG bailout, *Washington & Lee Law Review*, 66: 943–991.

Slaughter, Anne-Marie (2004), *A new world order*, Princeton: Princeton University Press.

Sloan, Alfred P., Jr (1964), *My years with General Motors*, New York: Doubleday.

Smith, Edward Bishop, and Gai, Shelby L. (2017), Institutional interruption: A relational account of the growth and decline of product heterogeneity in the global hedge fund industry, *Industrial and Corporate Change*, 26(6): 1039–1066.

Smith, James Allen (1991), *The idea brokers: Think tanks and the rise of the new policy elite*, New York: The Free Press.

Smith Hughes, Sally (2001), Making dollars out of DNA: The first major patent in biotechnology and the commercialization of molecular biology, 1974–1980, *Isis*, 92(3): 541–575.

Sockin, Michael, and Xiong, Wei (2015), Informational frictions and commodity markets, *Journal of Finance*, 70(5): 2063–2098.

Soederberg, Susanne (2008), A critique of the diagnosis and cure for "Enronitis": The Sarbanes–Oxley act and neoliberal governance of corporate America, *Critical Sociology*, 34(5): 657–680.

Sorkin, Andrew Ross (2009), *Too big to fail: The insider story of how Wall Street and Washington fought to save the financial system—and themselves*, New York: Viking.

Spira, Laura, and Page, Michael (2002), Risk management: The reinvention of internal control and the changing role of internal audit, *Accounting, Auditing and Accountability Journal*, 16(4), 640–661.

Star, Susan Leigh (1999), The ethnography of infrastructure, *American Behavioral Scientist*, 43(3): 377–391.

Stearns, Linda, and Allan, Kenneth D. (1996), Economic behavior in institutional environments: The merger wave of the 1980s, *American Sociological Review*, 61(4): 699–718.

Steiner, Christopher (2012), *Automate this: How algorithms came to rule our world*, New York: Penguin.

Stevens, Mitchel L. (2009), *Creating a class: College admissions and the education of elites*, Cambridge & London: Harvard University Press.

Stiglitz, Joseph E. (1993), Post Walrasian and post Marxian economics, *The Journal of Economic Perspectives*, 7(1): 109–114.

Stiglitz, Joseph E. (2010), *Freefall: America, free markets, and the sinking of the world economy*, New York & London: W.W. Norton.

Stillman, Peter G. (1988), Hegel's analysis of property in the *Philosophy of Right*, *Cardozo Law Review*, 10: 1031–1072.

Stockhammer, Engelbert (2004), Financialization and the slowdown of accumulation, *Cambridge Journal of Economics*, 28(5): 719–741.

Stockhammer, Engelbert (2015), Rising inequality as a cause of the present crisis, *Cambridge Journal of Economics*, 39: 935–958.

Stout, Lynn A. (2011), Derivatives and the legal origin of the 2008 credit crisis. *Harvard Business Law Review*, 1(1): 1–38.

Stout, Lynn A. (2012), *The shareholder value myth: How putting shareholders first harms investors, corporations and the public*, San Francisco: Berrett-Koehler.

Stout, Lynn A. (2013), Toxic side effects of shareholder primacy, *University of Pennsylvania Law Review*, 161(7): 2003–2023.

Strathern, Marilyn (2000), The tyranny of transparency, *British Educational Research Journal*, 26(3): 309–321.

Styhre, Alexander (2016), Coping with irrationality in orthodox economic theory: Moralization as expedient theorizing, *International Journal of Organizational Analysis*, 24(5): 792–810.

Suárez, Sandra L. (2014), Symbolic politics and the regulation of executive compensation: A comparison of the Great Depression and the Great Recession, *Politics and Society*, 3842(1) 73–105.

Sullivan, Teresa A., Warren, Elizabeth, and Westbrook, Jay Lawrence (2006), Less stigma and more financial distress: An empirical analysis of the extraordinary increase in bankruptcy filings, *Stanford Law Review*, 59(1): 213–256.

Sundberg, Mikaela (2009), The everyday world of simulation modeling: the Development of Parametization in meterology, *Social Studies of Science*, 34(2): 162–181.

Sundberg, Mikaela (2011), The dynamics of uncoordinated comparisons: How simulationists in astrophysics, oceanography and meteorology create standards for results, *Social Studies of Science*, 41(1): 107–125.

Svetlova, Ekaterina (2012), On the performative power of financial models, *Economy and Society*, 41(3): 418–434.

Tabb, William J. (2012), *The restructuring of capitalism*, New York: Columbia University Press.

Tang, Ke, and Xiong, Wei (2012), Index investment and the financialization of commodities, *Financial Analysts Journal*, 68(6): 54–74.

Thaler, Richard H., and Sunstein, Cass R. (2003), Libertarian paternalism, *The American Economic Review*, 93(2): 175–179.

Thiemann, Matthias, and Lepoutre, Jan (2017), Stitched on the edge: Rule evasion, embedded regulators, and the evolution of markets, *American Journal of Sociology*, 122(6): 1775–1821.

Thornburg, Steven, and Roberts, Robin W. (2008), Money, politics, and the regulation of public accounting services: Evidence from the Sarbanes–Oxley Act of 2002, *Accounting, Organizations and Society*, 33(2): 229–248.

Throsby, Karen (2009), The war on obesity as a moral project: Weight loss drugs, obesity surgery and negotiating failure, *Science as Culture*, 18(2): 210–216.

Tillman, Joseph A. (2012), Beyond the crisis: Dodd–Frank and private equity, *New York University Law Review*, 87: 1602–1640.

Tomaskovic-Devey, Donald, Lin, Ken-Hou, and Meyers, Nathan (2015), Did financialization reduce economic growth? *Socio-Economic Review*, 13(3): 525–548.

Topham, W. S. (2010), Re-regulating "financial weapons of mass destruction": Observations on repealing the commodity futures modernization act and future derivative regulation, *Willamette Law Review*, 47: 133–160.

Tregenna, Fiona (2012), The fat years: The structure and profitability of the US banking sector in the pre-crisis period, *Cambridge Journal of Economics*, 33(4): 609–632.

Tsui, Anne S., Enderle, Georges, and Jiang, Kaifeng (2018), Income inequality in the United States: Reflections on the role of corporations, *Academy of Management Review*, 43(1): 156–168.

Turco, Catherine J. (2012), Difficult decoupling: Employee resistance to the commercialization of personal settings, *American Journal of Sociology*, 118(2), 380–419.

Turner, Ralph H. (1976), The real self: From institution to impulse. *American Journal of Sociology*, 81(5): 989–1016.

Tversky, Amos and Kahneman, Daniel (1981), The framing of decisions and the psychology of choice, *Science*, 211(4481): 453–458.

Ulen, Thomas S. (1994) Rational choice and the economic analysis of law, *Law & Social Inquiry*, 19: 487–522.

Useem, Michael (1990), Business restructuring, management control, and corporate organization. *Theory and Society*, 19(6), 681–707.

Valdez, Zulema (2015), *Entrepreneurs and the search for the American dream*, New York & London: Routledge.

Vallas, Steven Peter, and Kleinman, Daniel Lee (2008), Contradiction, convergence and the knowledge economy: The confluence of academic and commercial biotechnology. *Socio-Economic Review*, 6(2): 283–311.

Van Arnum, Bradford M., and Naples Michele I. (2013), Financialization and income inequality in the United States, 1967–2010, *American Journal of Economics and Sociology*, 72(5): 1158–1182.

Van Horn, Robert, and Emmett, Ross B. (2015), Two trajectories of democratic capitalism in the post-war Chicago school: Frank Knight versus Aaron Director, *Cambridge Journal of Economics*, 39(5): 1443–1455.

Vaughan, Diana (1996), *The Challenger launch disaster: Risky technologies, culture, and deviance at NASA*, Chicago & London: The University of Chicago Press.

Veblen, Thorstein (1916), *The industry systems and the captains of industry*, New York: Oriole Chapbooks.

Veblen, Thorstein (1919/1964), *The vested interests and the common man*, New York: August M. Kelley.

Vidal, Jordi Blanes I., Draca, Mirko, and Fons-Rosen, Christian (2010), Revolving door lobbyists, *American Economic Review*, 102(7): 3731–3748.

Vogel, Steve K. (1996), *Freer markets, more rules: Regulatory reforms in advanced industrial countries*, Ithaca & London: Cornell University Press.

Volokh, Eugene (2003), The mechanisms of the slippery slope, *Harvard Law Review*, 116(4): 1026–1137.

Vuori, Timo O., and Huy, Quy N. (2016), Distributed attention and shared emotions in the innovation process: How Nokia lost the smartphone battle, *Administrative Science Quarterly*, 61(1): 9–51.

Wallerstein, Immanuel, Collins, Randall, Mann, Michael, Derluguian Georgi, and Calhoun, Craig (2013), *Does capitalism have a future?* New York & Oxford: Oxford University Press.

Warner, Mildred E. (2013), Private finance for public goods: Social impact bonds, *Journal of Economic Policy Reform*, 16(4): 303–319.

Watkins, S. (2003), Former Enron vicepresident Sherron Watkins on the Enron collapse, *Academy of Management Perspectives*, 17(4): 199–125.

Wedlin, Linda (2006), *Ranking business schools: Forming fields, identities and boundaries in international management education*, Cheltenham, UK and Northampton, MA, USA: Edward Elgar Publishing.

Weeden, Kim A., and Grusky, David B. (2014), Inequality and market failure, *American Behavioral Scientist*, 58: 473–491.

Weil, David (2014), *The fissured workplace: Why work became so bad for so many and what can be done about it*, Cambridge, MA & London: Harvard University Press.

Westphal, James D., and Bednar, Michael K. (2008), The pacification of institutional investors, *Administrative Science Quarterly*, 53(1): 29–72.

Westphal, James D., and Clement, Michael (2008), Sociopolitical dynamics in relations between top managers and security analysts: Favor rendering, reciprocity and analyst stock recommendations, *Academy of Management Journal*, 51(5): 873–897.

Westphal, James D., and Graebner, Melissa, E. (2010), A matter of appearance: How corporate leaders manage the impressions of financial analysis about the conducts of their boards, *Academy of Management Journal*, 53(1): 15–44.

Westphal, James D., and Khanna, Poonam (2003), Keeping directors in line: Social distancing as a control mechanism in the corporate elite, *Administrative Science Quarterly*, 48(3): 361–398.

Westphal, James, and Zajac, Edward (1998), The symbolic management of stockholders: Corporate governance reforms and shareholder reactions, *Administrative Science Quarterly*, 43: 127–153.

Westphal, James, and Zajac, Edward (2001), Decoupling policy from practice: The case of stock repurchase programs, *Administrative Science Quarterly*, 46(2): 202–228.

Westphal, James D., Park, Sun Hyun, McDonald, Michael L., and Hayward, Mathew L.A. (2012), Helping other CEOs avoid bad press: Social exchange and impression management support among CEOs in communications with journalists, *Administrative Science Quarterly*, 57(2): 217–268.

White, Lawrence J. (2009), The credit-rating agencies and the subprime debacle, *Critical Review*, 21(2–3): 389–399.

White, Lawrence J. (2013), Credit rating agencies: An overview, *Annual Review in Financial Economics*, 5: 93–122.

Whitehead, Alfred North (1925), *Science and the modern world*, Cambridge: Cambridge University Press.

Williams, James W. (2013), Regulatory technologies, risky subjects, and financial boundaries: Governing "fraud" in the financial markets, *Accounting, Organizations and Society*, 39(6–7): 544–558.

Williams, James W. (2014), Feeding finance: A critical account of the shifting relationships between finance, food and farming, *Economy and Society*, 43(3), 401–431.

Williams, James W., and Cook, Nikolai M. (2016), Econometrics as evidence? Examining the "causal" connections between financial speculation and commodities prices, *Social Studies of Science*, 46(5): 701–724.

Williamson, Oliver E. (1981), The modern corporation: Origins, evaluations, attributions, *Journal of Economic Literature*, 19: 1537–1568.

Wilmarth, Arthur E., Jr (2013), Turning a blind eye: Why Washington keeps giving in to Wall Street, *University of Cincinnati Law Review*, 81(4): 1283–1445.

Wilson, Rick K. (2011), The contribution of behavioral economics to political science, *Annual Review of Political Science*,14: 201–223.

Wodtke, Geoffrey T. (2016), Social class and income inequality in the United States: Ownership, authority, and personal income distribution from 1980 to 2010, *American Journal of Sociology*, 121(5): 1375–1415.

Wolff, Edward N. (2003), What's behind the rise in profitability in the US in the 1980s and 1990s? *Cambridge Journal of Economics*, 27(4): 479–499.

Wood, B. Dan, and Anderson, James E. (1993), The politics of U.S antitrust regulation, *American Journal of Political Science*, 37(1): 1–39.

Zalewski, David A., and Whalen, Charles J. (2010), Financialization and income inequality: A post Keynesian institutionalist analysis, *Journal of Economic Perspectives*, 44(3): 757–777.

Zarsky, Tal (2016), The trouble with algorithmic decisions: An analytic road map to examine efficiency and fairness in automated and opaque decision making. *Science, Technology, & Human Values*, 41(1): 118–132.

Zelizer, Vivianne (2005), *The purchase of intimacy*, Princeton: Princeton University Press.

Zelner, Bennet A., Henisz, Witold, and Holburn, Guy L.F. (2009), Contentious implementation and retrenchment in neoliberal policy reform: The global electric power industry, 1989–2001. *Administrative Science Quarterly*, 54(3): 379–412.

Ziewitz, Malte (2016), Governing algorithms: Myth, mess, and methods, *Science, Technology, & Human Values*, 41(1): 3–16.

Ziliak, Stephen T., and McCloskey, Dierdre N. (2008), *The cult of statistical significance: How the standard error costs us jobs, justice, and lives*, Ann Arbor: The University of Michigan Press.

Zinman, Jonathan (2015), Household debt: Facts, puzzles, theories, and policies, *Annual Review of Economics*, 7: 251–276.

Zorn, Dirk, Dobbin, Frank, Dierkes, Julian, and Kwok, Man-shan (2005), Managing investors: How financial markets reshaped the American firm, in Knorr Cetina, Karin, and Preda, Alex, eds. (2005), *The sociology of financial markets*, Oxford & New York. Oxford University Press (pp. 269–289).

Index